Love and Leftovers

by Ayumi Komura

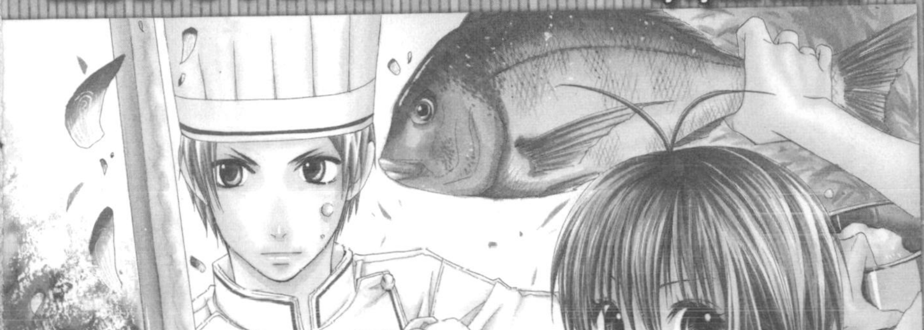

Hanayu Ashitaba is the daughter of a celebrated baker but dreams of being a sushi chef. Hayato Hyuga is the son of a sushi master and wants to become a pastry chef! Will these star-crossed gourmands fulfill their cuisine dreams?

Find out in *Mixed Vegetables*— manga available now!

Shojo Beat
MANGA from the HEART

P9-DWI-927

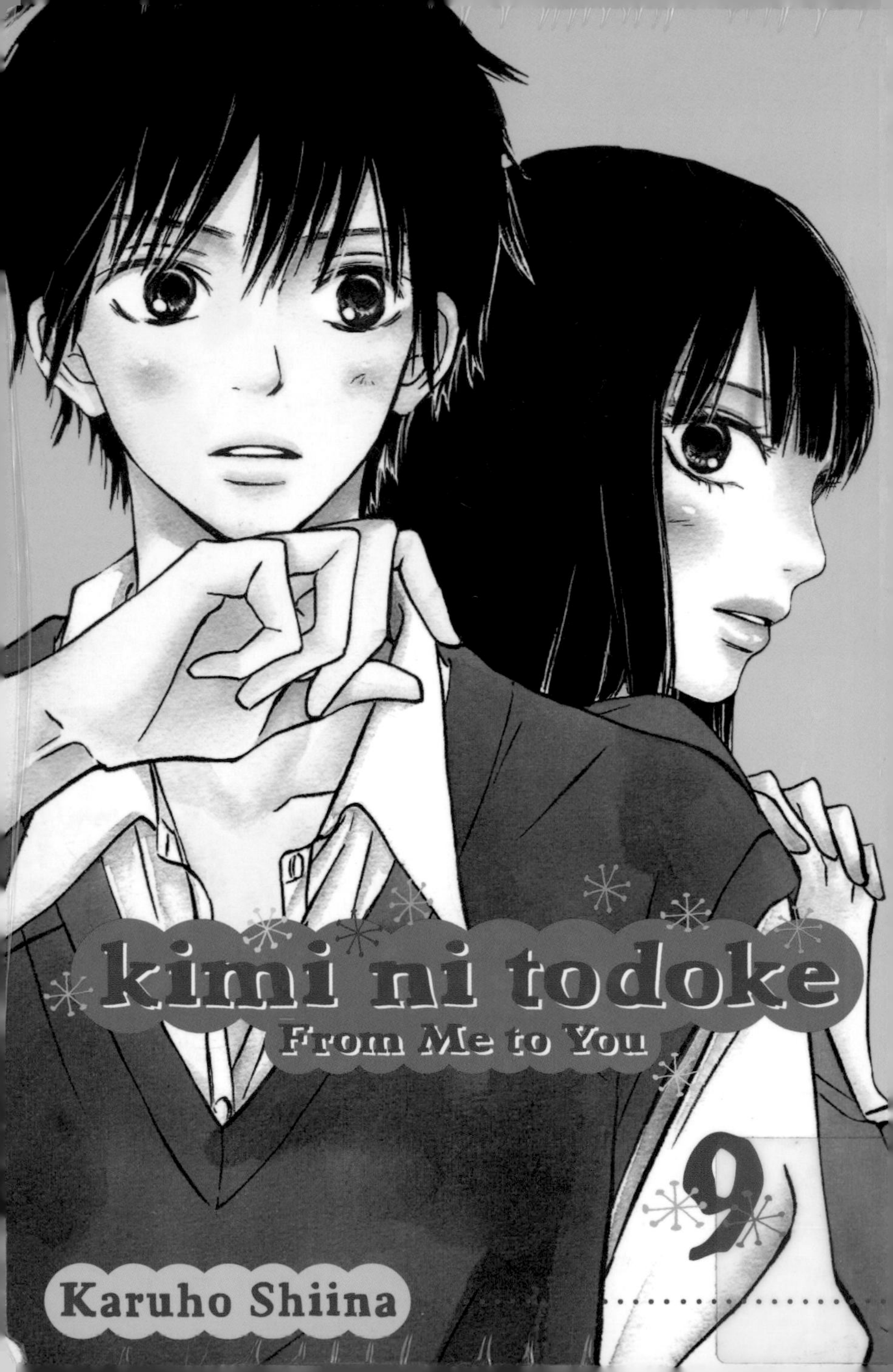
kimi ni todoke
From Me to You
9
Karuho Shiina

Shojo Beat

kimi ni todoke
From Me to You

Vol. 9
Story & Art by
Karuho Shiina

Volume 9

Contents

Story Thus Far

Sawako Kuronuma has always been a loner. Though not by choice, this optimistic 15-year-old can't seem to make any friends. Stuck with the unfortunate nickname "Sadako" after the haunting movie character, rumors about her summoning spirits have been greatly exaggerated. With her shy personality and scary looks, most of her classmates will barely talk to her, much less look into her eyes for more than three seconds lest they be cursed. Drawn out of her shell by her popular classmate Shota Kazehaya, Sawako is no longer an outcast. Thanks to her friends Ayane and Chizu, Sawako spends time alone with Kazehaya on New Year's Eve, which is also her birthday. Sawako has a good time, but can't bring herself to give chocolate to Kazehaya on Valentine's Day. Kazehaya is confused, and now their new classmate Kento is being very friendly to Sawako. Spurred on by their teacher, who teases Kazehaya about his feelings for Sawako, Kazehaya decides to tell her how he feels...

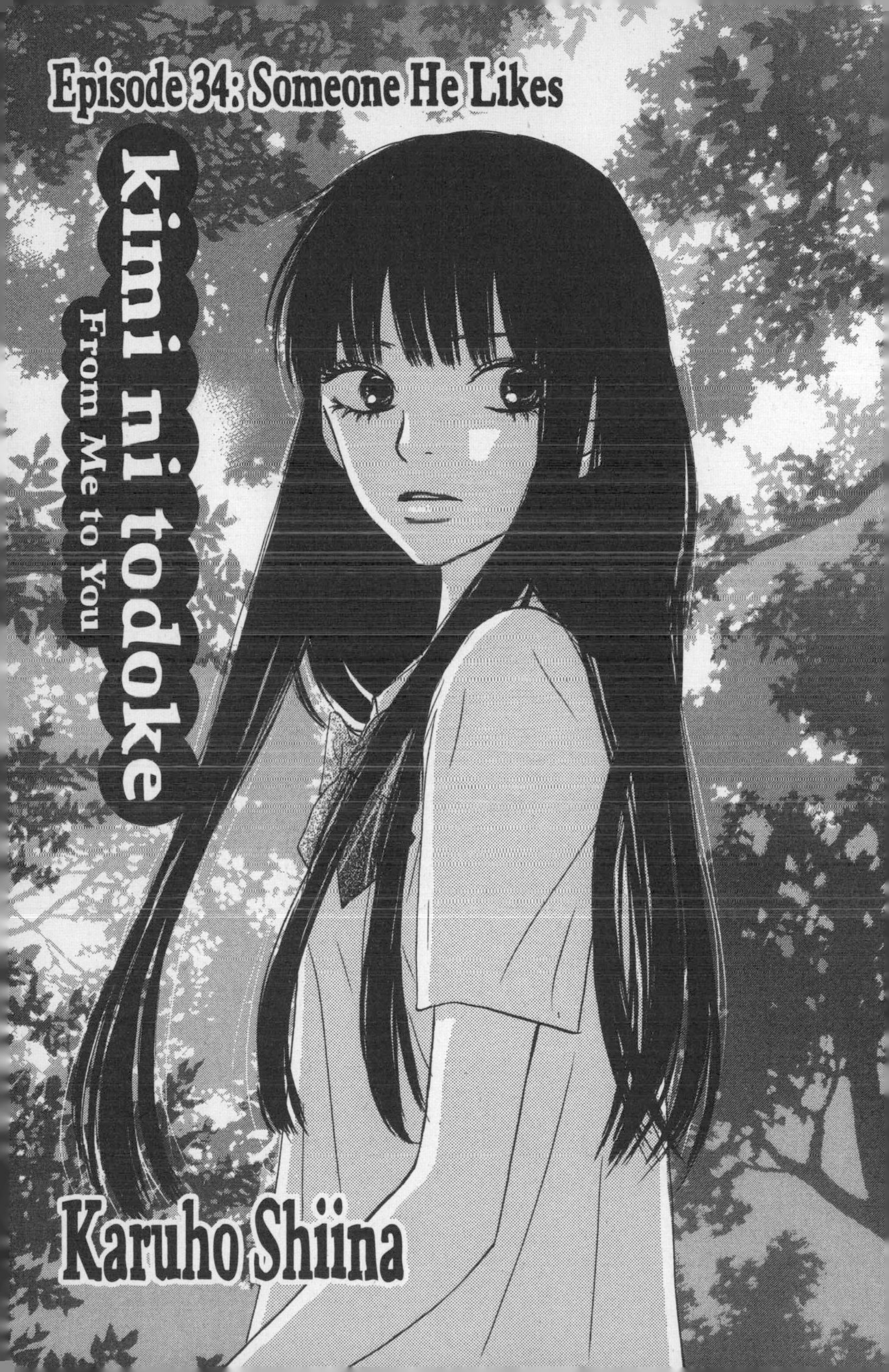
Episode 34: Someone He Likes
Kimi ni todoke
From Me to You
Karuho Shiina

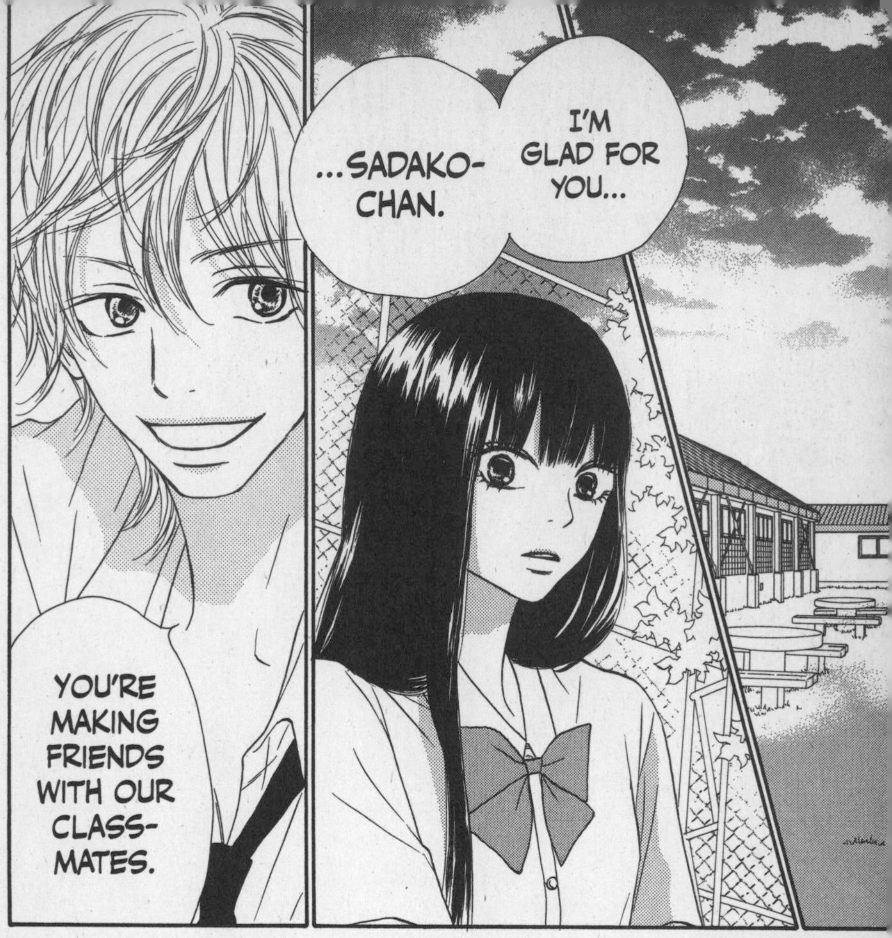
I'M GLAD FOR YOU...
...SADAKO-CHAN.
YOU'RE MAKING FRIENDS WITH OUR CLASS-MATES.

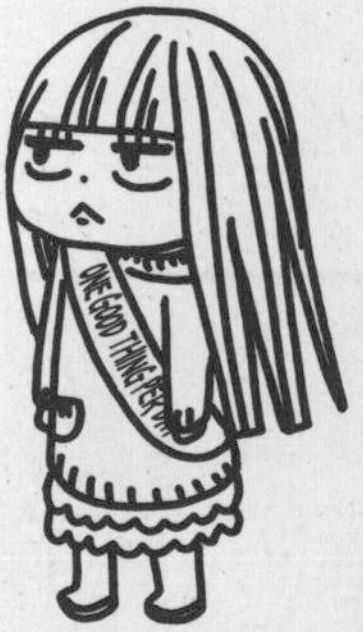

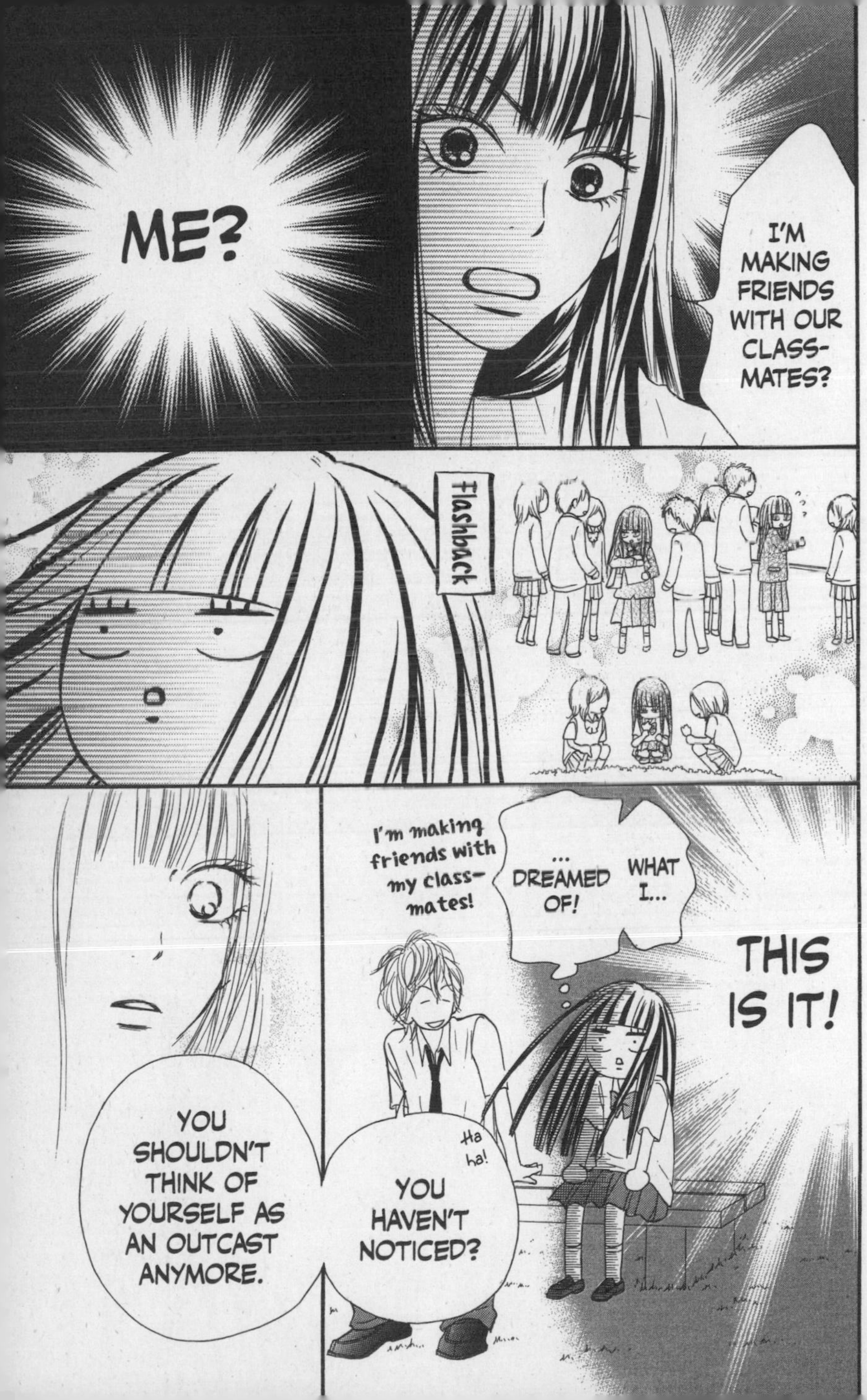
I'M MAKING FRIENDS WITH OUR CLASS-MATES?
ME?
Flashback
THIS IS IT!
WHAT I...
... DREAMED OF!
I'm making friends with my class-mates!
Ha ha!
YOU HAVEN'T NOTICED?
YOU SHOULDN'T THINK OF YOURSELF AS AN OUTCAST ANYMORE.

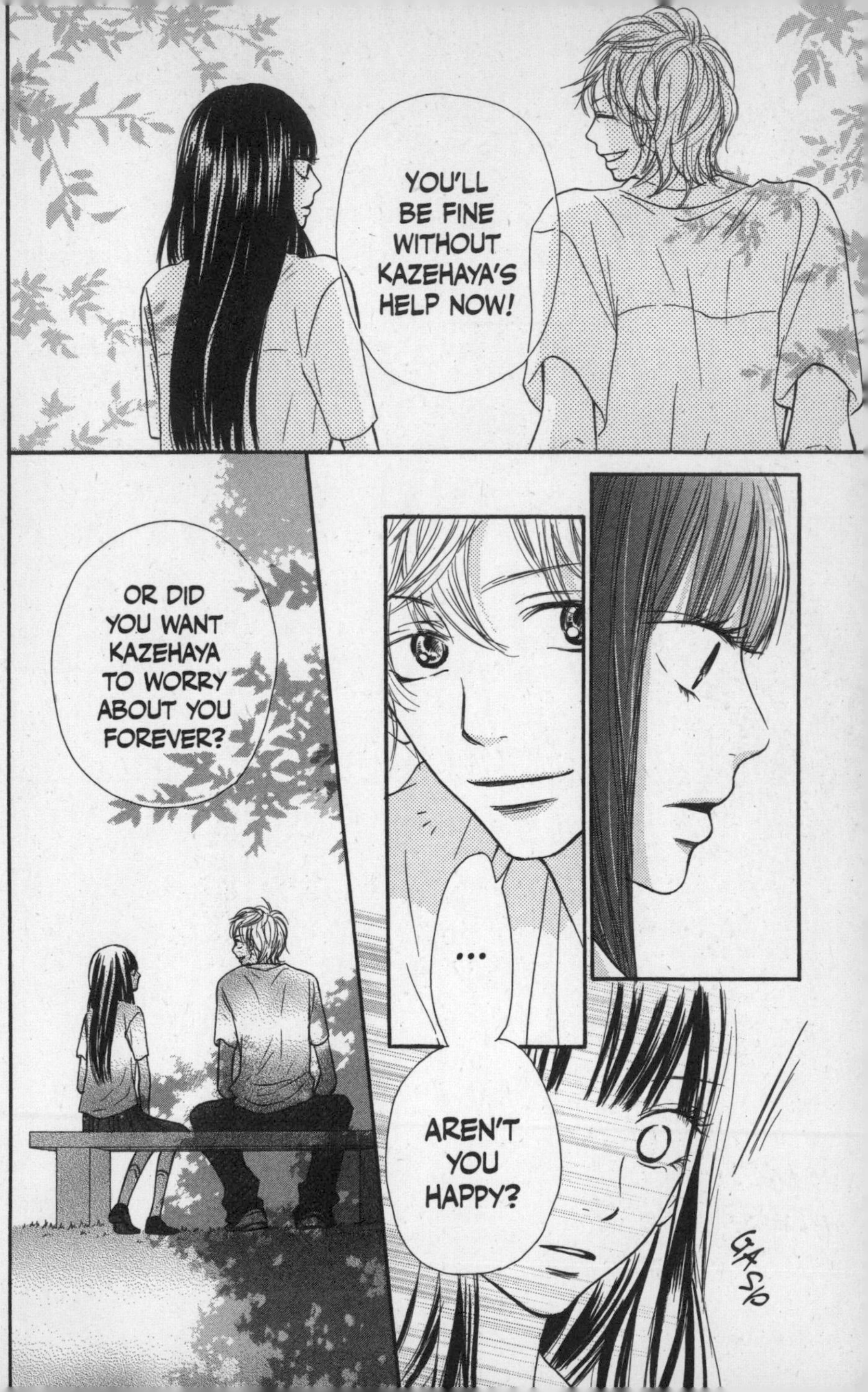
YOU'LL BE FINE WITHOUT KAZEHAYA'S HELP NOW!
OR DID YOU WANT KAZEHAYA TO WORRY ABOUT YOU FOREVER?
...
AREN'T YOU HAPPY?
GASP

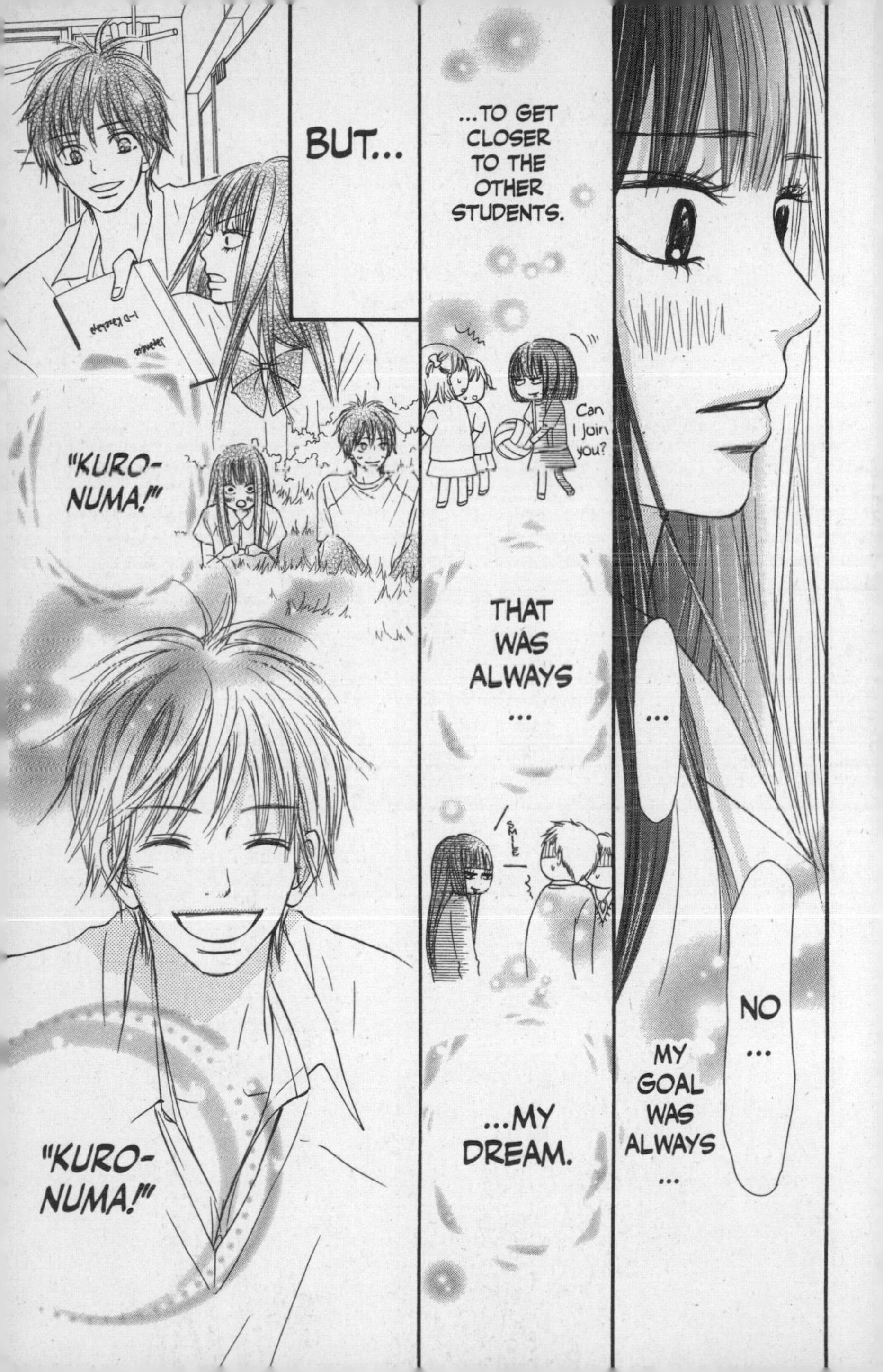
...
NO ...
MY GOAL WAS ALWAYS ...
...TO GET CLOSER TO THE OTHER STUDENTS.
Can I join you?
THAT WAS ALWAYS ...
SMILE
...MY DREAM.
BUT...
"KURO-NUMA!"
"KURO-NUMA!"

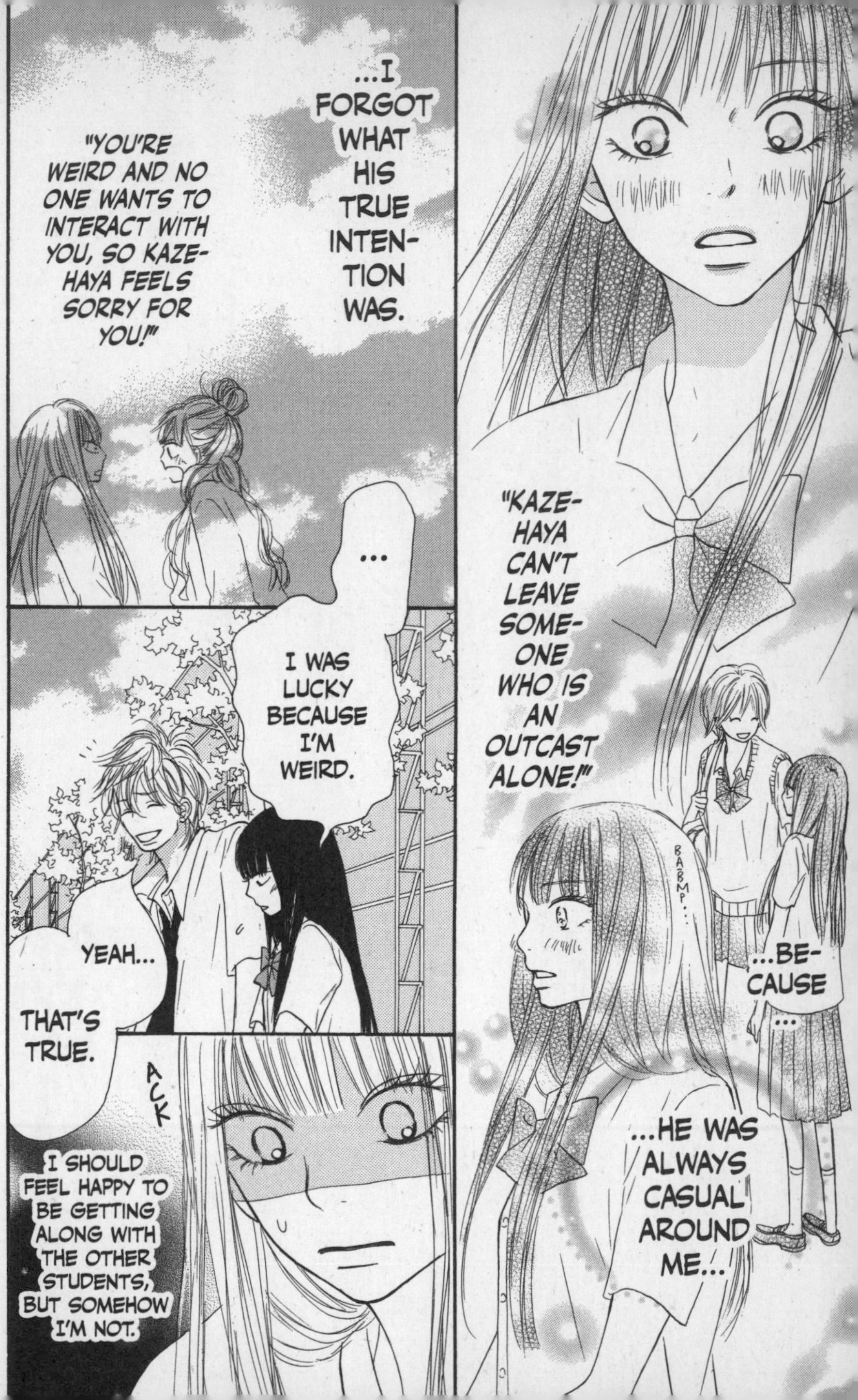
"KAZE-HAYA CAN'T LEAVE SOME-ONE WHO IS AN OUTCAST ALONE!"
BA-BUMP...
...BE-CAUSE...
...HE WAS ALWAYS CASUAL AROUND ME...
...I FORGOT WHAT HIS TRUE INTEN-TION WAS.
"YOU'RE WEIRD AND NO ONE WANTS TO INTERACT WITH YOU, SO KAZE-HAYA FEELS SORRY FOR YOU!"
...
I WAS LUCKY BECAUSE I'M WEIRD.
YEAH...
THAT'S TRUE.
ACK
I SHOULD FEEL HAPPY TO BE GETTING ALONG WITH THE OTHER STUDENTS, BUT SOMEHOW I'M NOT.

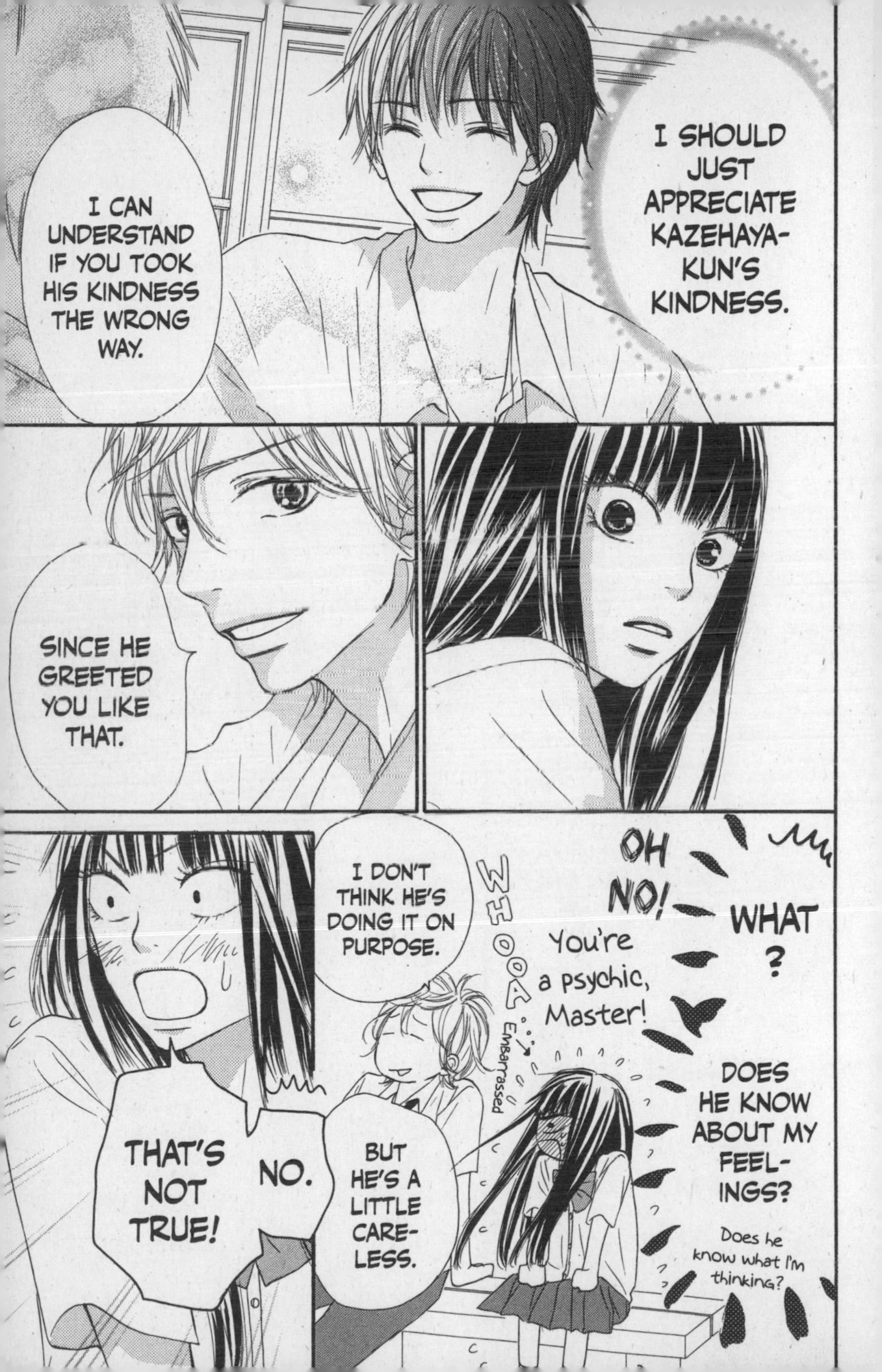

I SHOULD JUST APPRECIATE KAZEHAYA-KUN'S KINDNESS.
I CAN UNDERSTAND IF YOU TOOK HIS KINDNESS THE WRONG WAY.
SINCE HE GREETED YOU LIKE THAT.
WHAT?
OH NO!
You're a psychic, Master!
I DON'T THINK HE'S DOING IT ON PURPOSE.
WHOA
DOES HE KNOW ABOUT MY FEEL-INGS?
Does he know what I'm thinking?
Embarrassed
BUT HE'S A LITTLE CARE-LESS.
NO.
THAT'S NOT TRUE!

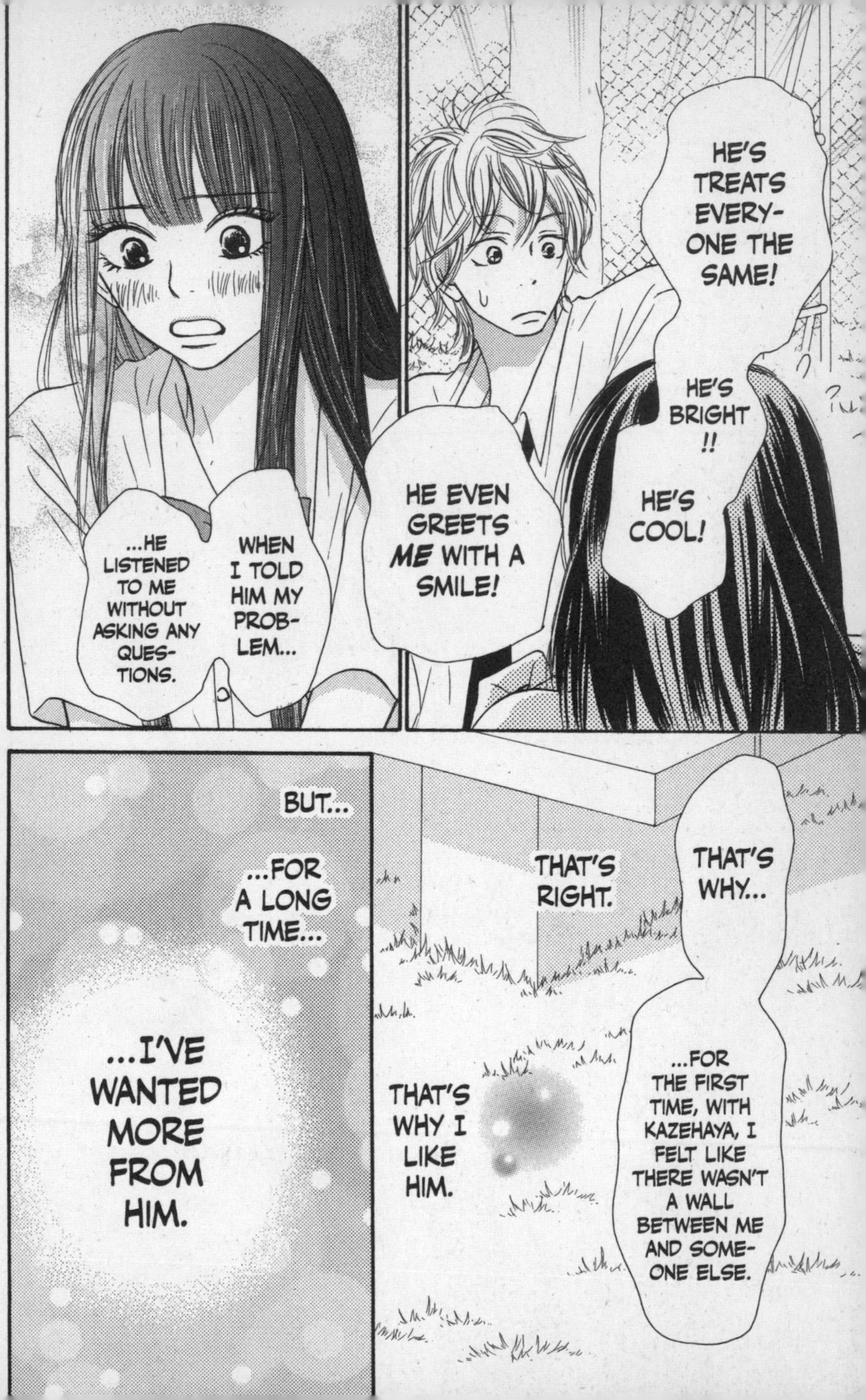
HE'S TREATS EVERY-ONE THE SAME!
HE'S BRIGHT !!
HE'S COOL!
HE EVEN GREETS *ME* WITH A SMILE!
WHEN I TOLD HIM MY PROB-LEM...
...HE LISTENED TO ME WITHOUT ASKING ANY QUES-TIONS.
THAT'S WHY...
...FOR THE FIRST TIME, WITH KAZEHAYA, I FELT LIKE THERE WASN'T A WALL BETWEEN ME AND SOME-ONE ELSE.
THAT'S RIGHT.
THAT'S WHY I LIKE HIM.
BUT...
...FOR A LONG TIME...
...I'VE WANTED MORE FROM HIM.

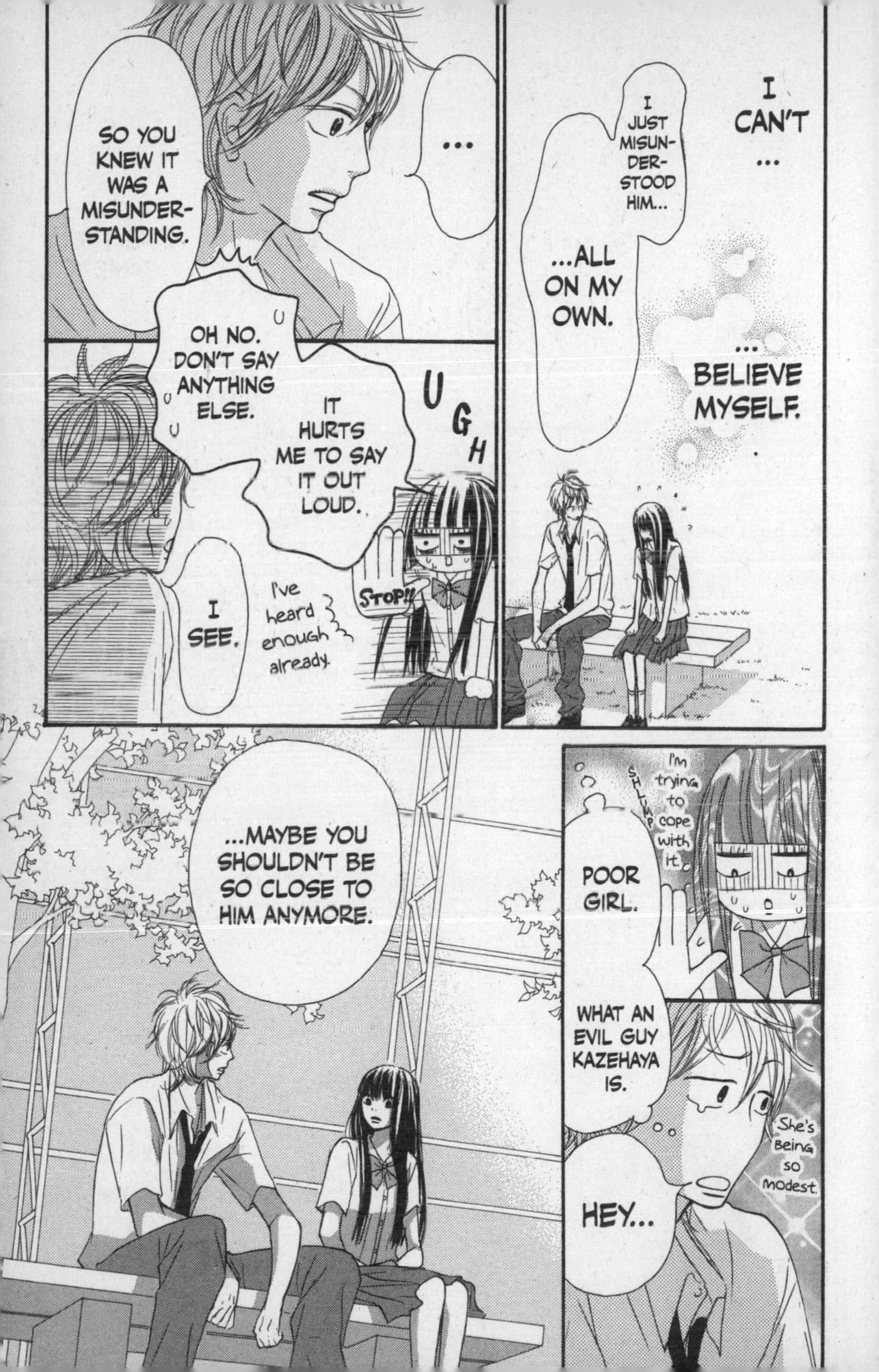
I CAN'T ...
... BELIEVE MYSELF.
I JUST MISUNDERSTOOD HIM...
...ALL ON MY OWN.
...
SO YOU KNEW IT WAS A MISUNDERSTANDING.
OH NO. DON'T SAY ANYTHING ELSE.
IT HURTS ME TO SAY IT OUT LOUD.
UGH
STOP!!
I've heard enough already.
I SEE.
I'm trying to cope with it.
SHLUMP
POOR GIRL.
WHAT AN EVIL GUY KAZEHAYA IS.
She's being so modest.
HEY...
...MAYBE YOU SHOULDN'T BE SO CLOSE TO HIM ANYMORE.

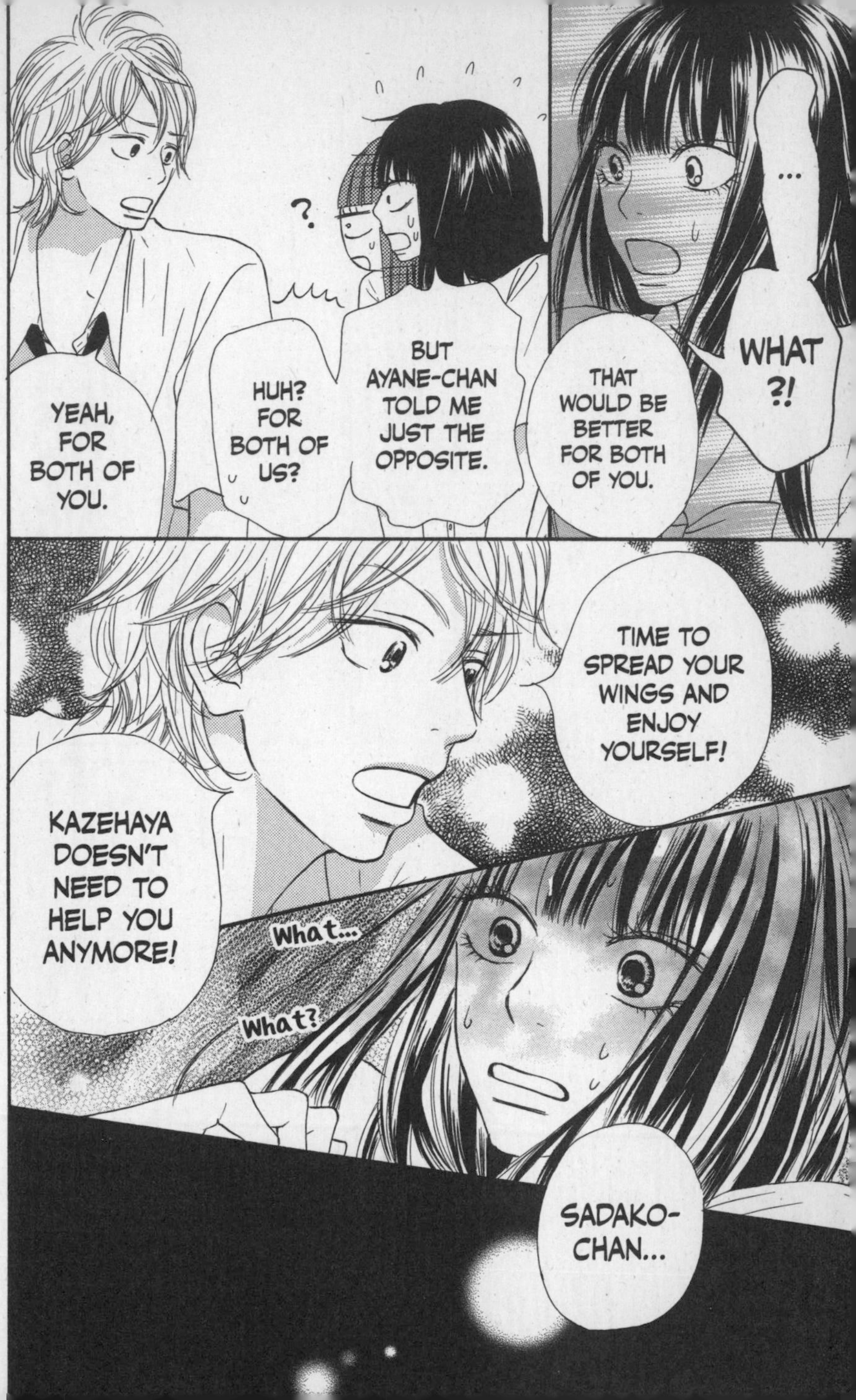
...
WHAT ?!
THAT WOULD BE BETTER FOR BOTH OF YOU.
BUT AYANE-CHAN TOLD ME JUST THE OPPOSITE.
HUH? FOR BOTH OF US?
YEAH, FOR BOTH OF YOU.
TIME TO SPREAD YOUR WINGS AND ENJOY YOURSELF!
KAZEHAYA DOESN'T NEED TO HELP YOU ANYMORE!
What...
What?
SADAKO-CHAN...

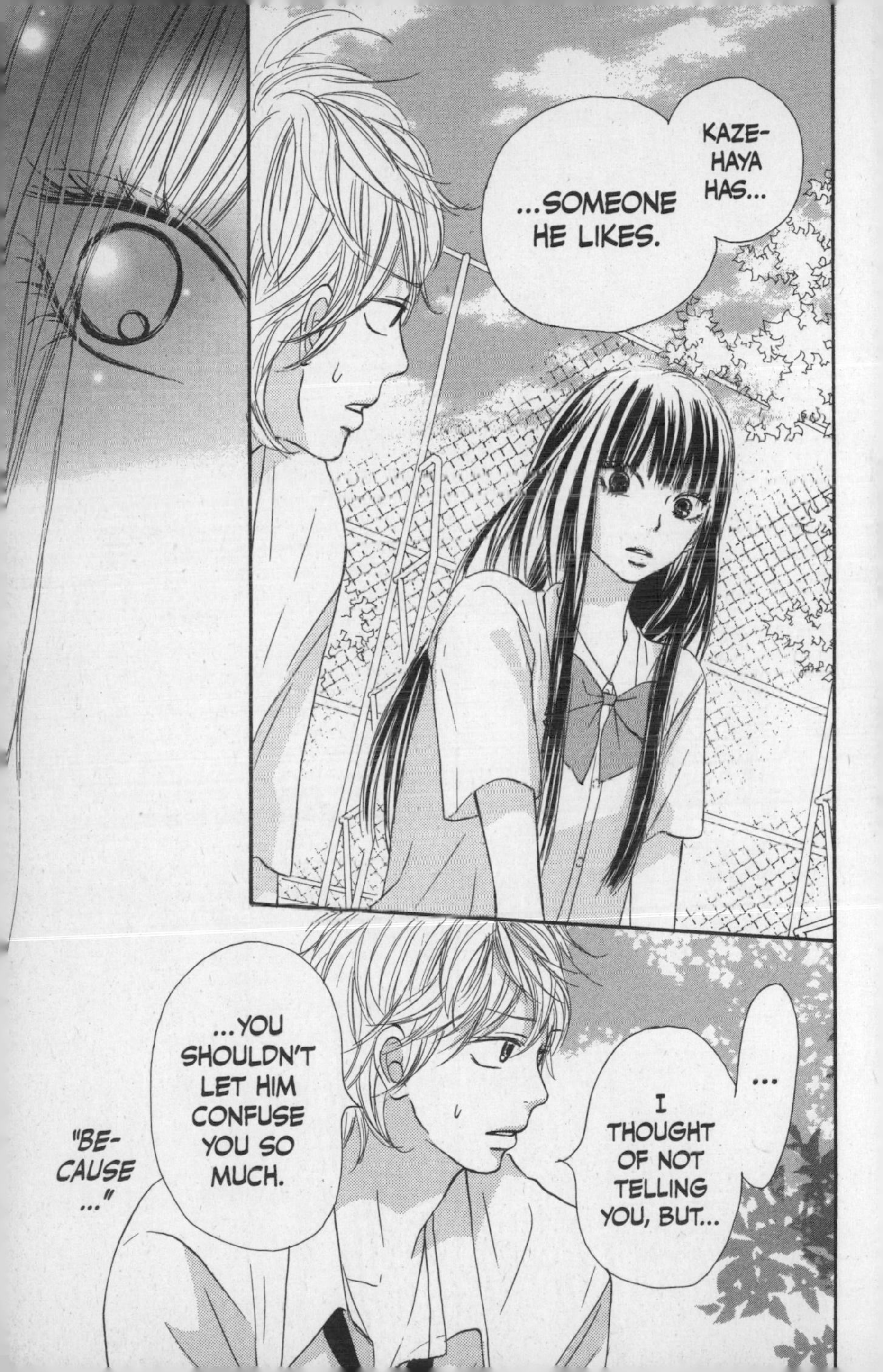
KAZE-HAYA HAS... ...SOMEONE HE LIKES.
...
I THOUGHT OF NOT TELLING YOU, BUT...
...YOU SHOULDN'T LET HIM CONFUSE YOU SO MUCH.
"BE-CAUSE ..."

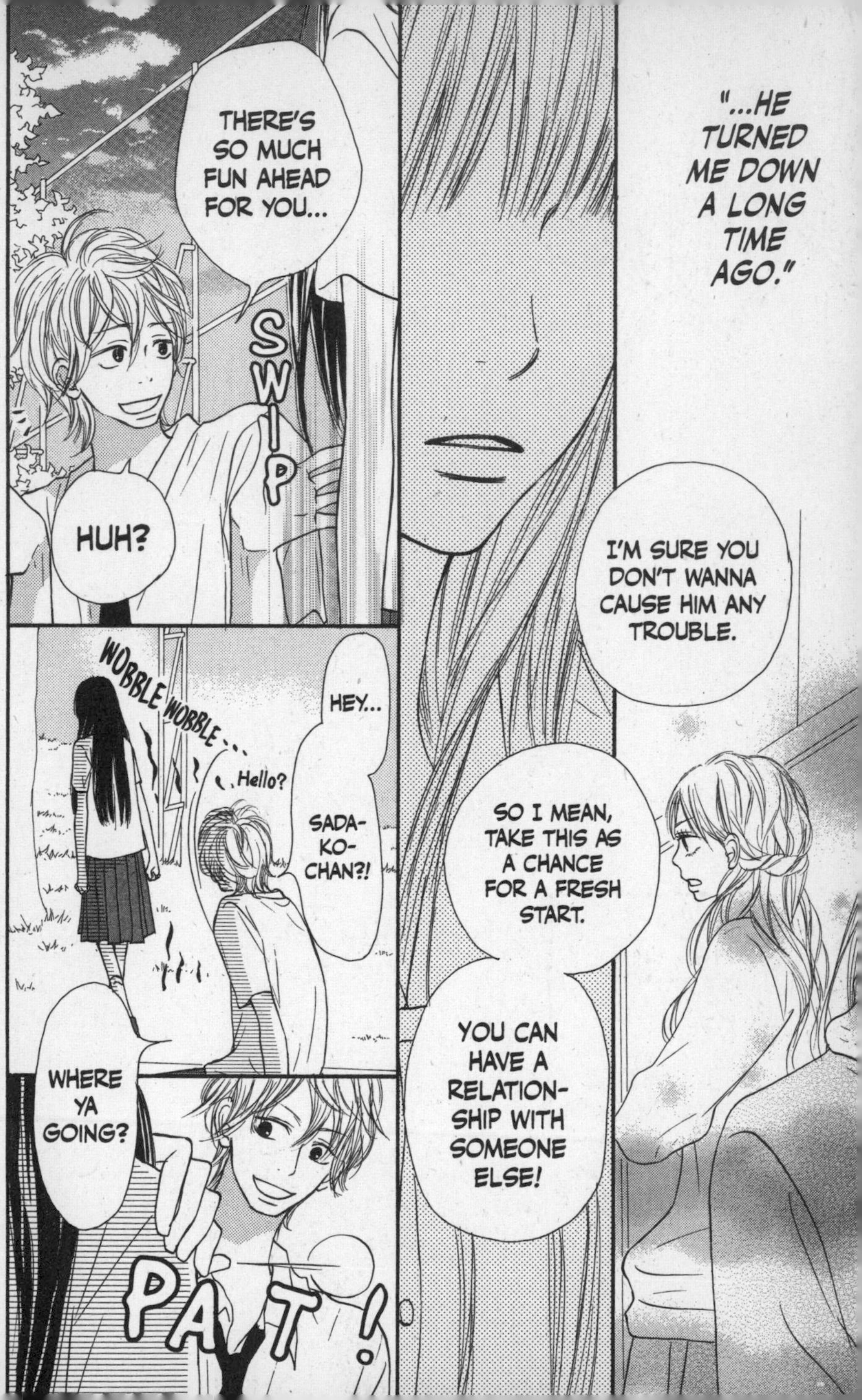
"...HE TURNED ME DOWN A LONG TIME AGO."
I'M SURE YOU DON'T WANNA CAUSE HIM ANY TROUBLE.
SO I MEAN, TAKE THIS AS A CHANCE FOR A FRESH START.
YOU CAN HAVE A RELATION-SHIP WITH SOMEONE ELSE!
THERE'S SO MUCH FUN AHEAD FOR YOU...
SWIP
HUH?
HEY...
SADA-KO-CHAN?!
Hello?
WOBBLE WOBBLE...
WHERE YA GOING?
PAT!

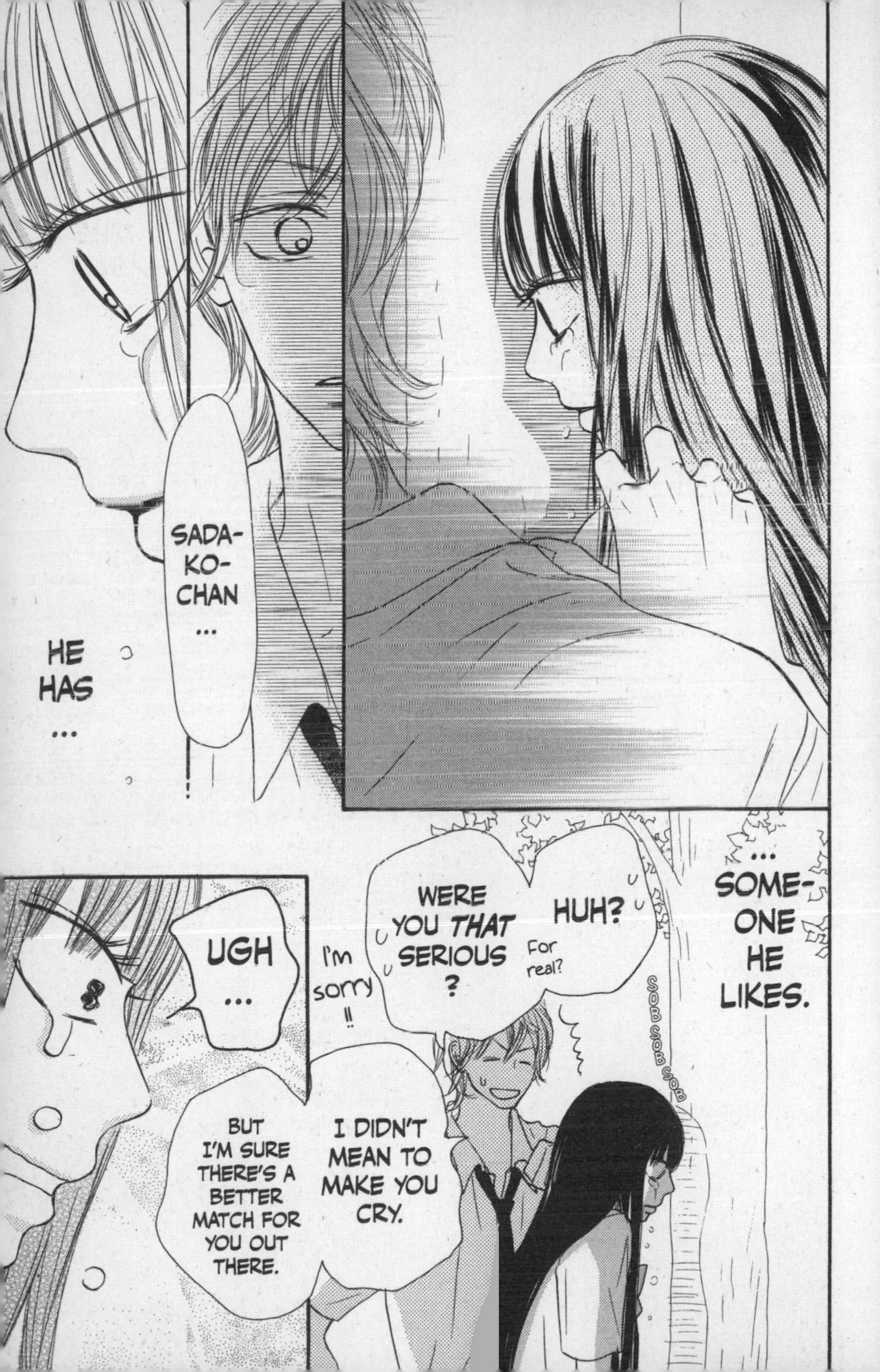
SADA-KO-CHAN...
HE HAS...
...SOME-ONE HE LIKES.
HUH?
For real?
WERE YOU THAT SERIOUS?
I'm sorry!!
SOB SOB SOB
I DIDN'T MEAN TO MAKE YOU CRY.
BUT I'M SURE THERE'S A BETTER MATCH FOR YOU OUT THERE.
UGH...

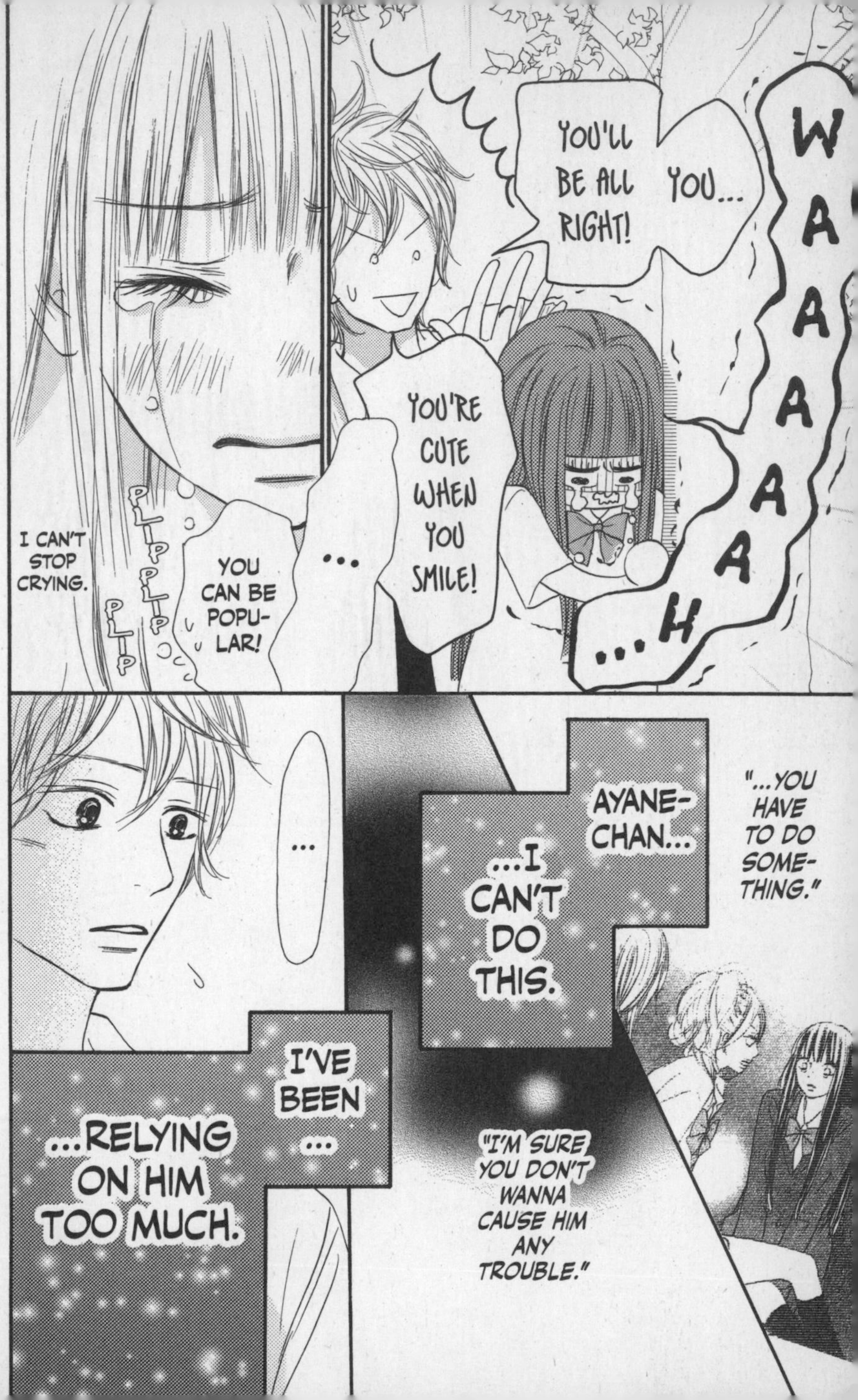
WAAAAAH...
YOU...
YOU'LL BE ALL RIGHT!
YOU'RE CUTE WHEN YOU SMILE!
...
YOU CAN BE POPULAR!
PLIP PLIP PLIP
I CAN'T STOP CRYING.
"...YOU HAVE TO DO SOMETHING."
AYANE-CHAN...
...I CAN'T DO THIS.
"I'M SURE YOU DON'T WANNA CAUSE HIM ANY TROUBLE."
...
I'VE BEEN...
...RELYING ON HIM TOO MUCH.

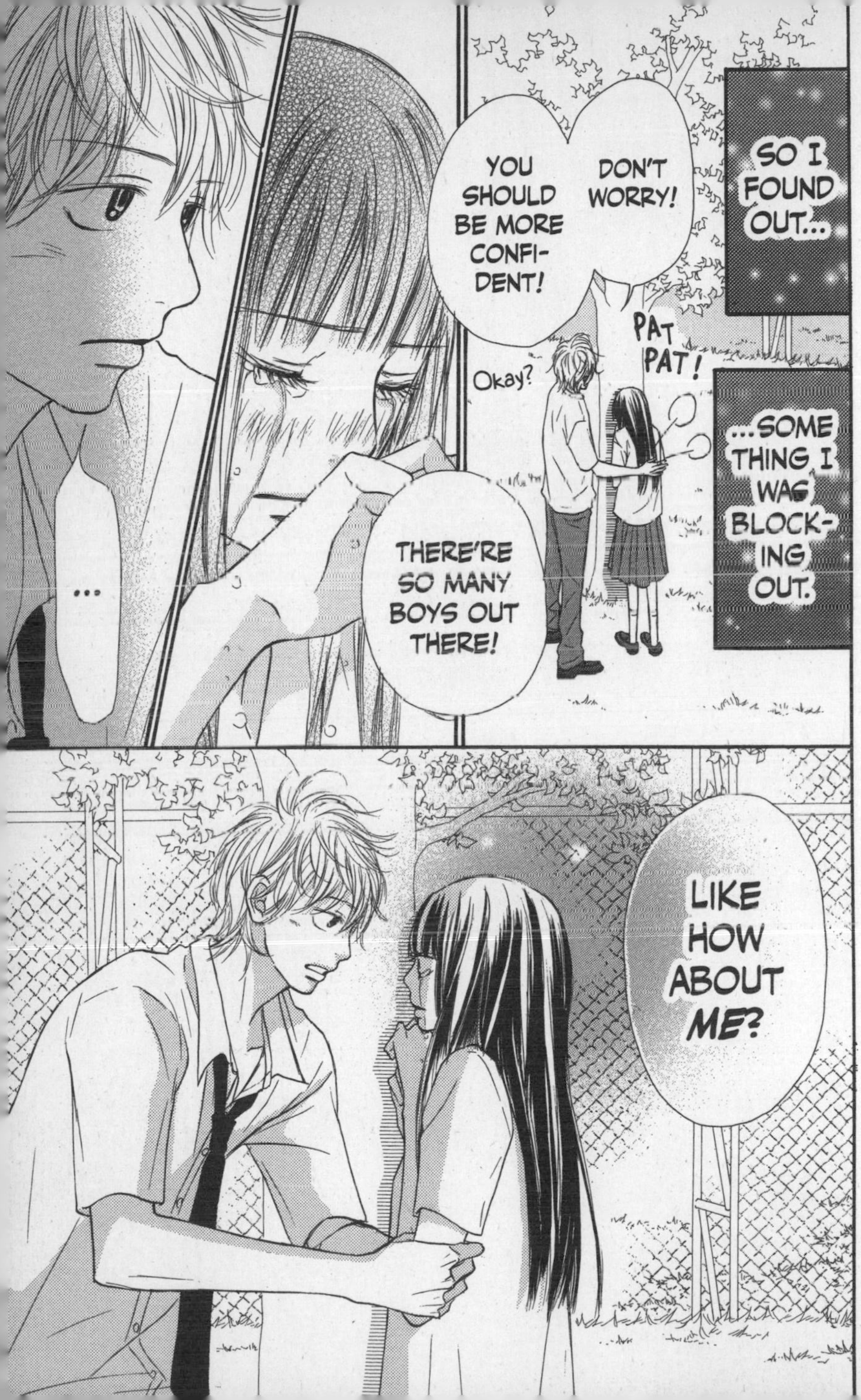
SO I FOUND OUT...
DON'T WORRY!
YOU SHOULD BE MORE CONFI-DENT!
PAT PAT!
...SOME THING I WAS BLOCK-ING OUT.
Okay?
THERE'RE SO MANY BOYS OUT THERE!
...
LIKE HOW ABOUT *ME*?

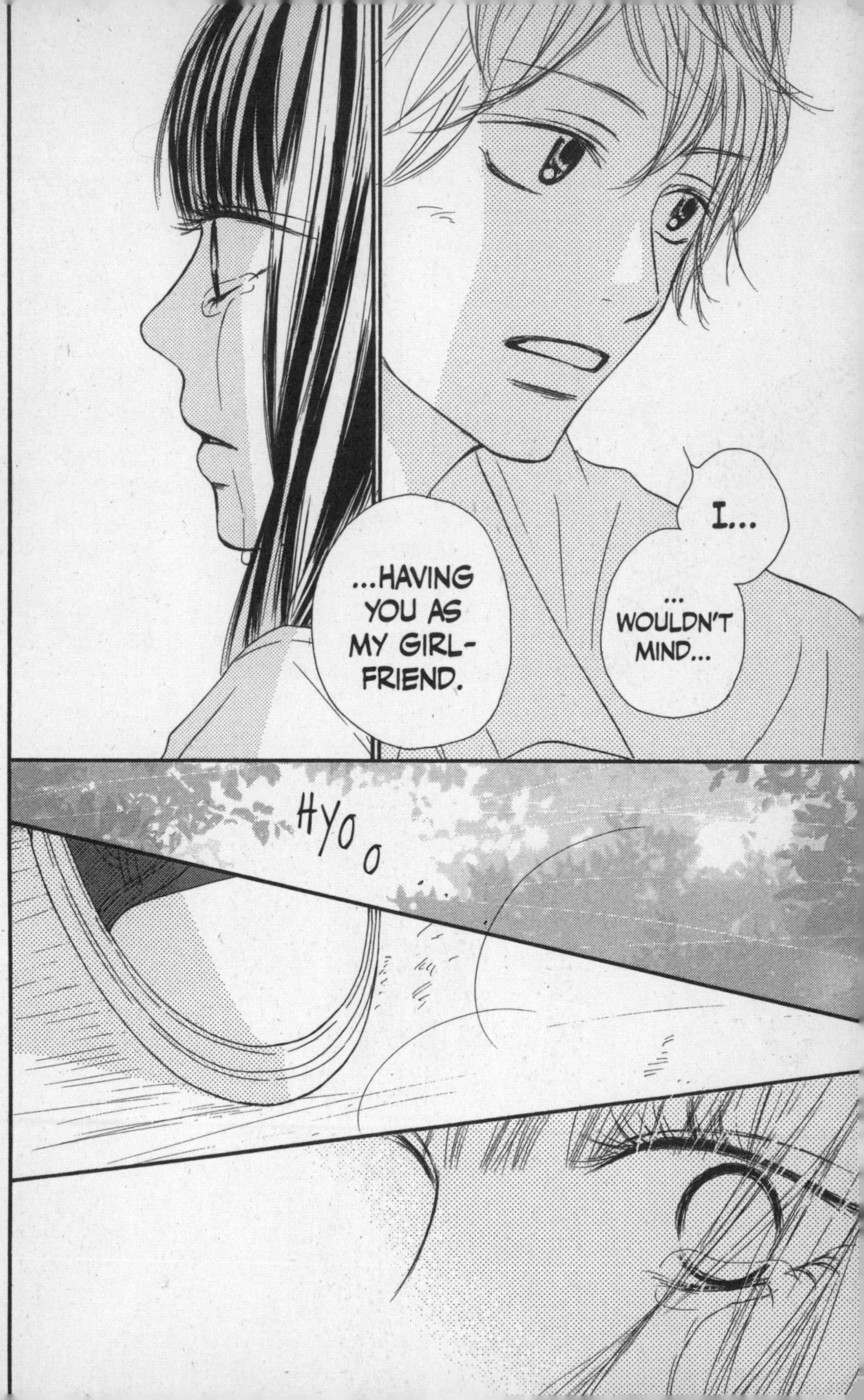
I...
...WOULDN'T MIND...
...HAVING YOU AS MY GIRL-FRIEND.
HYOO

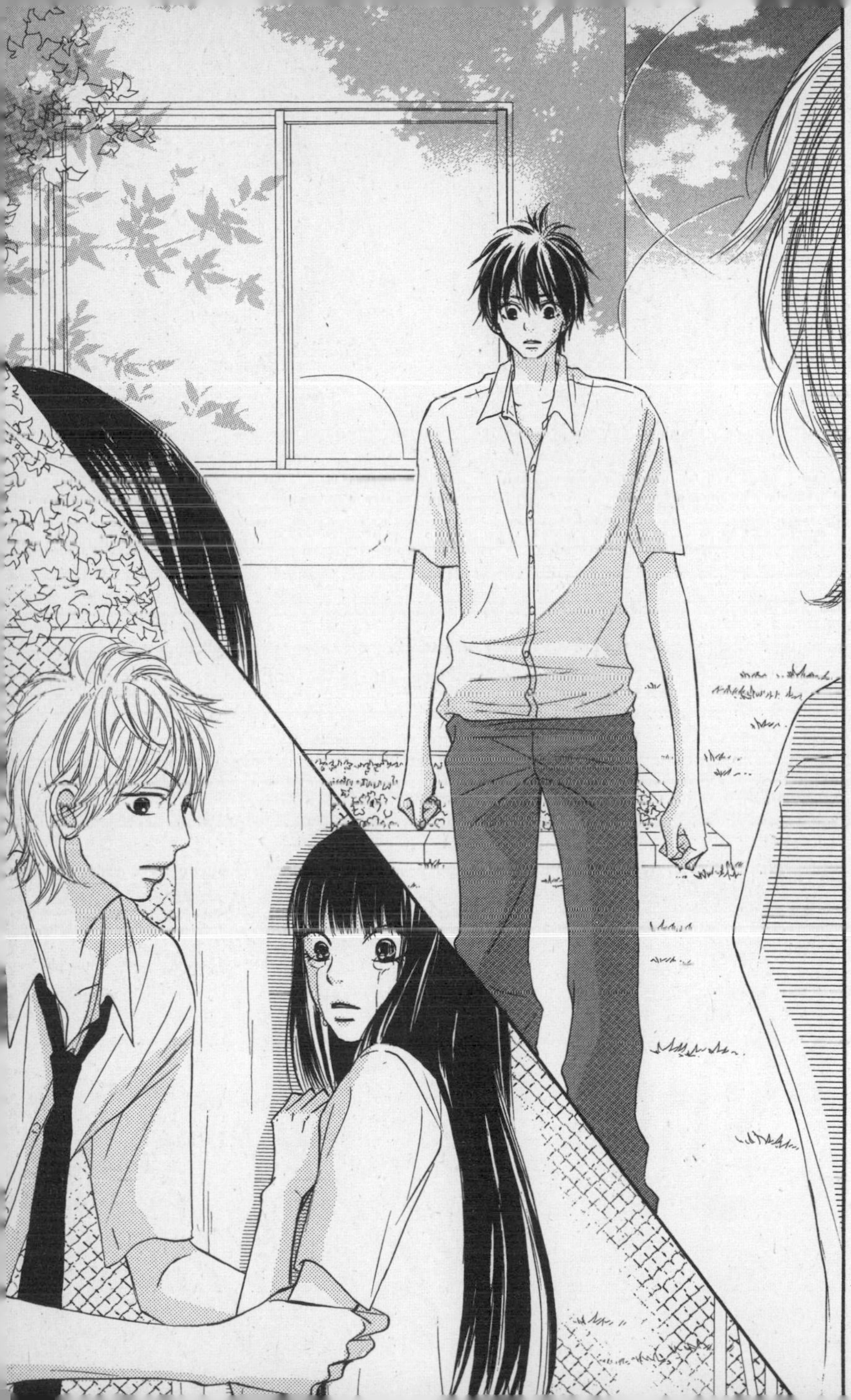

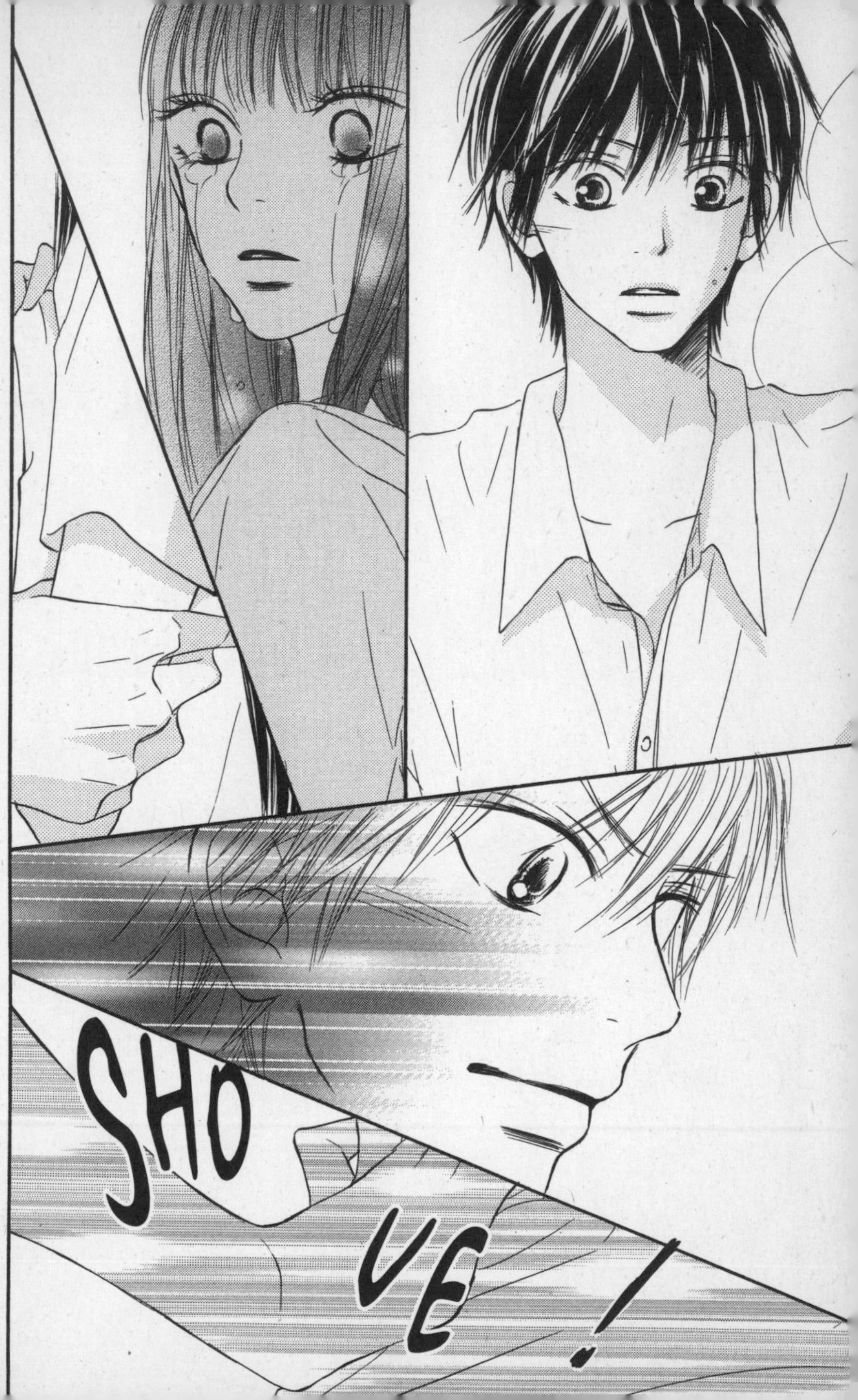
SHOVE!

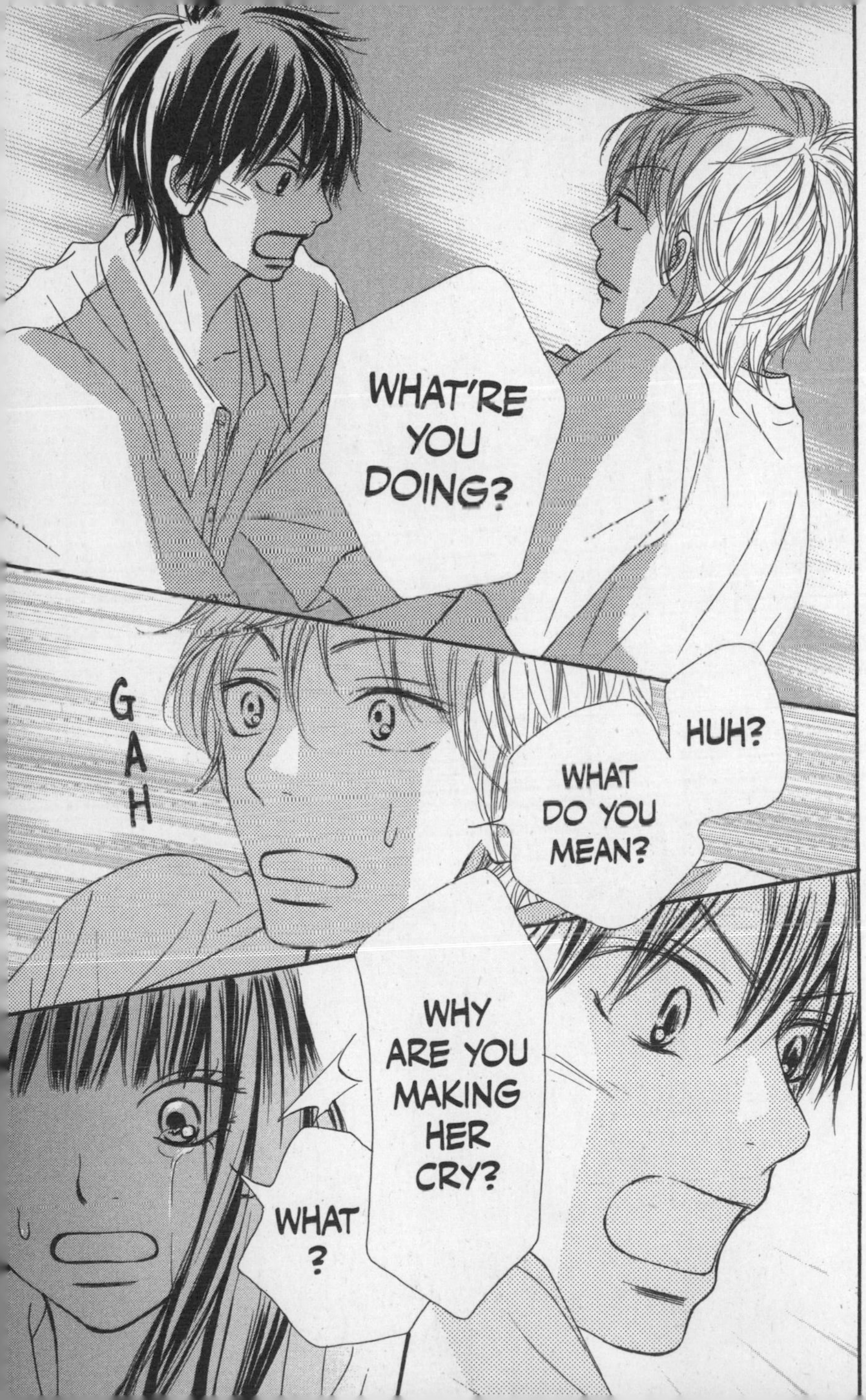
WHAT'RE YOU DOING?
HUH?
WHAT DO YOU MEAN?
GAH
WHY ARE YOU MAKING HER CRY?
WHAT?

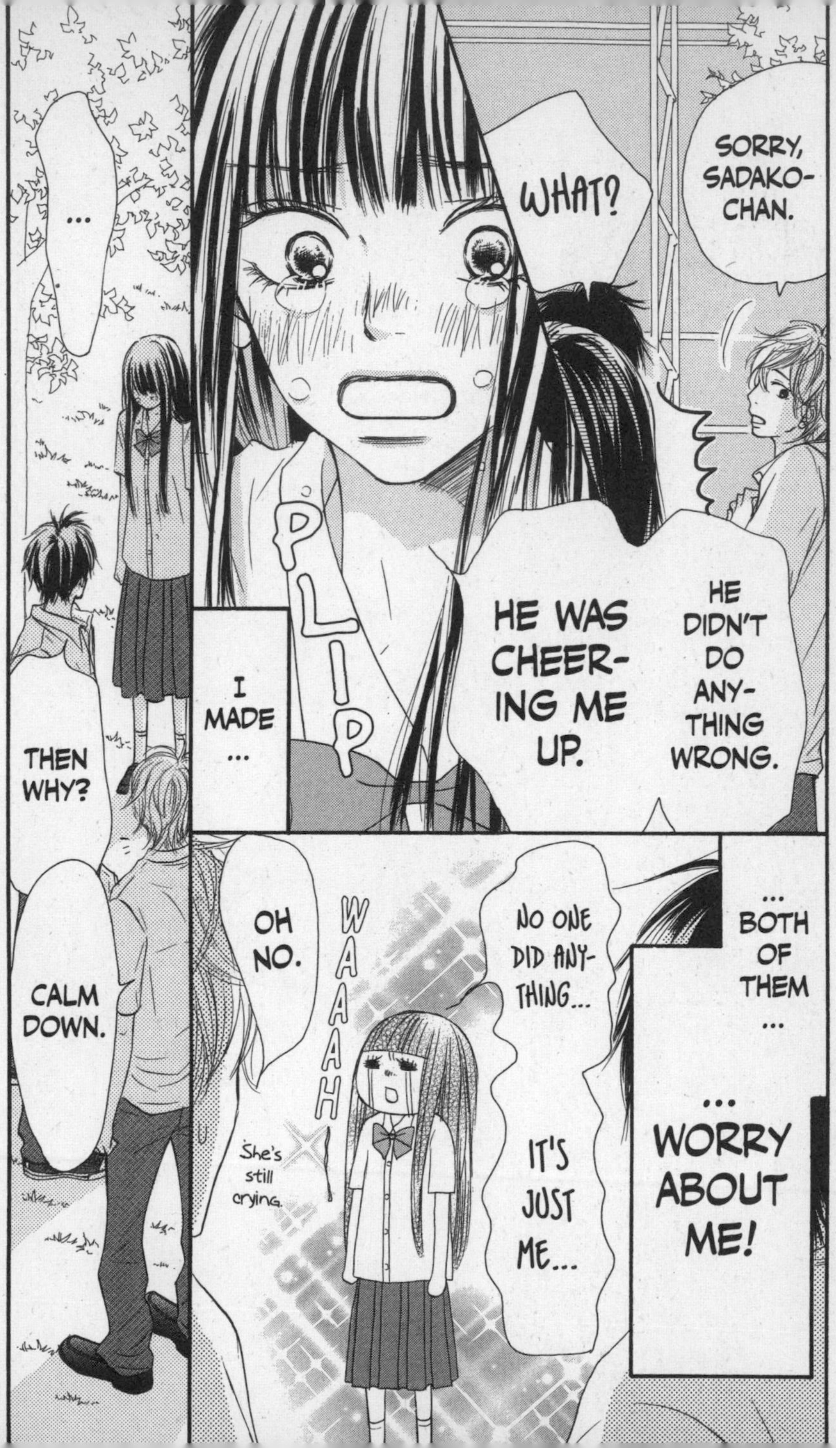
SORRY, SADAKO-CHAN.
WHAT?
HE DIDN'T DO ANY-THING WRONG.
HE WAS CHEER-ING ME UP.
I MADE ...
PLIP
... BOTH OF THEM ...
... WORRY ABOUT ME!
NO ONE DID ANY-THING...
IT'S JUST ME...
WAAAAH
OH NO.
She's still crying.
...
THEN WHY?
CALM DOWN.

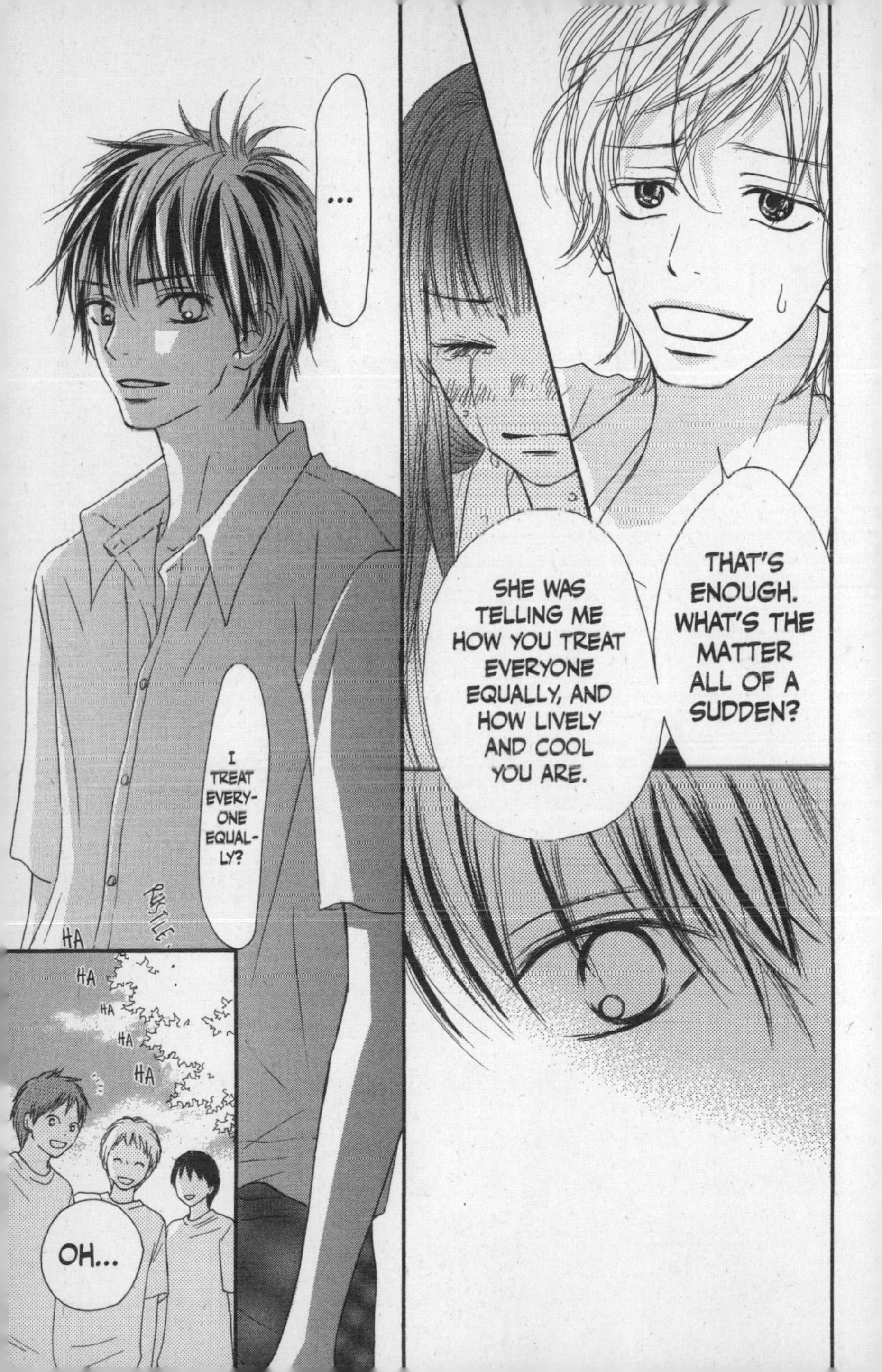
THAT'S ENOUGH. WHAT'S THE MATTER ALL OF A SUDDEN?
SHE WAS TELLING ME HOW YOU TREAT EVERYONE EQUALLY, AND HOW LIVELY AND COOL YOU ARE.
...
I TREAT EVERY-ONE EQUAL-LY?
RUSTLE
HA
HA
HA
HA
HA
OH...

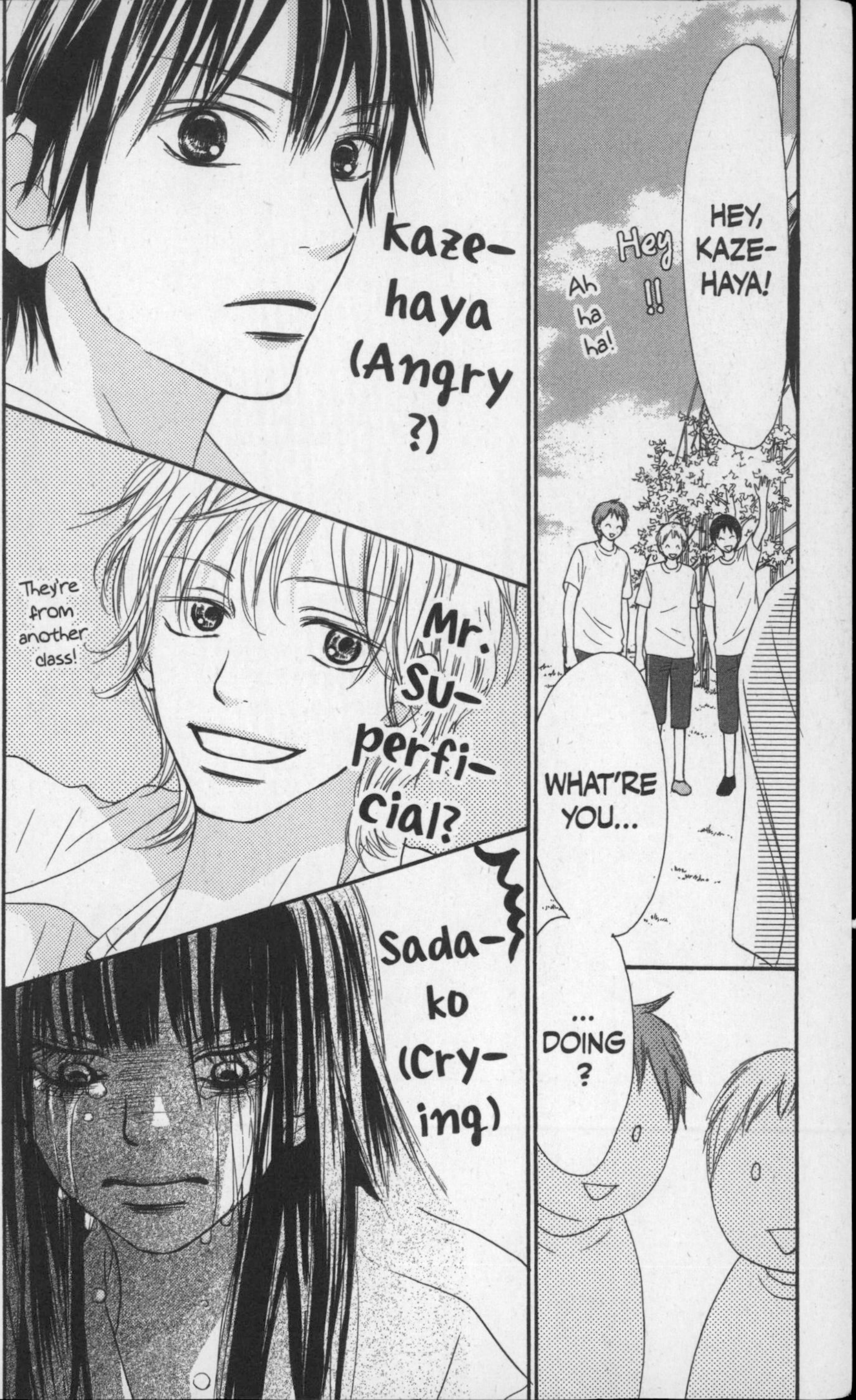
HEY, KAZE-HAYA!
Hey !!
Ah ha ha!
WHAT'RE YOU...
... DOING ?
kaze-haya (Angry ?)
Mr. Su-perfi-cial?
They're from another class!
Sada-ko (Cry-ing)

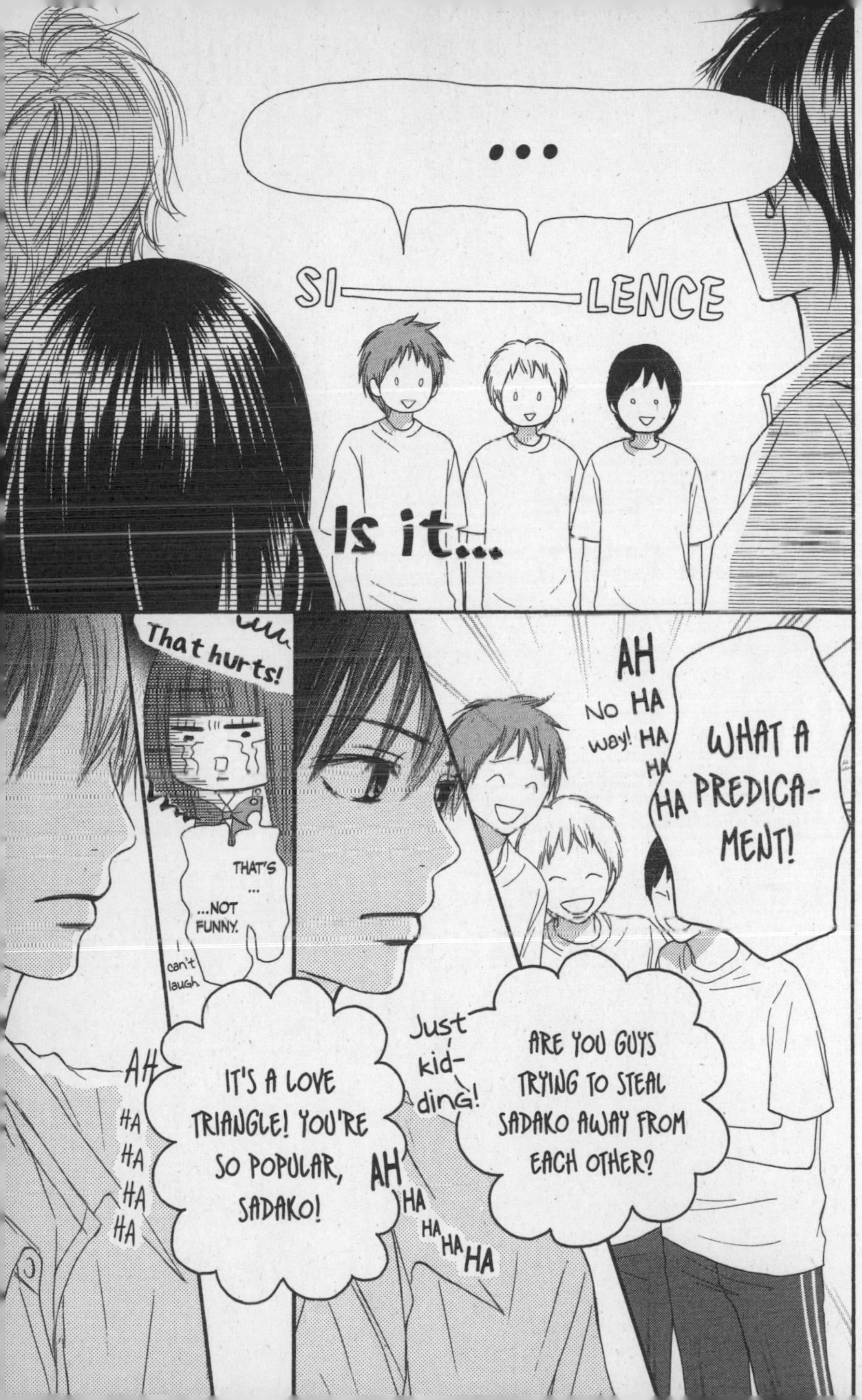
...
SI———LENCE
Is it...
AH HA HA HA HA
No way!
WHAT A PREDICAMENT!
ARE YOU GUYS TRYING TO STEAL SADAKO AWAY FROM EACH OTHER?
Just kidding!
AH HA HA HA HA
IT'S A LOVE TRIANGLE! YOU'RE SO POPULAR, SADAKO!
That hurts!
THAT'S ... ...NOT FUNNY.
I can't laugh.
AH HA HA HA HA

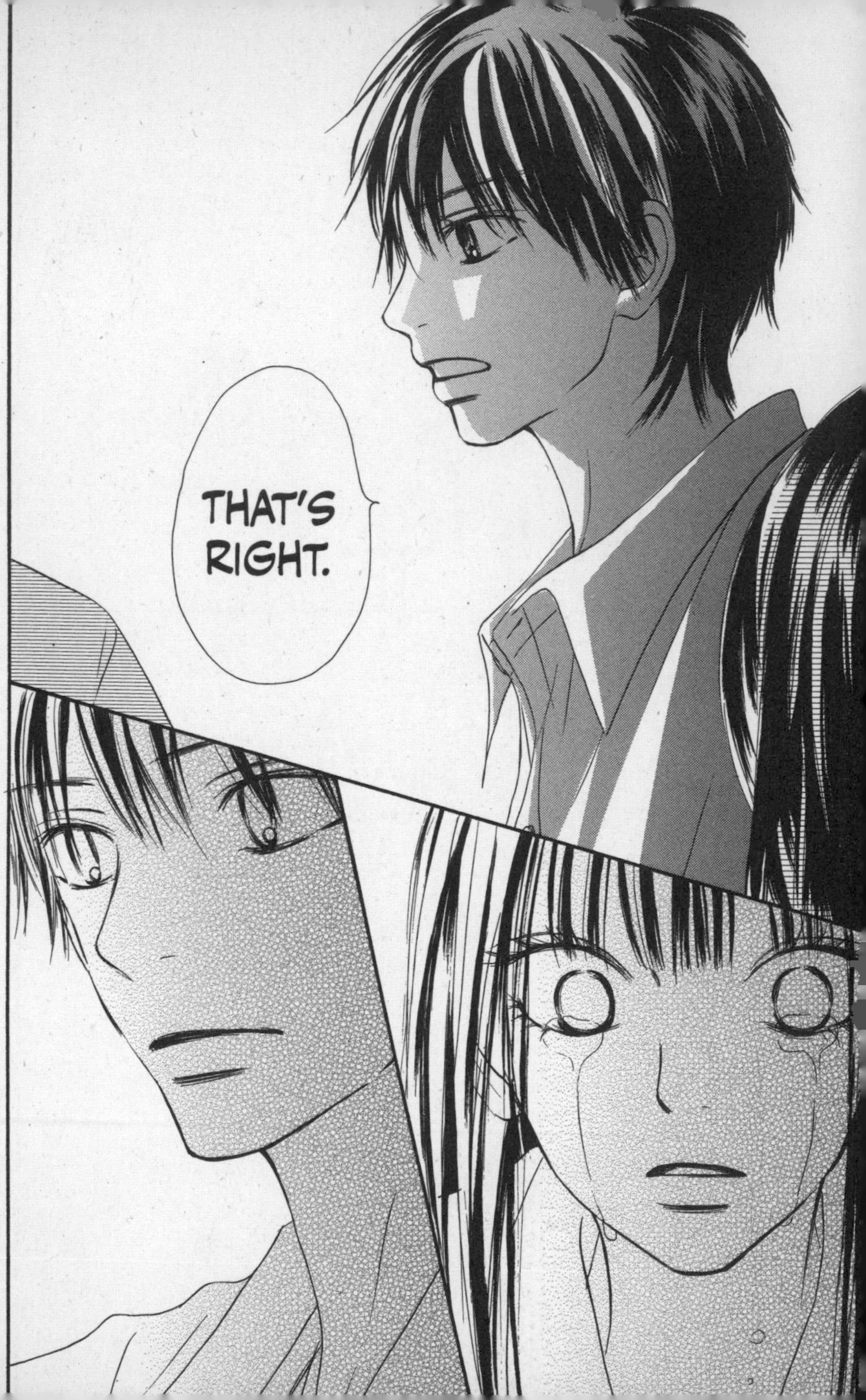
THAT'S RIGHT.

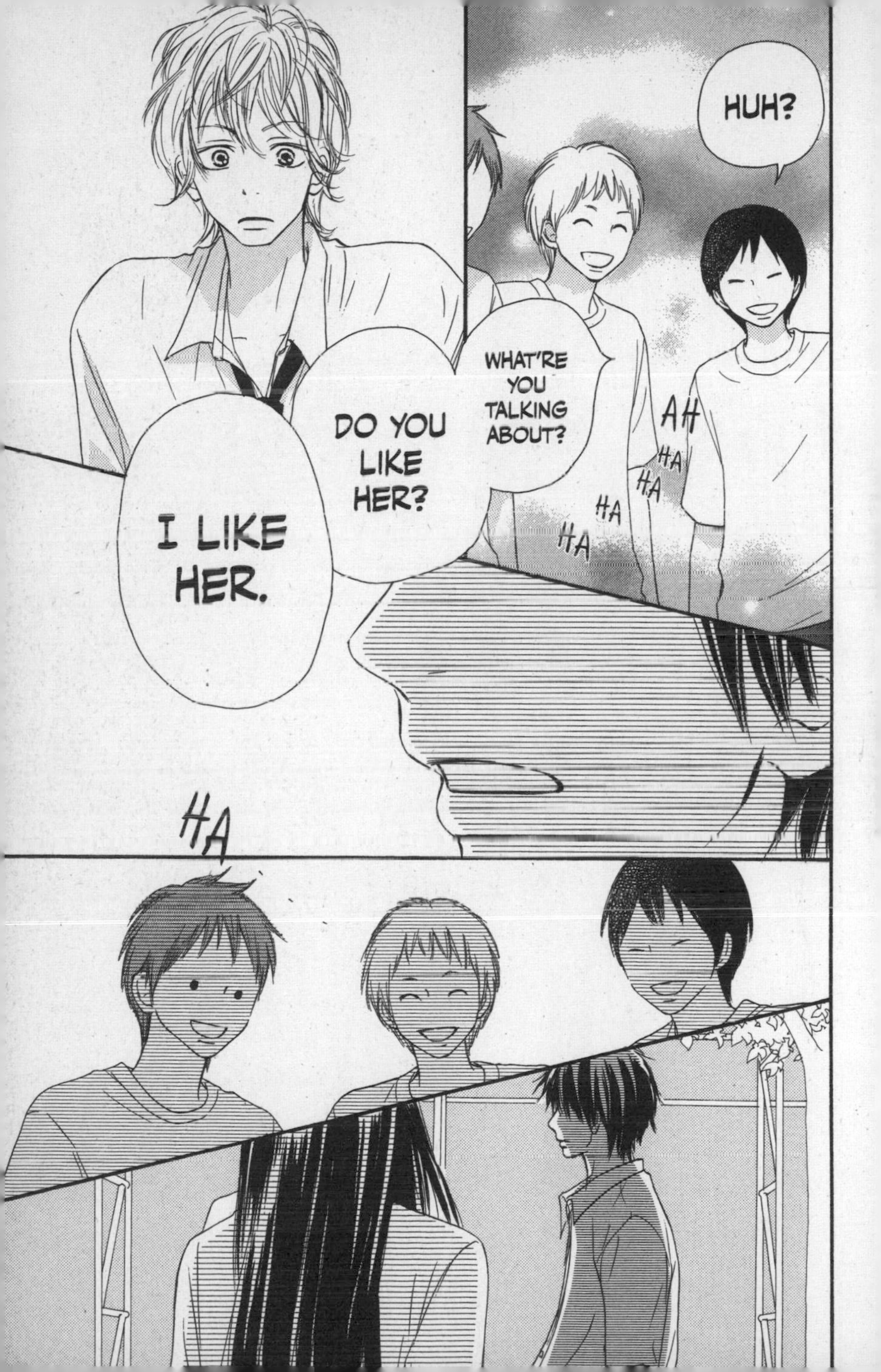
HUH?
WHAT'RE YOU TALKING ABOUT?
AH HA HA HA HA
DO YOU LIKE HER?
I LIKE HER.
HA

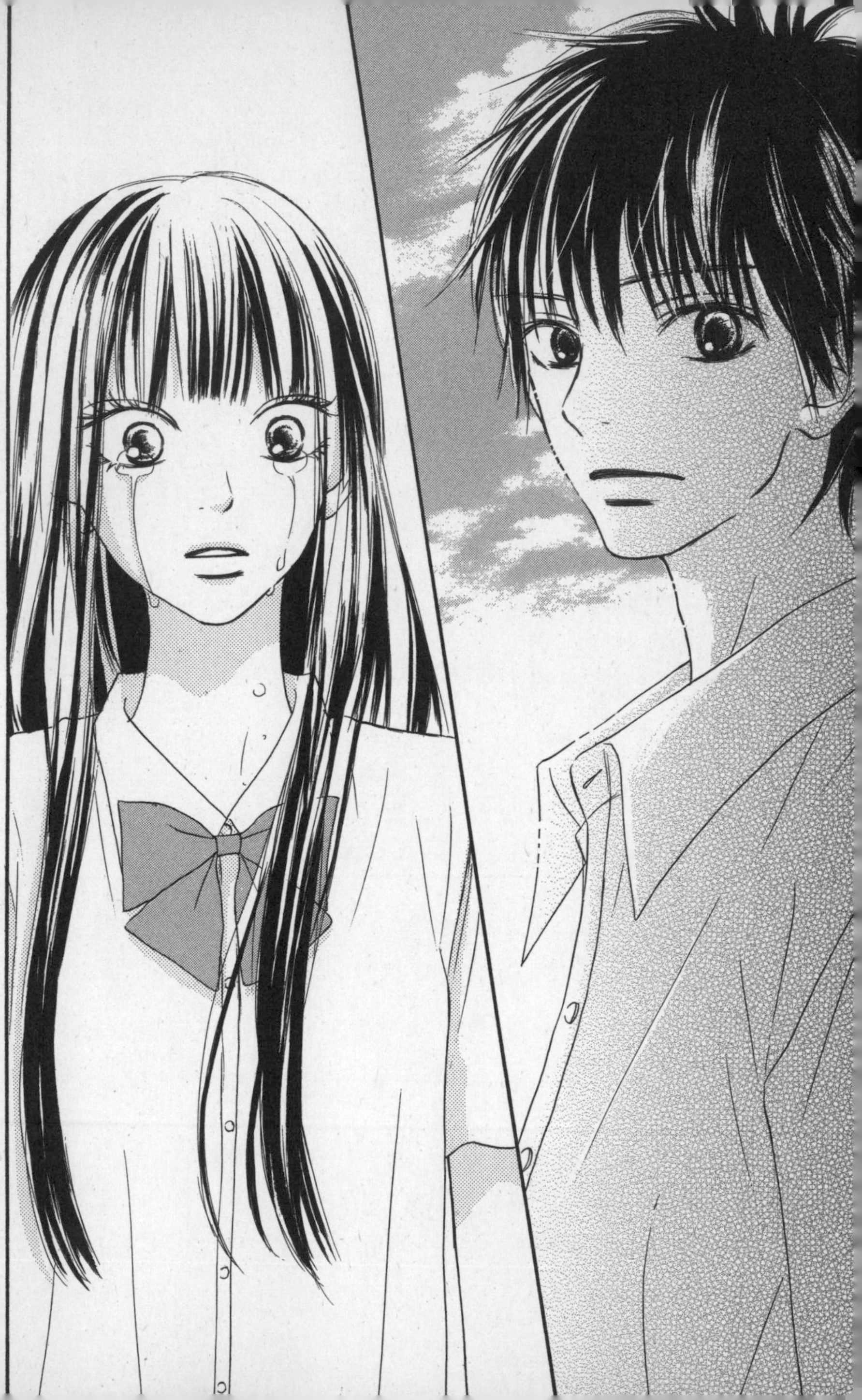

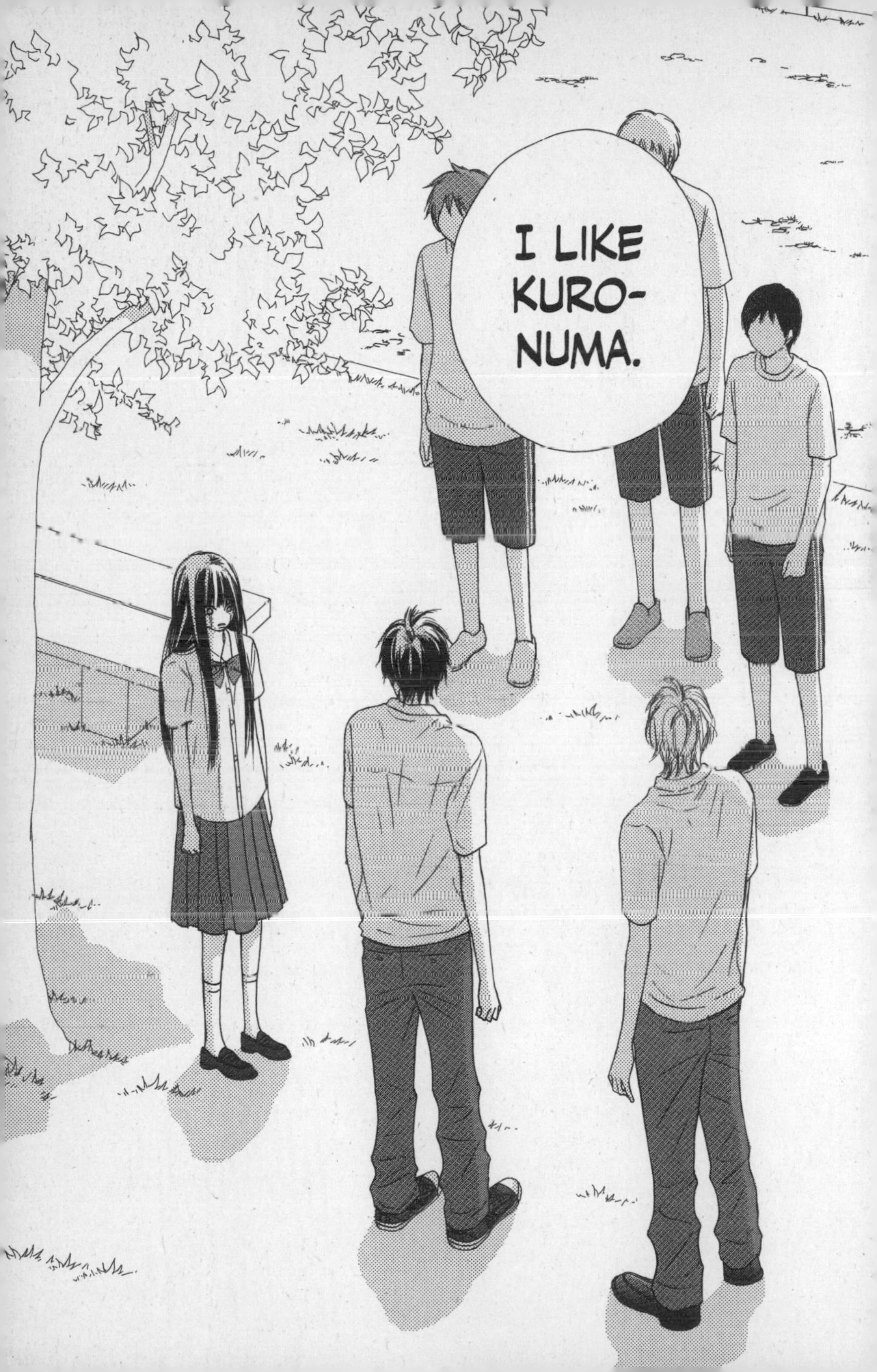
I LIKE KURO-NUMA.

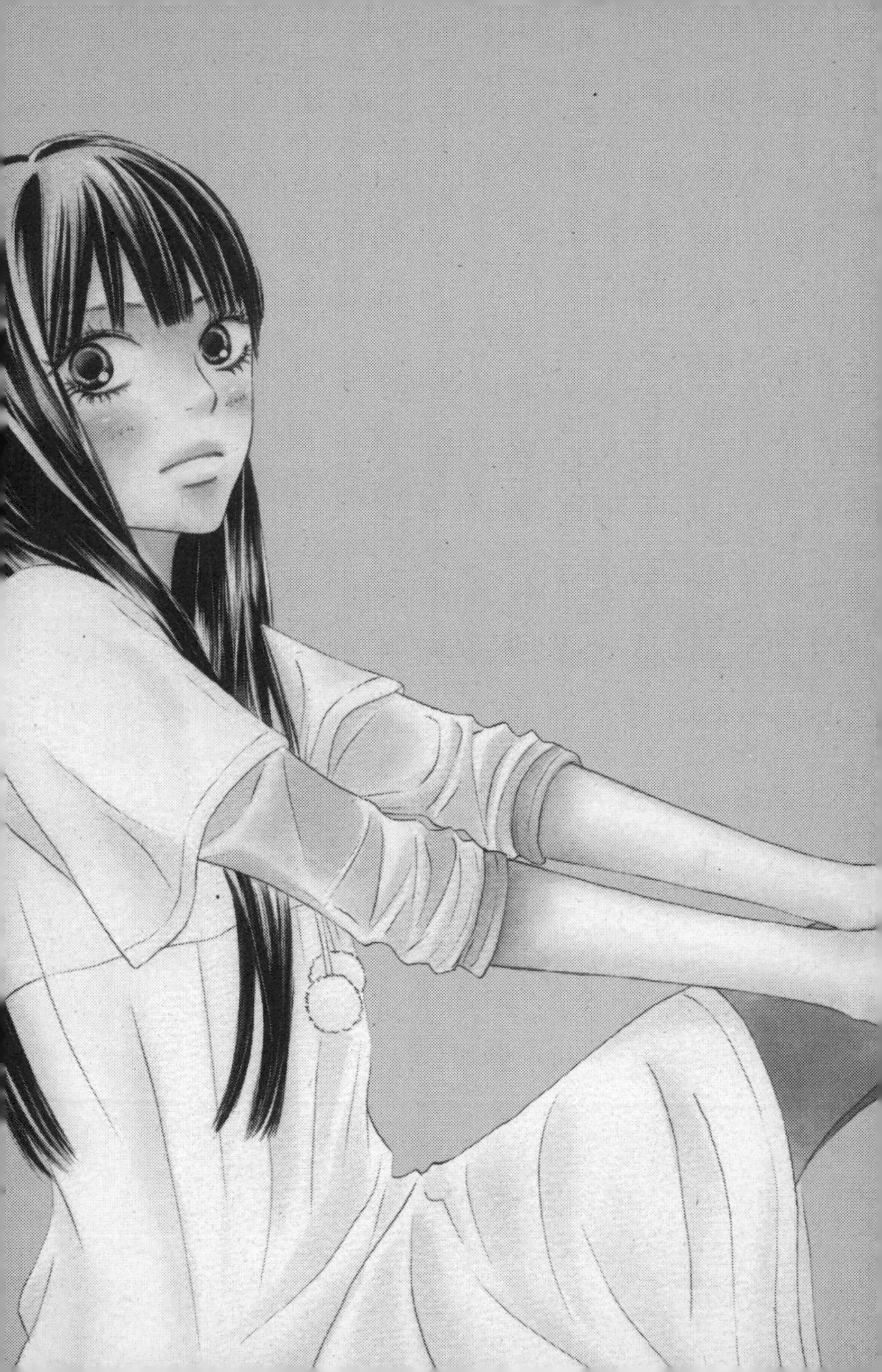

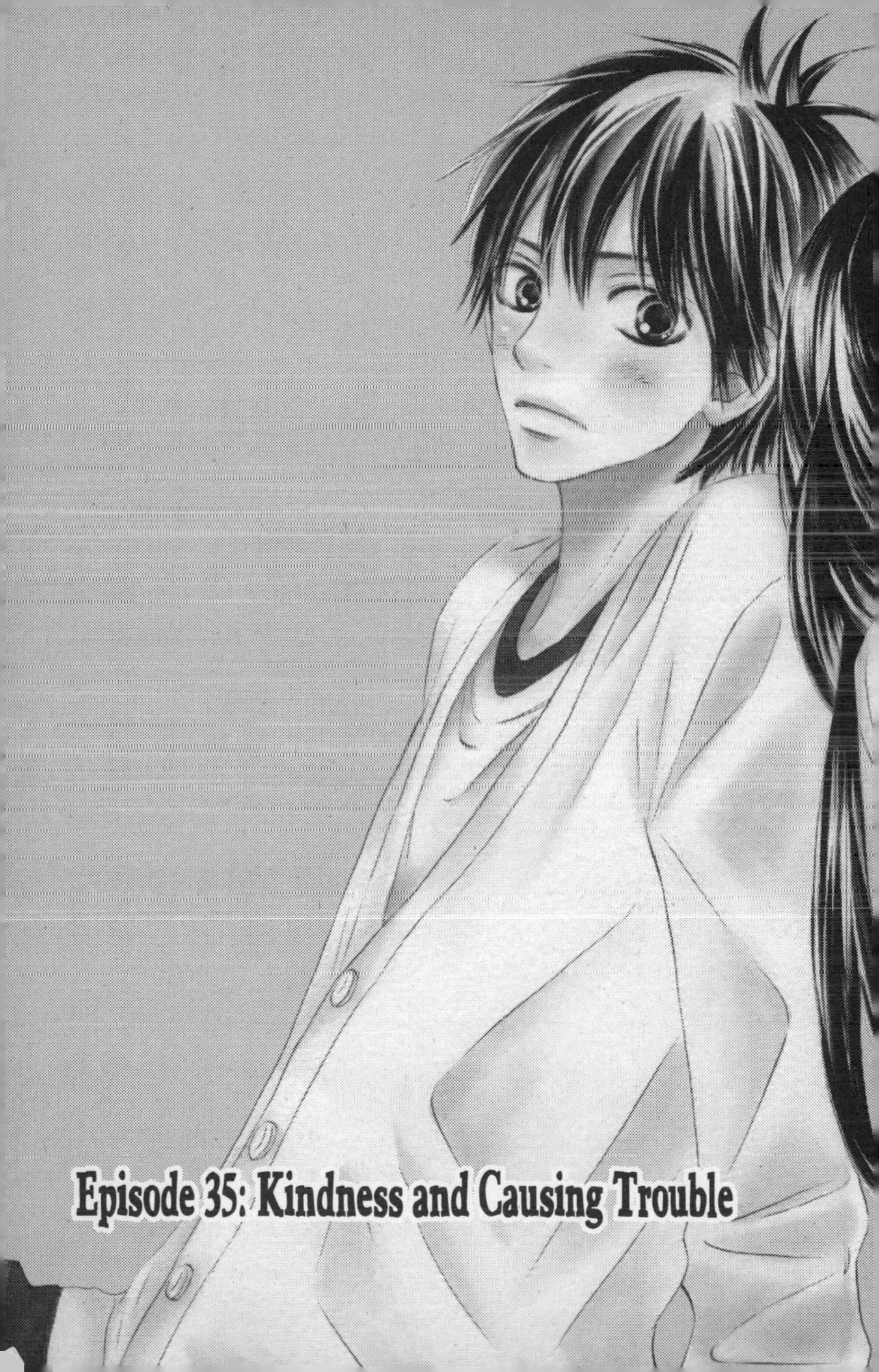

Episode 35: Kindness and Causing Trouble

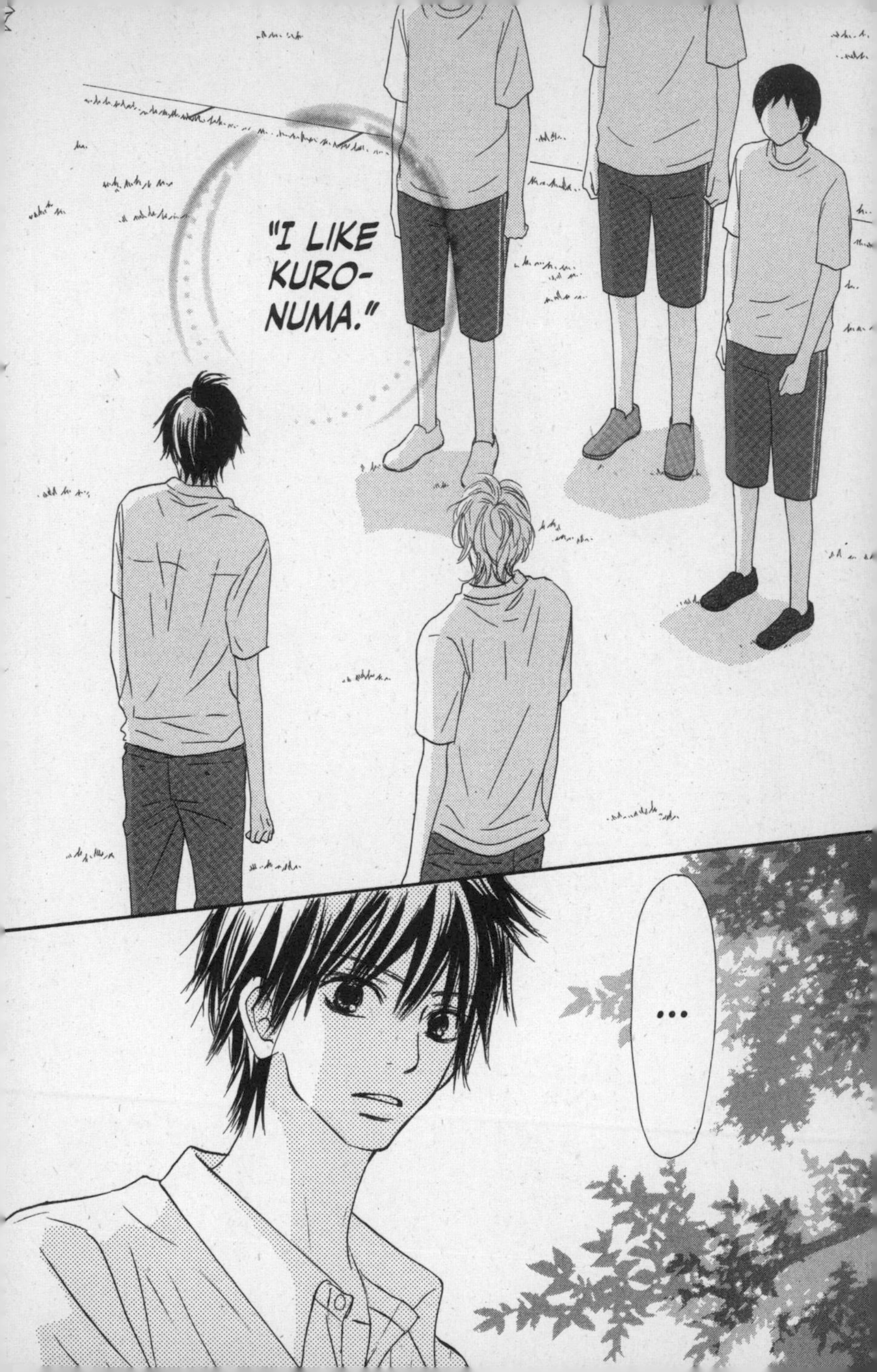
"I LIKE KURO-NUMA."
...

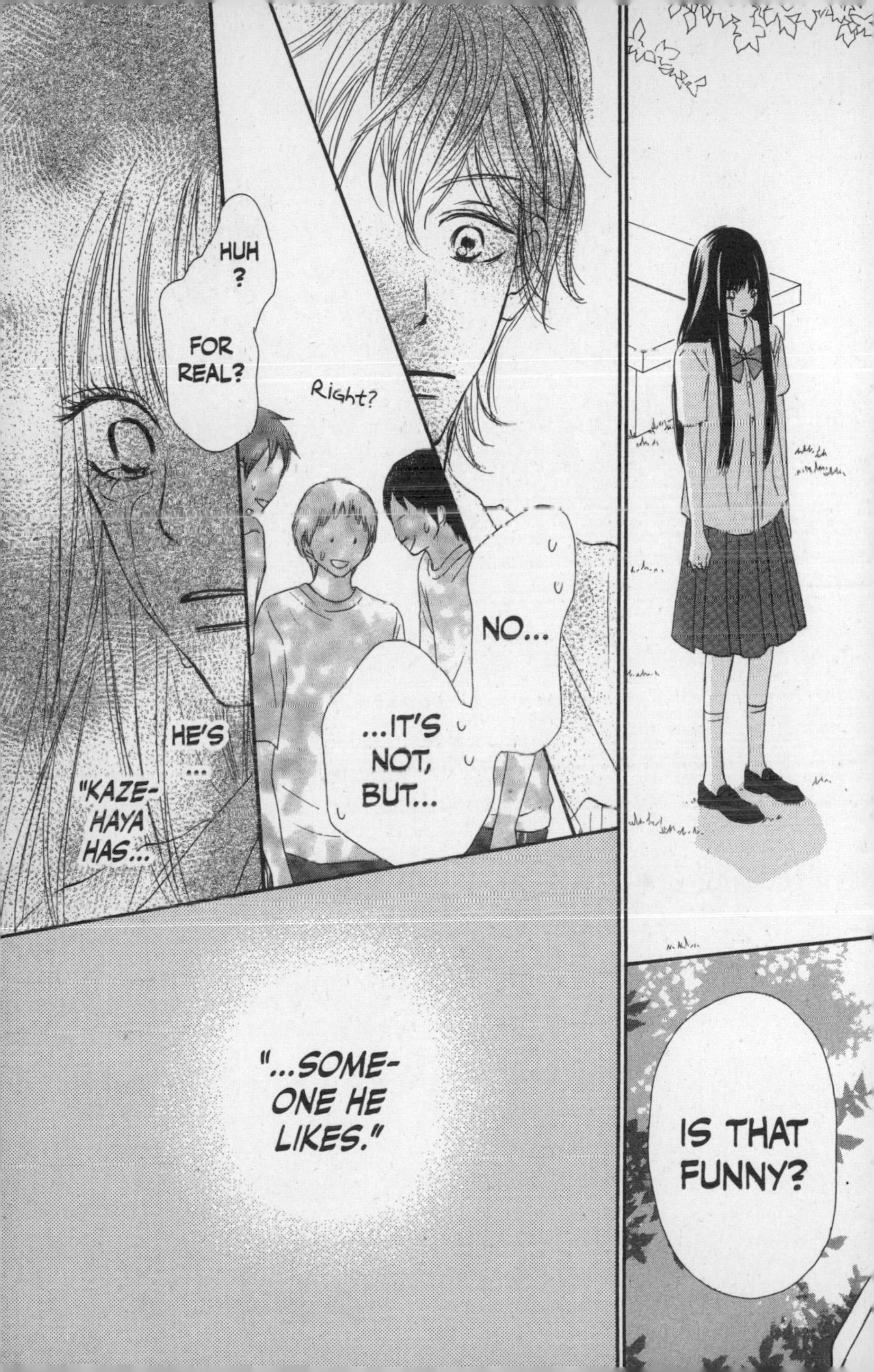
IS THAT FUNNY?
HUH? FOR REAL?
Right?
NO...
...IT'S NOT, BUT...
HE'S...
"KAZE-HAYA HAS...
"...SOME-ONE HE LIKES."

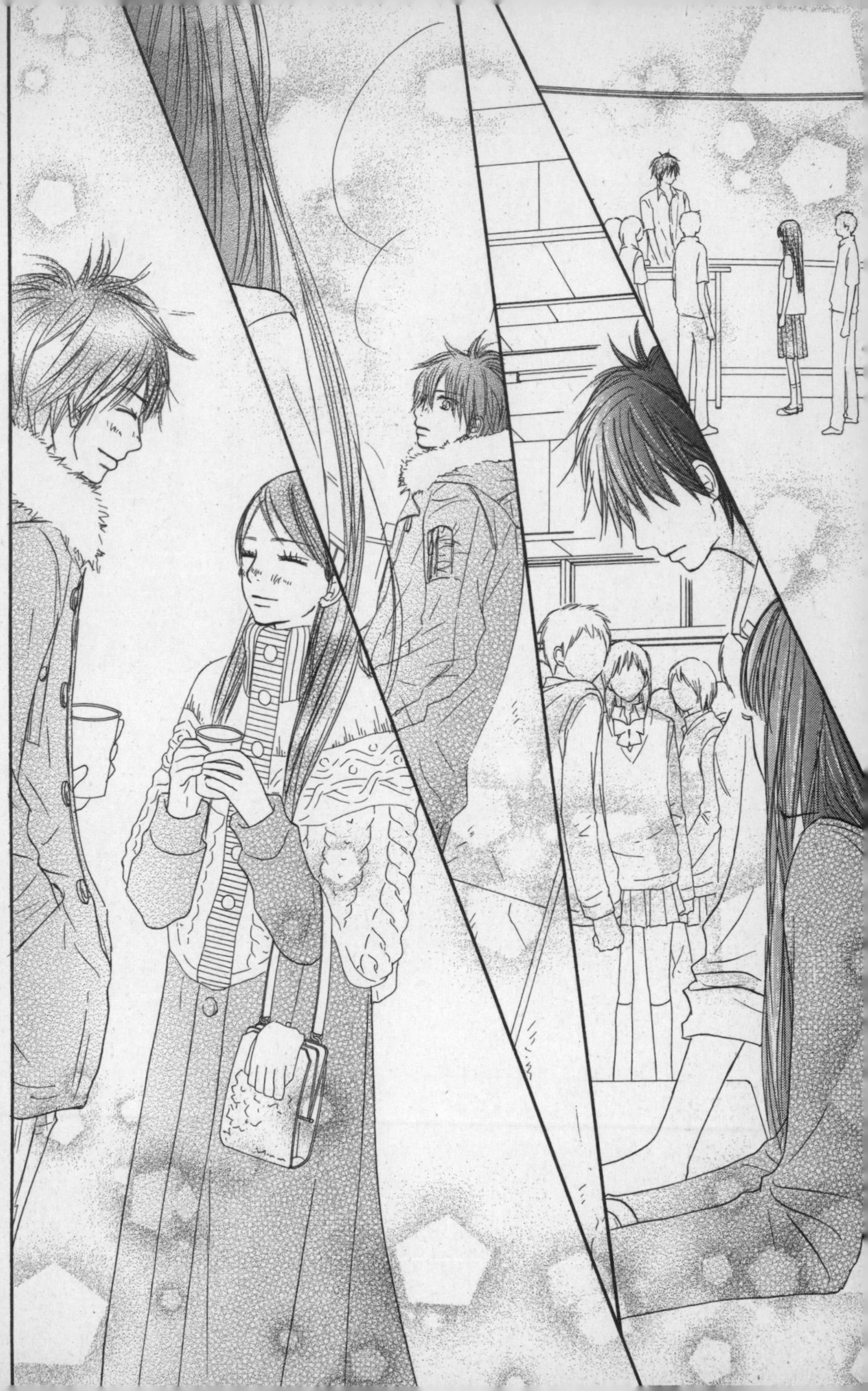

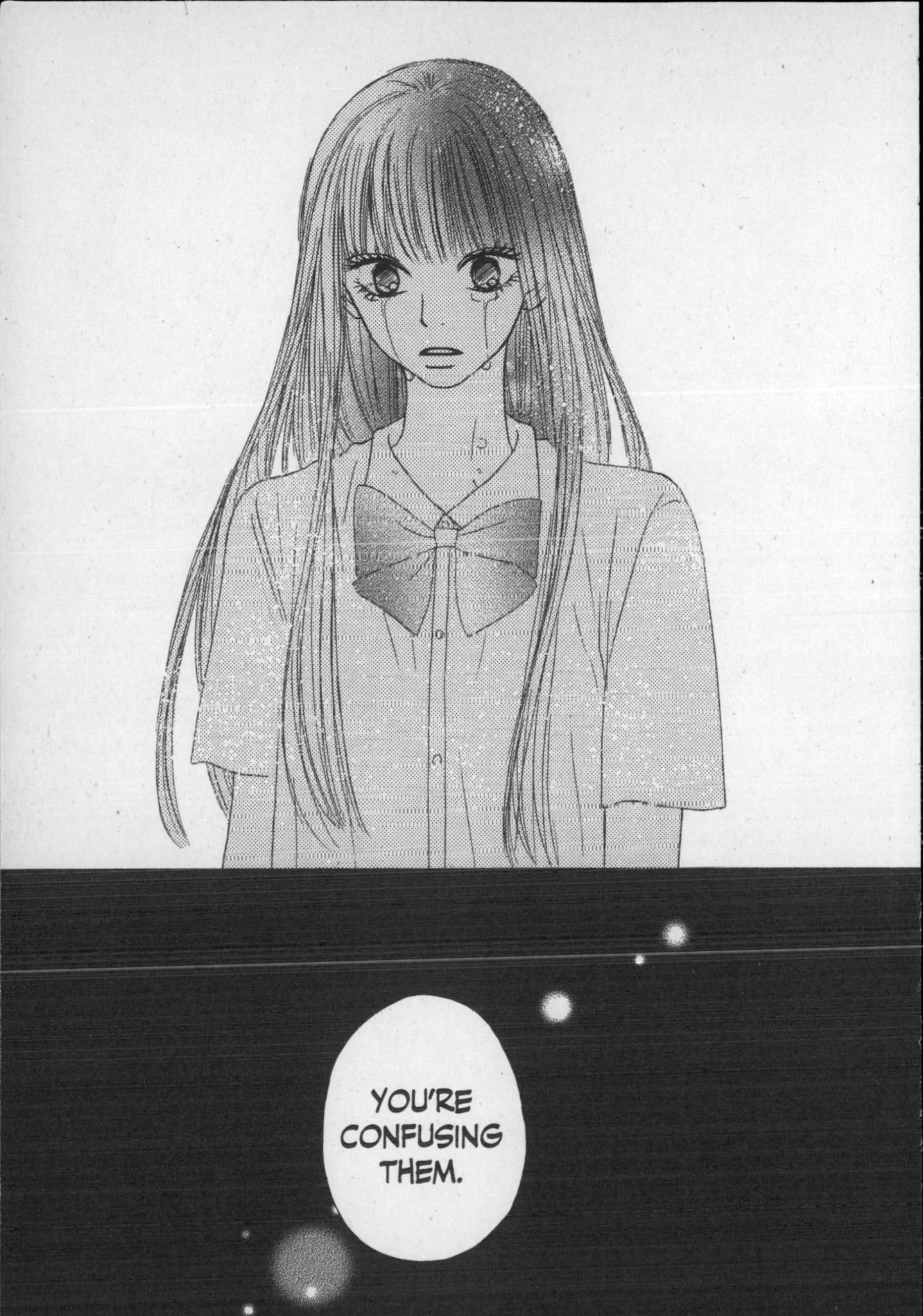
YOU'RE CONFUSING THEM.

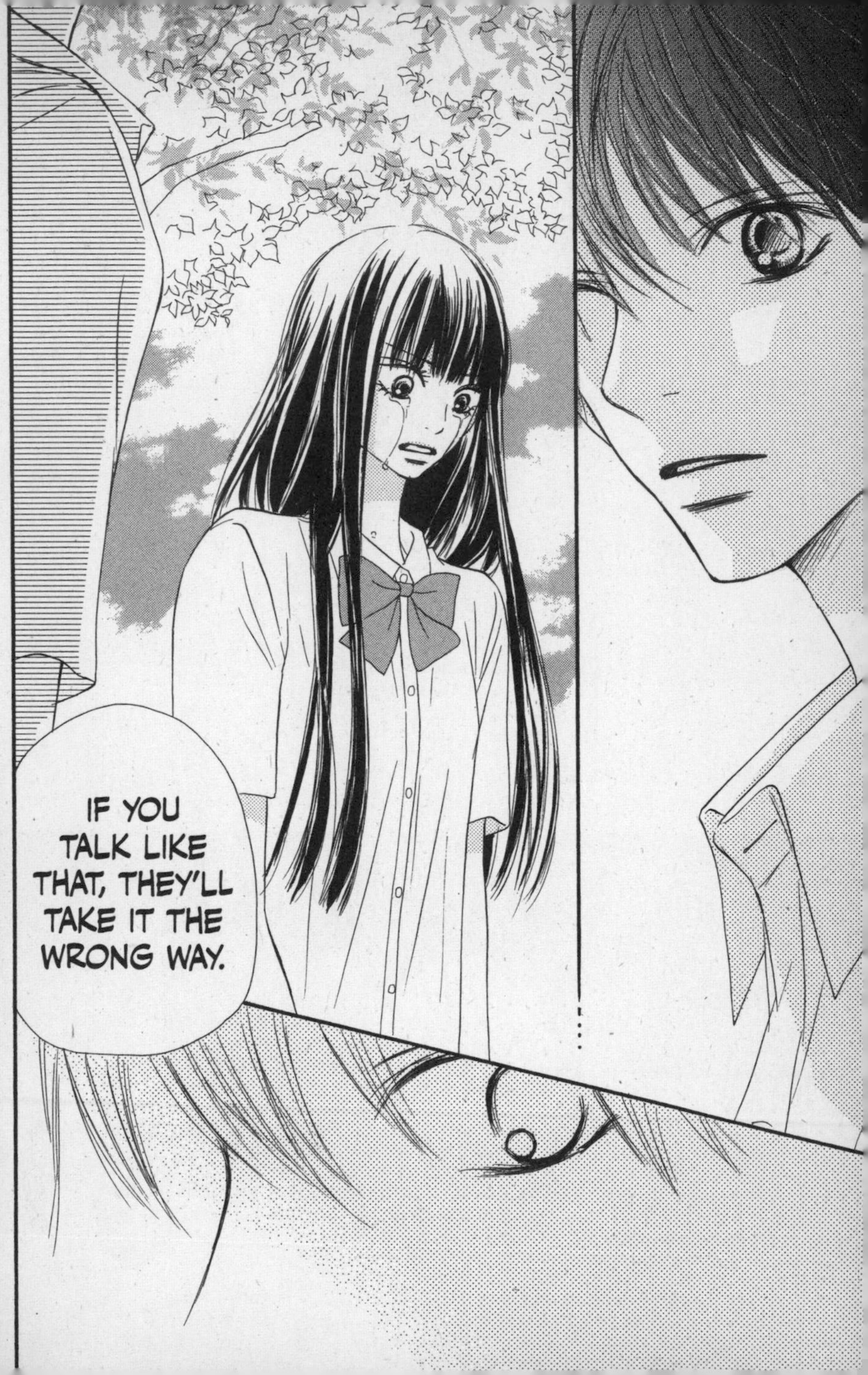
IF YOU TALK LIKE THAT, THEY'LL TAKE IT THE WRONG WAY.
...

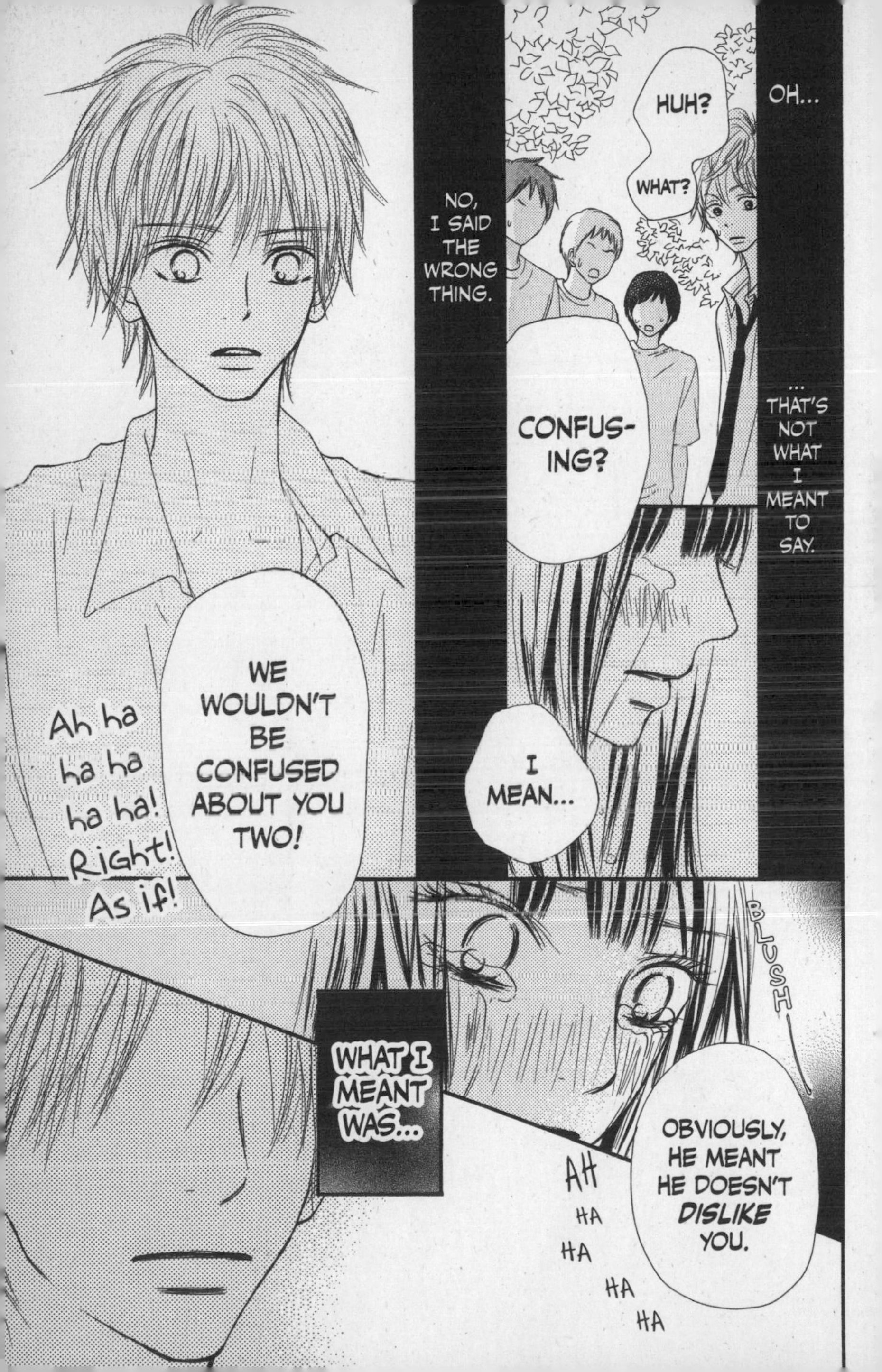

OH...
HUH?
WHAT?
CONFUSING?
NO, I SAID THE WRONG THING.
...THAT'S NOT WHAT I MEANT TO SAY.
I MEAN...
WE WOULDN'T BE CONFUSED ABOUT YOU TWO!
Ah ha ha ha ha ha! Right! As if!
BLUSH
OBVIOUSLY, HE MEANT HE DOESN'T *DISLIKE* YOU.
AH HA HA HA HA
WHAT I MEANT WAS...

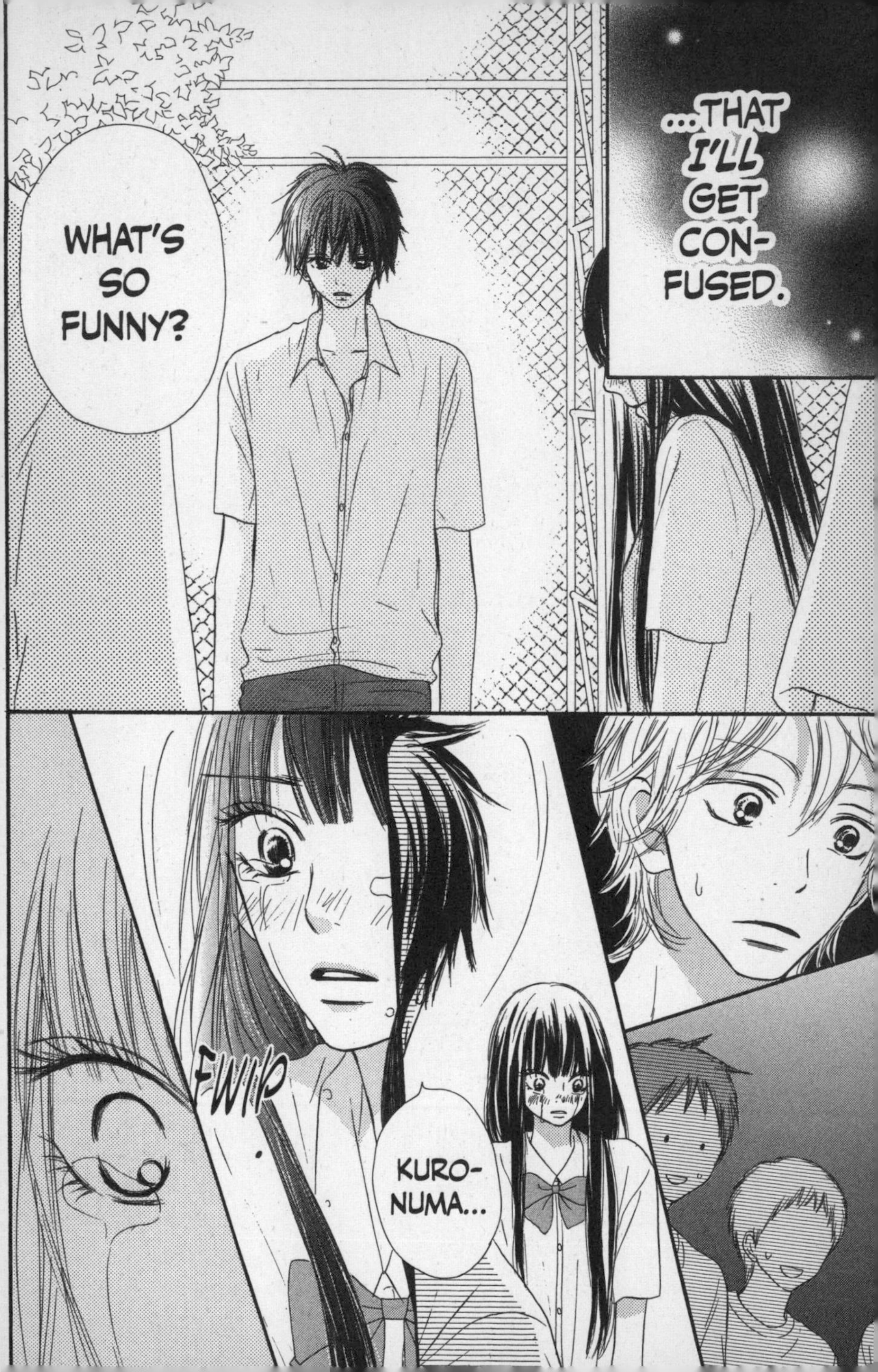
...THAT I'LL GET CON-FUSED.
WHAT'S SO FUNNY?
FWIP
KURO-NUMA...

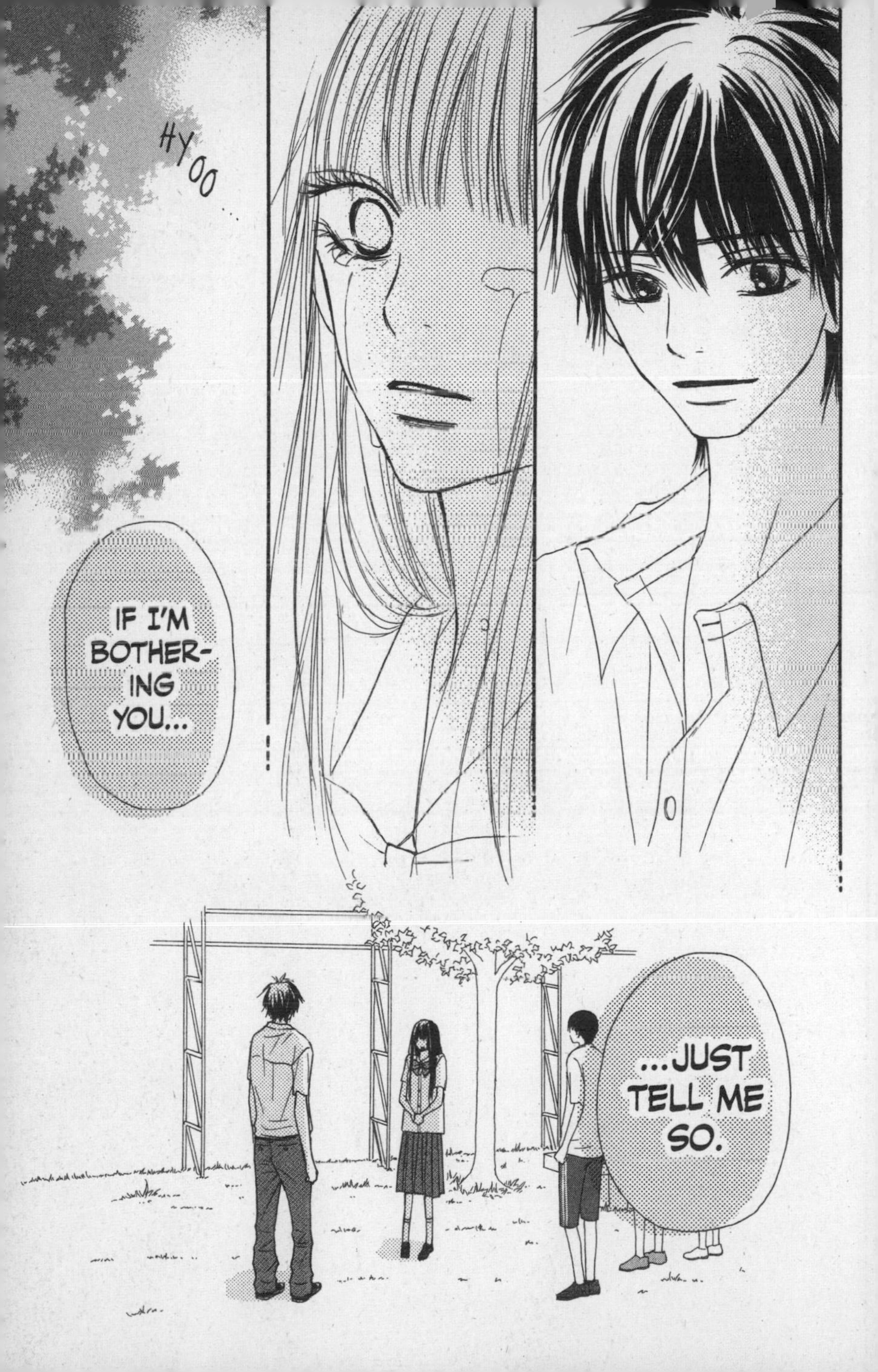
HYOO...
IF I'M BOTHERING YOU...
...JUST TELL ME SO.

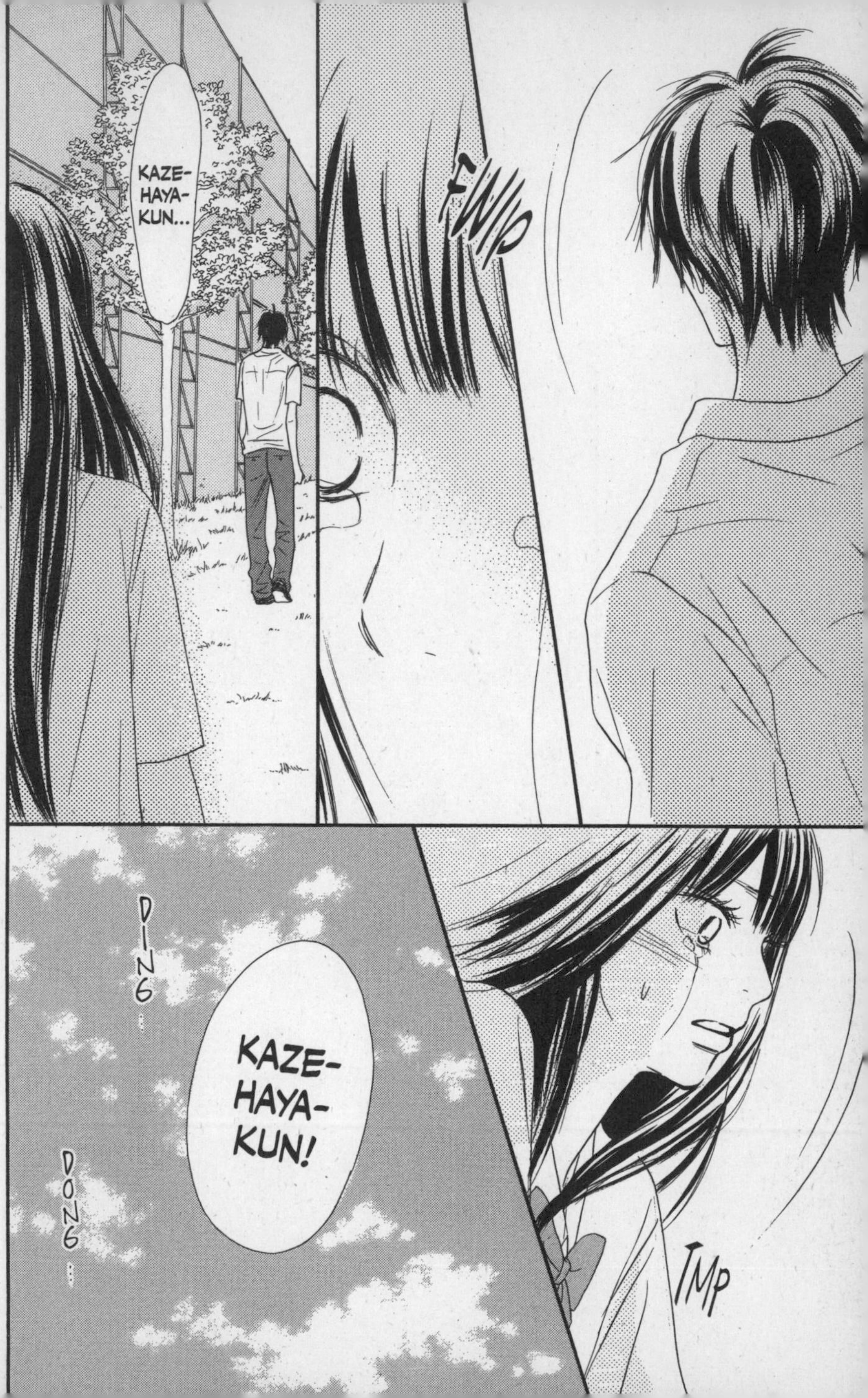
FWIP
KAZE-HAYA-KUN...
KAZE-HAYA-KUN!
TMP
DING...
DONG...

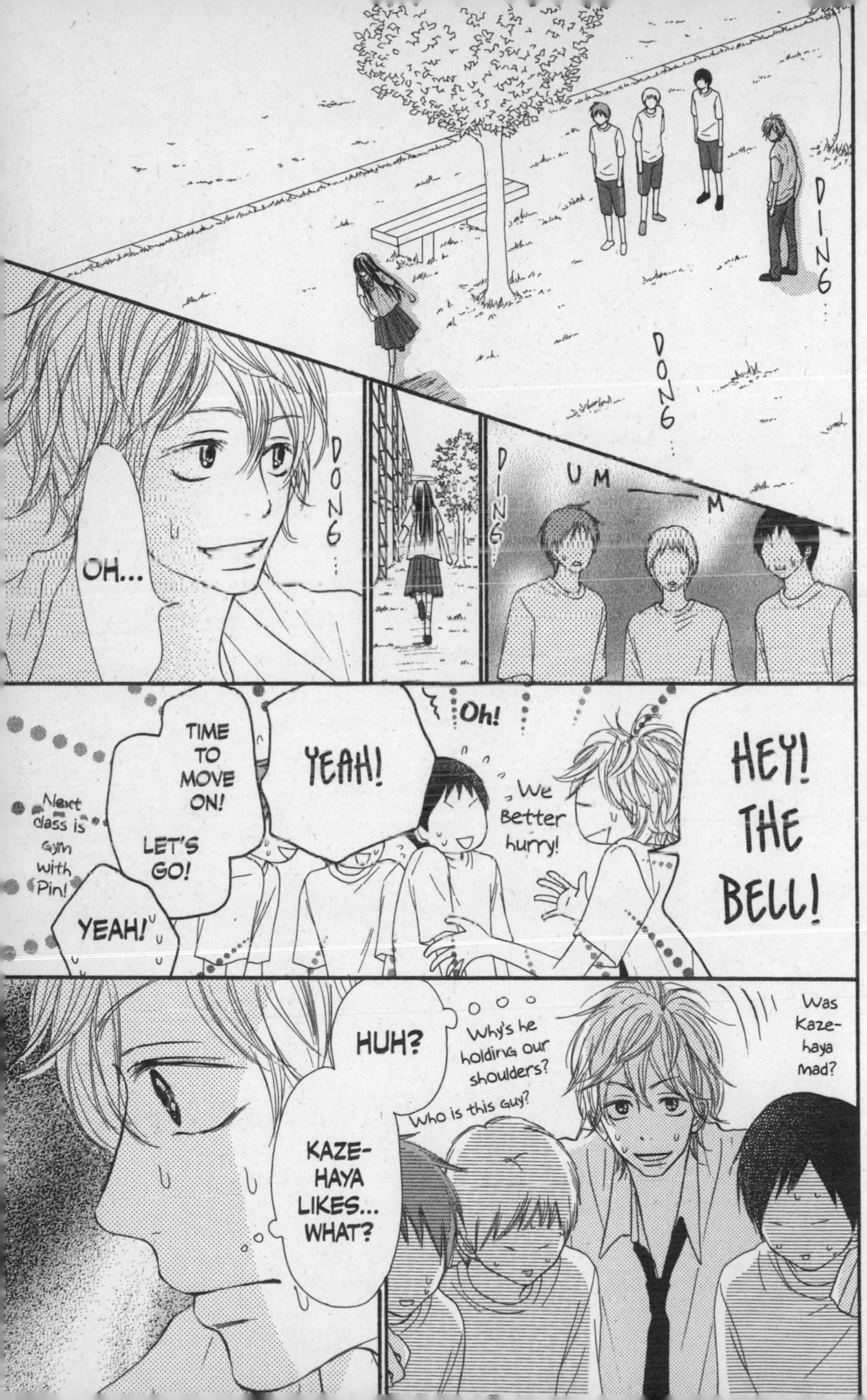
DING...
DONG...
UM—M
DING...
DONG...
OH...
HEY! THE BELL!
We Better hurry!
Oh!
YEAH!
TIME TO MOVE ON!
LET'S GO!
Next class is gym with Pin!
YEAH!
Was Kaze-haya mad?
Why's he holding our shoulders?
Who is this guy?
HUH?
KAZE-HAYA LIKES... WHAT?

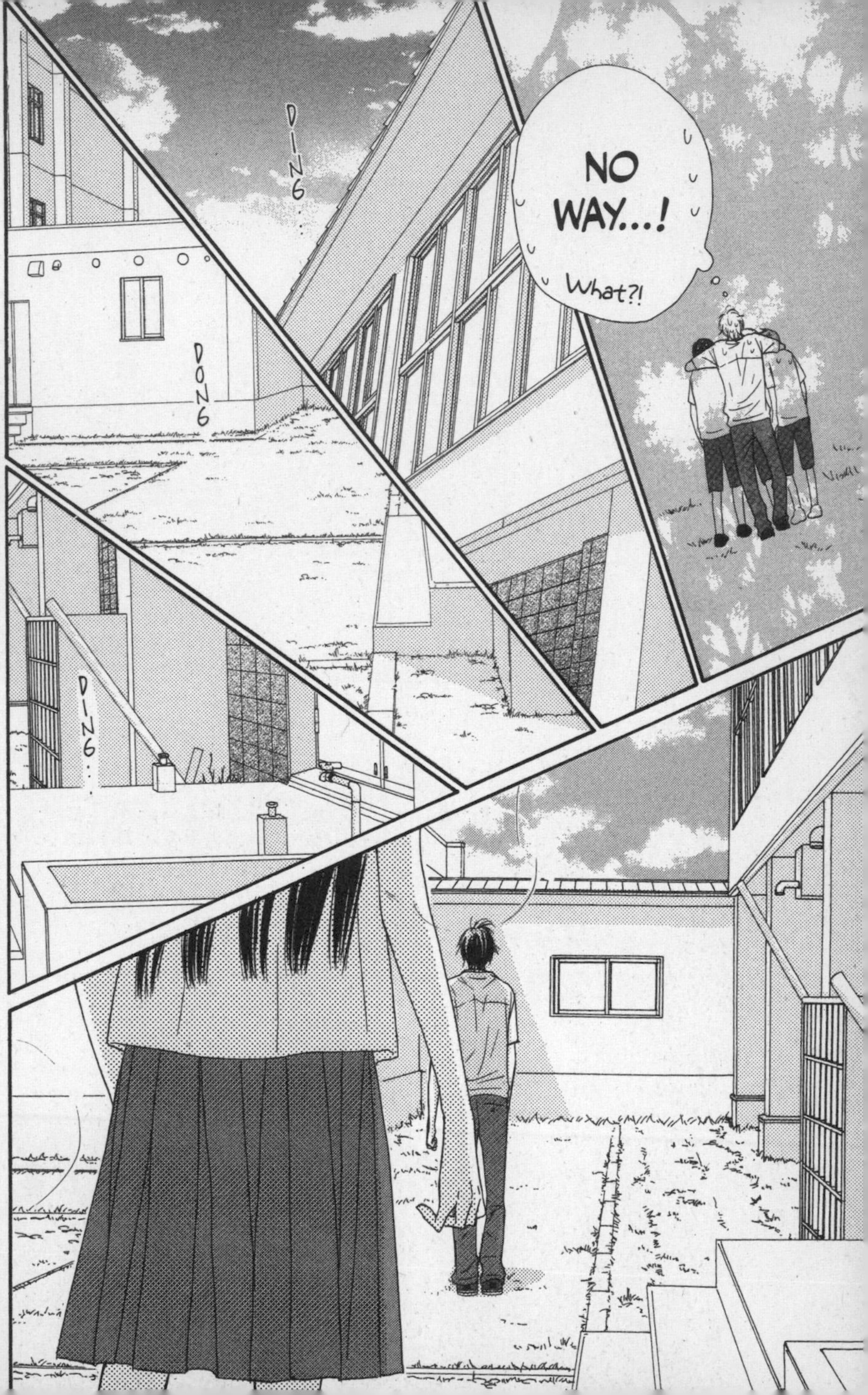
NO WAY...!
What?!
DING
DONG
DING...

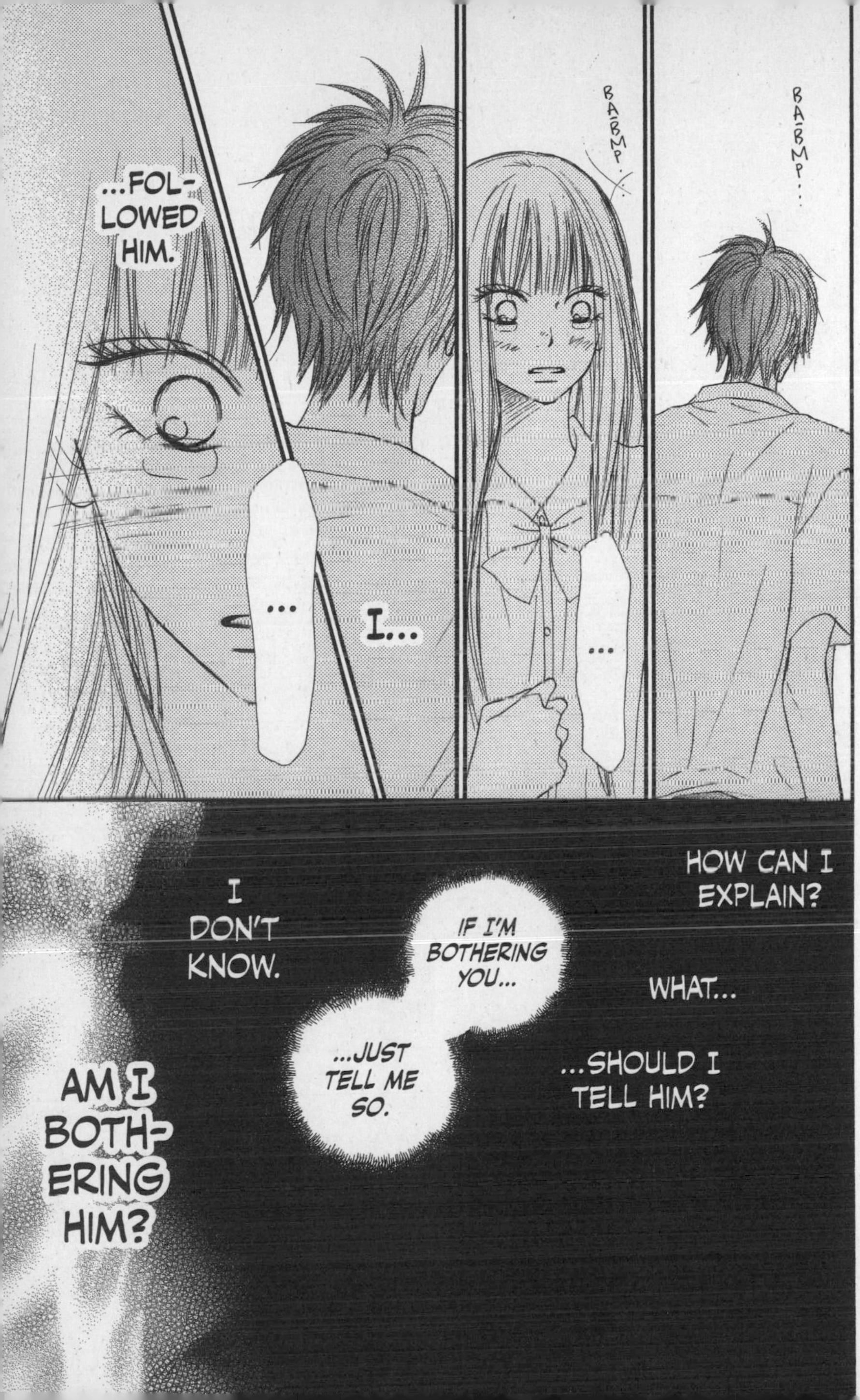
BA-BUMP...
BA-BUMP...
...
I...
...FOL-LOWED HIM.
...
HOW CAN I EXPLAIN?
WHAT...
...SHOULD I TELL HIM?
I DON'T KNOW.
IF I'M BOTHERING YOU...
...JUST TELL ME SO.
AM I BOTH-ERING HIM?

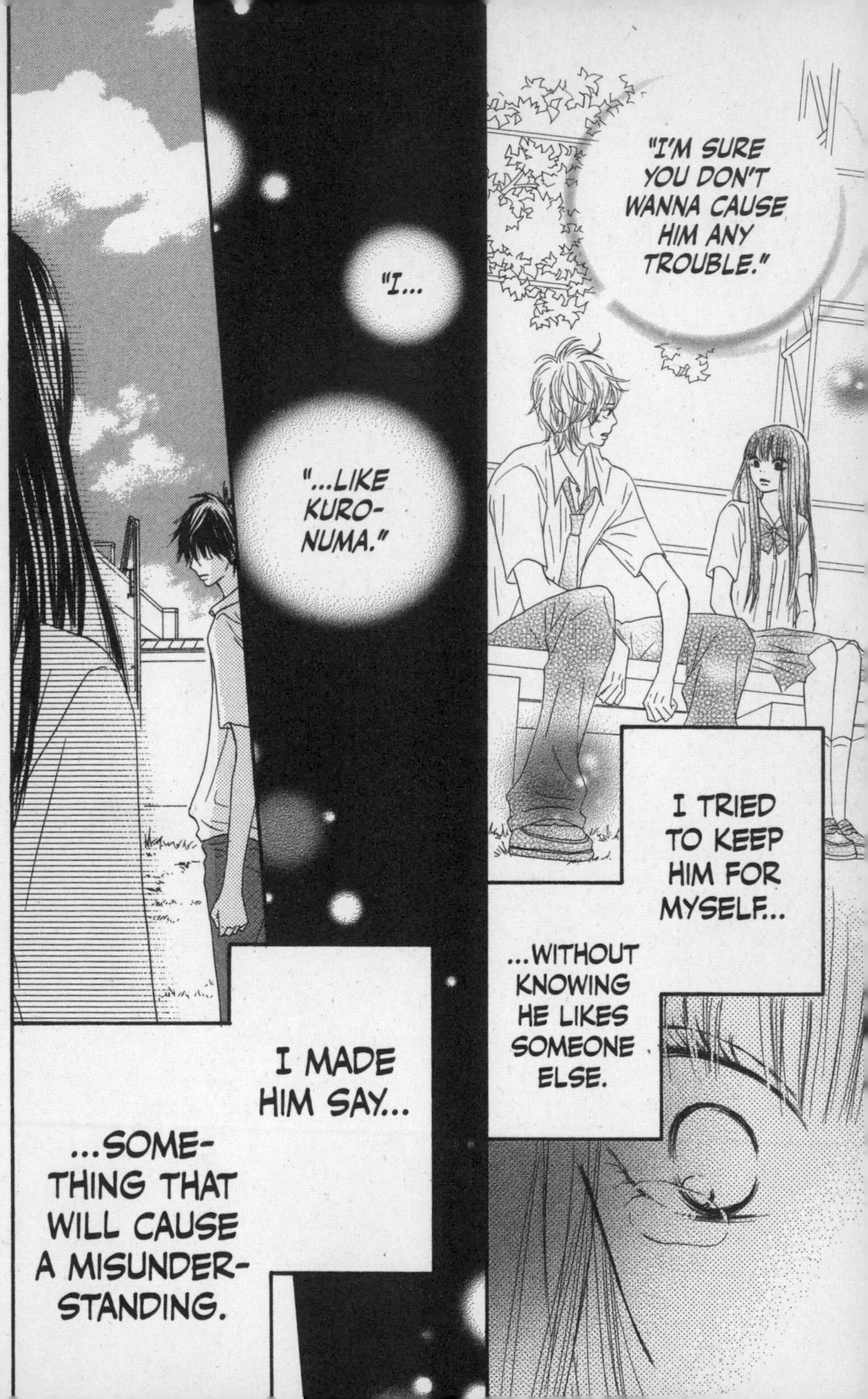
"I'M SURE YOU DON'T WANNA CAUSE HIM ANY TROUBLE."
I TRIED TO KEEP HIM FOR MYSELF...
...WITHOUT KNOWING HE LIKES SOMEONE ELSE.
"I...
"...LIKE KURO-NUMA."
I MADE HIM SAY...
...SOME-THING THAT WILL CAUSE A MISUNDER-STANDING.

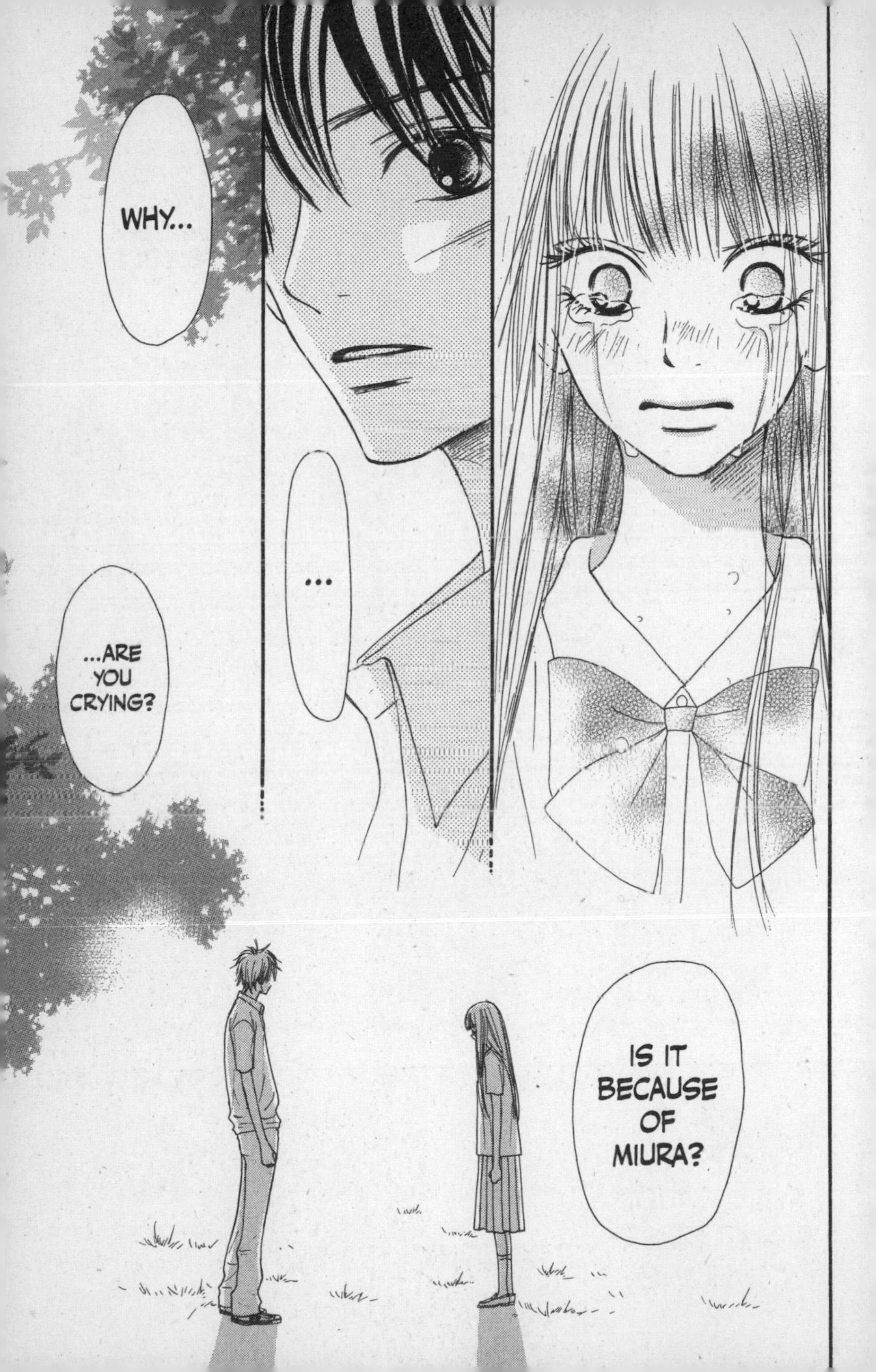
...
WHY...
...ARE YOU CRYING?
IS IT BECAUSE OF MIURA?

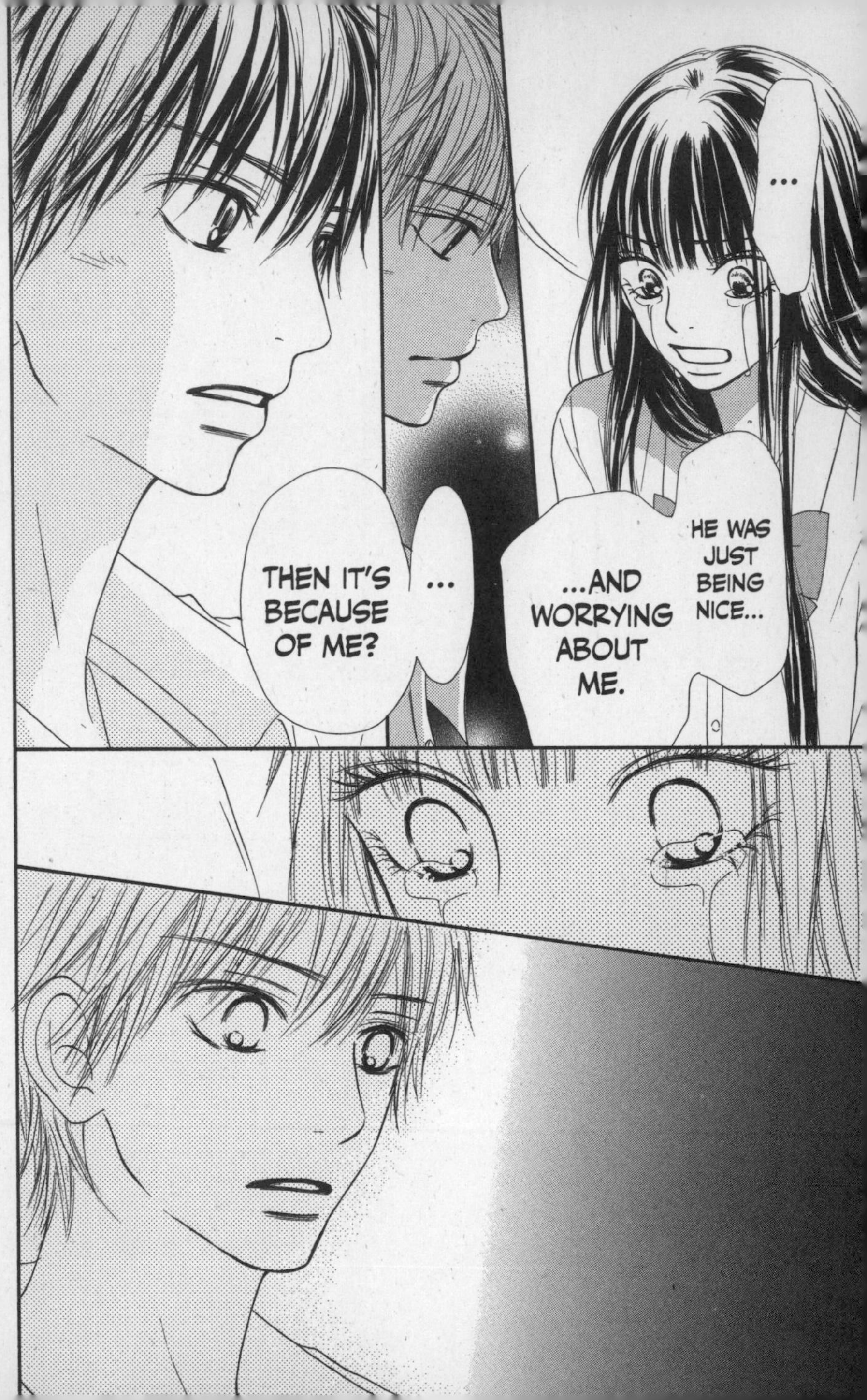
...
HE WAS JUST BEING NICE...
...AND WORRYING ABOUT ME.
...
THEN IT'S BECAUSE OF ME?

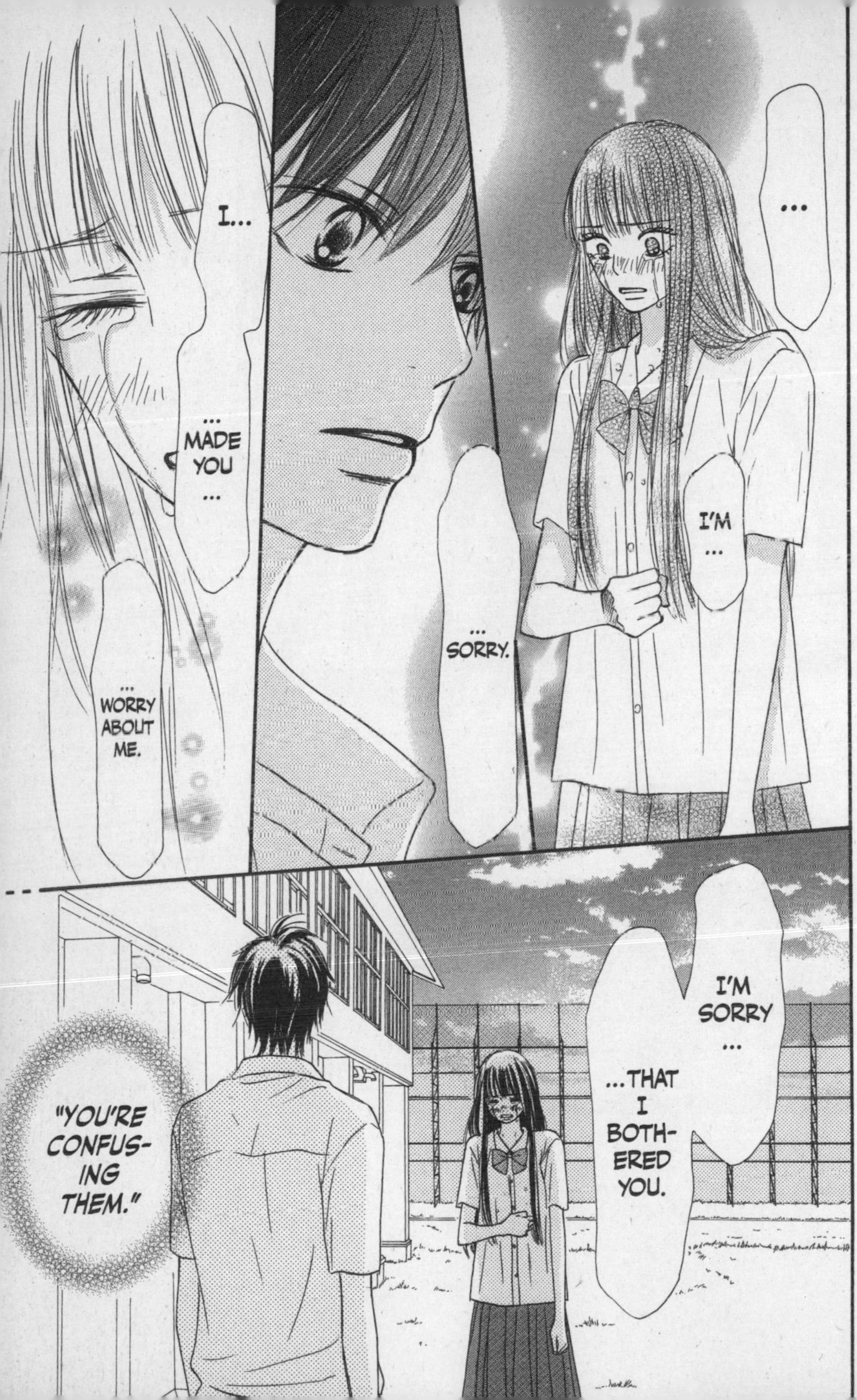
...
I'M ...
... SORRY.
I...
... MADE YOU ...
... WORRY ABOUT ME.
I'M SORRY ...
... THAT I BOTHERED YOU.
"YOU'RE CONFUSING THEM."

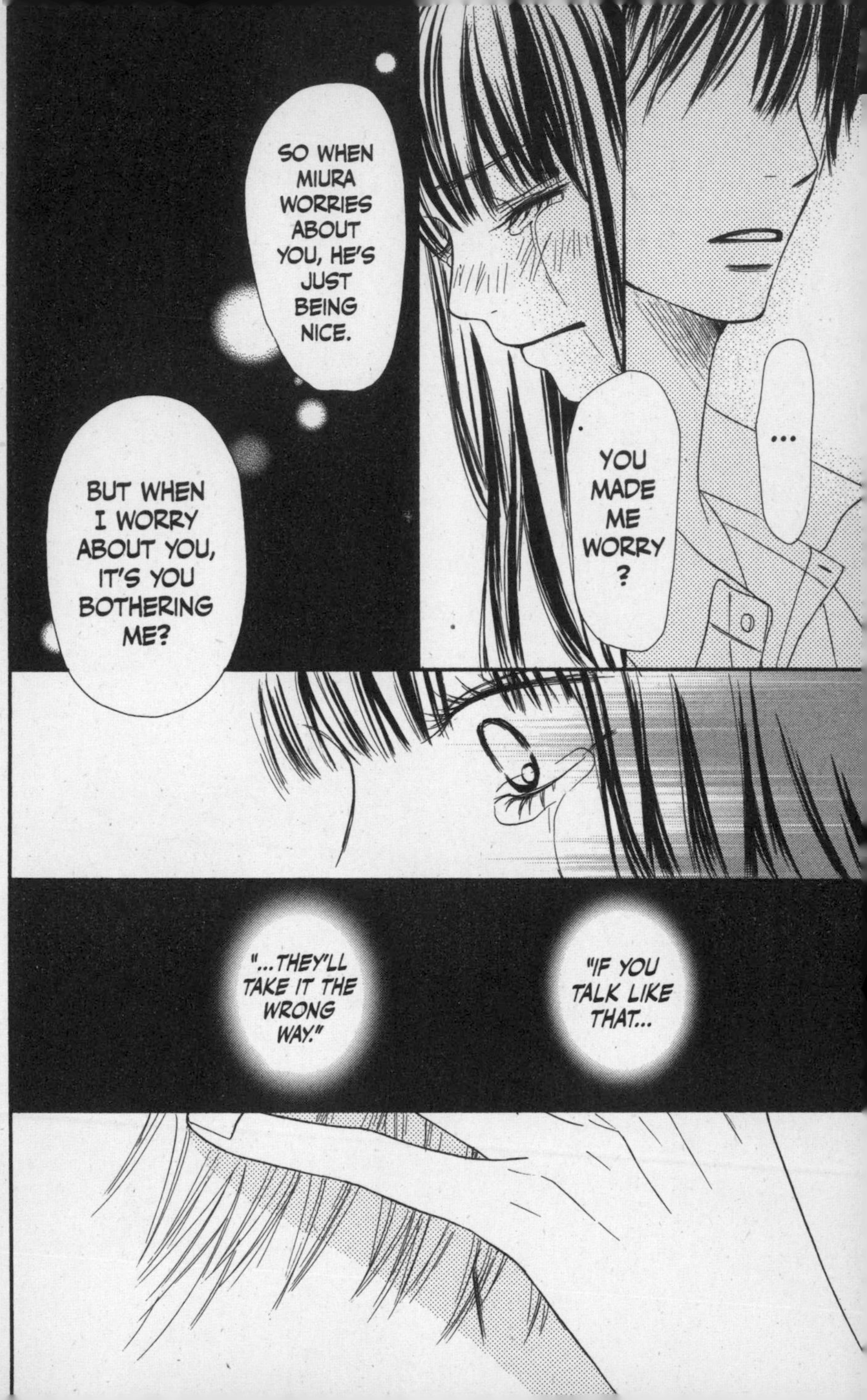
...
YOU MADE ME WORRY?
SO WHEN MIURA WORRIES ABOUT YOU, HE'S JUST BEING NICE.
BUT WHEN I WORRY ABOUT YOU, IT'S YOU BOTHERING ME?
"IF YOU TALK LIKE THAT...
"...THEY'LL TAKE IT THE WRONG WAY."

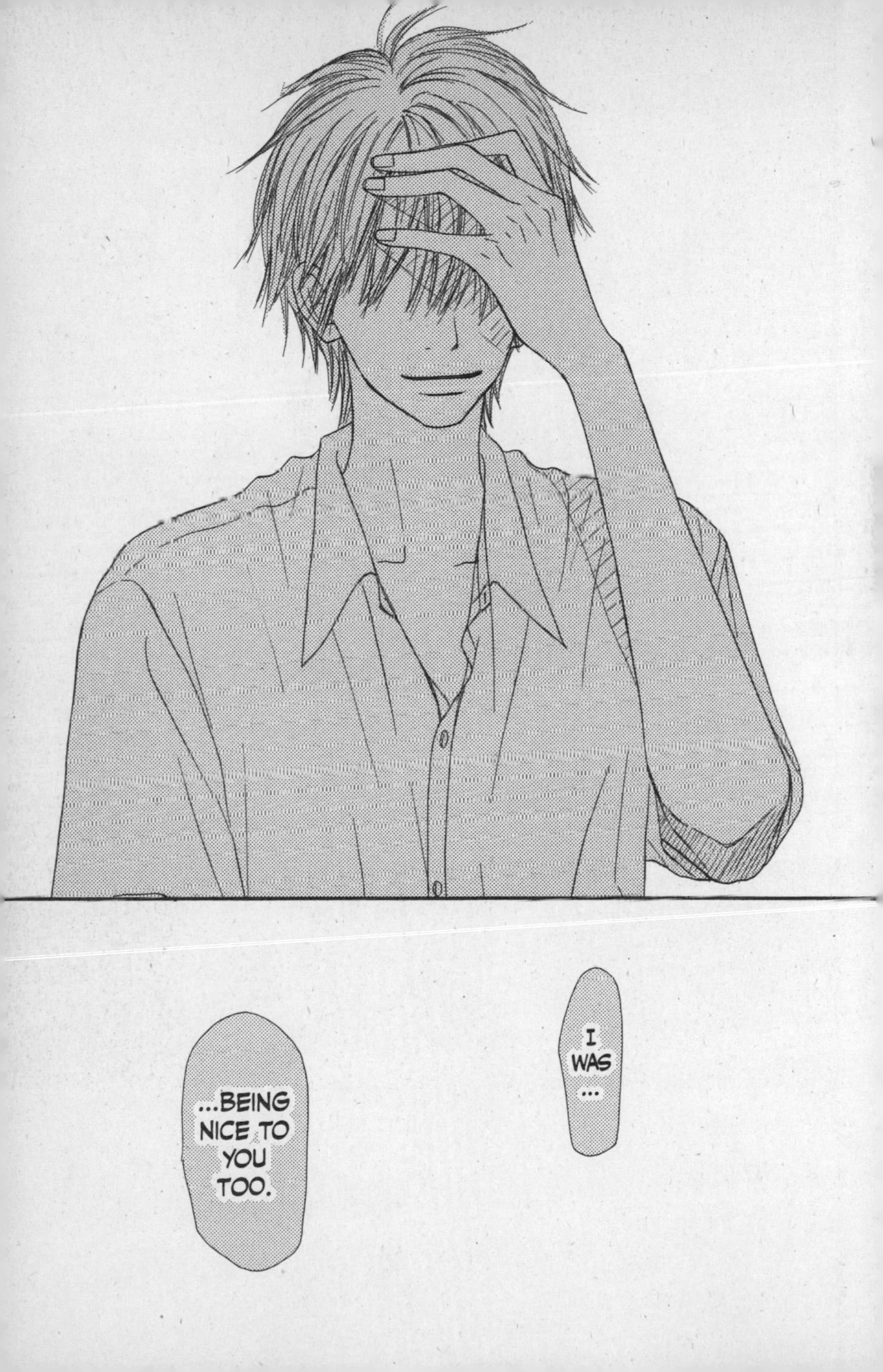
I WAS ...
...BEING NICE TO YOU TOO.

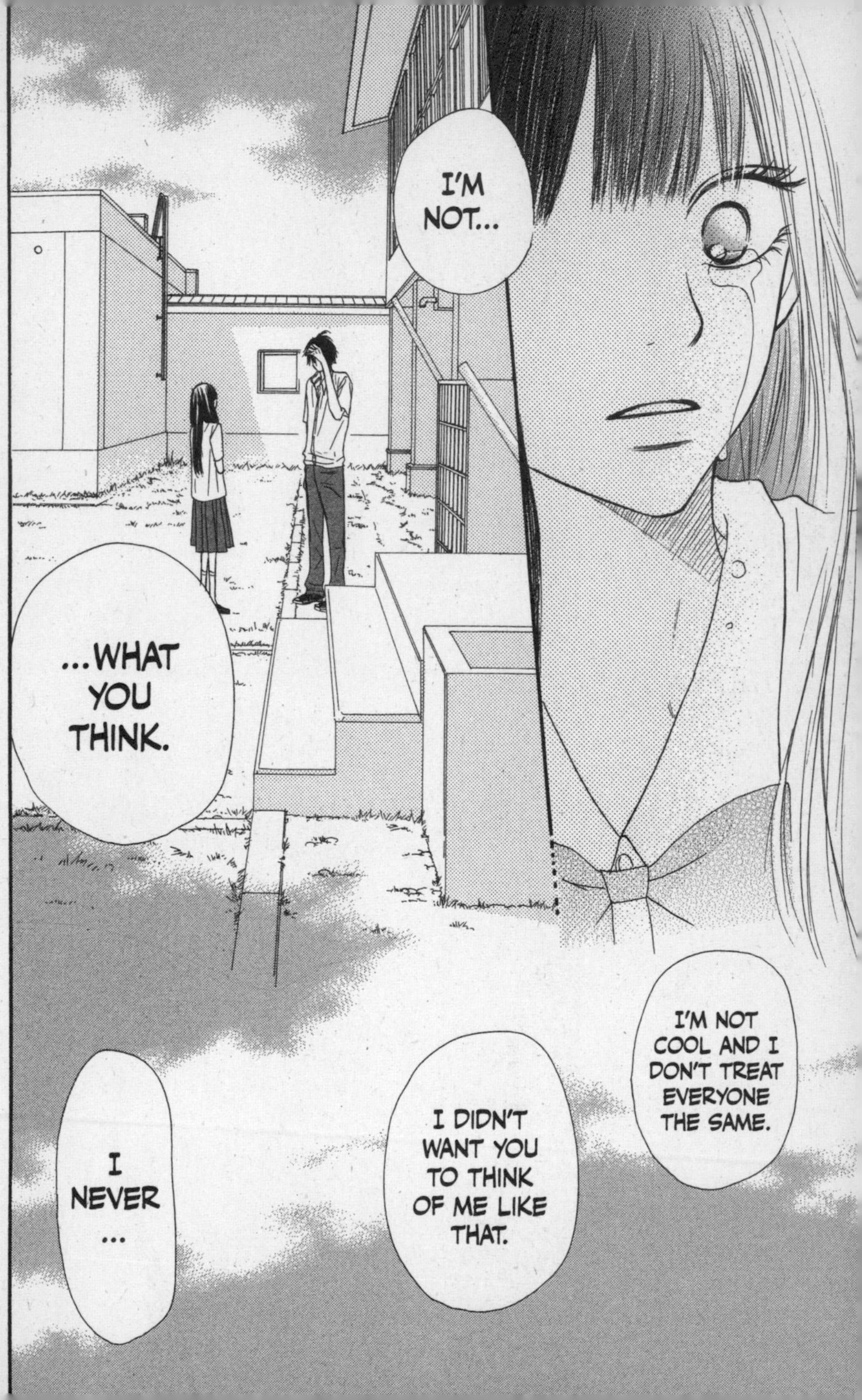
I'M NOT...
...WHAT YOU THINK.
I'M NOT COOL AND I DON'T TREAT EVERYONE THE SAME.
I DIDN'T WANT YOU TO THINK OF ME LIKE THAT.
I NEVER ...

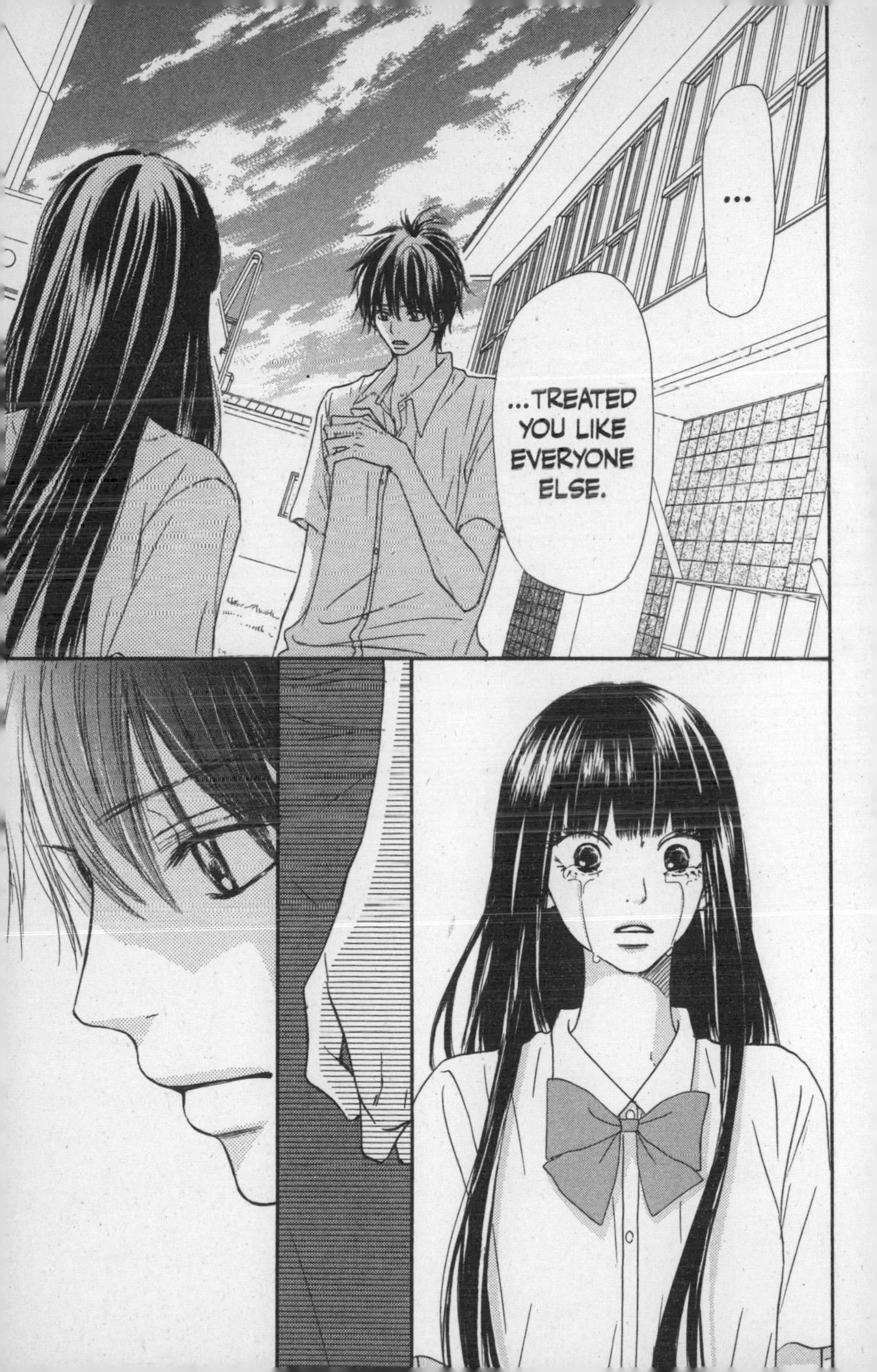
...
...TREATED YOU LIKE EVERYONE ELSE.

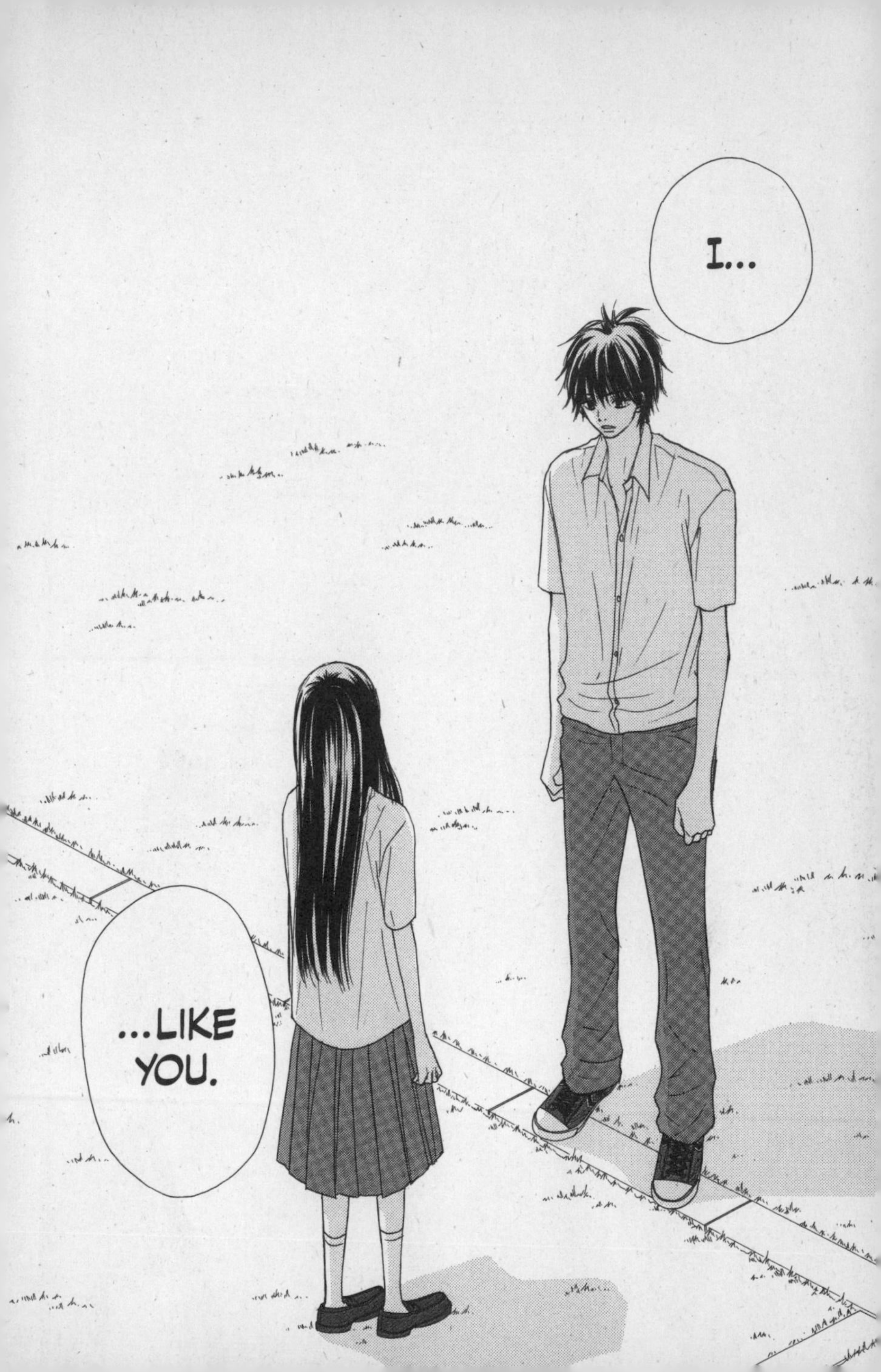
I...
...LIKE YOU.

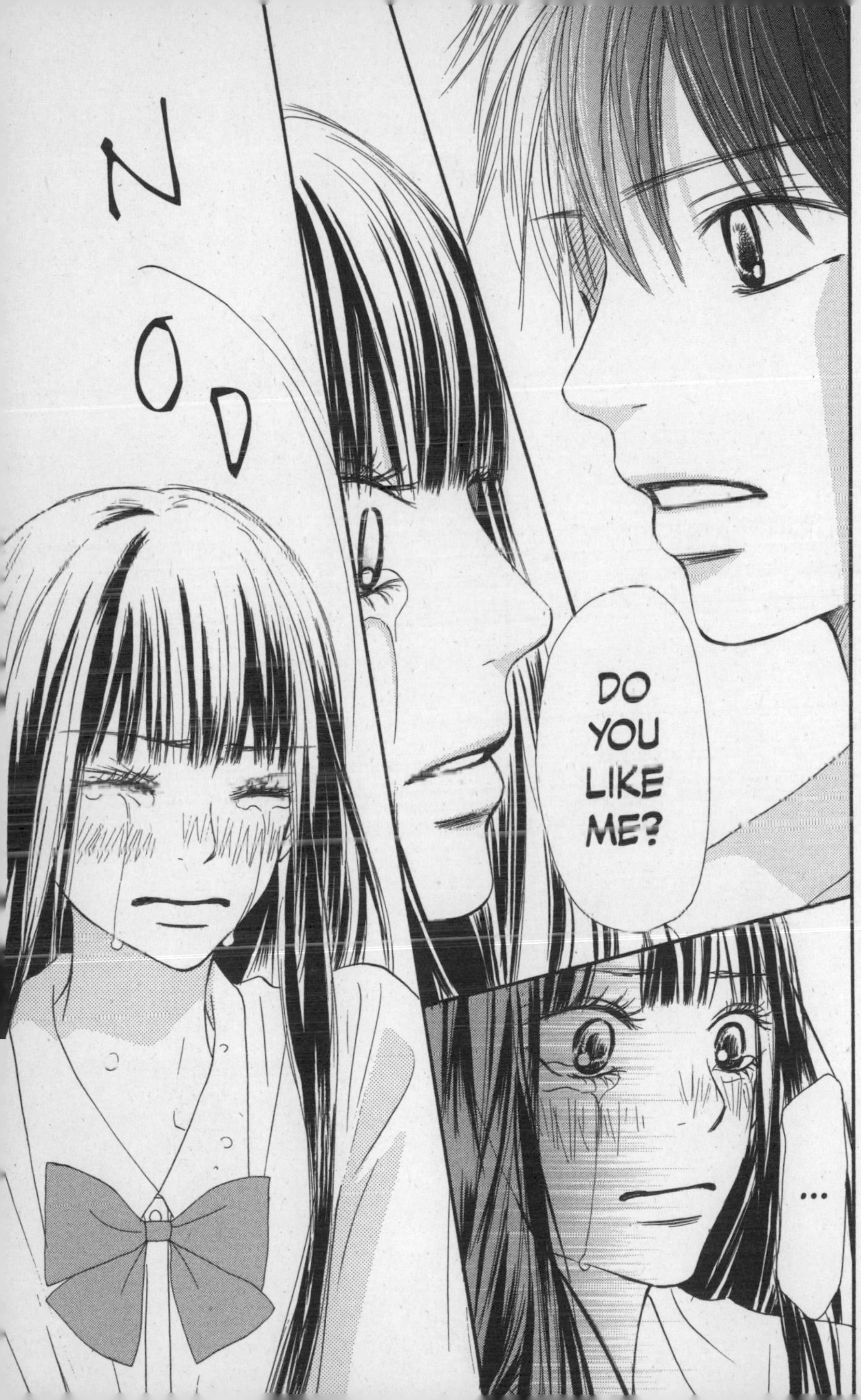
DO YOU LIKE ME?
...
NOD

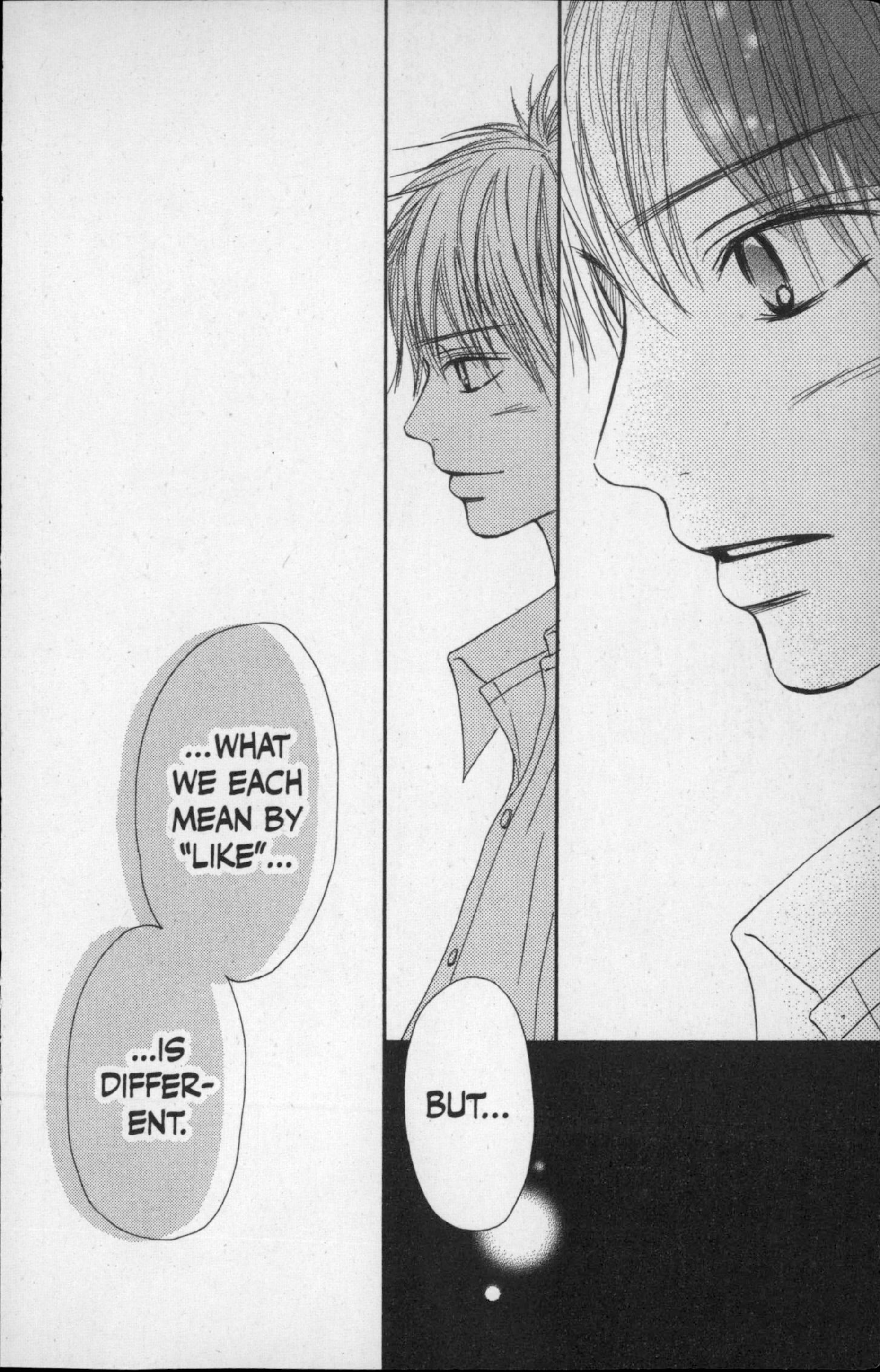
BUT...
...WHAT WE EACH MEAN BY "LIKE"...
...IS DIFFER-ENT.

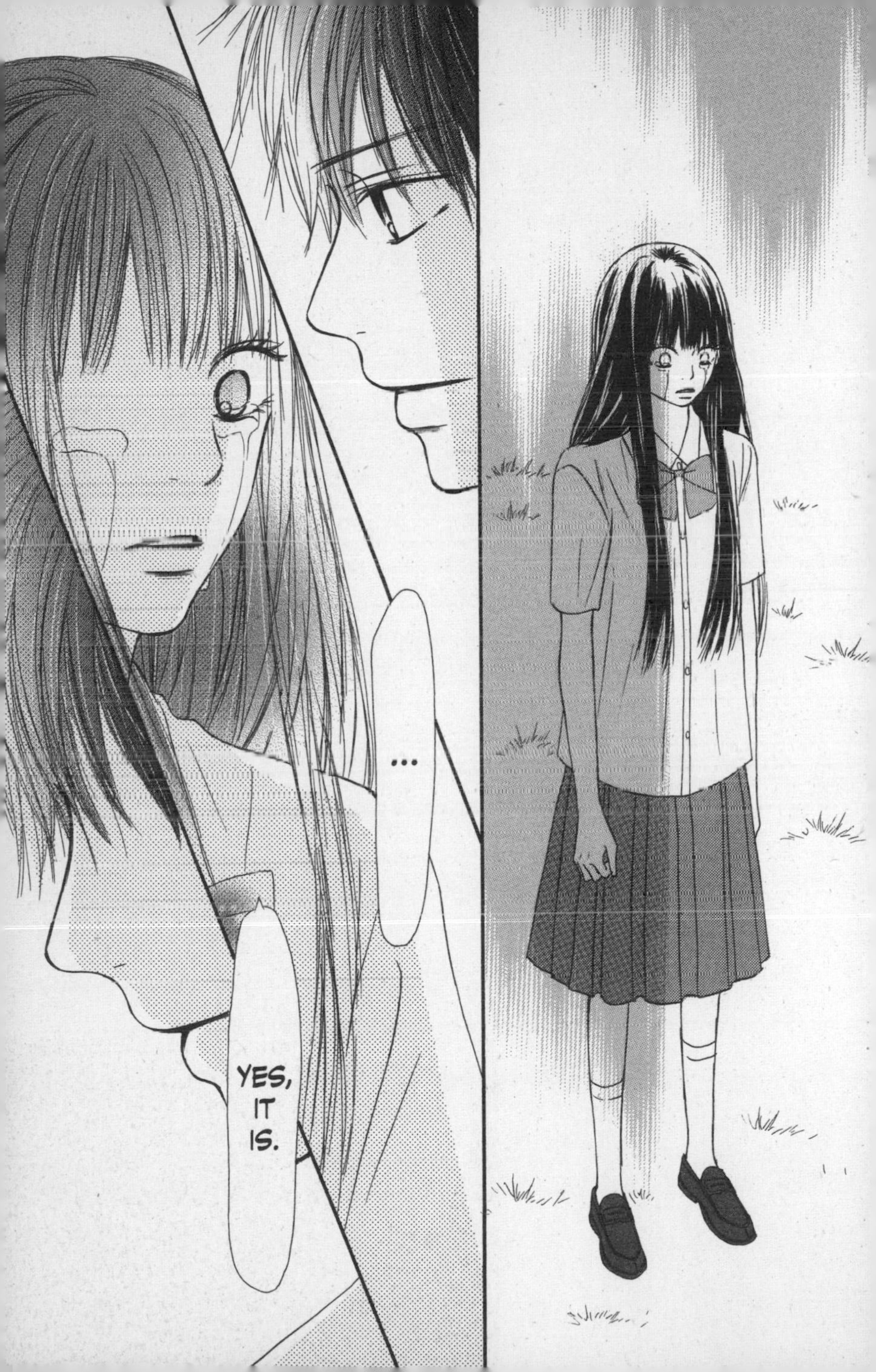
...
YES, IT IS.

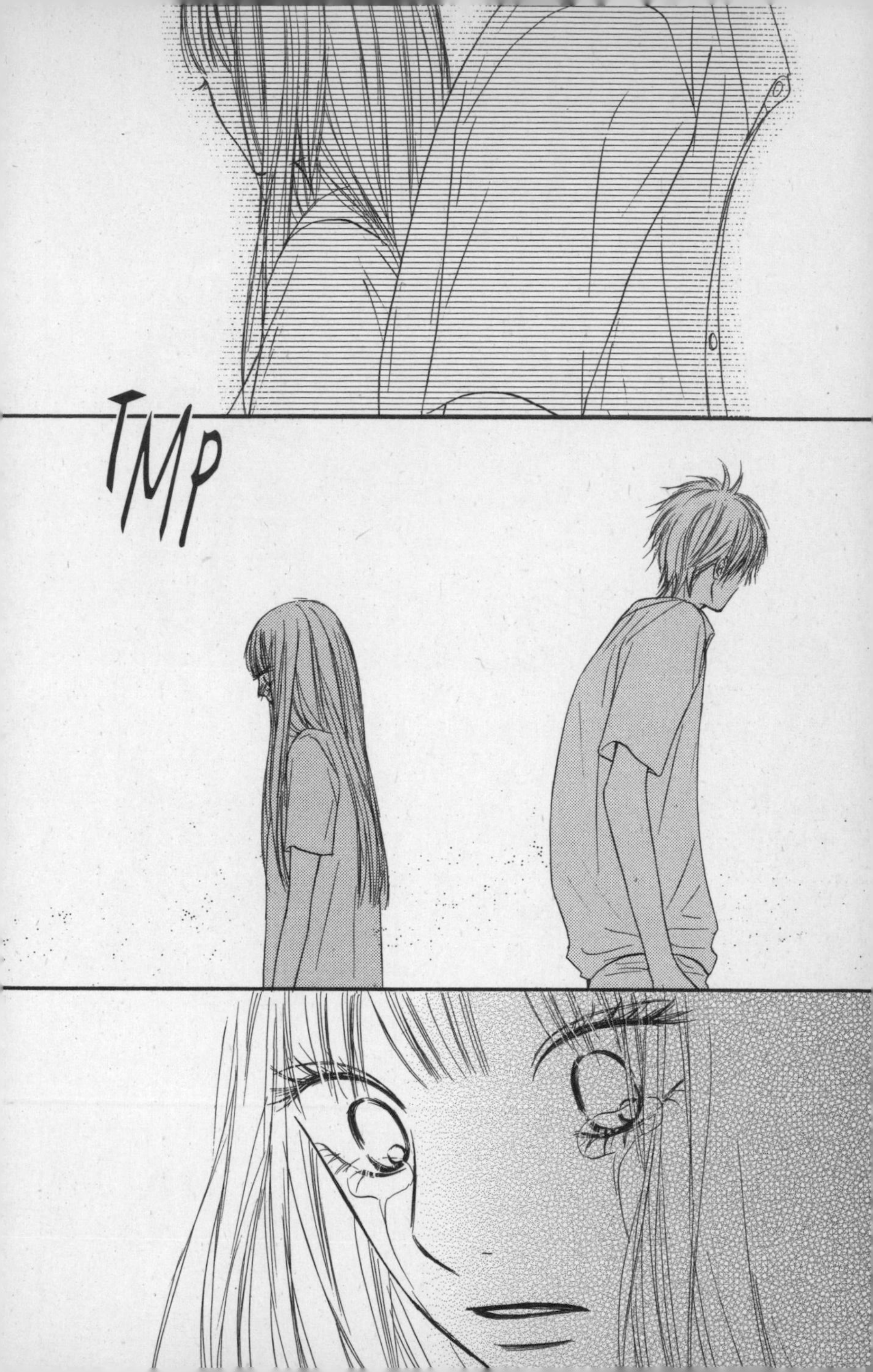
TMP

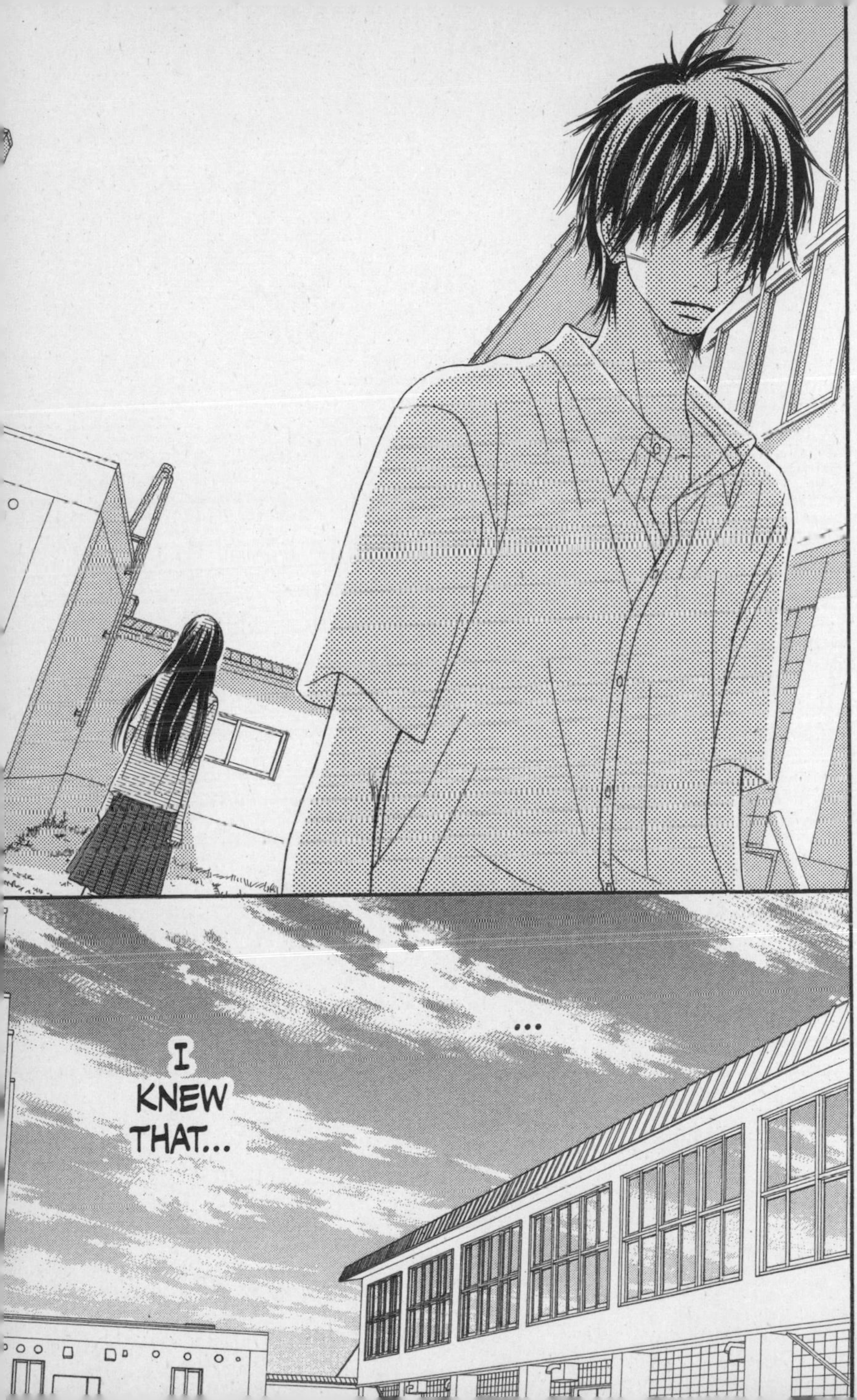
...
I KNEW THAT...

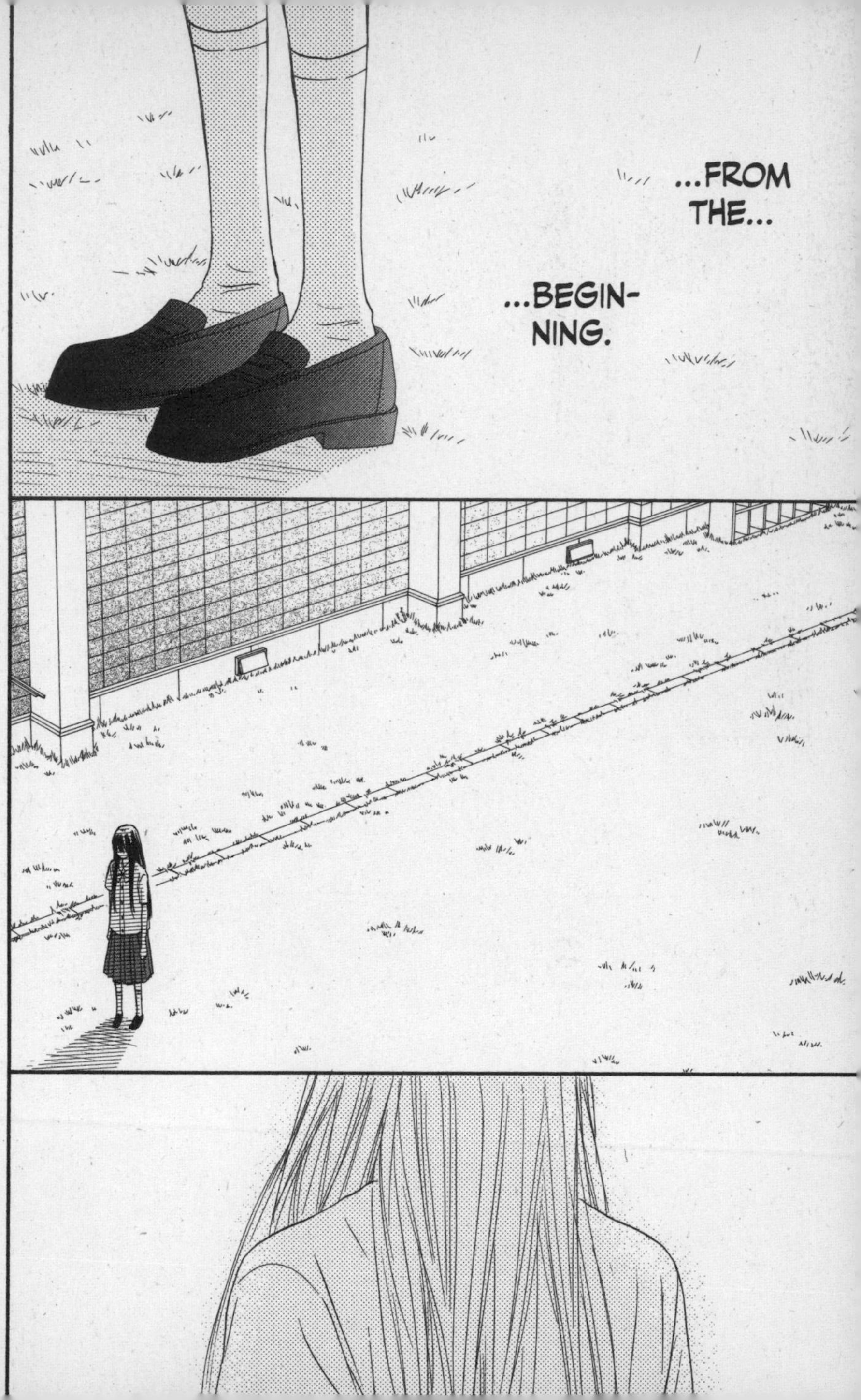
...FROM THE...
...BEGIN-NING.

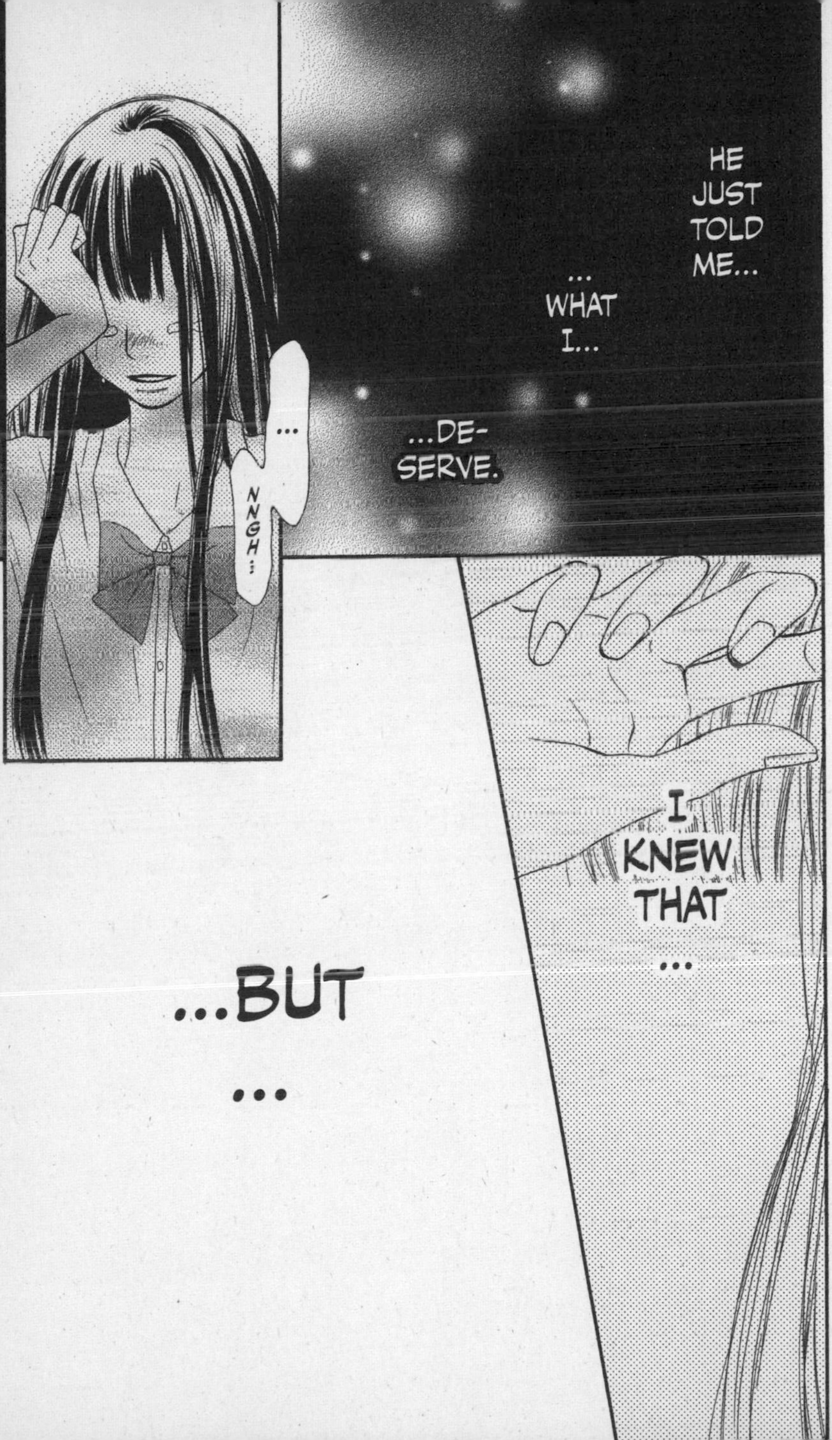
HE JUST TOLD ME...
...WHAT I...
...DE-SERVE.
...
NNGH...
I KNEW THAT ...
...BUT ...

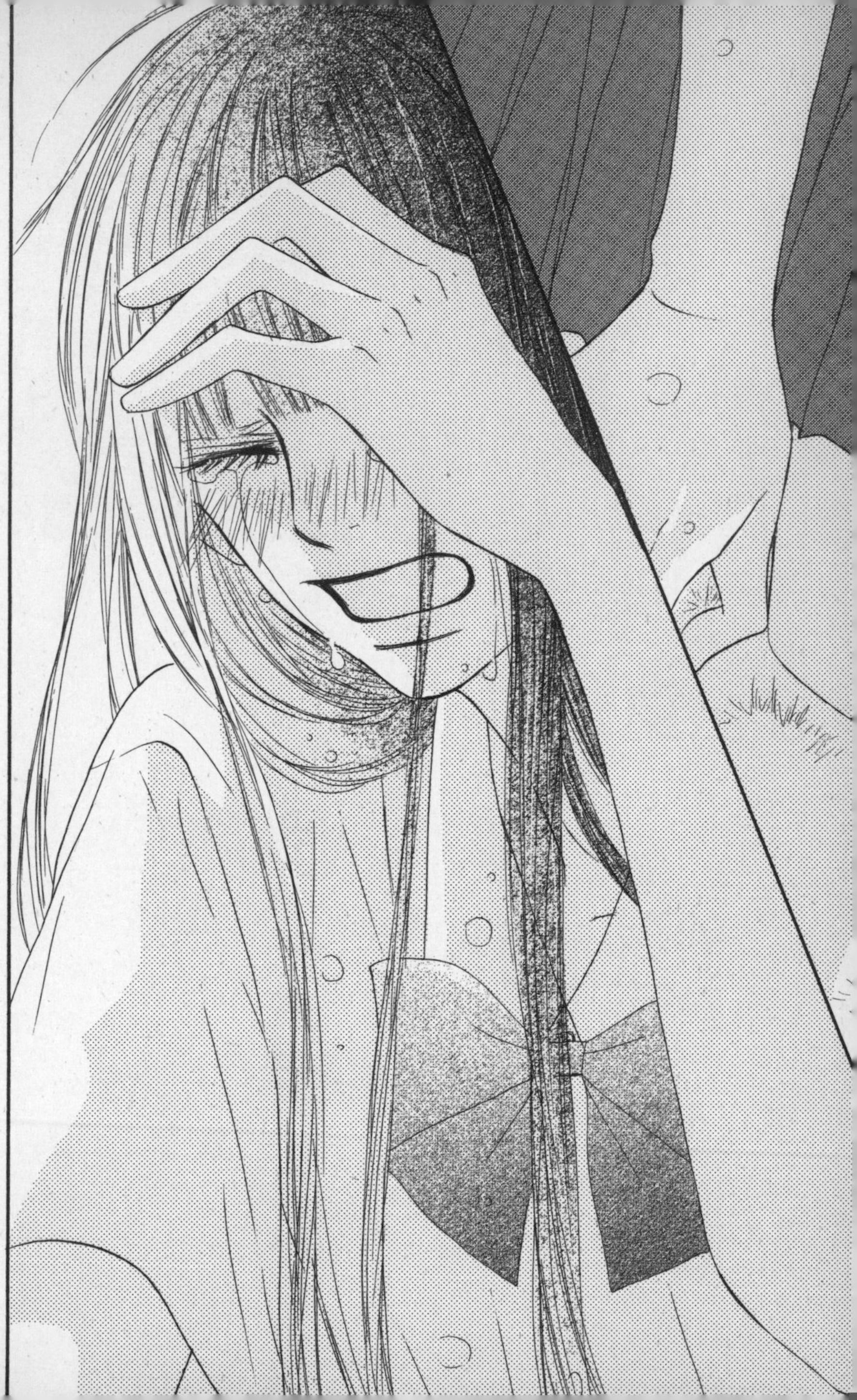

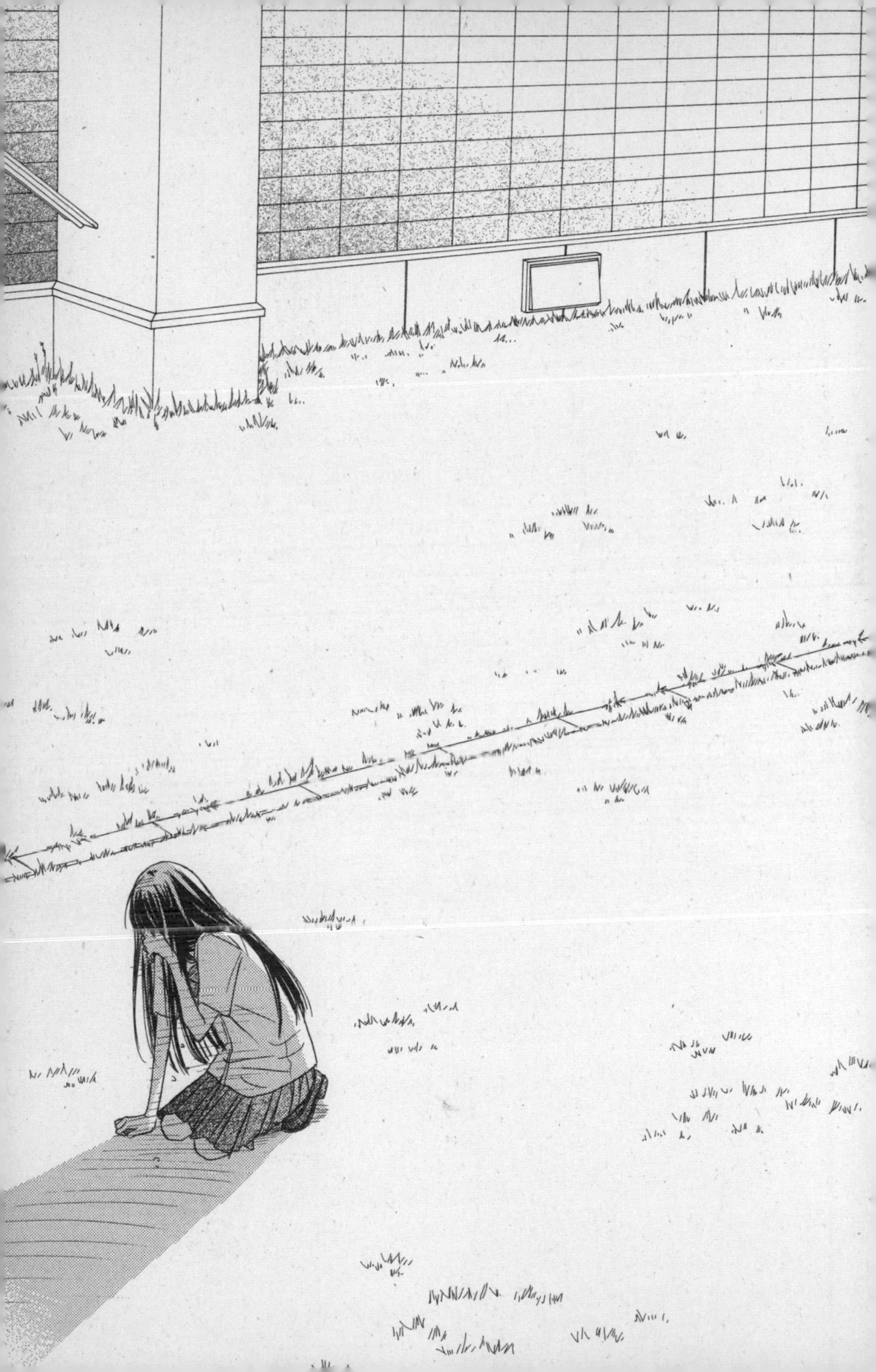

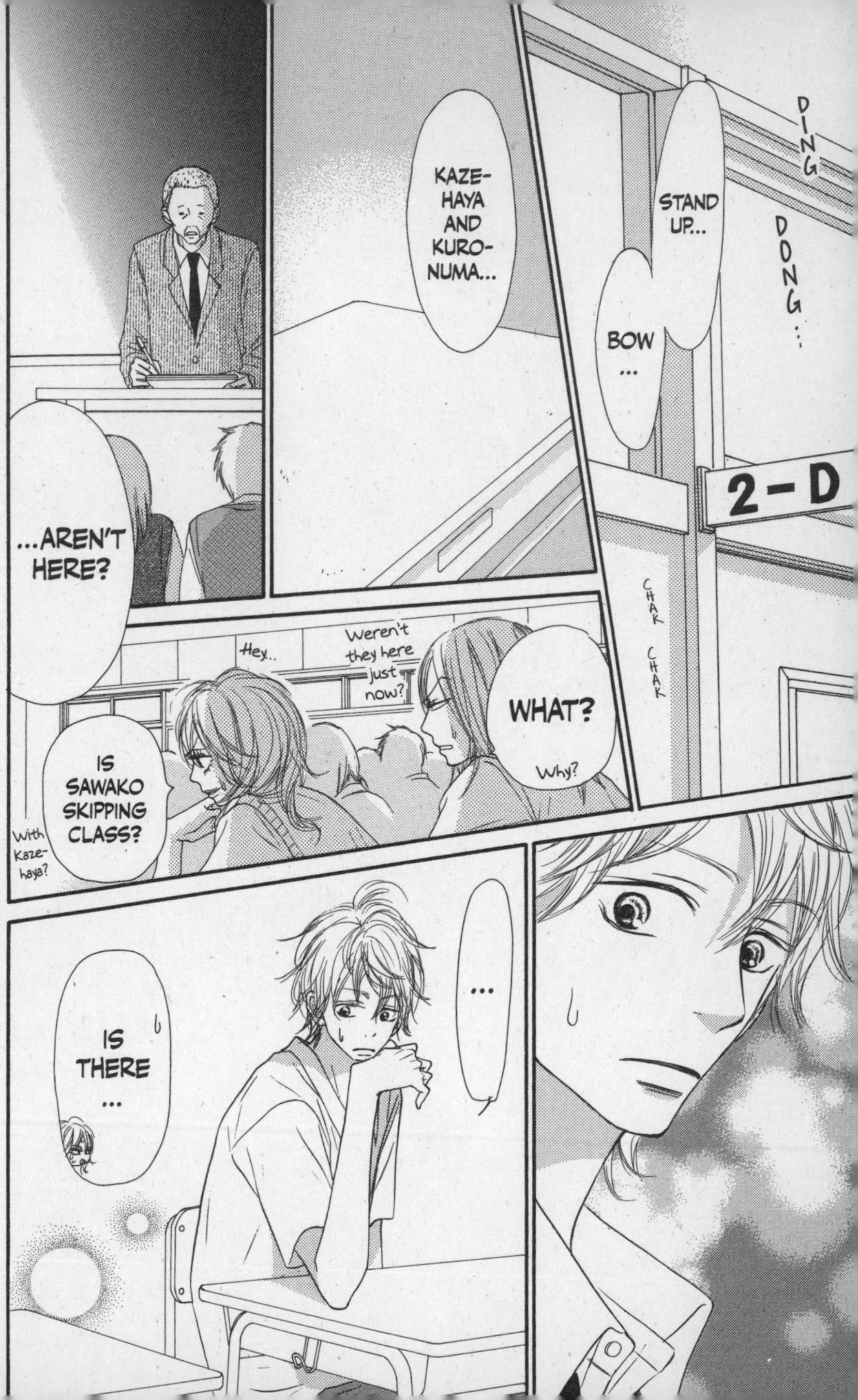
DING DONG...
STAND UP...
BOW...
2-D
CHAK CHAK
KAZE-HAYA AND KURO-NUMA...
...AREN'T HERE?
WHAT?
Why?
Weren't they here just now?
Hey...
IS SAWAKO SKIPPING CLASS?
With Kaze-haya?
...
IS THERE ...

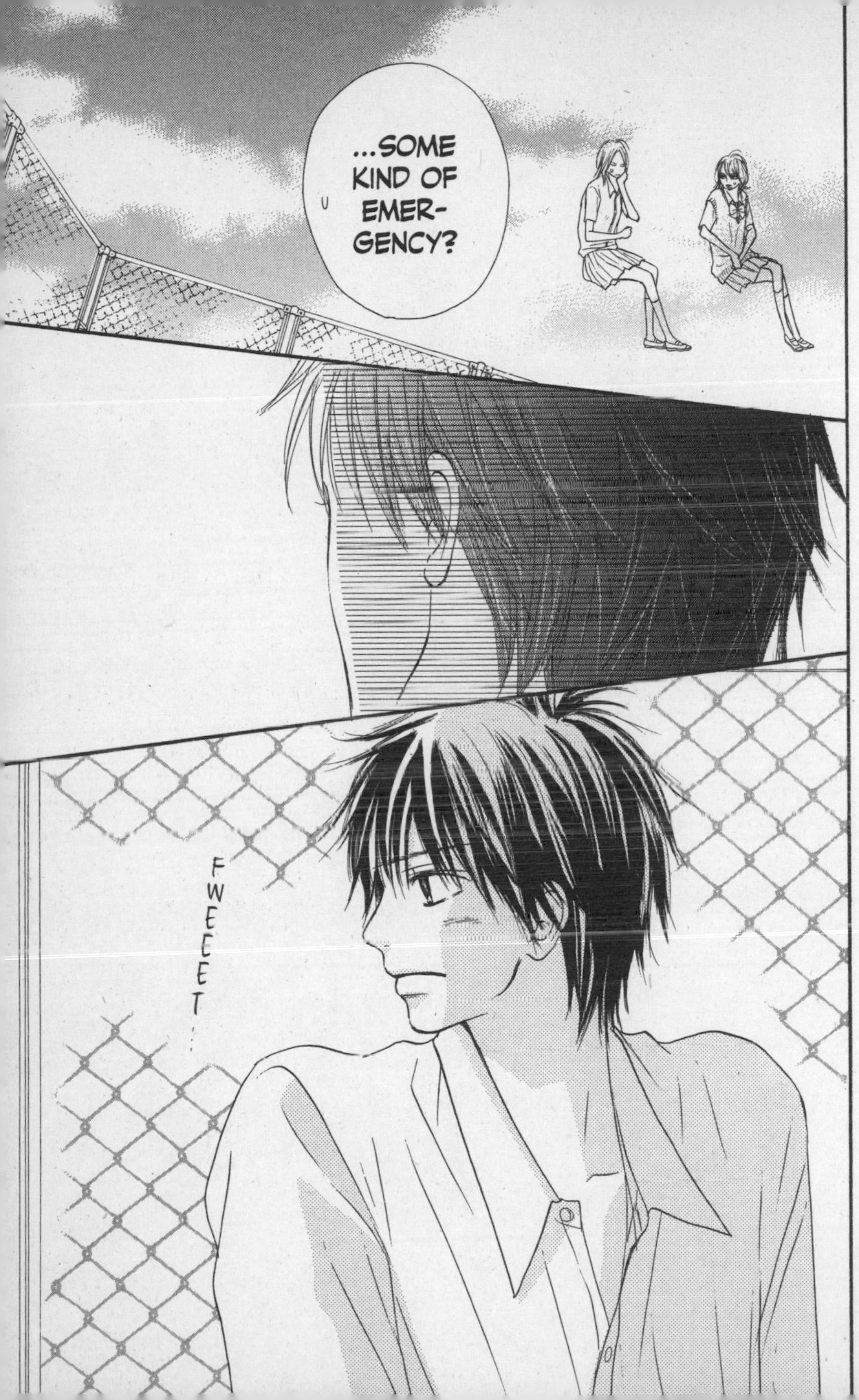
...SOME KIND OF EMER-GENCY?
FWEEET

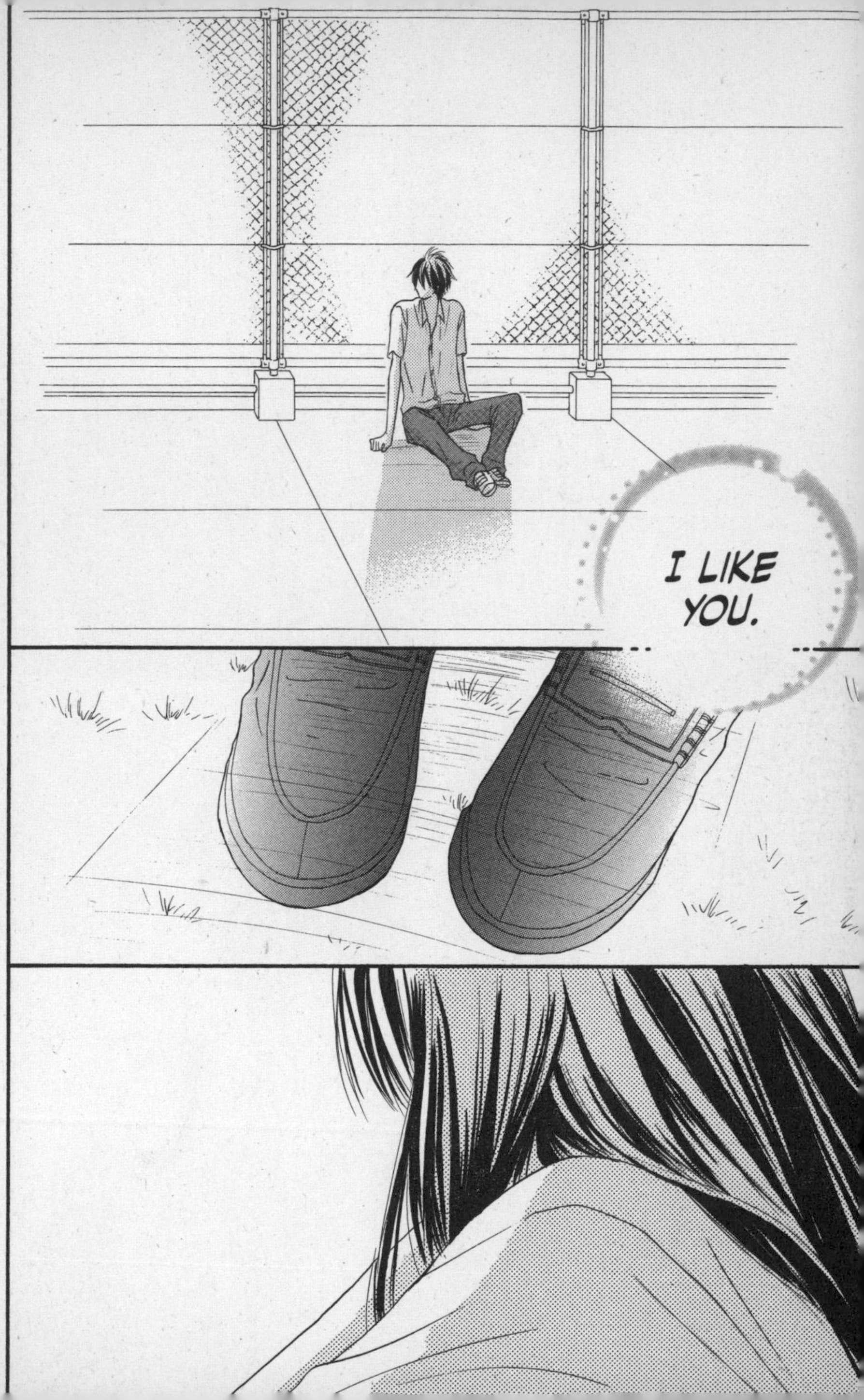
I LIKE YOU.

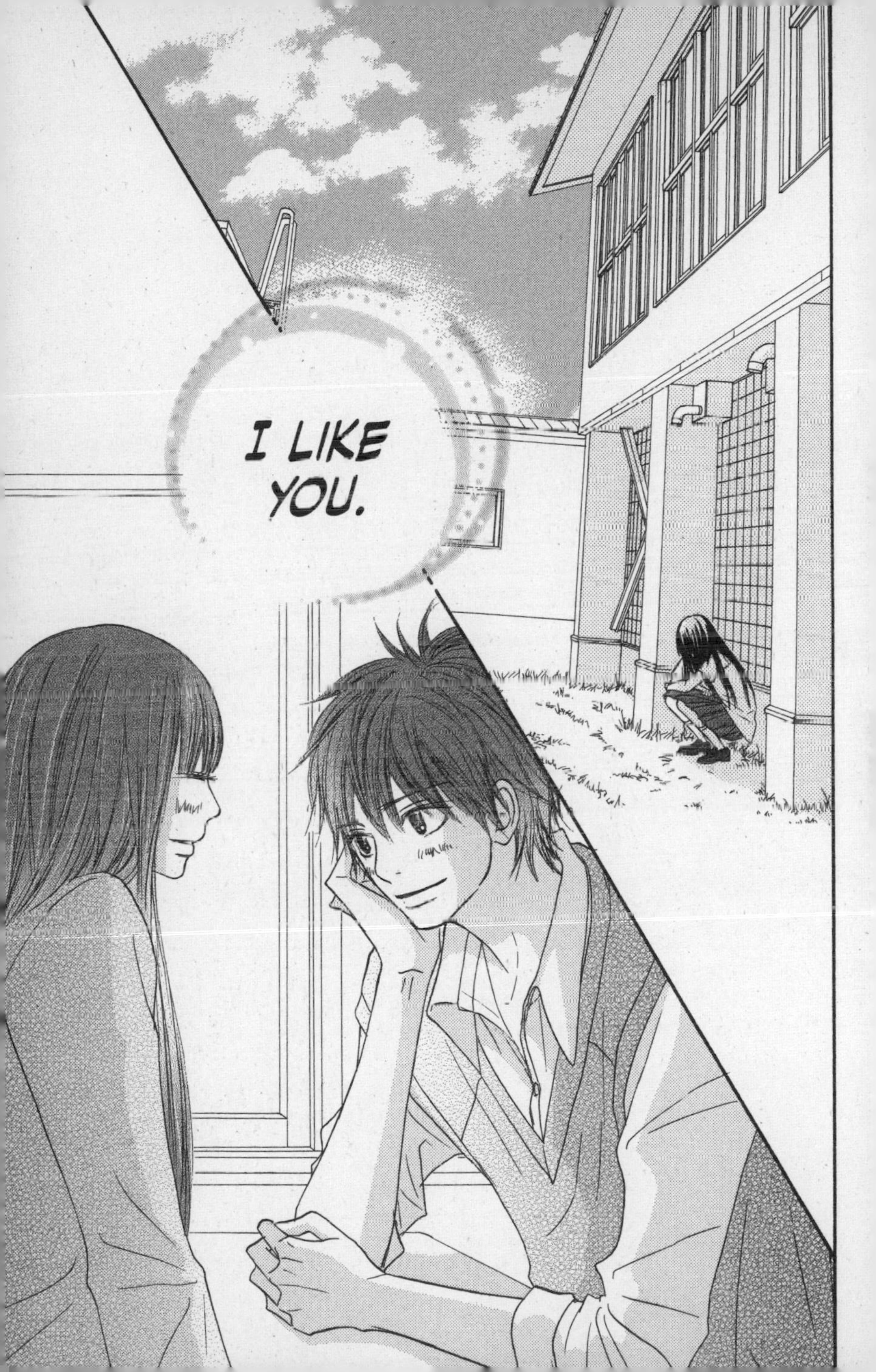
I LIKE YOU.

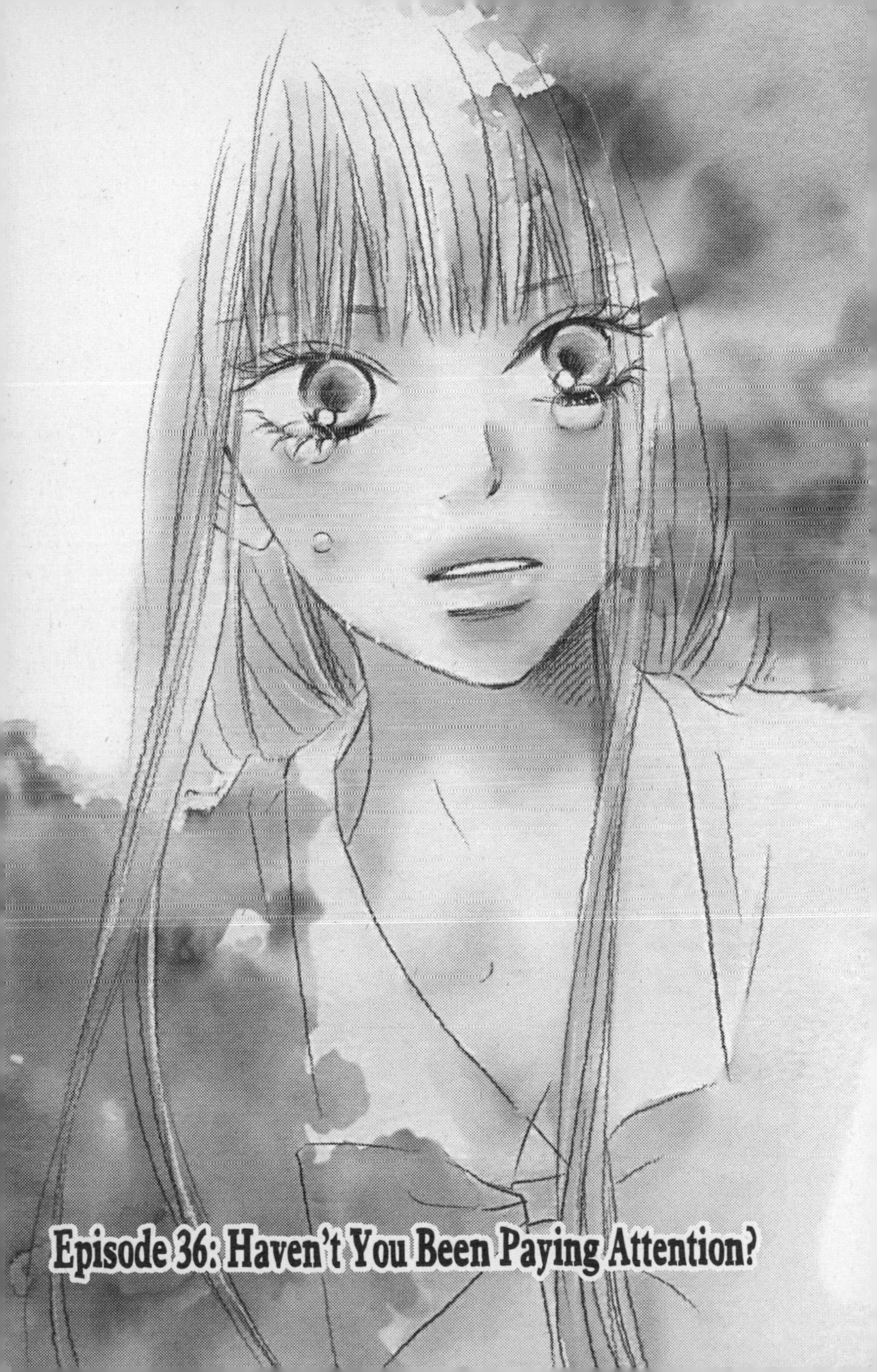
Episode 36: Haven't You Been Paying Attention?

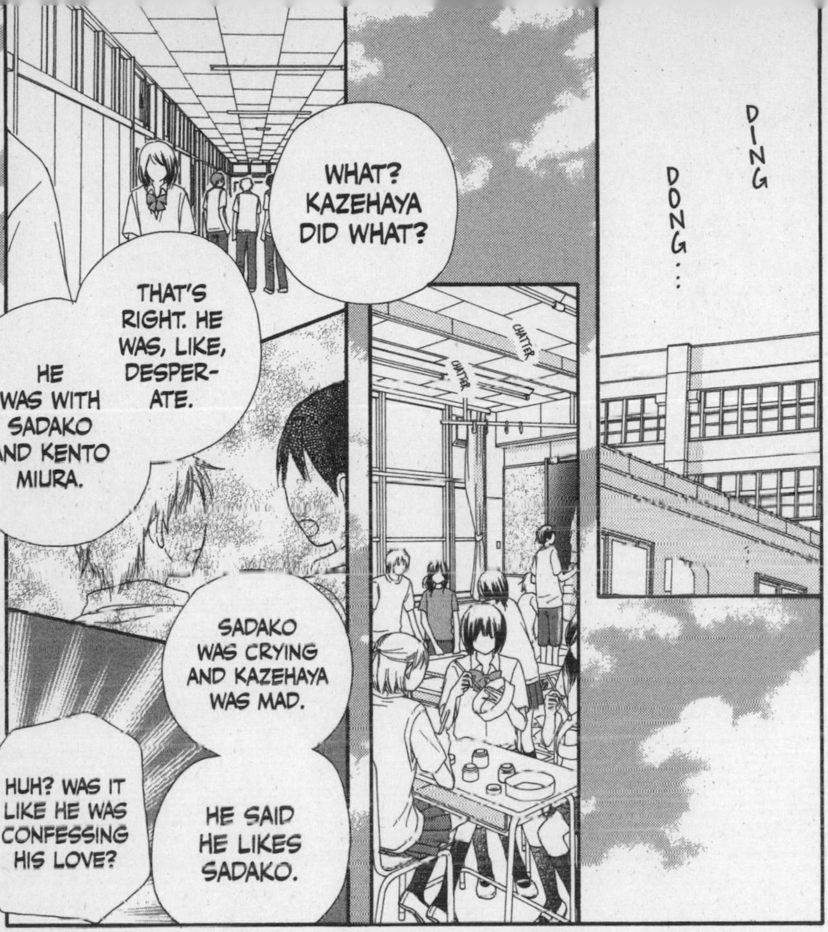
DING DONG...
CHATTER
CHATTER
WHAT? KAZEHAYA DID WHAT?
THAT'S RIGHT. HE WAS, LIKE, DESPERATE.
HE WAS WITH SADAKO AND KENTO MIURA.
SADAKO WAS CRYING AND KAZEHAYA WAS MAD.
HE SAID HE LIKES SADAKO.
HUH? WAS IT LIKE HE WAS CONFESSING HIS LOVE?

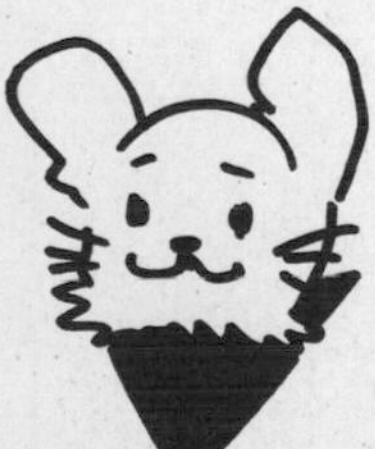

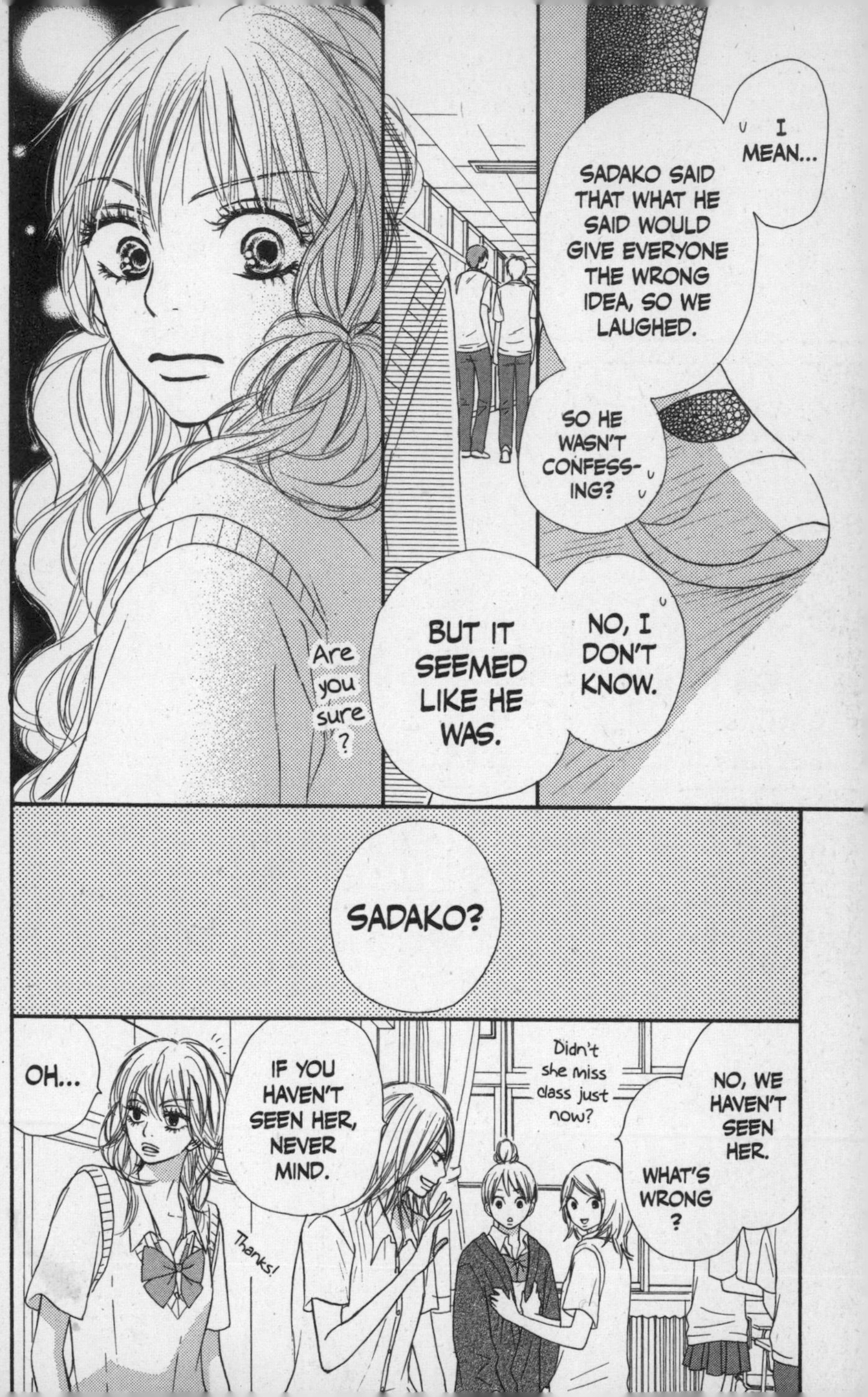
I MEAN...
SADAKO SAID THAT WHAT HE SAID WOULD GIVE EVERYONE THE WRONG IDEA, SO WE LAUGHED.
SO HE WASN'T CONFESS-ING?
NO, I DON'T KNOW.
BUT IT SEEMED LIKE HE WAS.
Are you sure?
SADAKO?
NO, WE HAVEN'T SEEN HER.
WHAT'S WRONG?
Didn't she miss class just now?
IF YOU HAVEN'T SEEN HER, NEVER MIND.
Thanks!
OH...

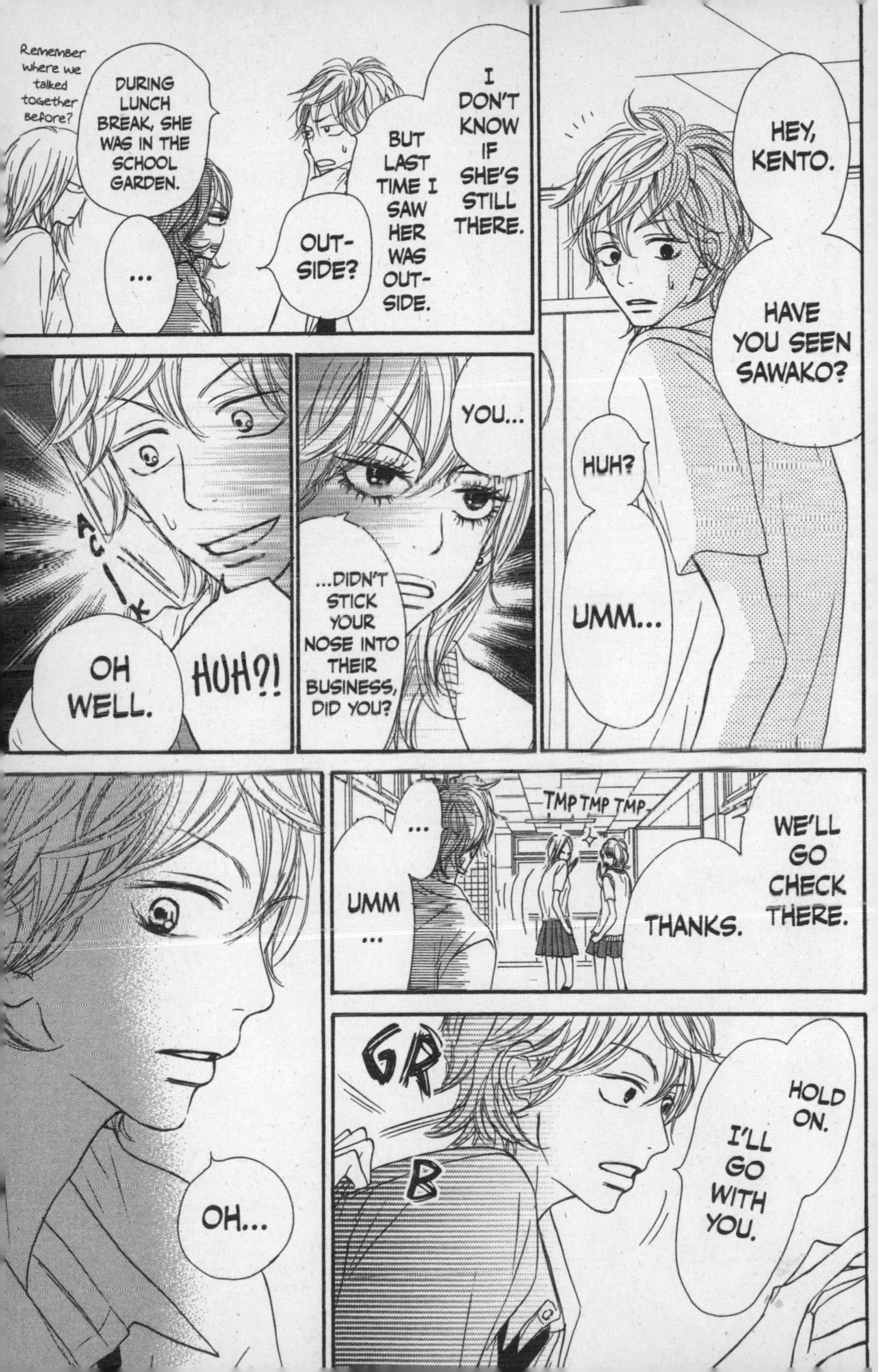
HEY, KENTO.
HAVE YOU SEEN SAWAKO?
HUH?
UMM...
I DON'T KNOW IF SHE'S STILL THERE.
BUT LAST TIME I SAW HER WAS OUT-SIDE.
OUT-SIDE?
DURING LUNCH BREAK, SHE WAS IN THE SCHOOL GARDEN.
Remember where we talked together before?
...
YOU...
...DIDN'T STICK YOUR NOSE INTO THEIR BUSINESS, DID YOU?
HUH?!
OH WELL.
WE'LL GO CHECK THERE.
THANKS.
TMP TMP TMP
...
UMM ...
HOLD ON. I'LL GO WITH YOU.
GR
B
OH...

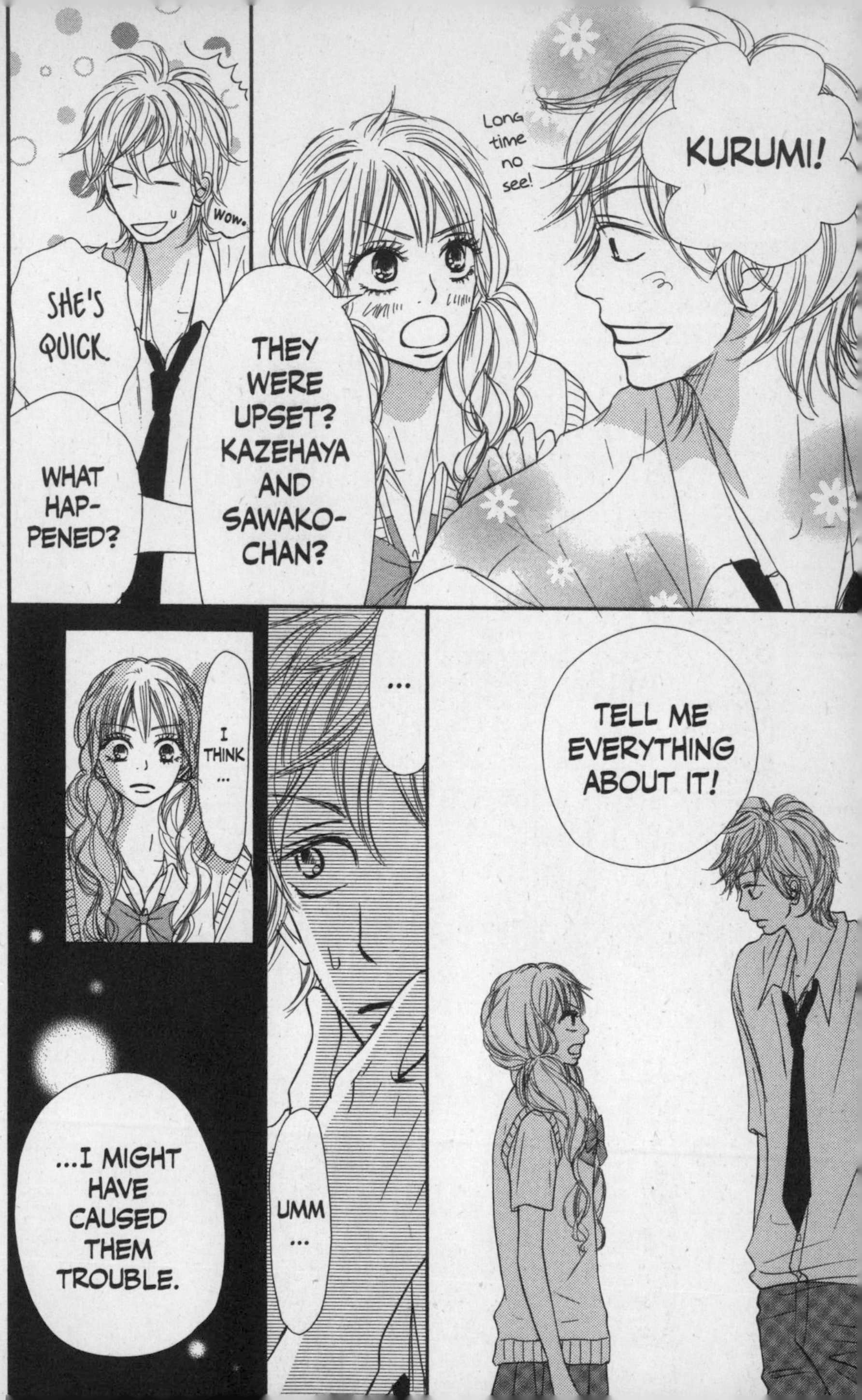
KURUMI!
Long time no see!
WOW.
SHE'S QUICK.
WHAT HAP-PENED?
THEY WERE UPSET? KAZEHAYA AND SAWAKO-CHAN?
TELL ME EVERYTHING ABOUT IT!
...
UMM ...
I THINK ...
...I MIGHT HAVE CAUSED THEM TROUBLE.

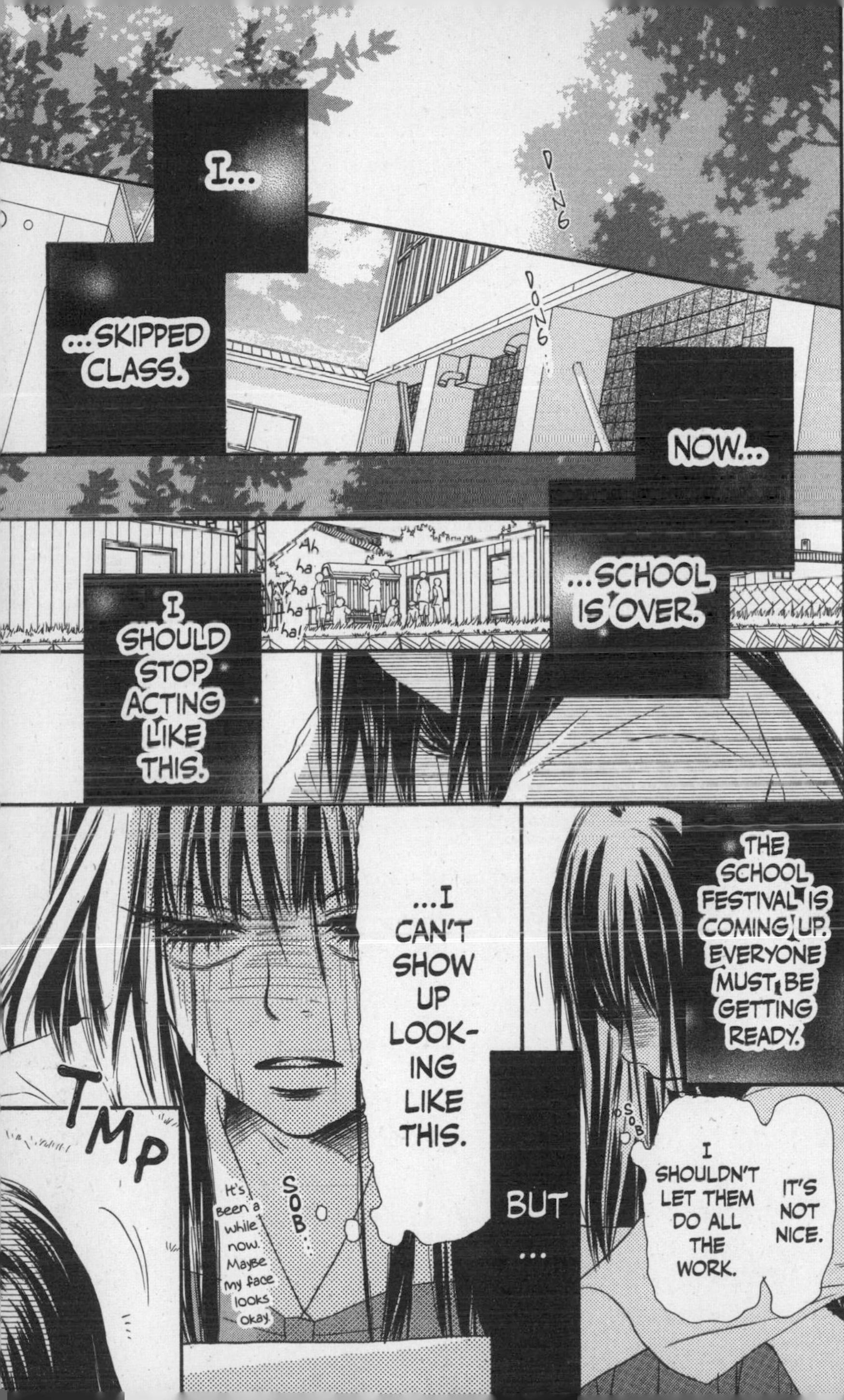
DING
DONG
I...
...SKIPPED CLASS.
NOW...
...SCHOOL IS OVER.
Ah ha ha ha ha!
I SHOULD STOP ACTING LIKE THIS.
THE SCHOOL FESTIVAL IS COMING UP. EVERYONE MUST BE GETTING READY.
SOB
IT'S NOT NICE.
I SHOULDN'T LET THEM DO ALL THE WORK.
BUT...
...I CAN'T SHOW UP LOOKING LIKE THIS.
SOB...
It's been a while now. Maybe my face looks okay.
TMP

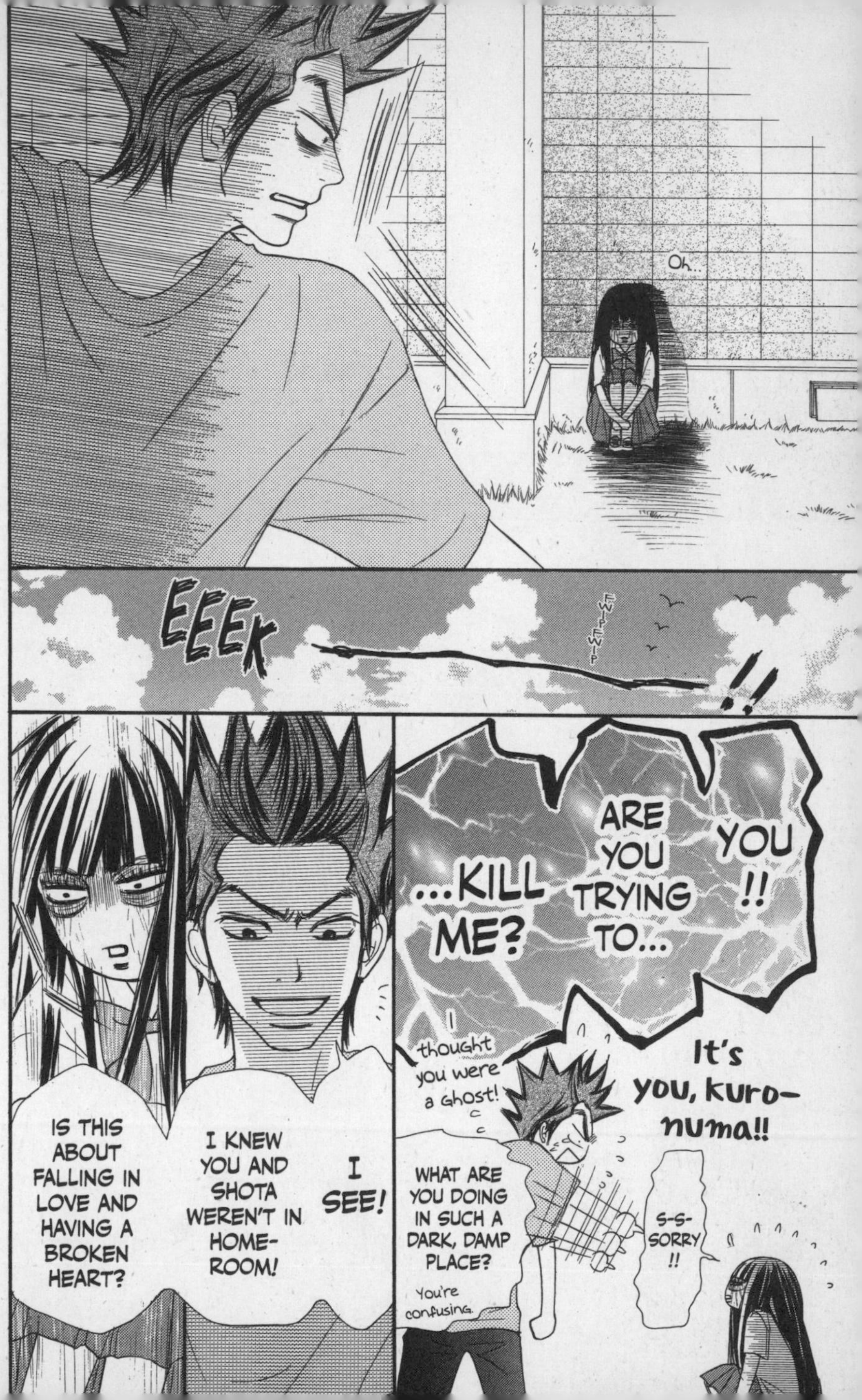
Oh...
EEEK
FWIP FWIP
!!
YOU!! ARE YOU TRYING TO... ...KILL ME?
It's you, kuro-numa!!
I thought you were a ghost!
S-S-SORRY!!
WHAT ARE YOU DOING IN SUCH A DARK, DAMP PLACE?
You're confusing.
I SEE!
I KNEW YOU AND SHOTA WEREN'T IN HOME-ROOM!
IS THIS ABOUT FALLING IN LOVE AND HAVING A BROKEN HEART?

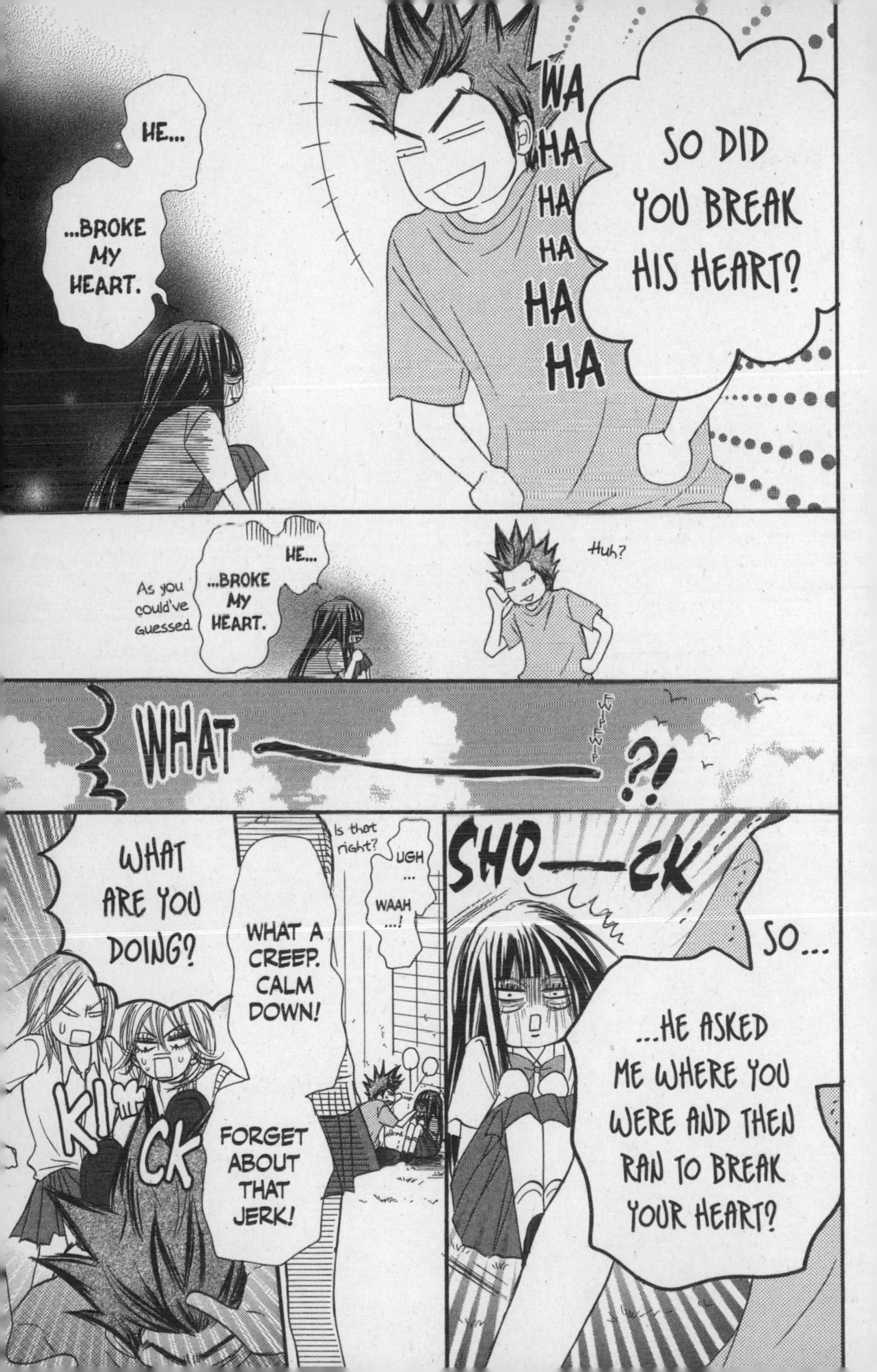

SO DID YOU BREAK HIS HEART?
WA HA HA HA HA HA
HE...
...BROKE MY HEART.
Huh?
HE...
...BROKE MY HEART.
As you could've guessed.
WHAT——?!
FWIP FWIP
SHO—CK
SO...
...HE ASKED ME WHERE YOU WERE AND THEN RAN TO BREAK YOUR HEART?
Is that right?
UGH... WAAH...!
WHAT A CREEP. CALM DOWN!
FORGET ABOUT THAT JERK!
WHAT ARE YOU DOING?
KICK

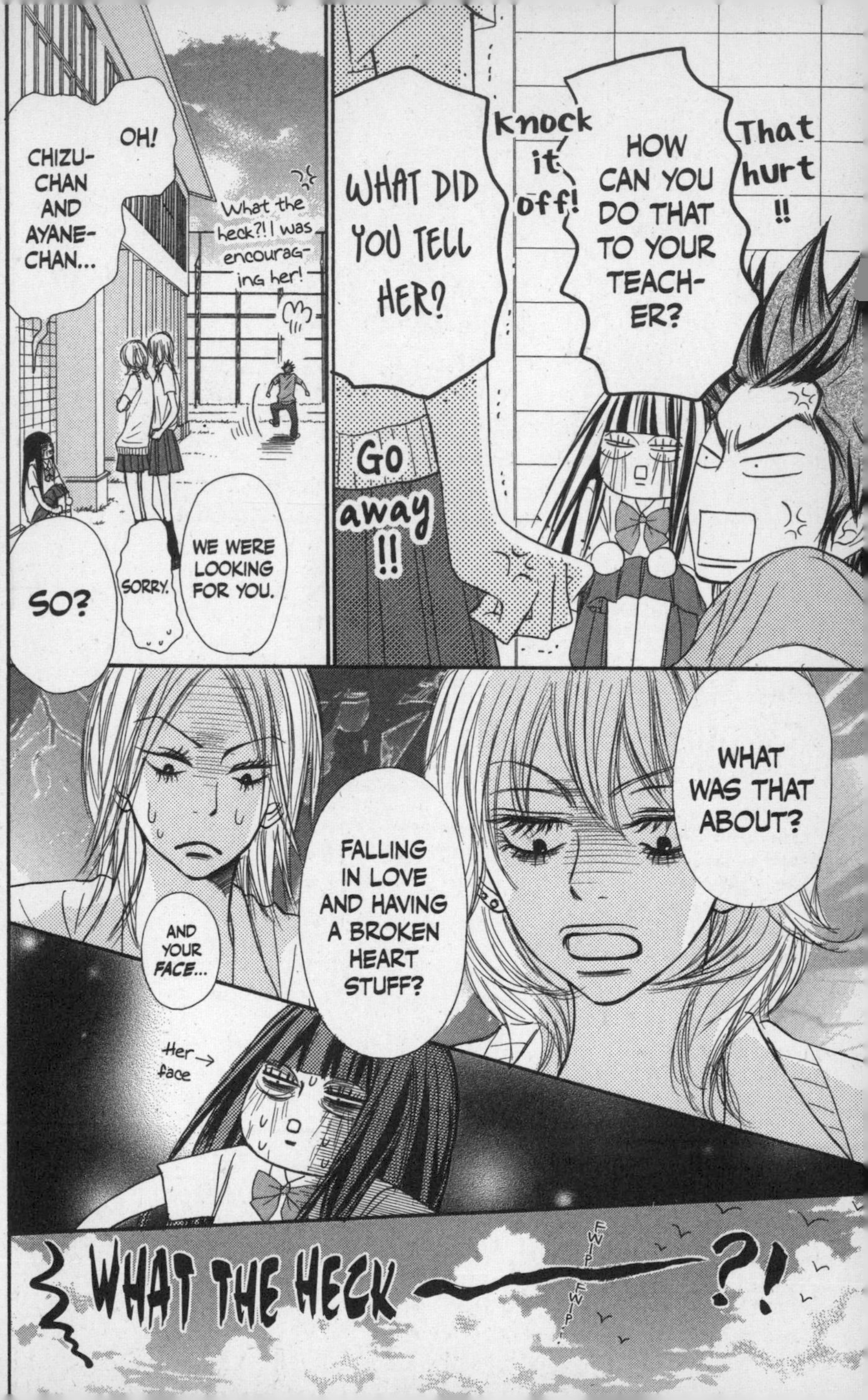
That hurt!!
HOW CAN YOU DO THAT TO YOUR TEACHER?
Knock it off!
WHAT DID YOU TELL HER?
Go away!!
OH!
CHIZU-CHAN AND AYANE-CHAN...
What the heck?! I was encouraging her!
WE WERE LOOKING FOR YOU.
SORRY.
SO?
WHAT WAS THAT ABOUT?
FALLING IN LOVE AND HAVING A BROKEN HEART STUFF?
AND YOUR FACE...
Her → face
FWIP FWIP
WHAT THE HECK——?!

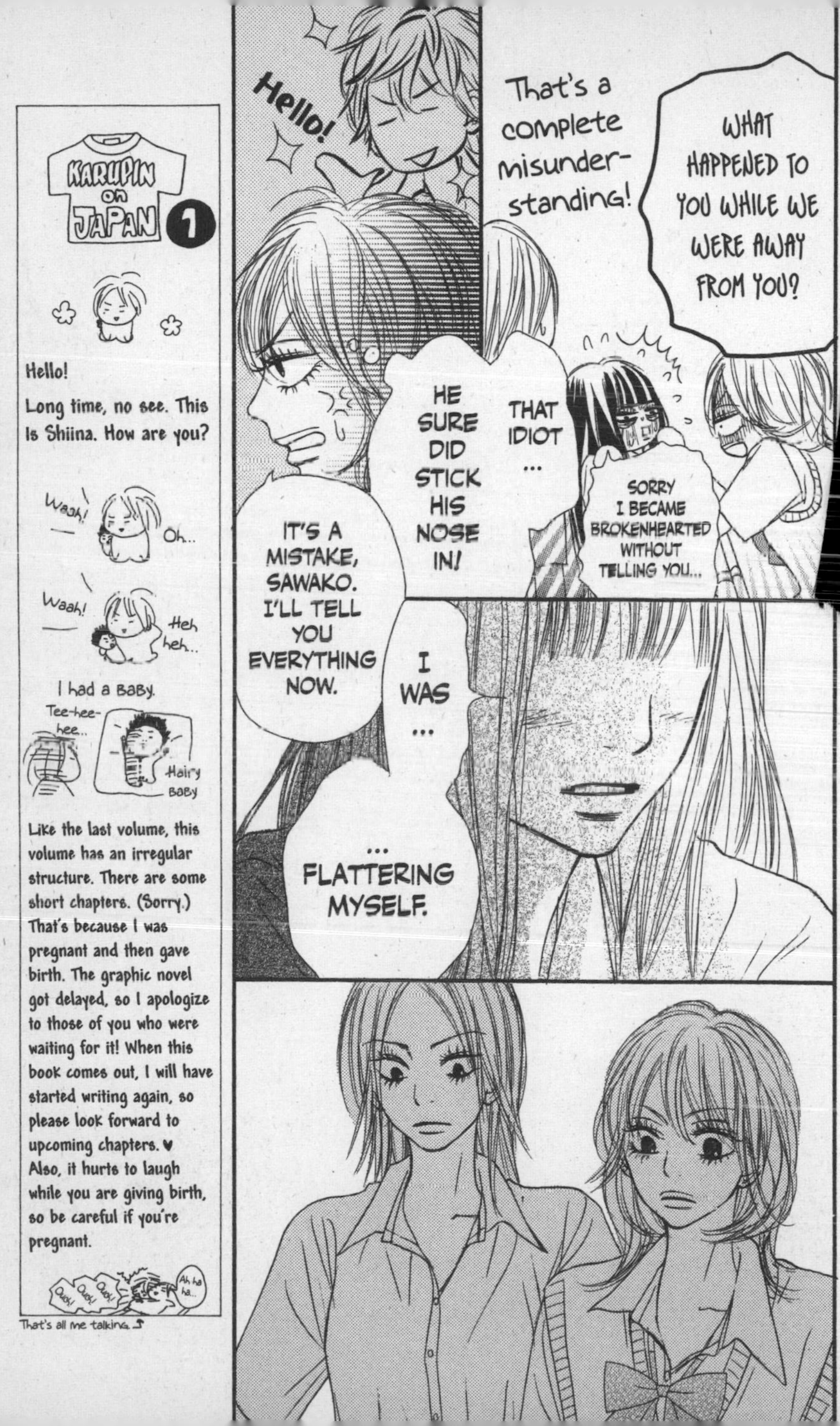
WHAT HAPPENED TO YOU WHILE WE WERE AWAY FROM YOU?
That's a complete misunder-standing!
SORRY I BECAME BROKENHEARTED WITHOUT TELLING YOU...
THAT IDIOT...
HE SURE DID STICK HIS NOSE IN!
Hello!
IT'S A MISTAKE, SAWAKO. I'LL TELL YOU EVERYTHING NOW.
I WAS...
...FLATTERING MYSELF.

KARUPIN on JAPAN 1

Hello!

Long time, no see. This Is Shiina. How are you?

Waah! Oh...

Waah! Heh heh...

I had a baby.

Tee-hee-hee... Hairy baby

Like the last volume, this volume has an irregular structure. There are some short chapters. (Sorry.) That's because I was pregnant and then gave birth. The graphic novel got delayed, so I apologize to those of you who were waiting for it! When this book comes out, I will have started writing again, so please look forward to upcoming chapters. ♥ Also, it hurts to laugh while you are giving birth, so be careful if you're pregnant.

Ouch! Ouch! Ouch! Ouch! Ah ha ha...

That's all me talking.

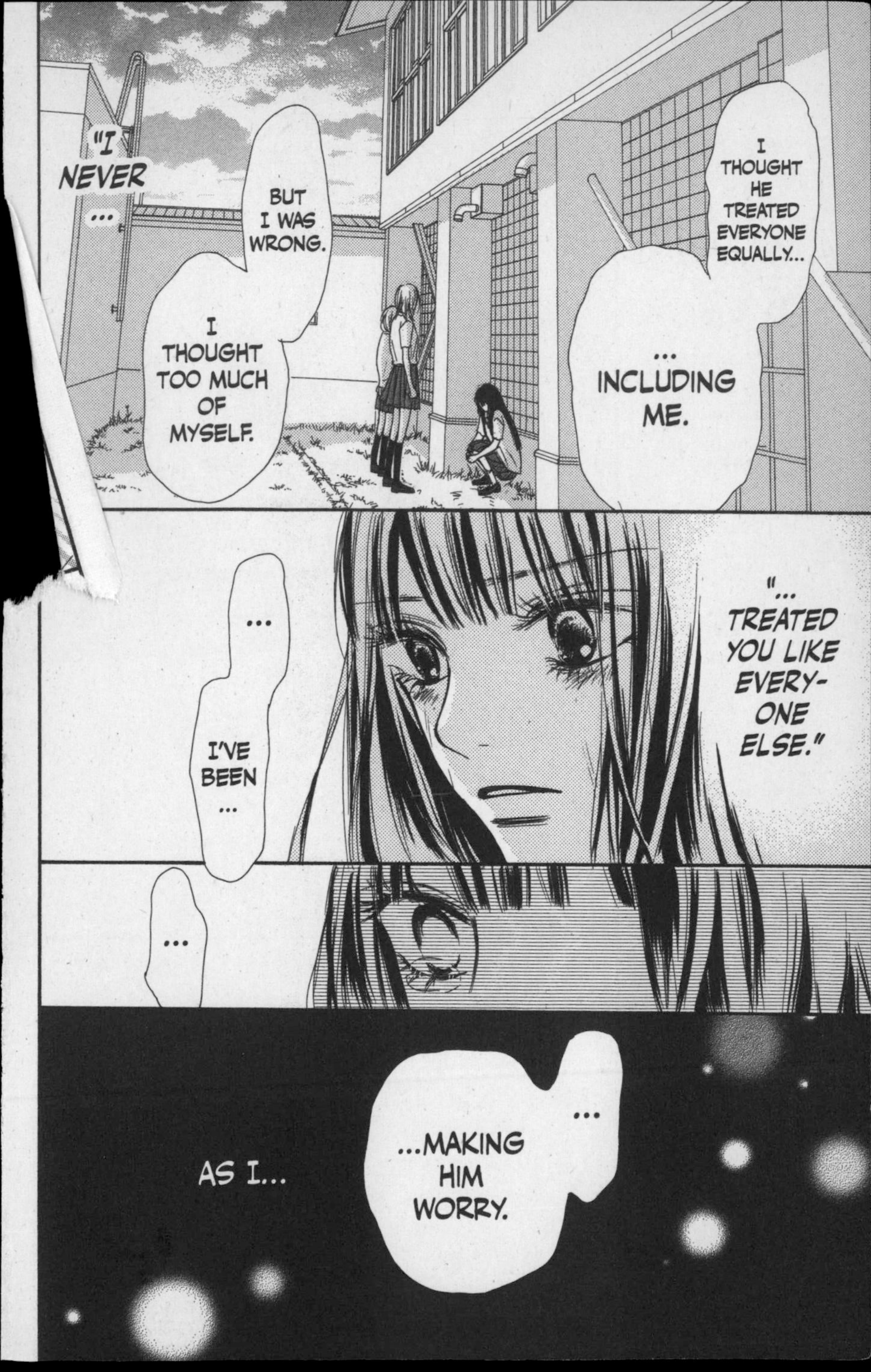
I THOUGHT HE TREATED EVERYONE EQUALLY...
... INCLUDING ME.
BUT I WAS WRONG.
I THOUGHT TOO MUCH OF MYSELF.
"I NEVER ...
"... TREATED YOU LIKE EVERY-ONE ELSE."
...
I'VE BEEN ...
...
...
...MAKING HIM WORRY.
AS I...

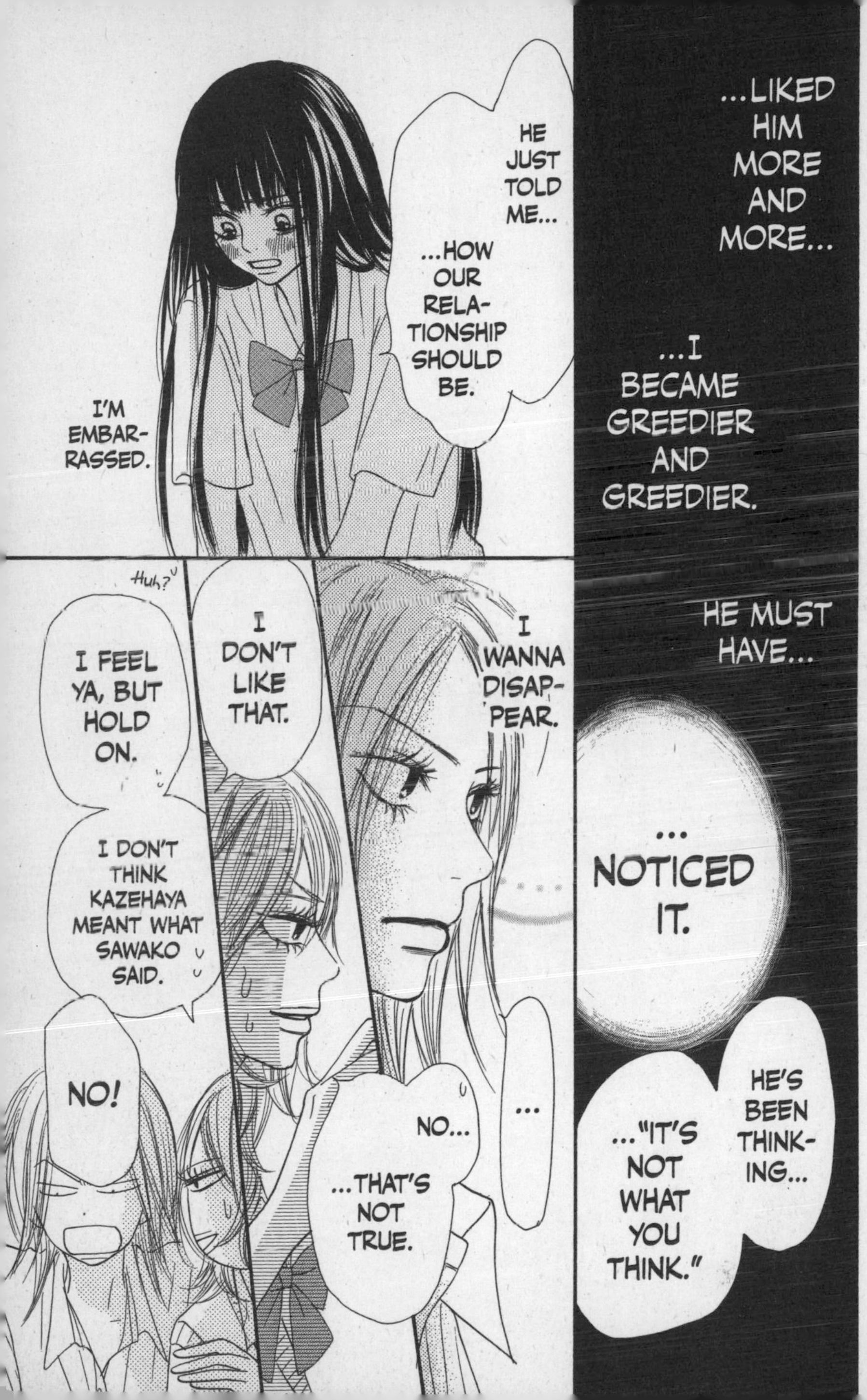
...LIKED HIM MORE AND MORE...
...I BECAME GREEDIER AND GREEDIER.
HE MUST HAVE...
...NOTICED IT.
HE'S BEEN THINKING...
..."IT'S NOT WHAT YOU THINK."
HE JUST TOLD ME...
...HOW OUR RELATIONSHIP SHOULD BE.
I'M EMBARRASSED.
I WANNA DISAPPEAR.
...
NO...
...THAT'S NOT TRUE.
I DON'T LIKE THAT.
Huh?
I FEEL YA, BUT HOLD ON.
I DON'T THINK KAZEHAYA MEANT WHAT SAWAKO SAID.
NO!

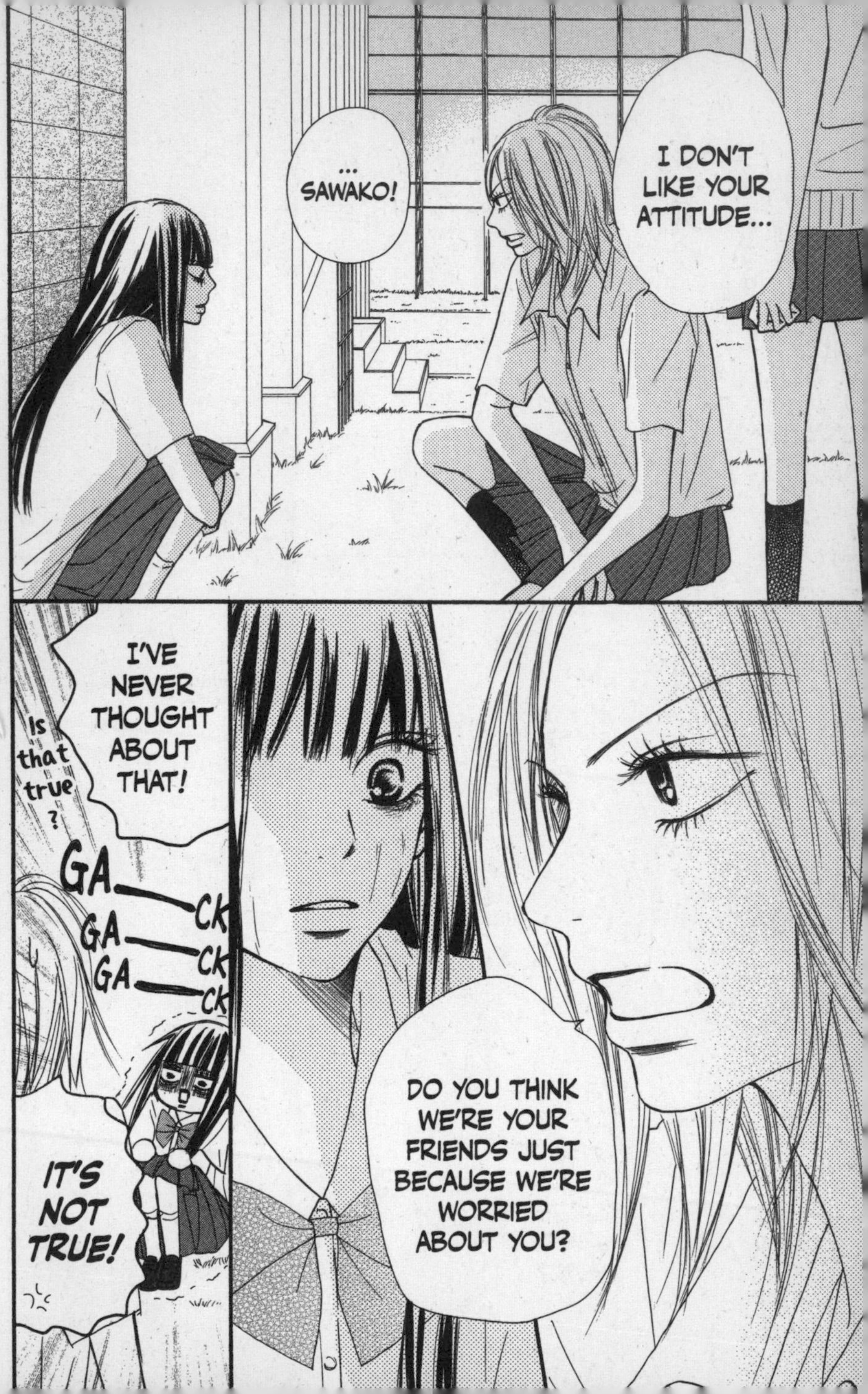
I DON'T LIKE YOUR ATTITUDE...
... SAWAKO!
DO YOU THINK WE'RE YOUR FRIENDS JUST BECAUSE WE'RE WORRIED ABOUT YOU?
I'VE NEVER THOUGHT ABOUT THAT!
Is that true?
GA—CK GA—CK GA—CK
IT'S NOT TRUE!

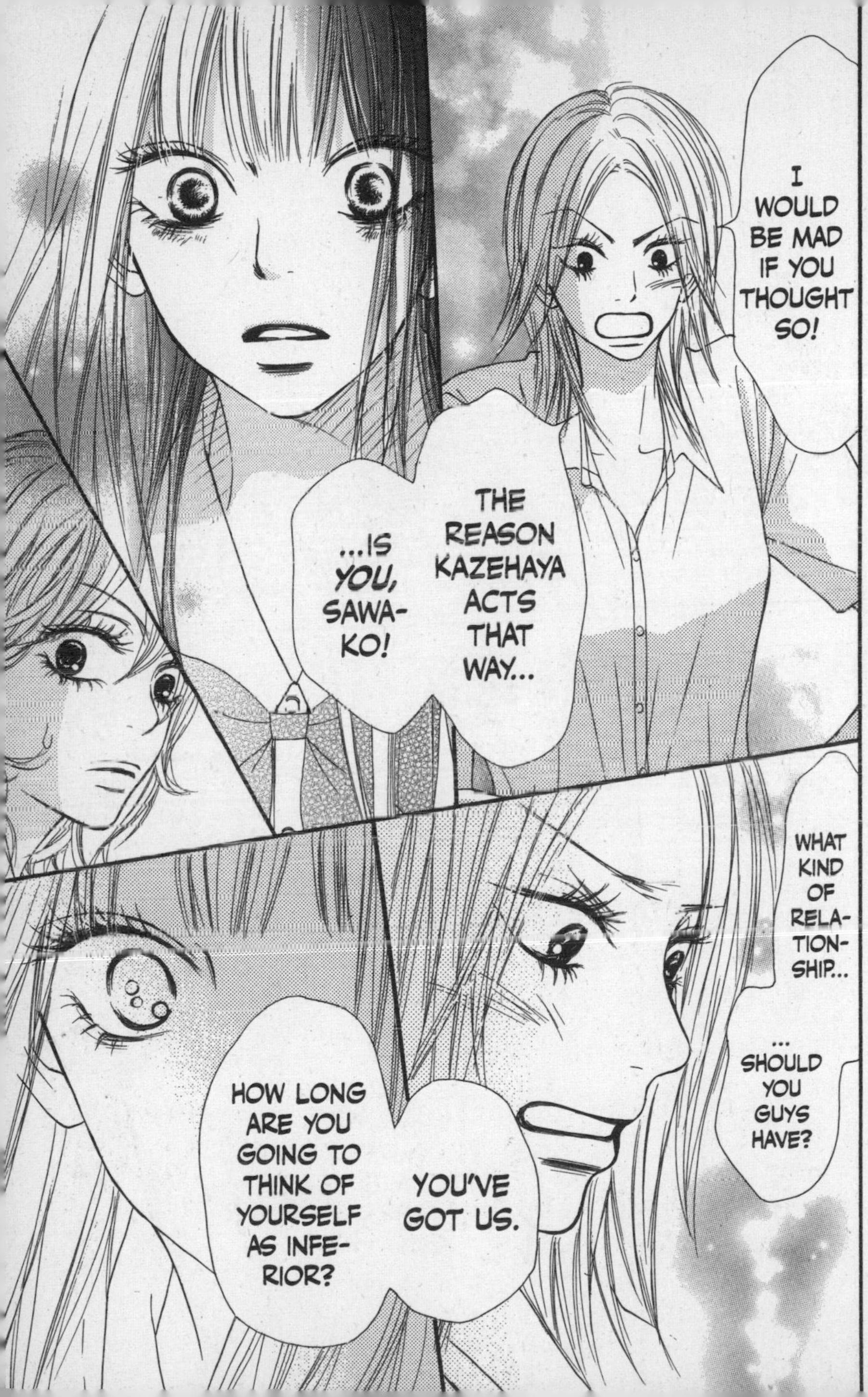
I WOULD BE MAD IF YOU THOUGHT SO!
THE REASON KAZEHAYA ACTS THAT WAY...
...IS *YOU*, SAWAKO!
WHAT KIND OF RELATIONSHIP...
...SHOULD YOU GUYS HAVE?
YOU'VE GOT US.
HOW LONG ARE YOU GOING TO THINK OF YOURSELF AS INFERIOR?

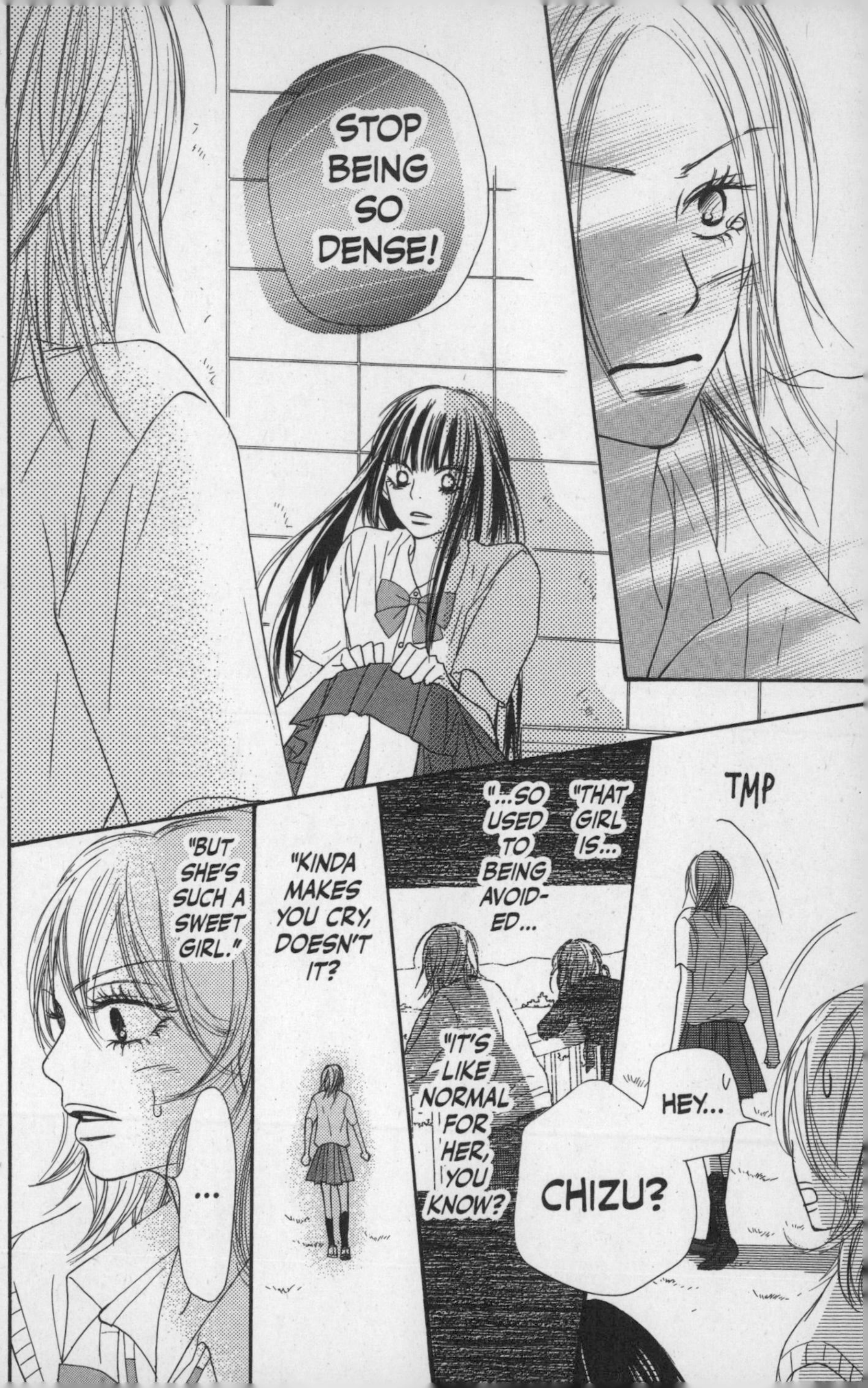
STOP BEING SO DENSE!
TMP
HEY...
CHIZU?
"THAT GIRL IS...
"...SO USED TO BEING AVOID-ED...
"IT'S LIKE NORMAL FOR HER, YOU KNOW?
"KINDA MAKES YOU CRY, DOESN'T IT?
"BUT SHE'S SUCH A SWEET GIRL."
...

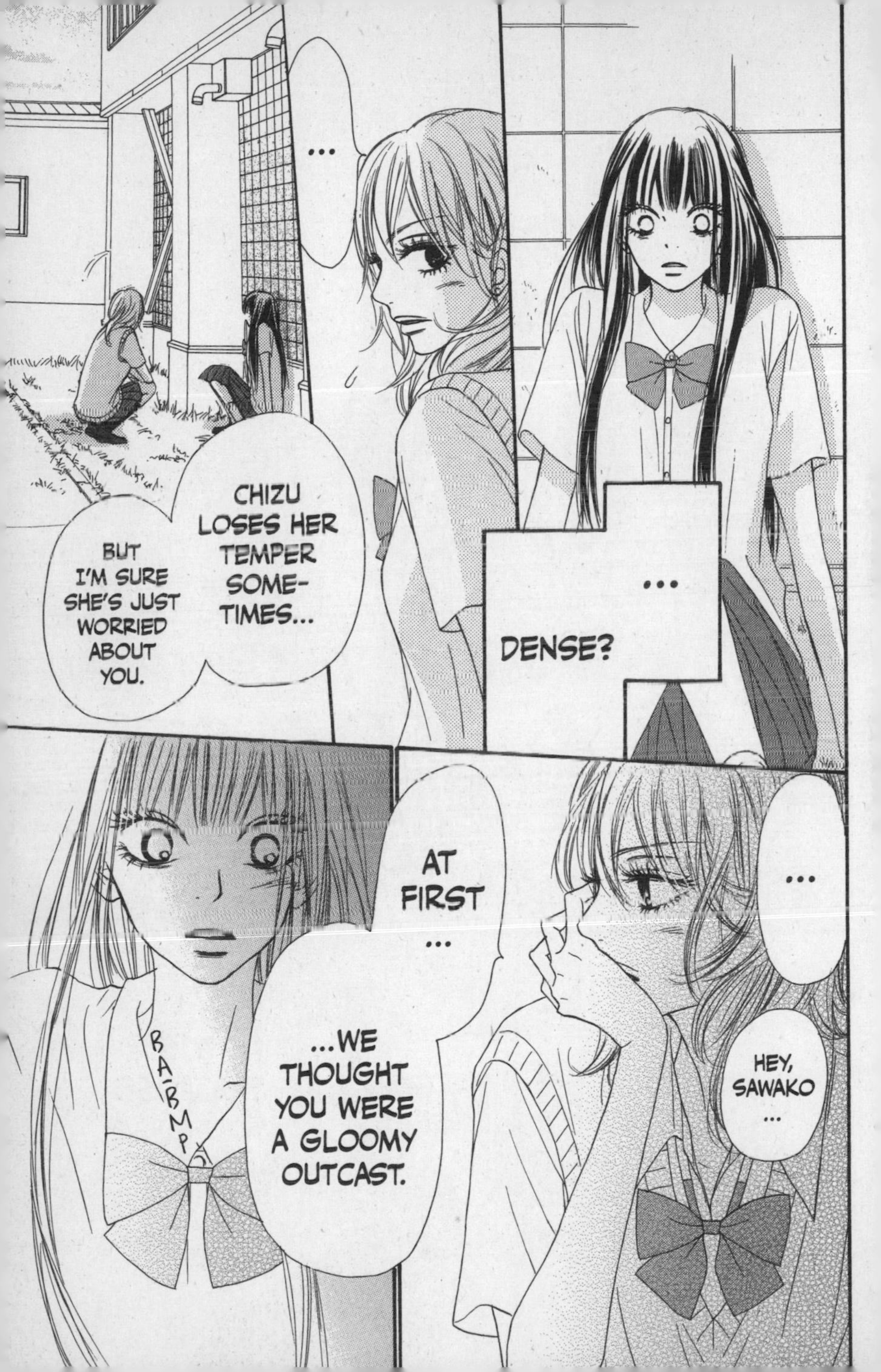
...
DENSE?
...
CHIZU LOSES HER TEMPER SOMETIMES...
BUT I'M SURE SHE'S JUST WORRIED ABOUT YOU.
...
HEY, SAWAKO ...
AT FIRST ...
...WE THOUGHT YOU WERE A GLOOMY OUTCAST.
BA-BMP

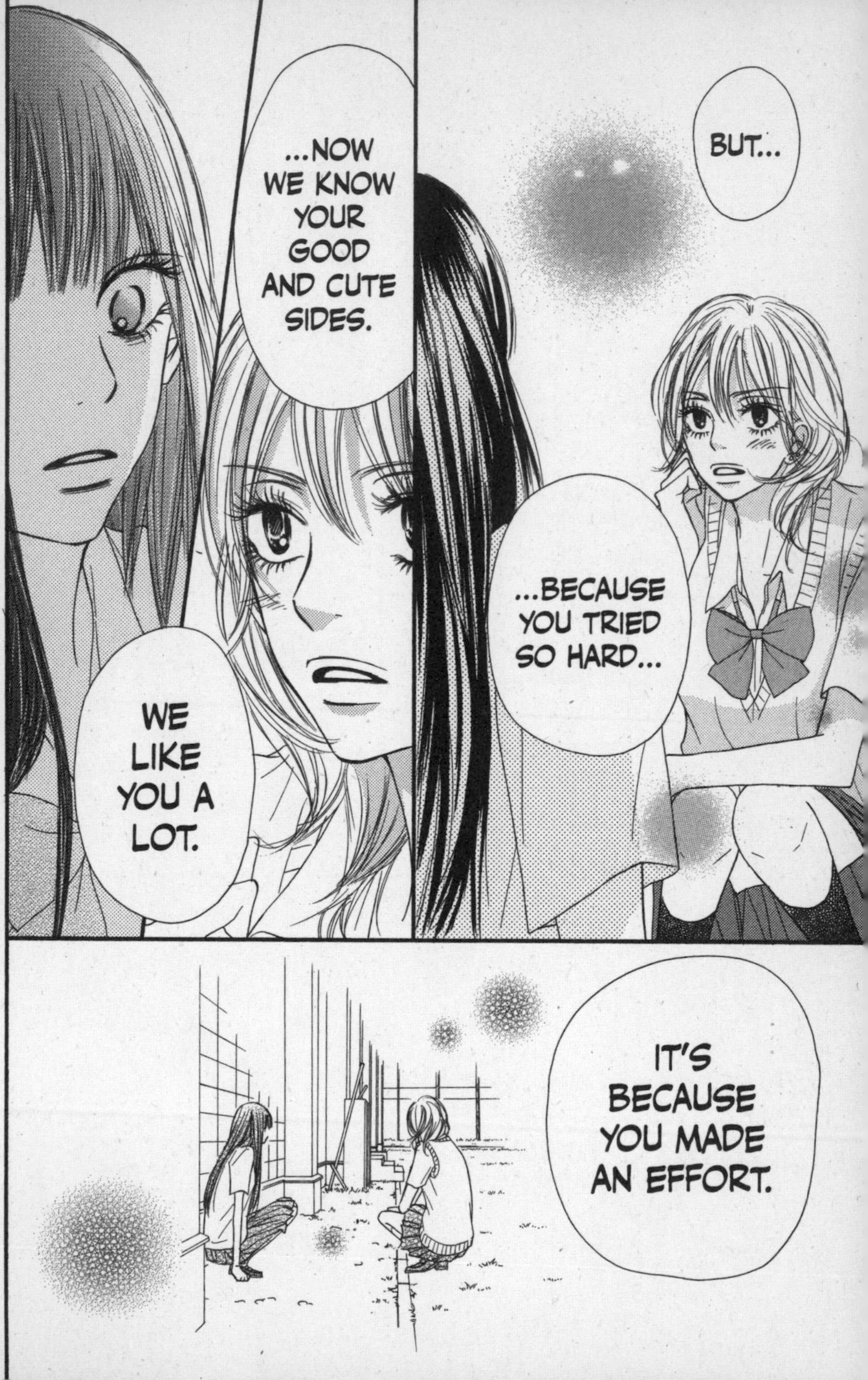
BUT...
...BECAUSE YOU TRIED SO HARD...
...NOW WE KNOW YOUR GOOD AND CUTE SIDES.
WE LIKE YOU A LOT.
IT'S BECAUSE YOU MADE AN EFFORT.

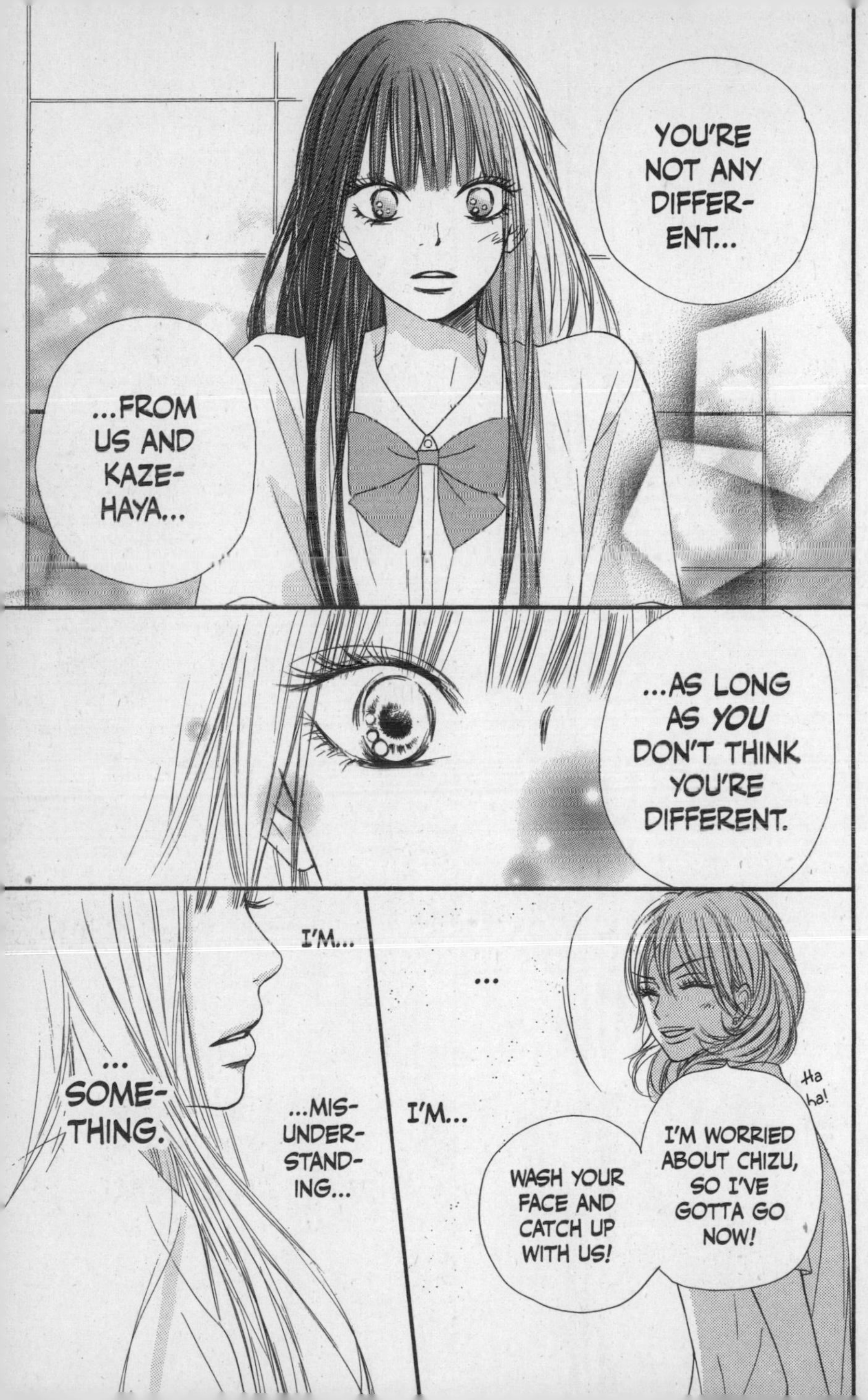
YOU'RE NOT ANY DIFFER-ENT...
...FROM US AND KAZE-HAYA...
...AS LONG AS *YOU* DON'T THINK YOU'RE DIFFERENT.
...
Ha ha!
I'M WORRIED ABOUT CHIZU, SO I'VE GOTTA GO NOW!
WASH YOUR FACE AND CATCH UP WITH US!
I'M...
I'M...
...MIS-UNDER-STAND-ING...
... SOME-THING.

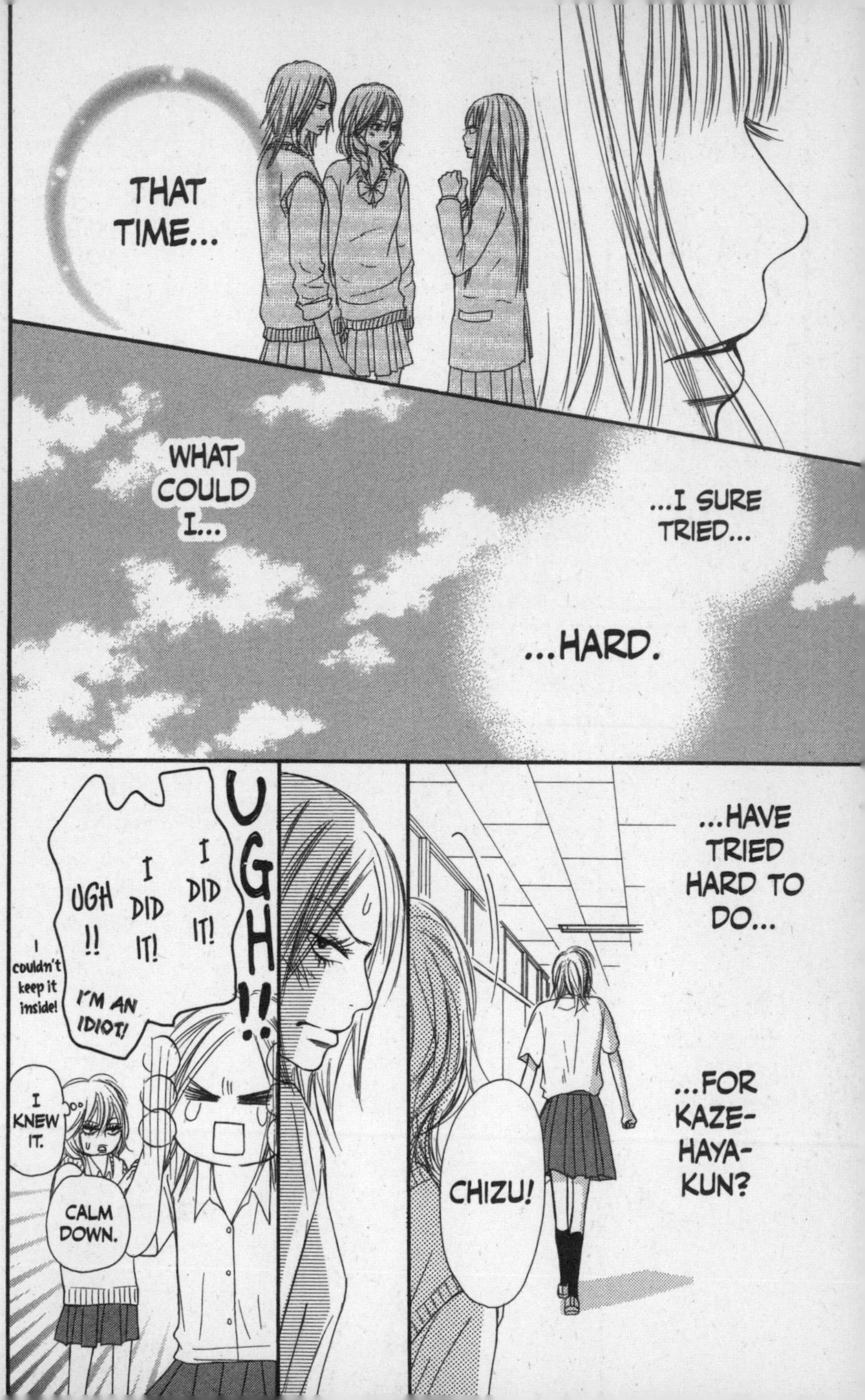
THAT TIME...
...I SURE TRIED...
...HARD.
WHAT COULD I...
...HAVE TRIED HARD TO DO...
...FOR KAZE-HAYA-KUN?
CHIZU!
UGH!!
I DID IT!
I DID IT!
UGH!!
I'M AN IDIOT!
I couldn't keep it inside!
I KNEW IT.
CALM DOWN.

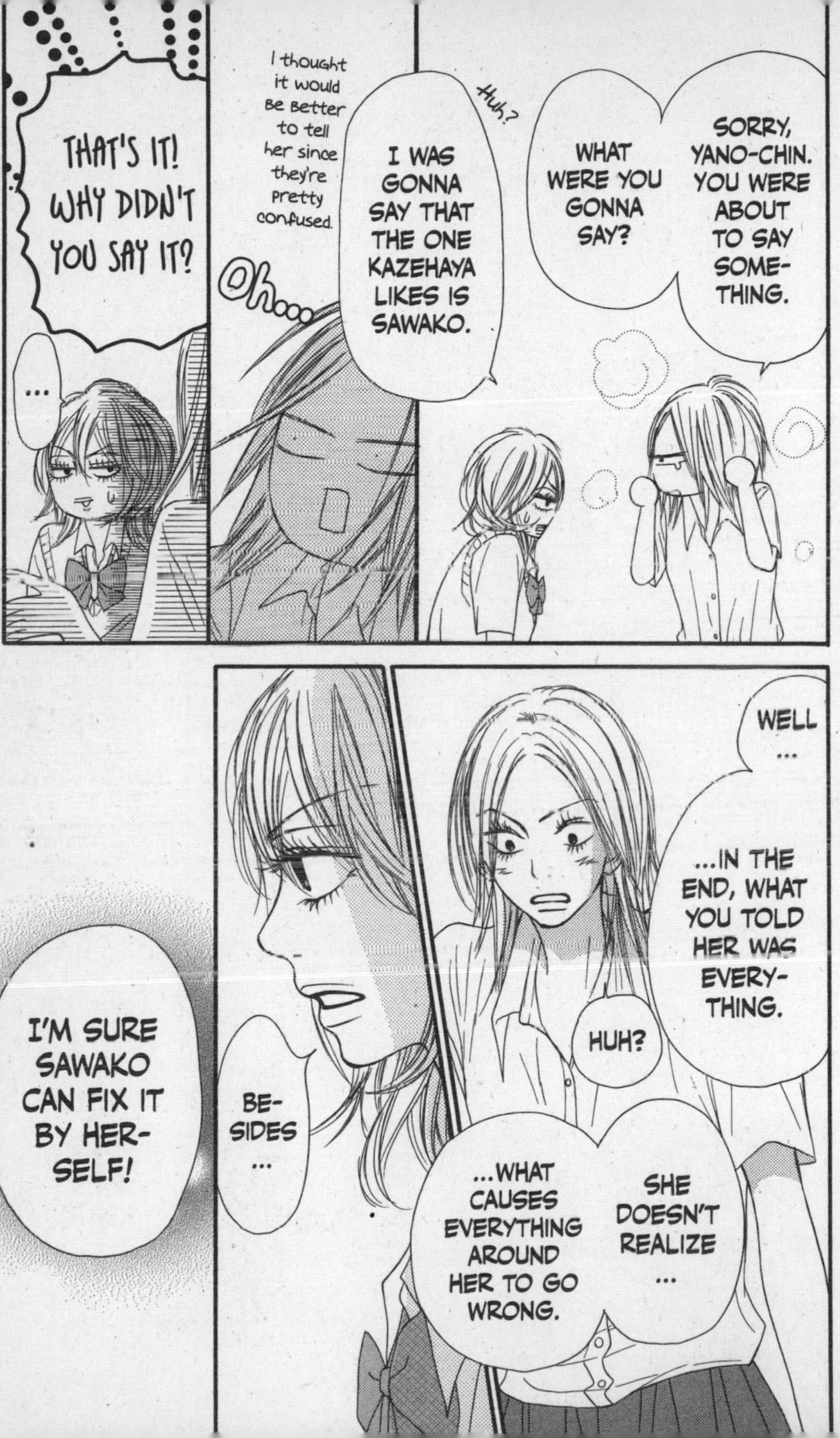
SORRY, YANO-CHIN. YOU WERE ABOUT TO SAY SOME-THING.
WHAT WERE YOU GONNA SAY?
Huh?
I WAS GONNA SAY THAT THE ONE KAZEHAYA LIKES IS SAWAKO.
I thought it would be better to tell her since they're pretty confused.
Oh...
THAT'S IT! WHY DIDN'T YOU SAY IT?
...
WELL...
...IN THE END, WHAT YOU TOLD HER WAS EVERY-THING.
HUH?
SHE DOESN'T REALIZE...
...WHAT CAUSES EVERYTHING AROUND HER TO GO WRONG.
BE-SIDES...
I'M SURE SAWAKO CAN FIX IT BY HER-SELF!

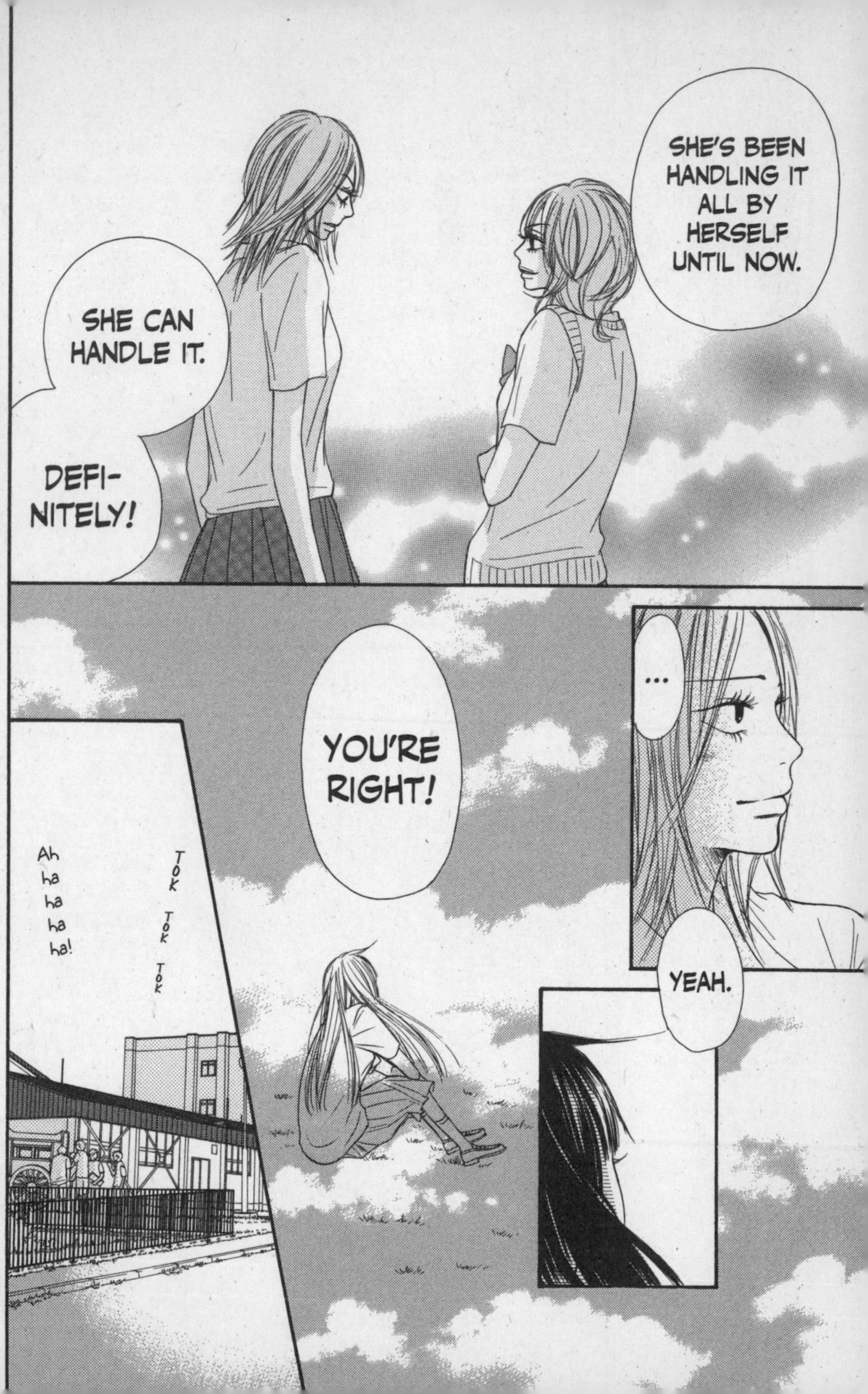

SHE'S BEEN HANDLING IT ALL BY HERSELF UNTIL NOW.
SHE CAN HANDLE IT.
DEFI- NITELY!
...
YEAH.
YOU'RE RIGHT!
TOK TOK TOK
Ah ha ha ha ha!

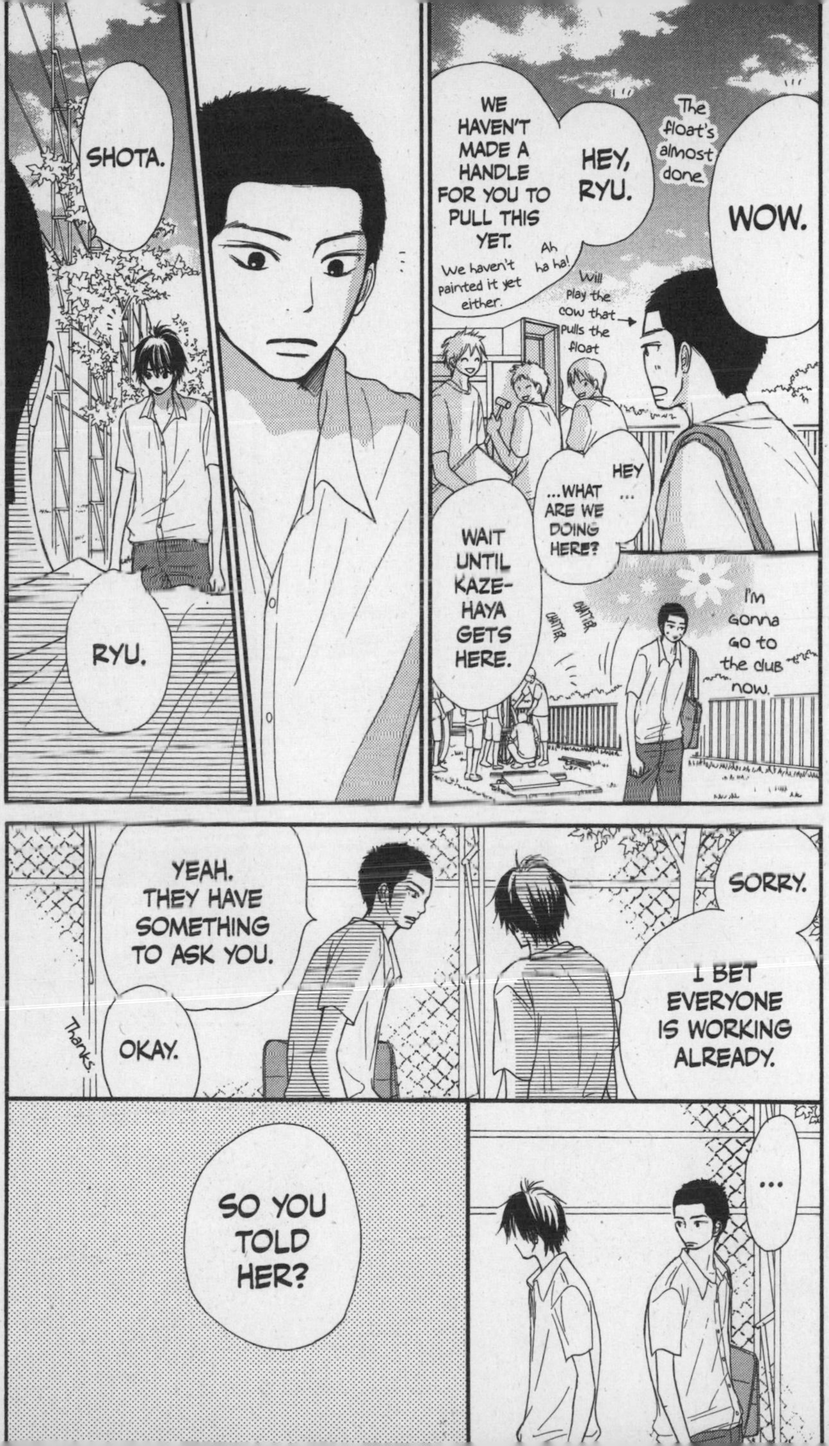
WOW.
The float's almost done.
HEY, RYU.
WE HAVEN'T MADE A HANDLE FOR YOU TO PULL THIS YET.
Ah ha ha!
We haven't painted it yet either.
Will play the cow that pulls the float
I'm gonna go to the club now.
HEY ...
...WHAT ARE WE DOING HERE?
WAIT UNTIL KAZE-HAYA GETS HERE.
CHATTER CHATTER
SHOTA.
RYU.
SORRY.
I BET EVERYONE IS WORKING ALREADY.
YEAH. THEY HAVE SOMETHING TO ASK YOU.
OKAY.
Thanks.
...
SO YOU TOLD HER?

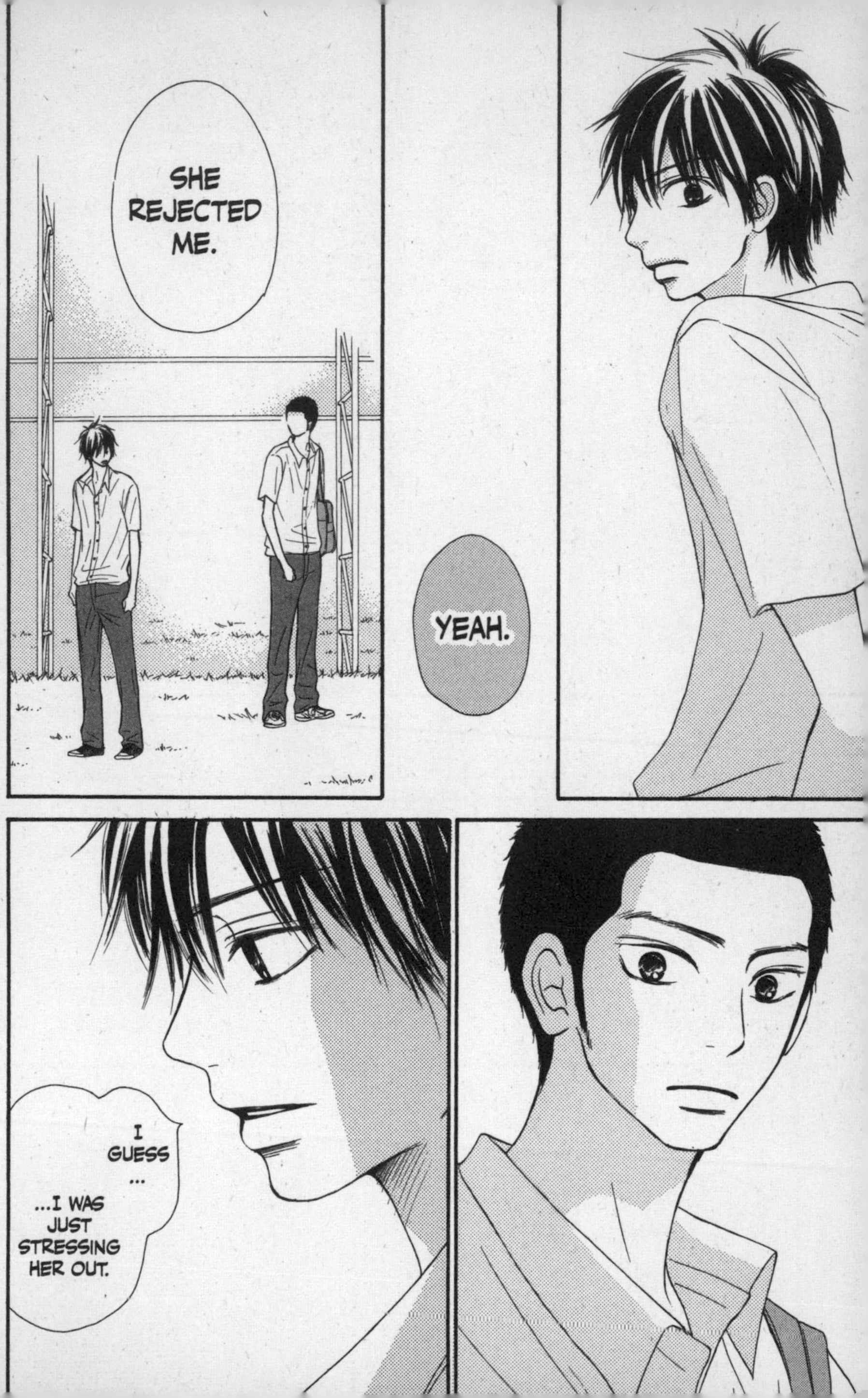
YEAH.
SHE REJECTED ME.
I GUESS...
...I WAS JUST STRESSING HER OUT.

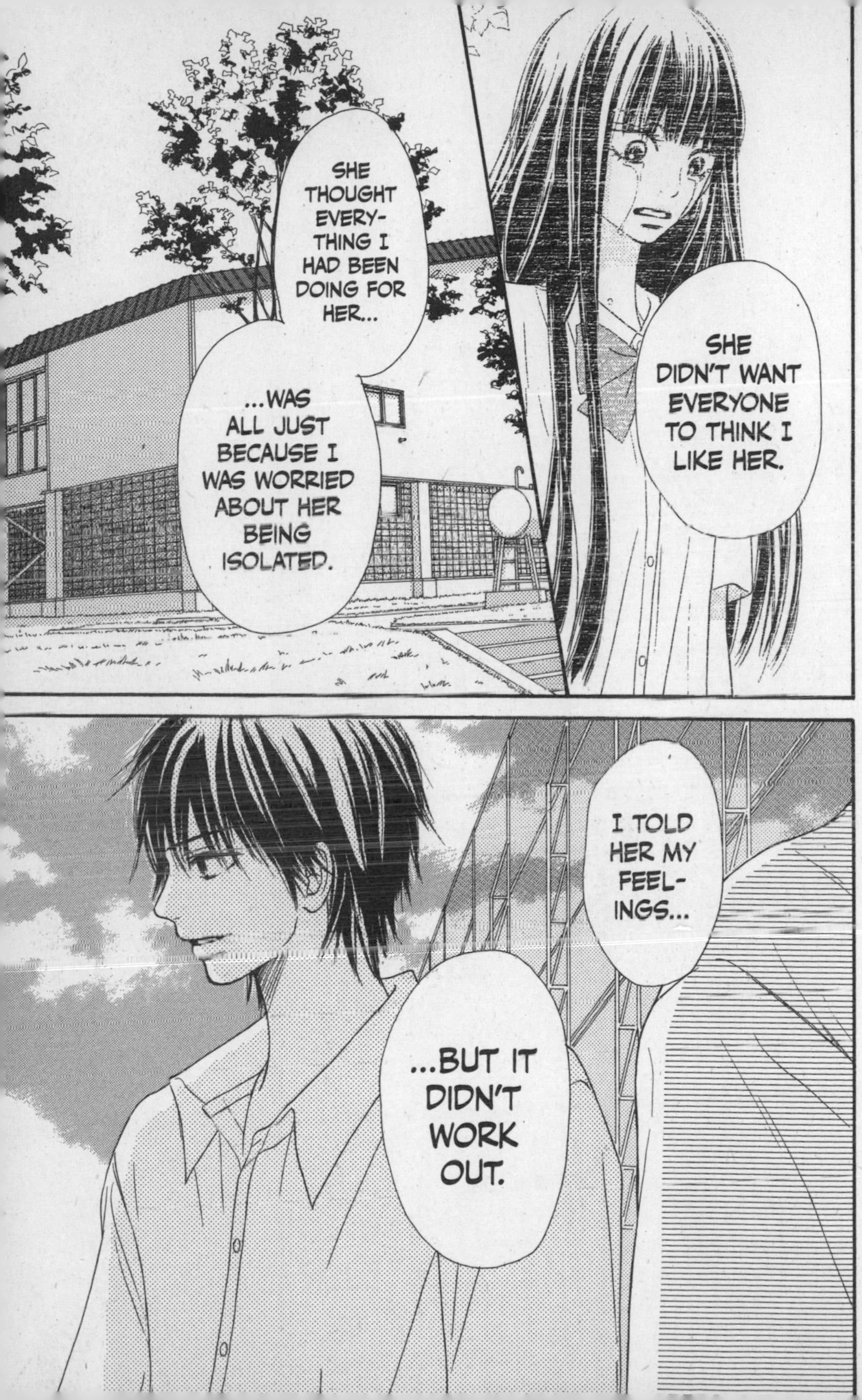
SHE DIDN'T WANT EVERYONE TO THINK I LIKE HER.
SHE THOUGHT EVERY-THING I HAD BEEN DOING FOR HER...
...WAS ALL JUST BECAUSE I WAS WORRIED ABOUT HER BEING ISOLATED.
I TOLD HER MY FEEL-INGS...
...BUT IT DIDN'T WORK OUT.

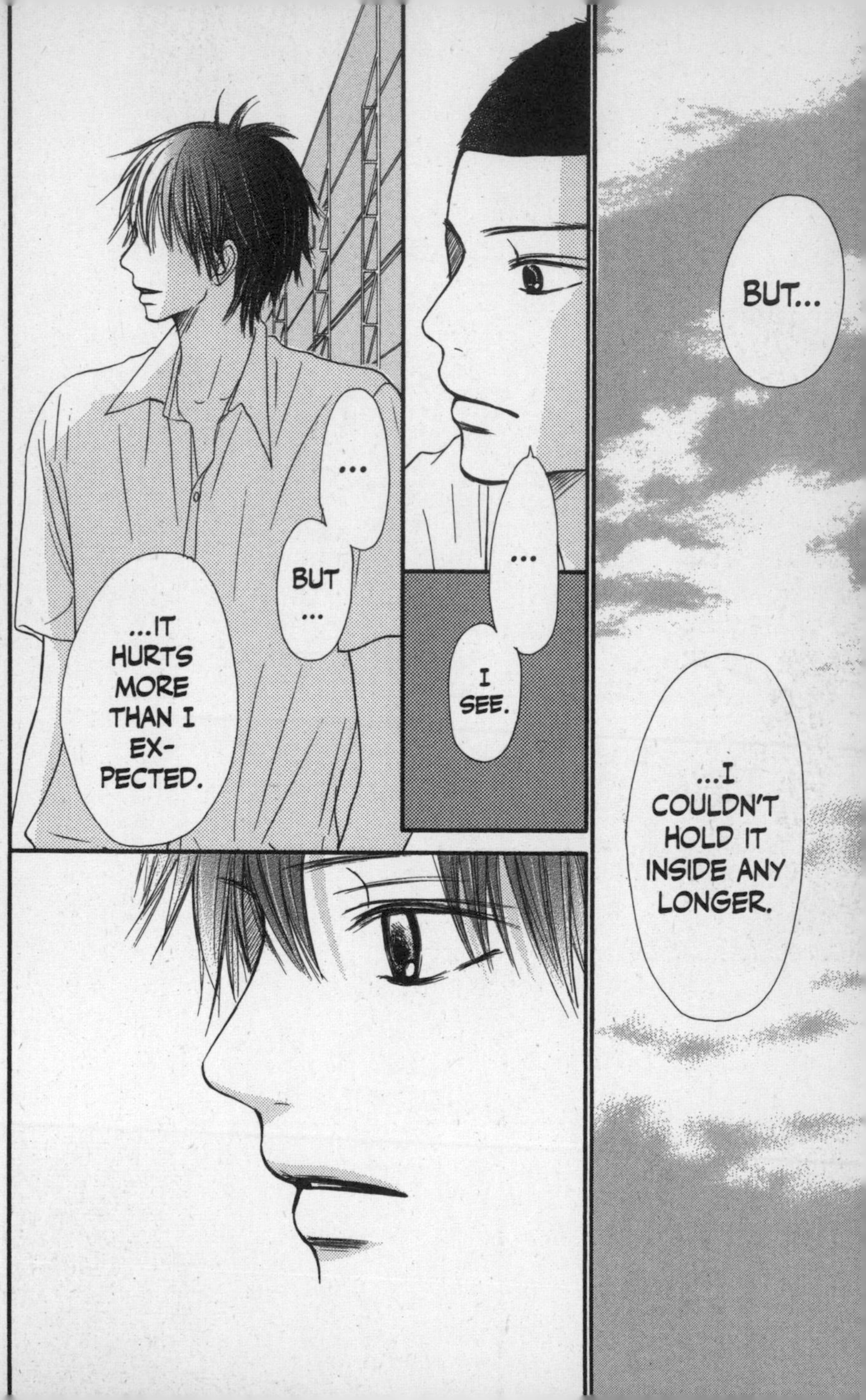
BUT...
...I COULDN'T HOLD IT INSIDE ANY LONGER.
...
I SEE.
...
BUT ...
...IT HURTS MORE THAN I EX-PECTED.

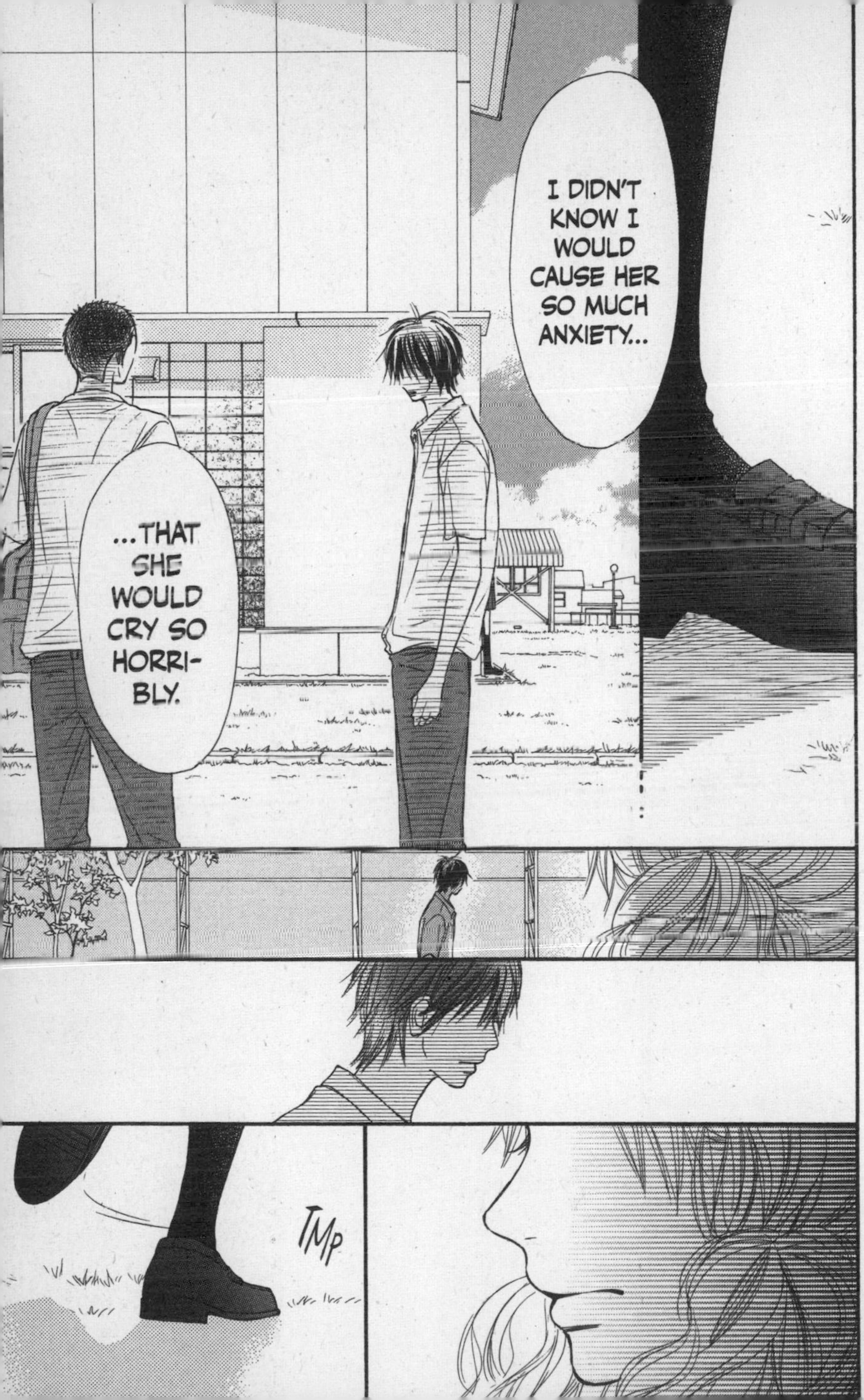
I DIDN'T KNOW I WOULD CAUSE HER SO MUCH ANXIETY...
...THAT SHE WOULD CRY SO HORRI-BLY.
TMP

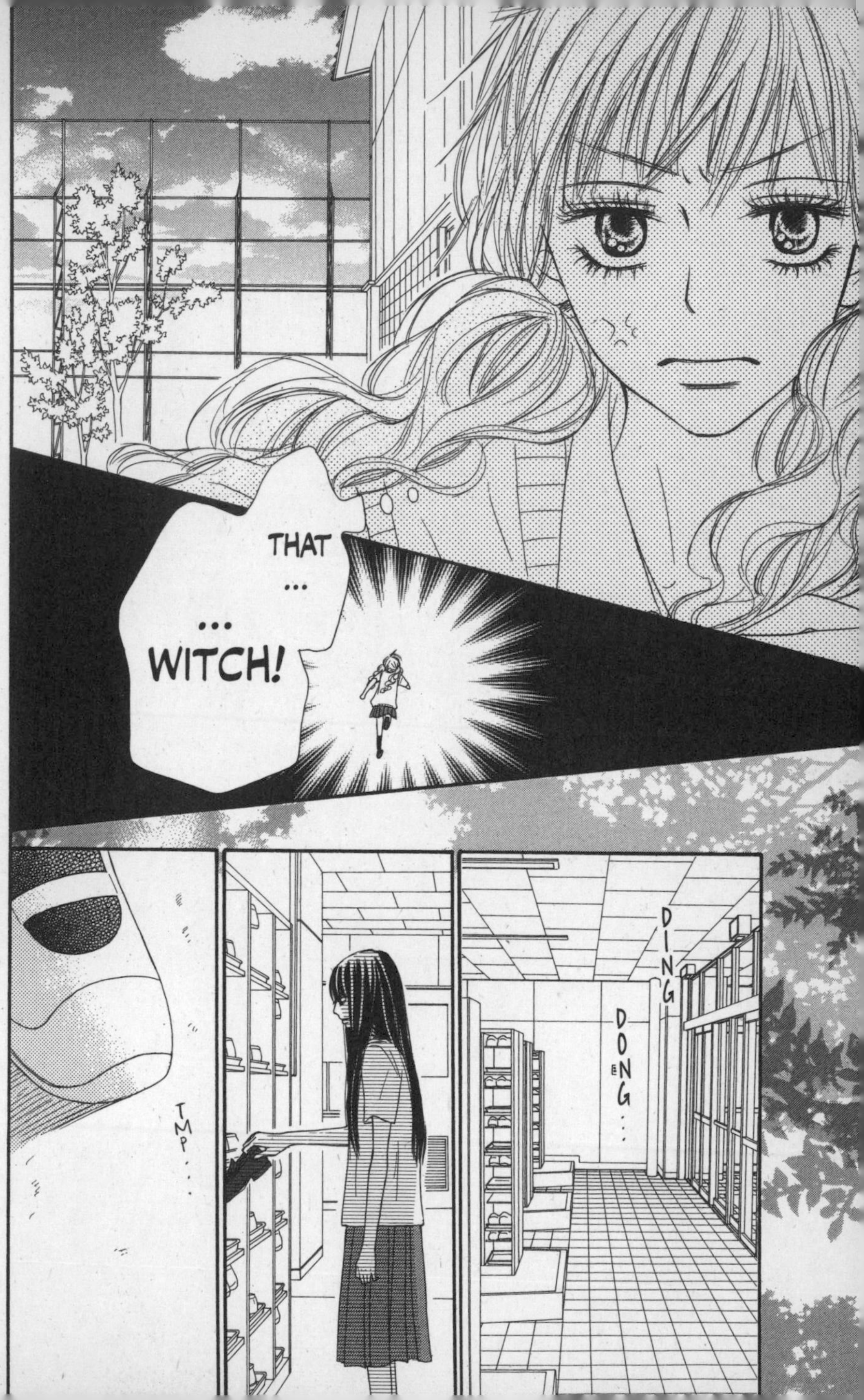
THAT ...
... WITCH!
DING DONG...
TMP...

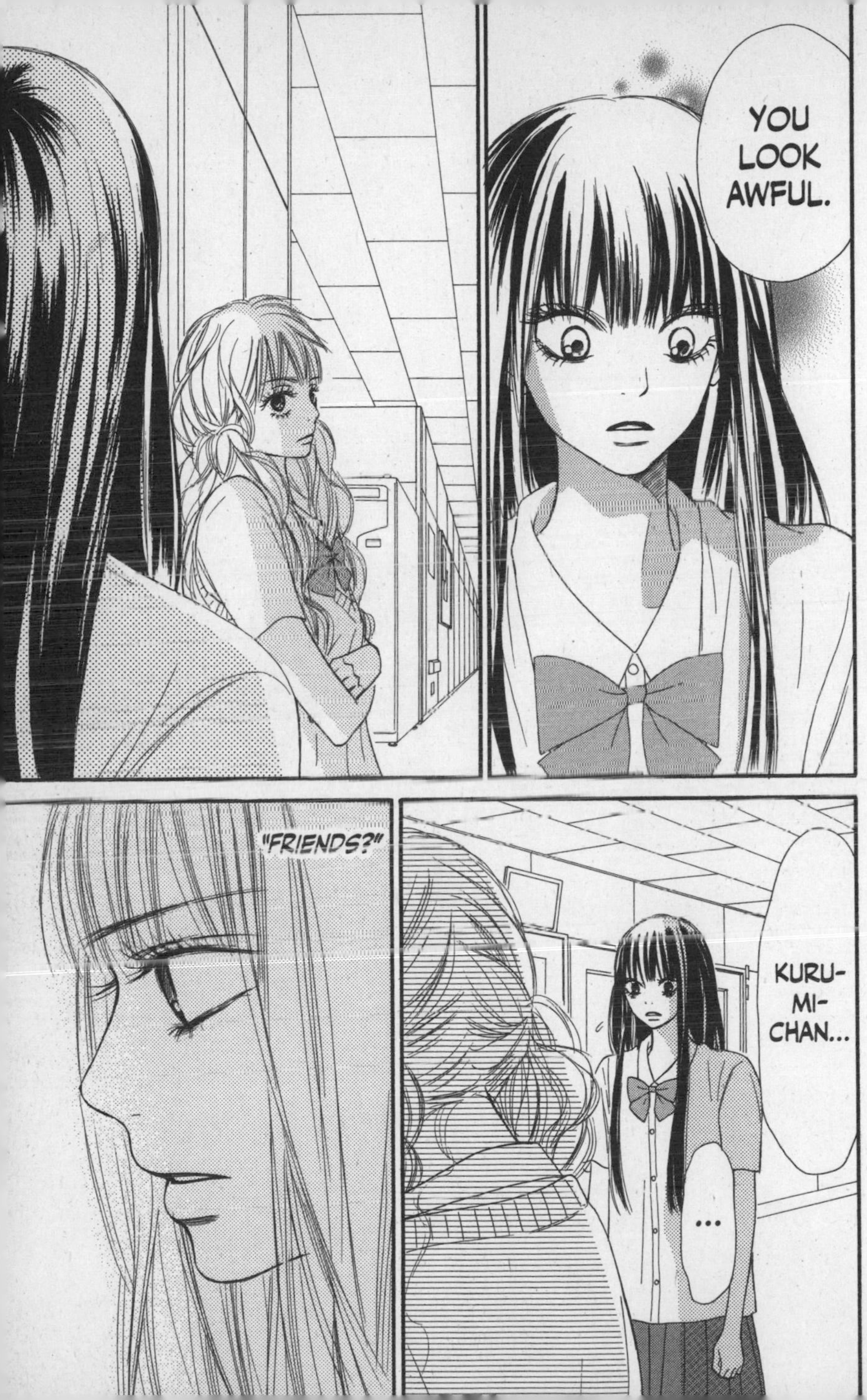
YOU LOOK AWFUL.
KURU-MI-CHAN...
...
"FRIENDS?"

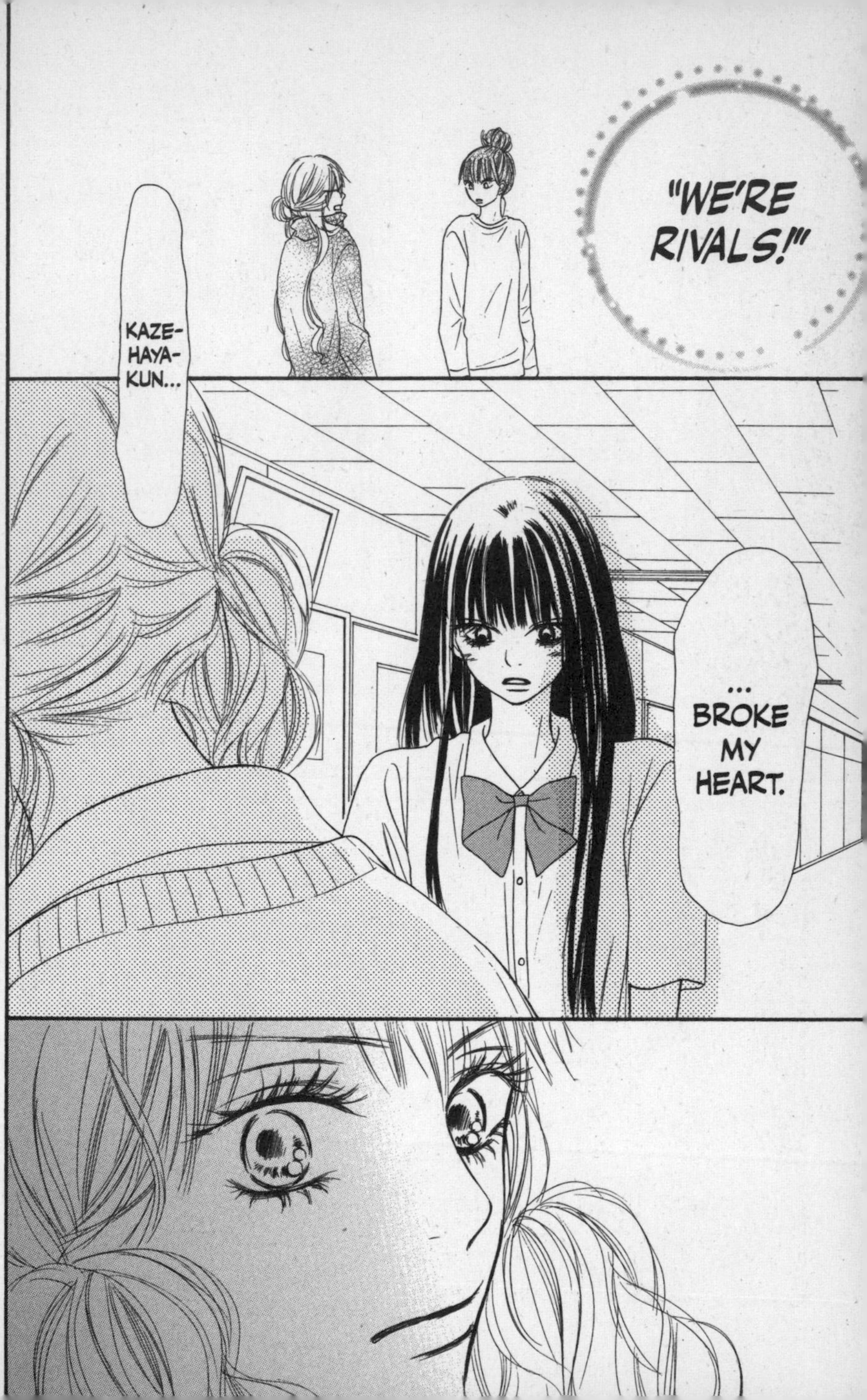
"WE'RE RIVALS!"
KAZE-HAYA-KUN...
... BROKE MY HEART.

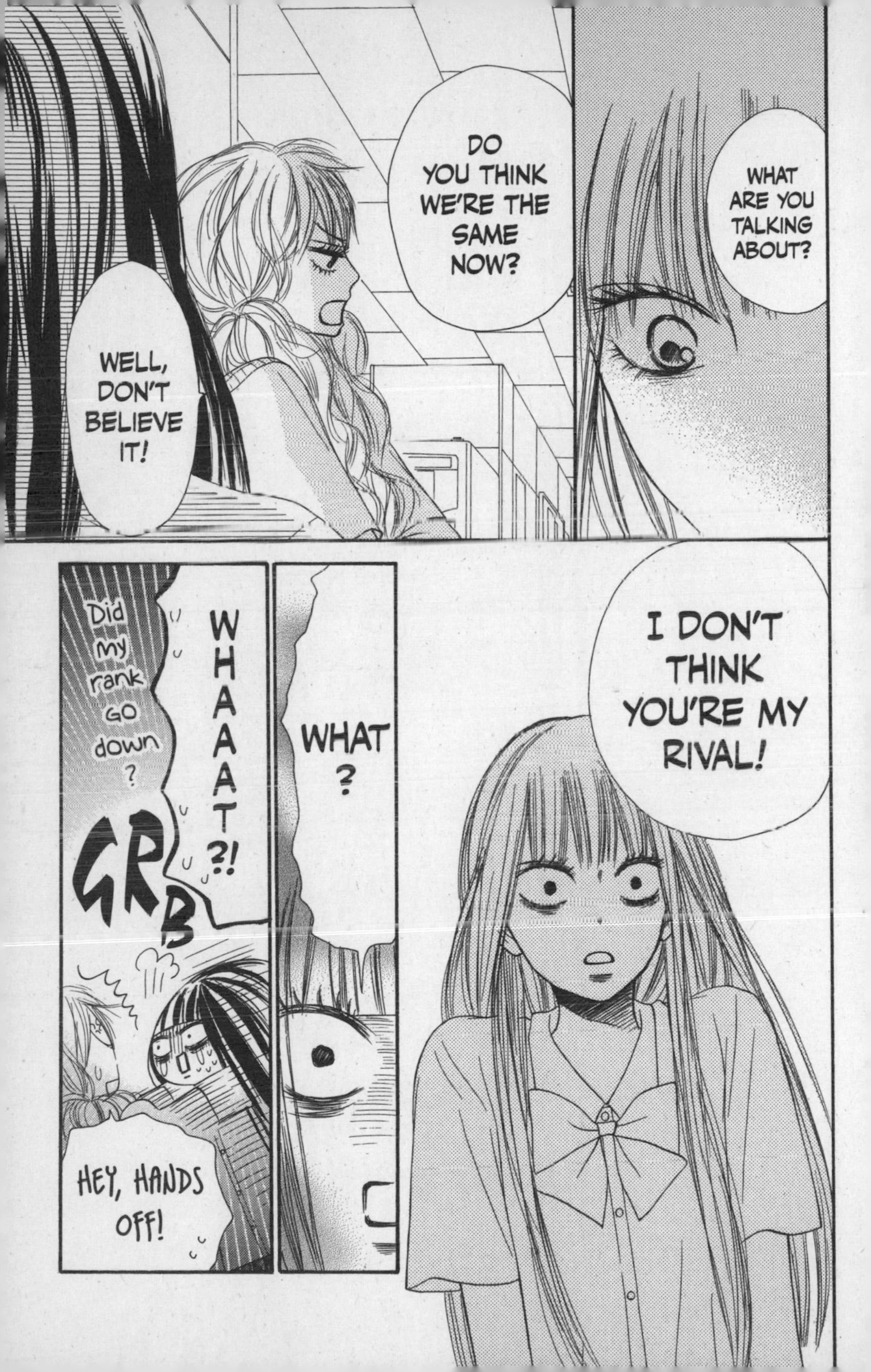
WHAT ARE YOU TALKING ABOUT?
DO YOU THINK WE'RE THE SAME NOW?
WELL, DON'T BELIEVE IT!
I DON'T THINK YOU'RE MY RIVAL!
WHAT?
WHAAAAT?!
Did my rank GO down?
GRB
HEY, HANDS OFF!

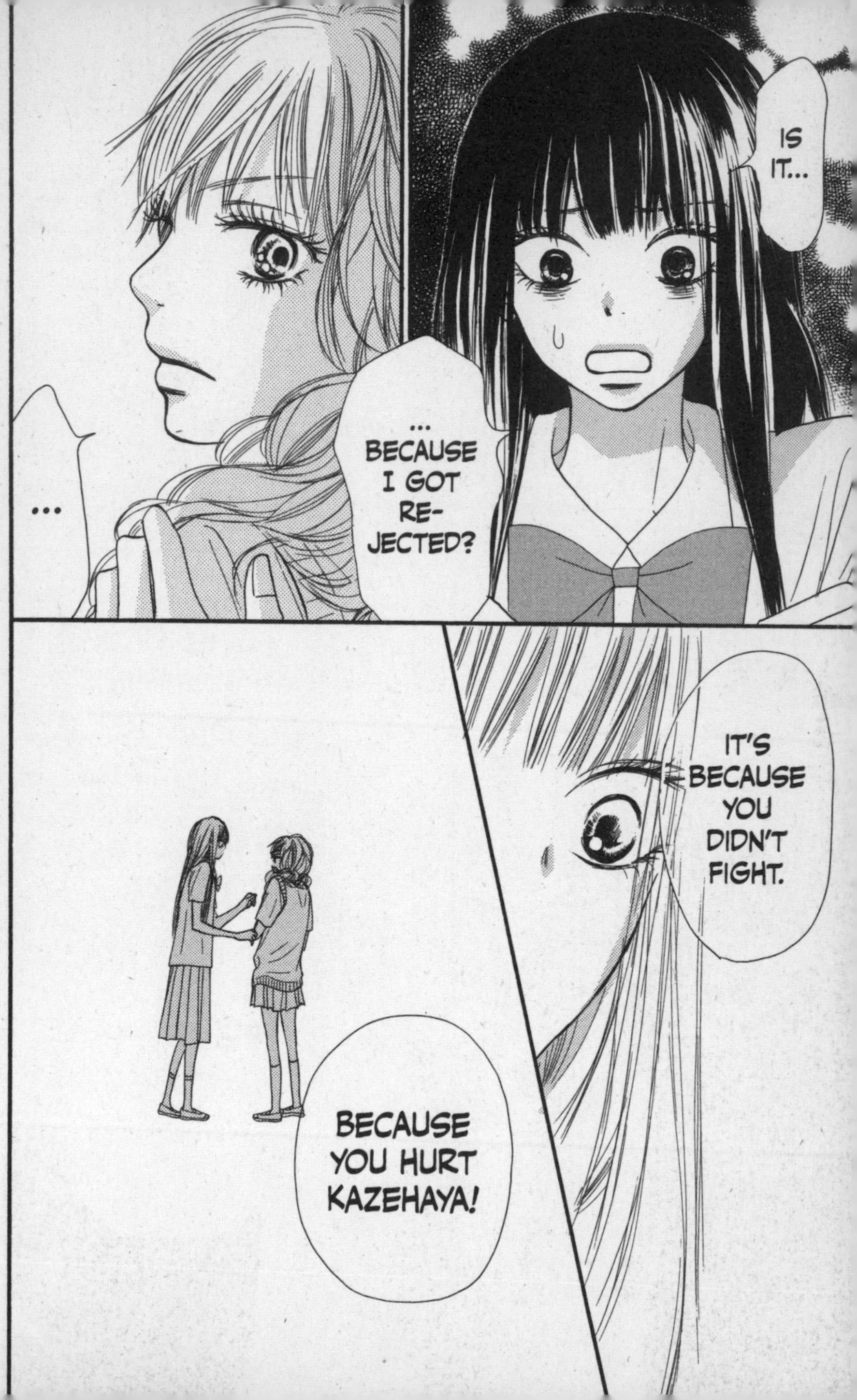
IS IT...
...BECAUSE I GOT RE-JECTED?
...
IT'S BECAUSE YOU DIDN'T FIGHT.
BECAUSE YOU HURT KAZEHAYA!

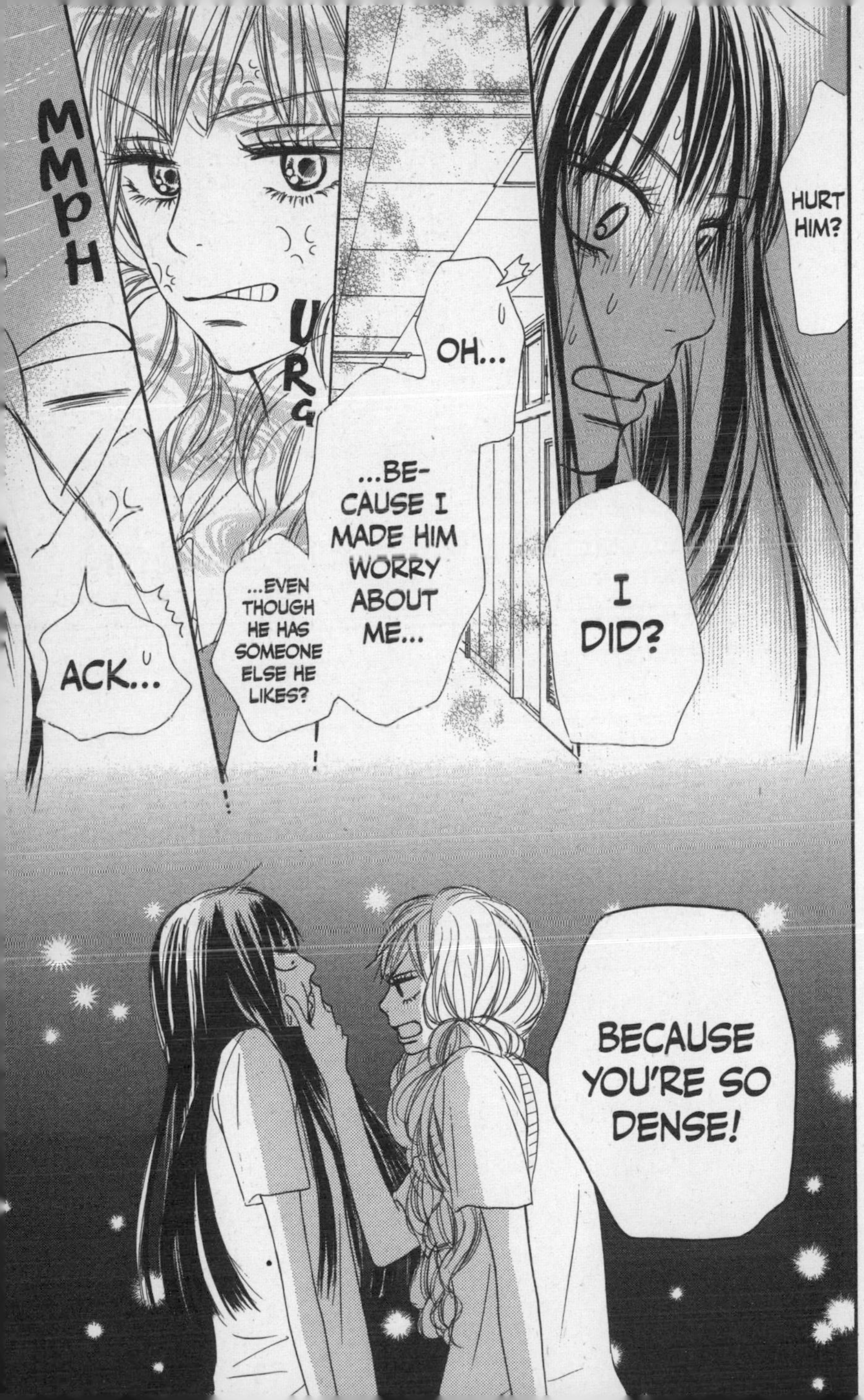
HURT HIM?
I DID?
OH...
...BE-CAUSE I MADE HIM WORRY ABOUT ME...
...EVEN THOUGH HE HAS SOMEONE ELSE HE LIKES?
URG
MMPH
ACK...
BECAUSE YOU'RE SO DENSE!

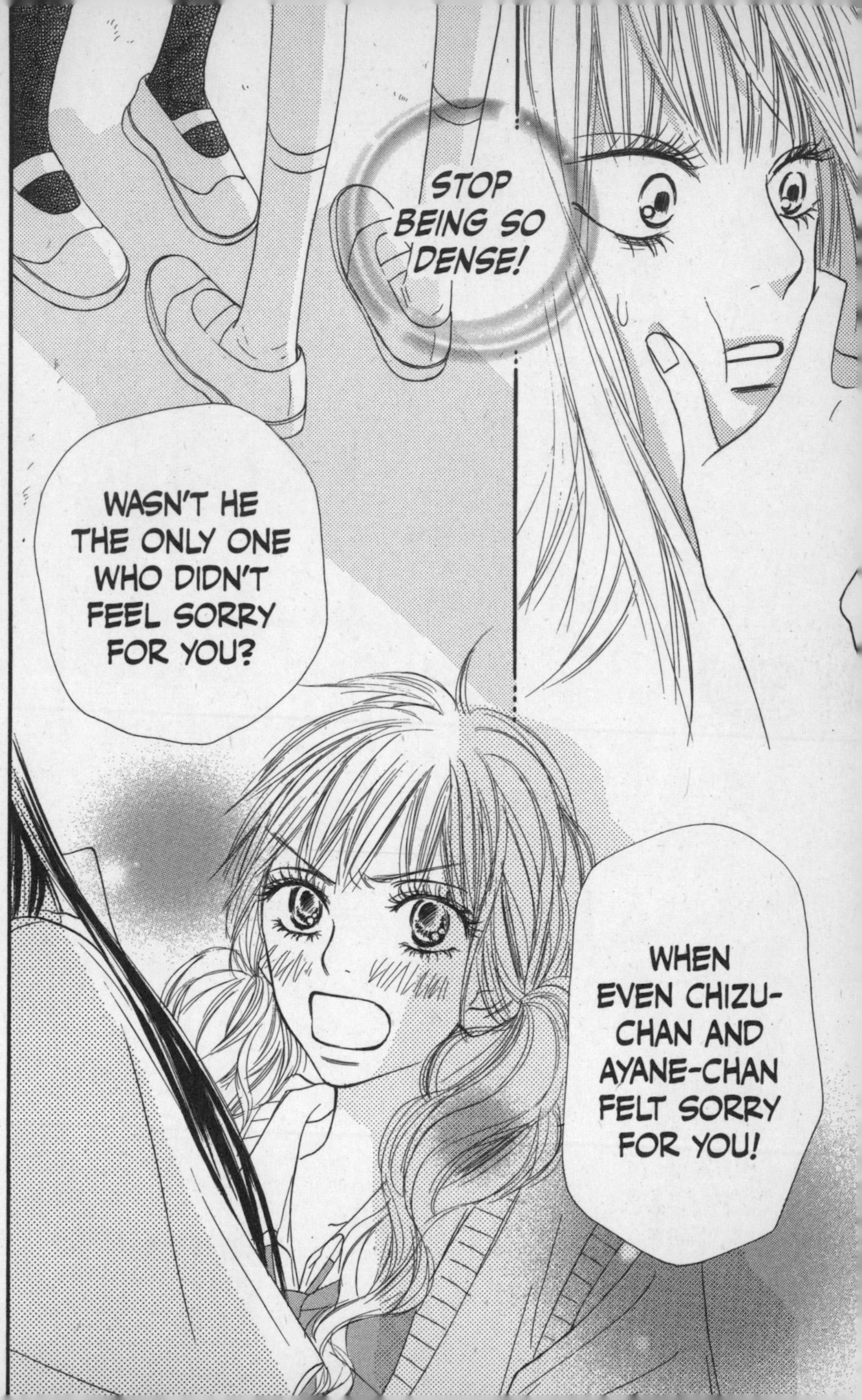
STOP BEING SO DENSE!
WASN'T HE THE ONLY ONE WHO DIDN'T FEEL SORRY FOR YOU?
WHEN EVEN CHIZU-CHAN AND AYANE-CHAN FELT SORRY FOR YOU!

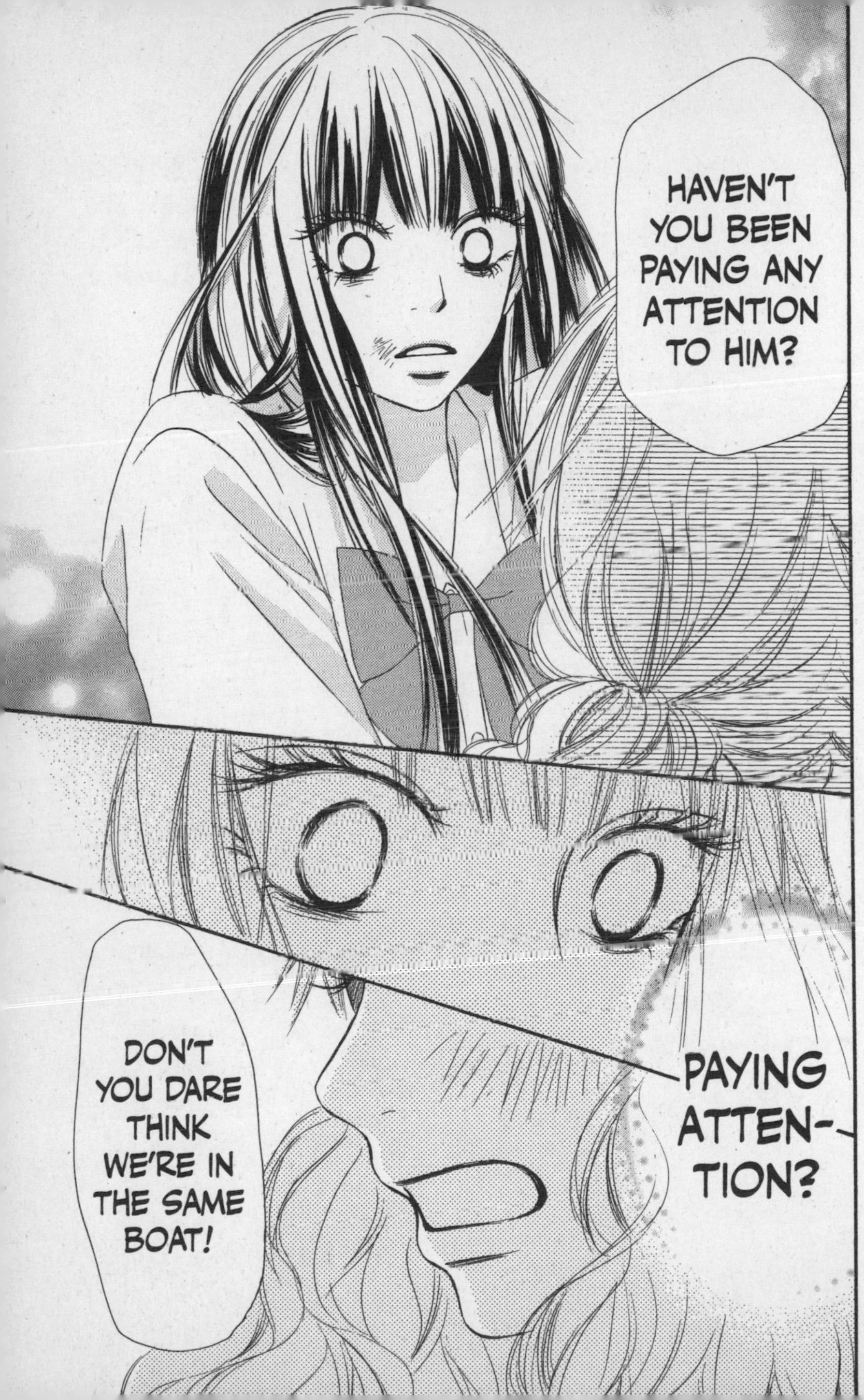
HAVEN'T YOU BEEN PAYING ANY ATTENTION TO HIM?
PAYING ATTEN-TION?
DON'T YOU DARE THINK WE'RE IN THE SAME BOAT!

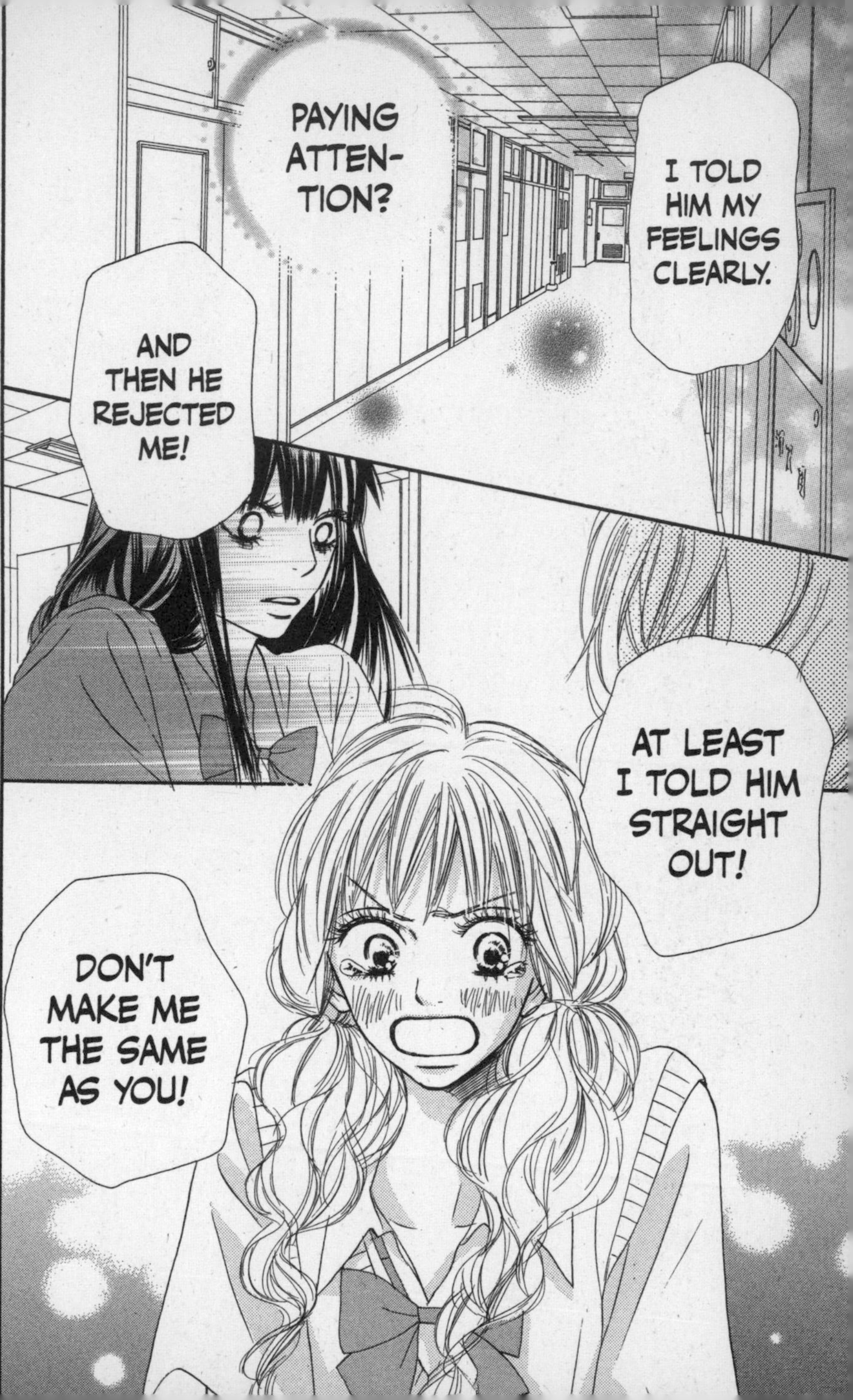
I TOLD HIM MY FEELINGS CLEARLY.
PAYING ATTEN-TION?
AND THEN HE REJECTED ME!
AT LEAST I TOLD HIM STRAIGHT OUT!
DON'T MAKE ME THE SAME AS YOU!

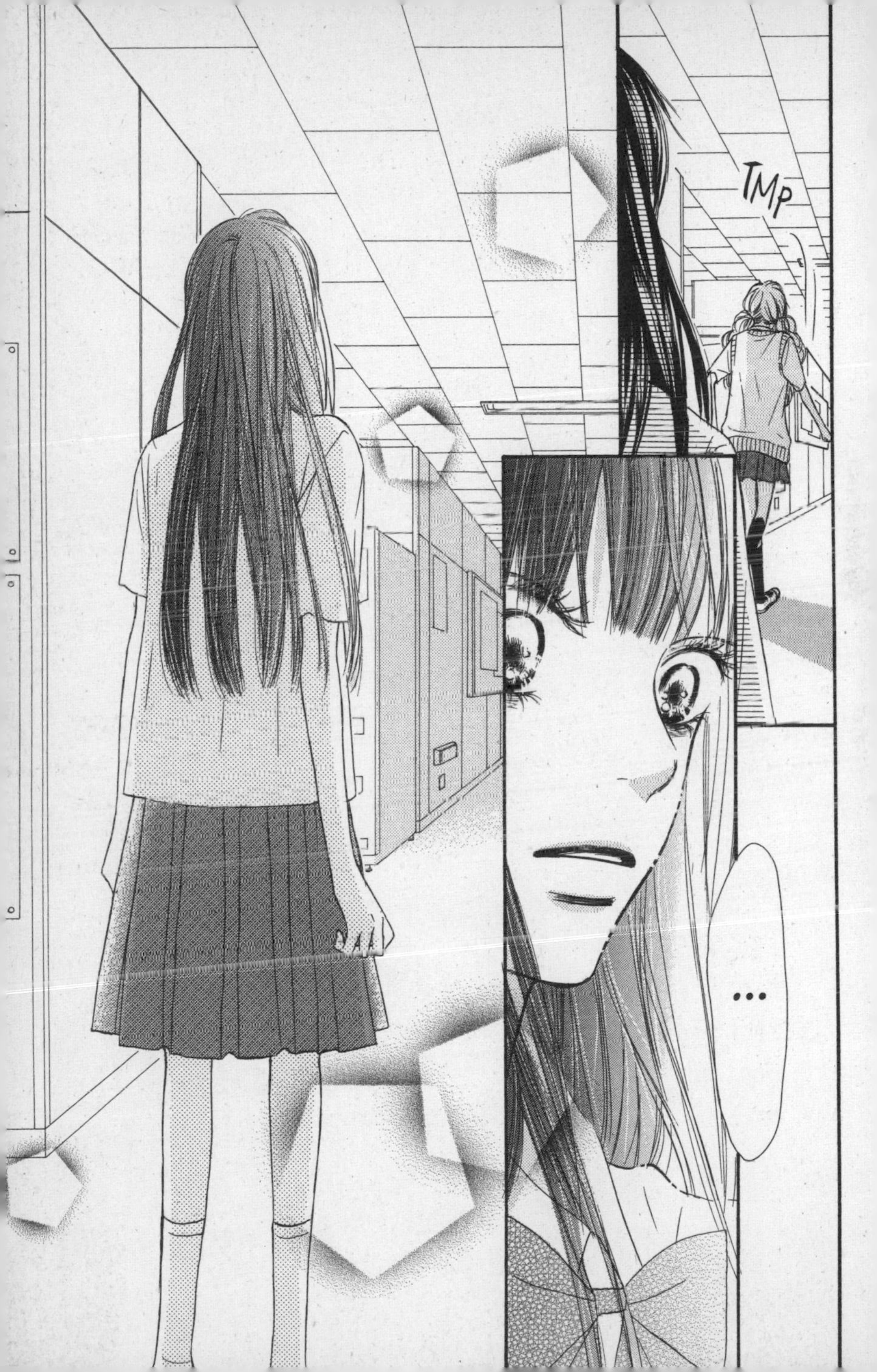
TMP
...

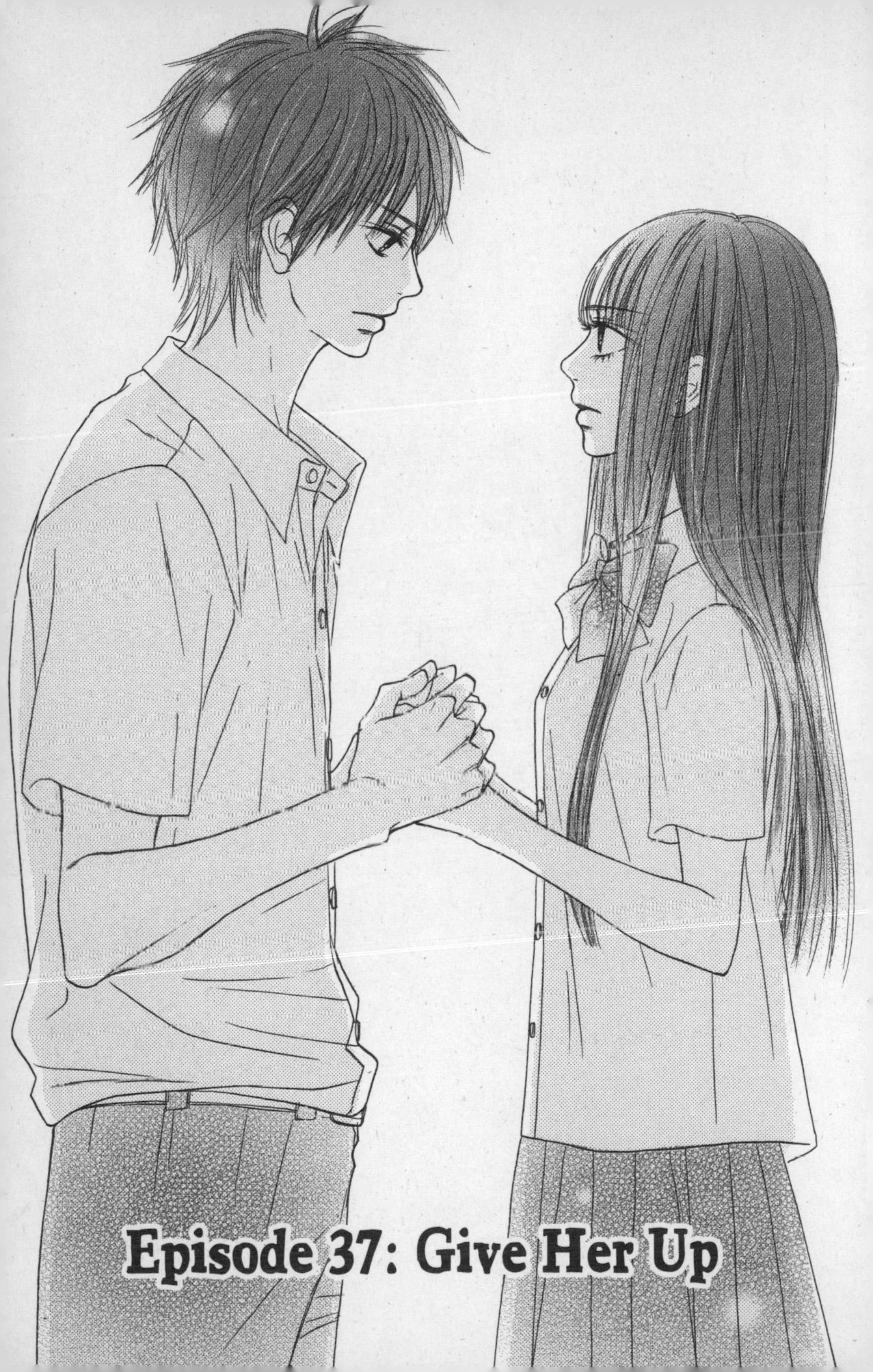
Episode 37: Give Her Up

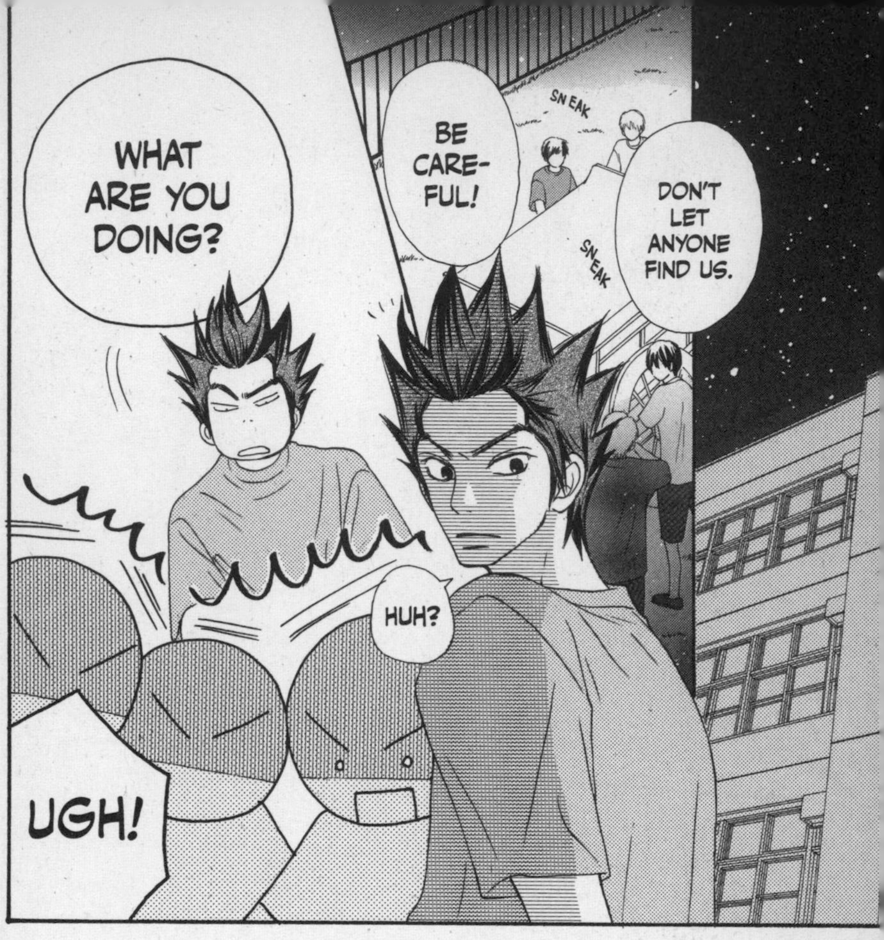
DON'T LET ANYONE FIND US.
SNEAK
SNEAK
BE CARE-FUL!
WHAT ARE YOU DOING?
HUH?
UGH!

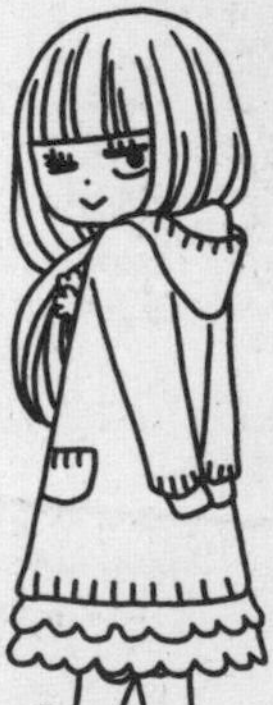

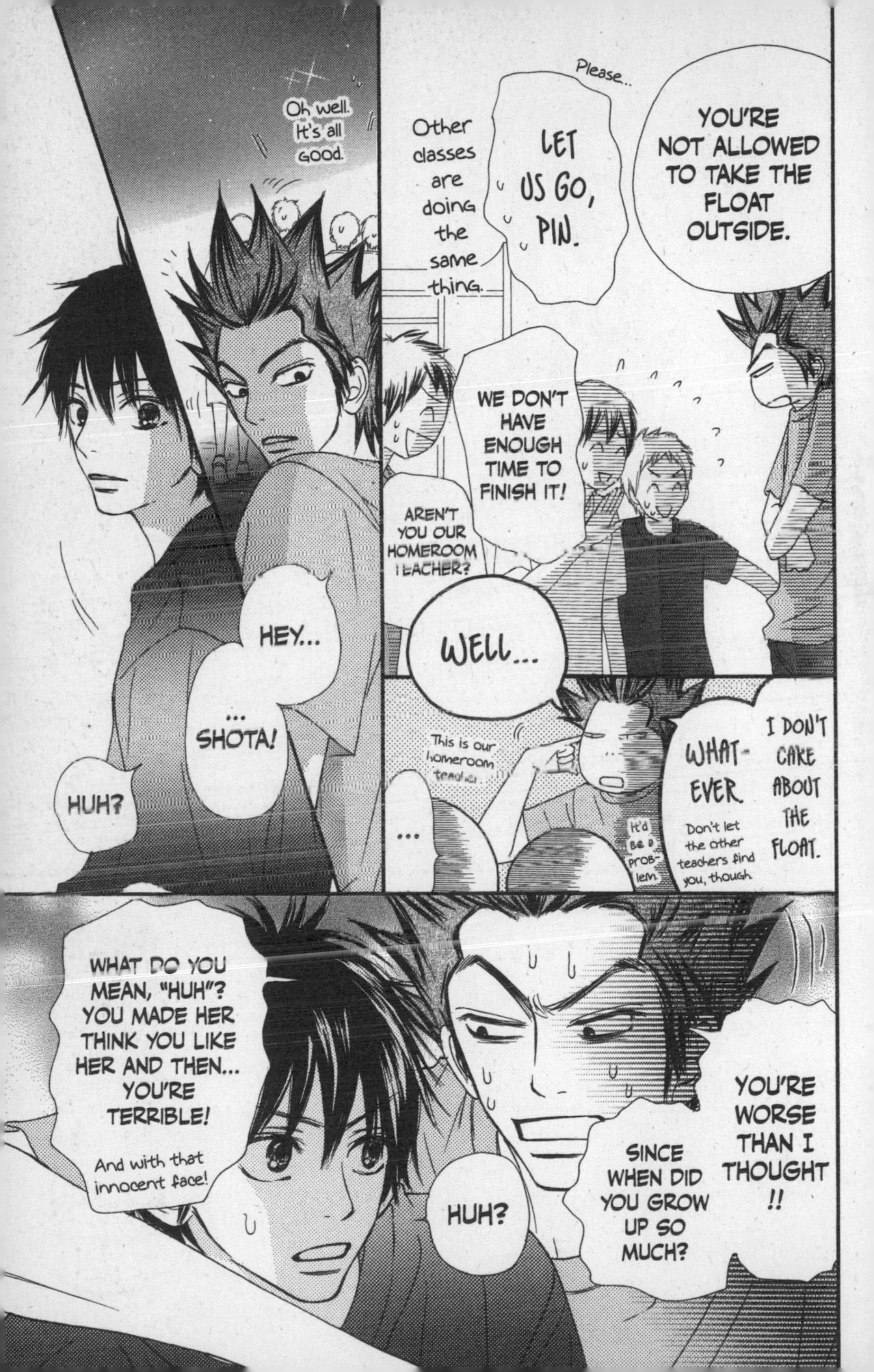
YOU'RE NOT ALLOWED TO TAKE THE FLOAT OUTSIDE.
Please... LET US GO, PIN.
Other classes are doing the same thing.
WE DON'T HAVE ENOUGH TIME TO FINISH IT!
AREN'T YOU OUR HOMEROOM TEACHER?
WELL...
I DON'T CARE ABOUT THE FLOAT.
WHATEVER.
Don't let the other teachers find you, though.
It'd be a problem.
This is our homeroom
...
Oh well. It's all good.
HEY...
...SHOTA!
HUH?
YOU'RE WORSE THAN I THOUGHT!!
SINCE WHEN DID YOU GROW UP SO MUCH?
HUH?
WHAT DO YOU MEAN, "HUH"? YOU MADE HER THINK YOU LIKE HER AND THEN... YOU'RE TERRIBLE!
And with that innocent face!

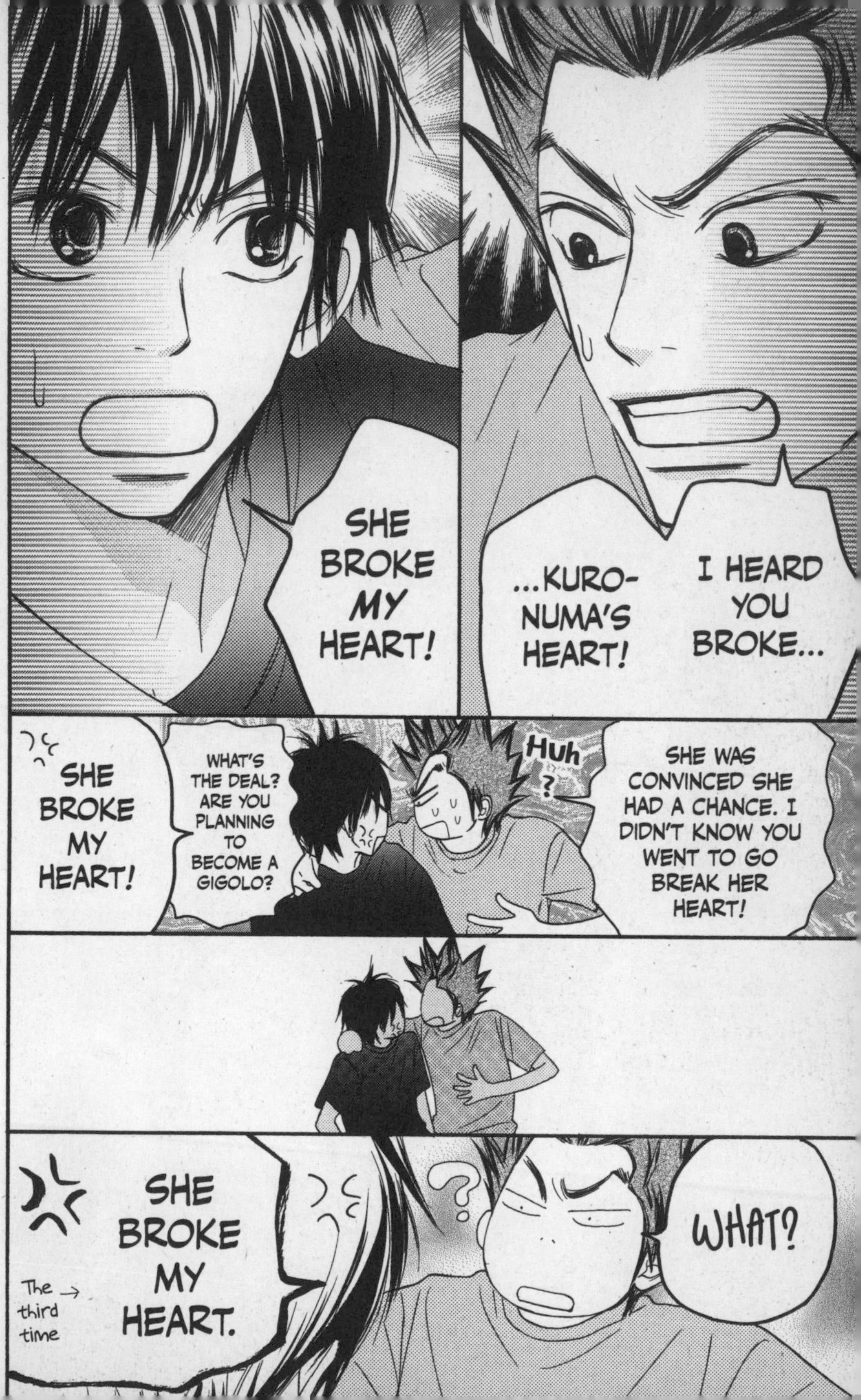
I HEARD YOU BROKE...
...KURO-NUMA'S HEART!
SHE BROKE MY HEART!
SHE WAS CONVINCED SHE HAD A CHANCE. I DIDN'T KNOW YOU WENT TO GO BREAK HER HEART!
Huh?
WHAT'S THE DEAL? ARE YOU PLANNING TO BECOME A GIGOLO?
SHE BROKE MY HEART!
WHAT?
SHE BROKE MY HEART.
The third time

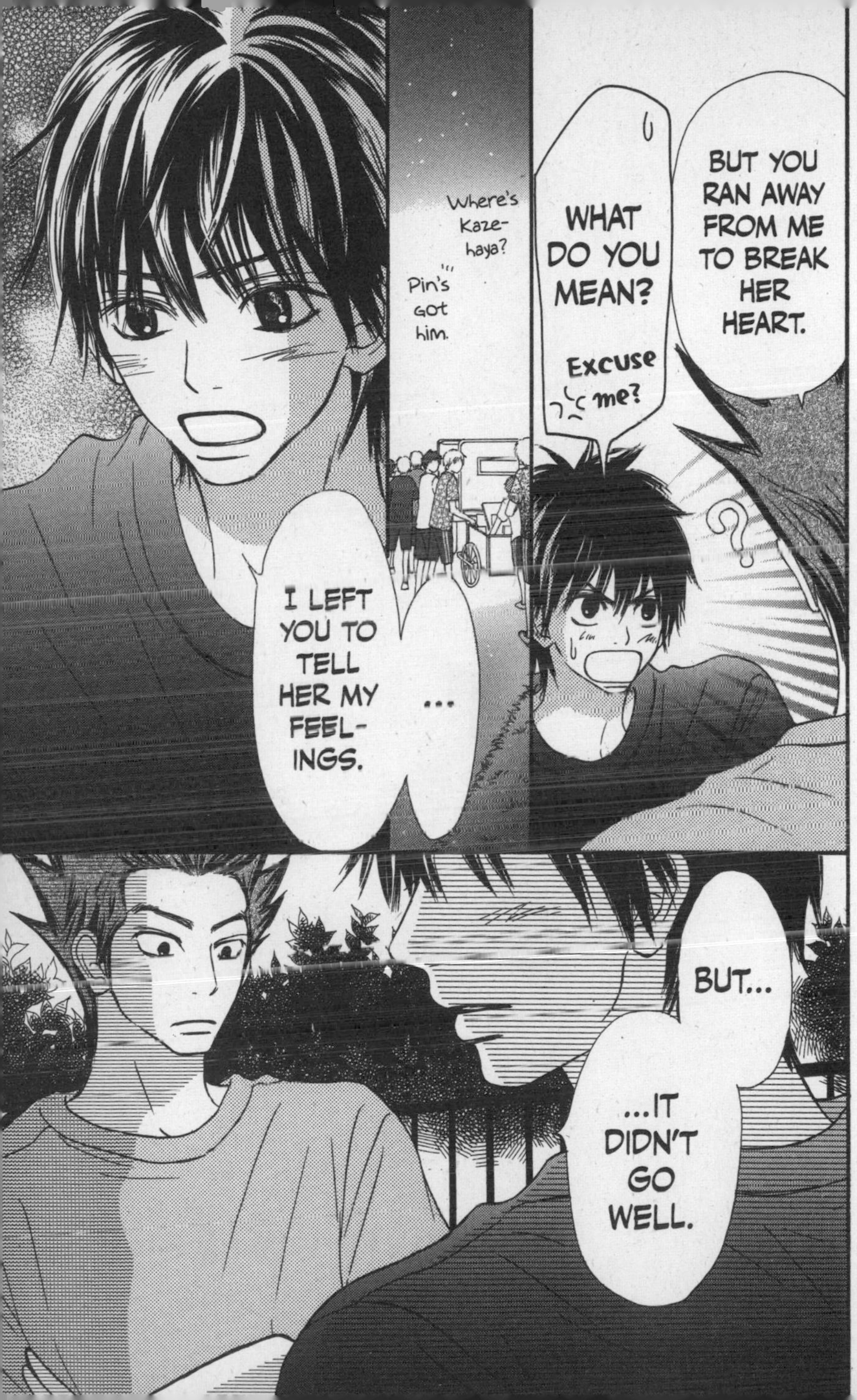
BUT YOU RAN AWAY FROM ME TO BREAK HER HEART.
WHAT DO YOU MEAN?
Excuse me?
Where's Kaze-haya?
Pin's got him.
I LEFT YOU TO TELL HER MY FEEL-INGS.
...
BUT...
...IT DIDN'T GO WELL.

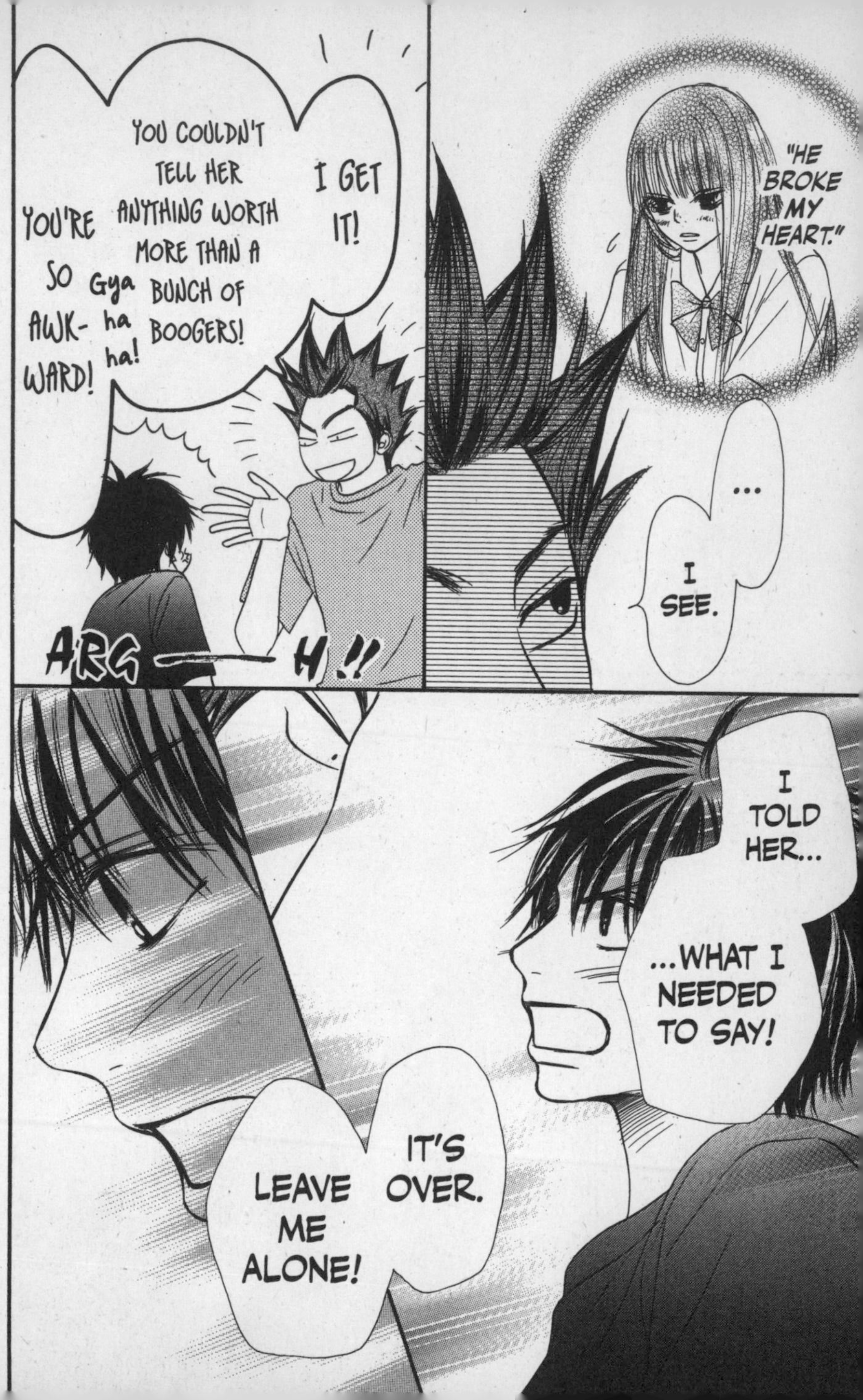
"HE BROKE MY HEART."
... I SEE.
I GET IT!
YOU COULDN'T TELL HER ANYTHING WORTH MORE THAN A BUNCH OF BOOGERS!
YOU'RE SO AWK-WARD!
Gya ha ha!
ARG——H!!
I TOLD HER...
...WHAT I NEEDED TO SAY!
IT'S OVER.
LEAVE ME ALONE!

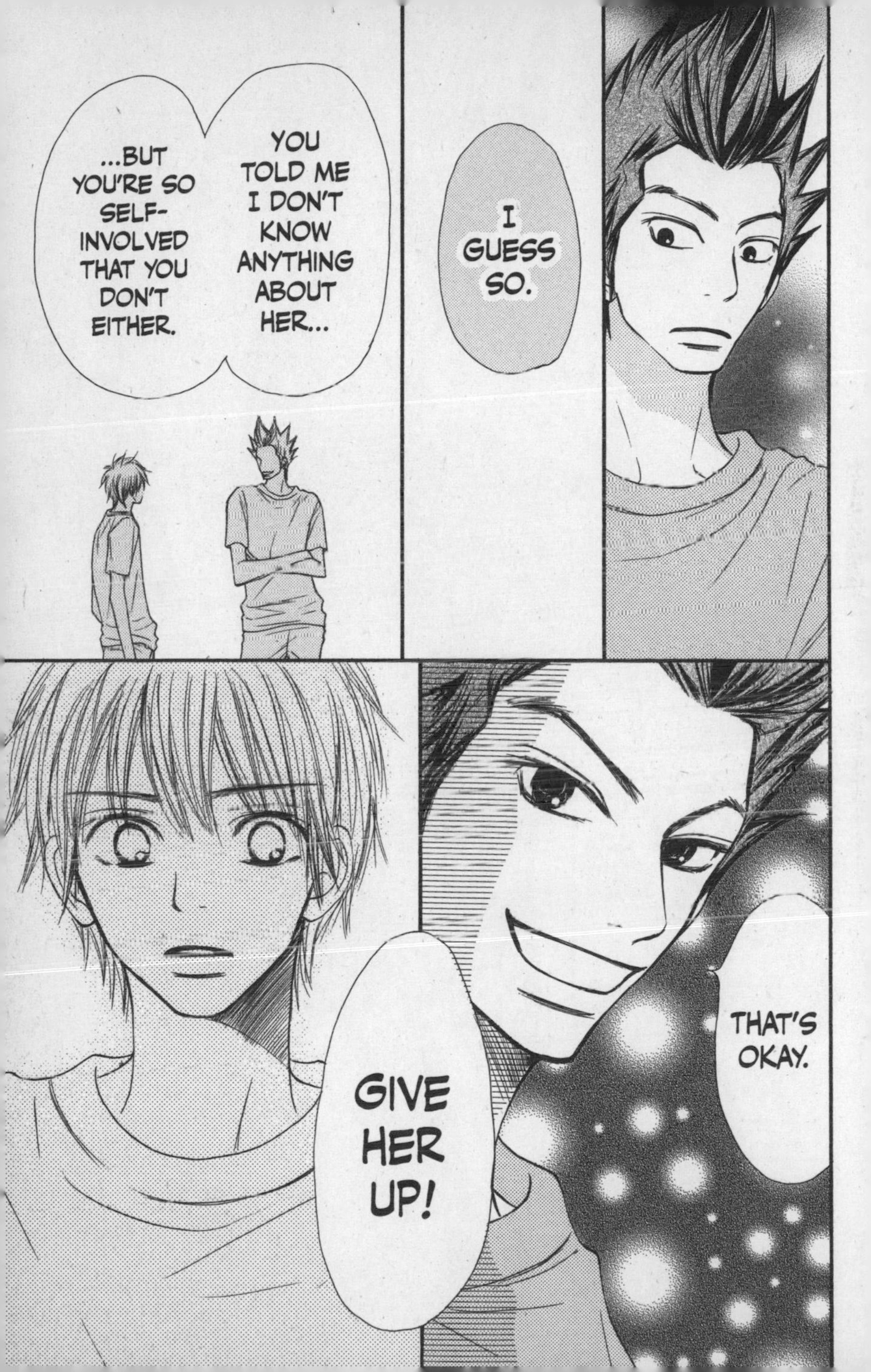
I GUESS SO.
YOU TOLD ME I DON'T KNOW ANYTHING ABOUT HER...
...BUT YOU'RE SO SELF-INVOLVED THAT YOU DON'T EITHER.
THAT'S OKAY.
GIVE HER UP!

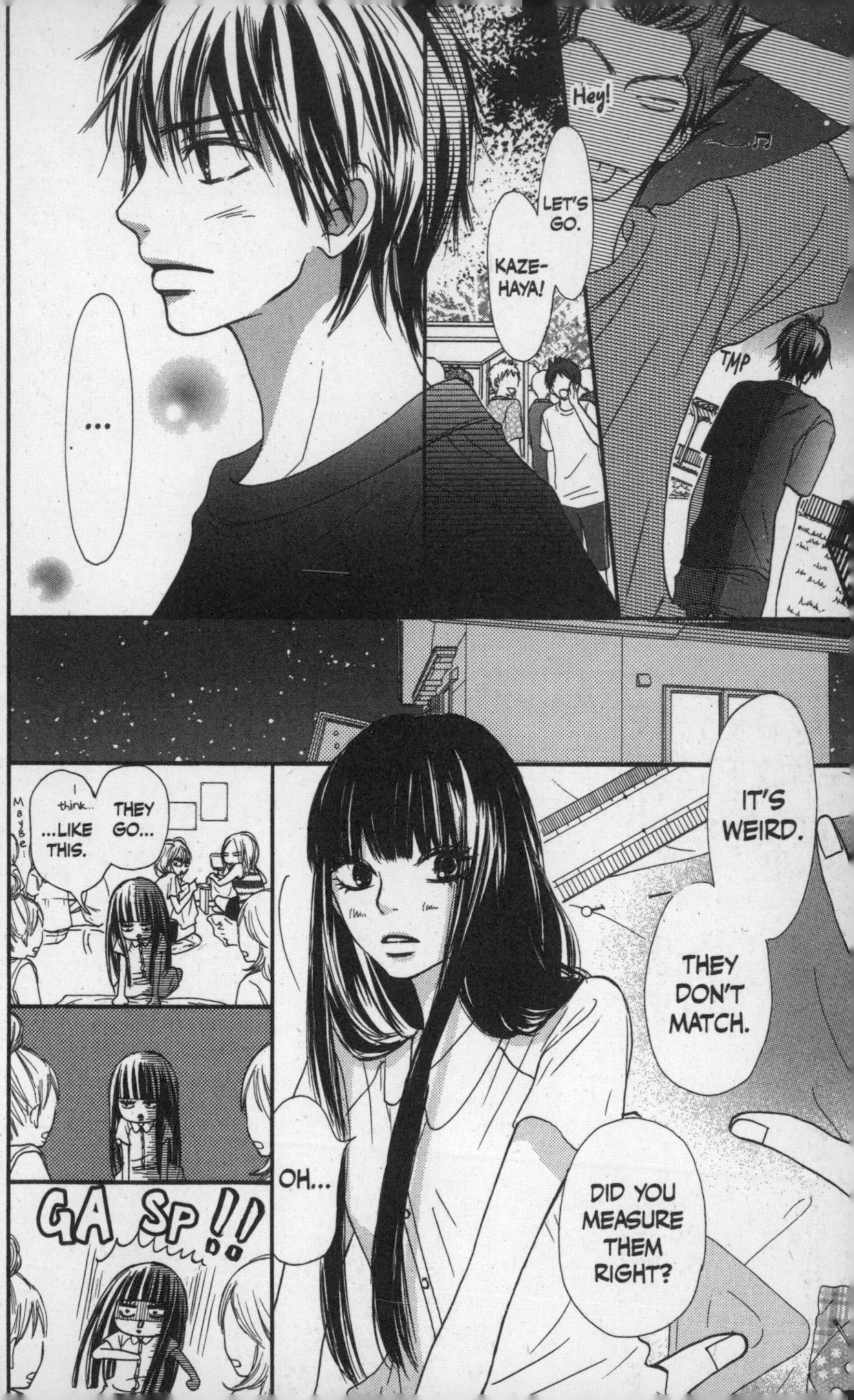
Hey!
LET'S GO.
KAZE-HAYA!
TMP
...
IT'S WEIRD.
THEY DON'T MATCH.
DID YOU MEASURE THEM RIGHT?
OH...
THEY GO...
I think... ...LIKE THIS.
Maybe...
GASP!!

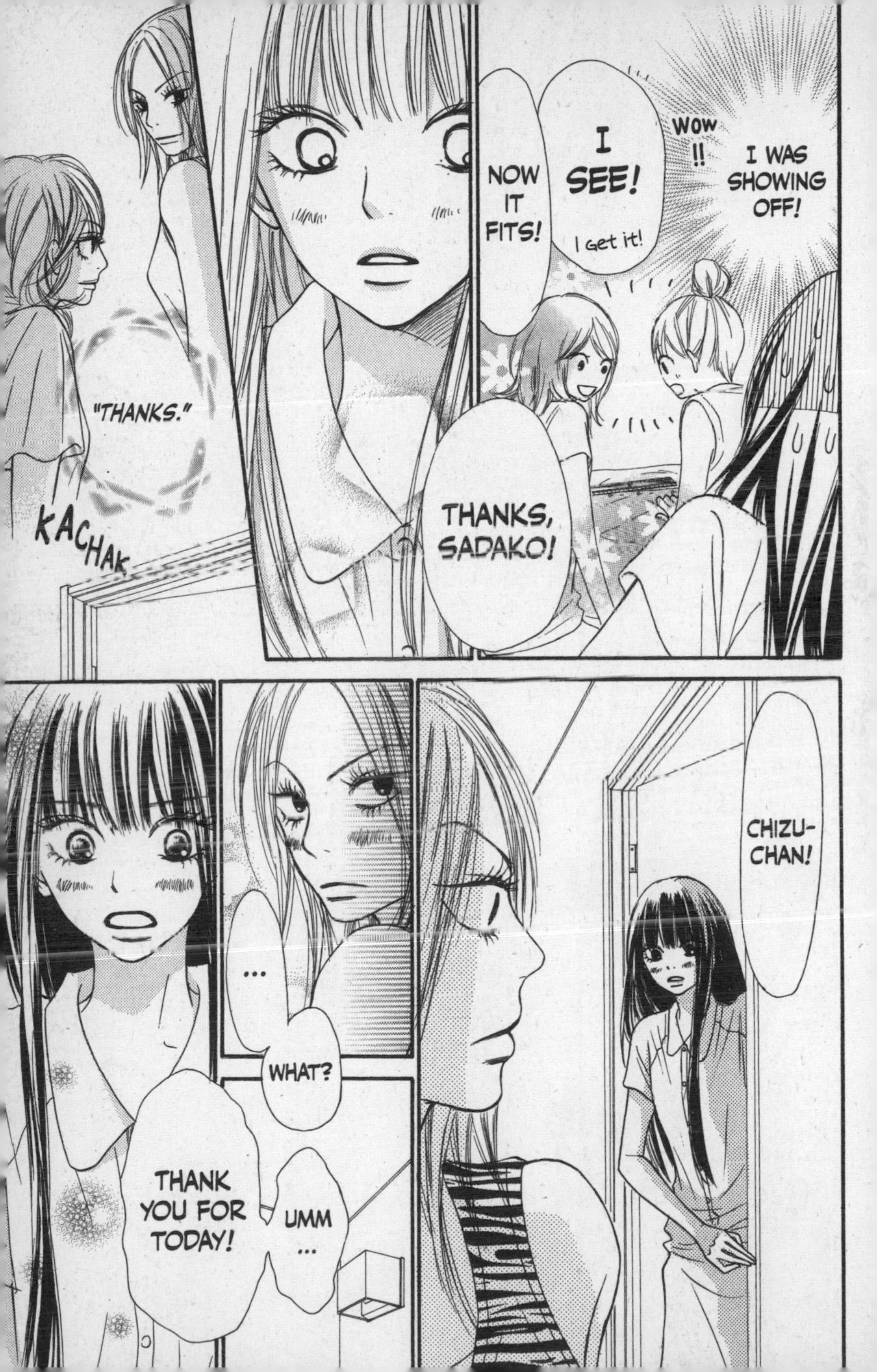
I WAS SHOWING OFF!
WOW !!
I SEE!
I get it!
NOW IT FITS!
THANKS, SADAKO!
"THANKS."
KACHAK
CHIZU-CHAN!
...
WHAT?
UMM ...
THANK YOU FOR TODAY!

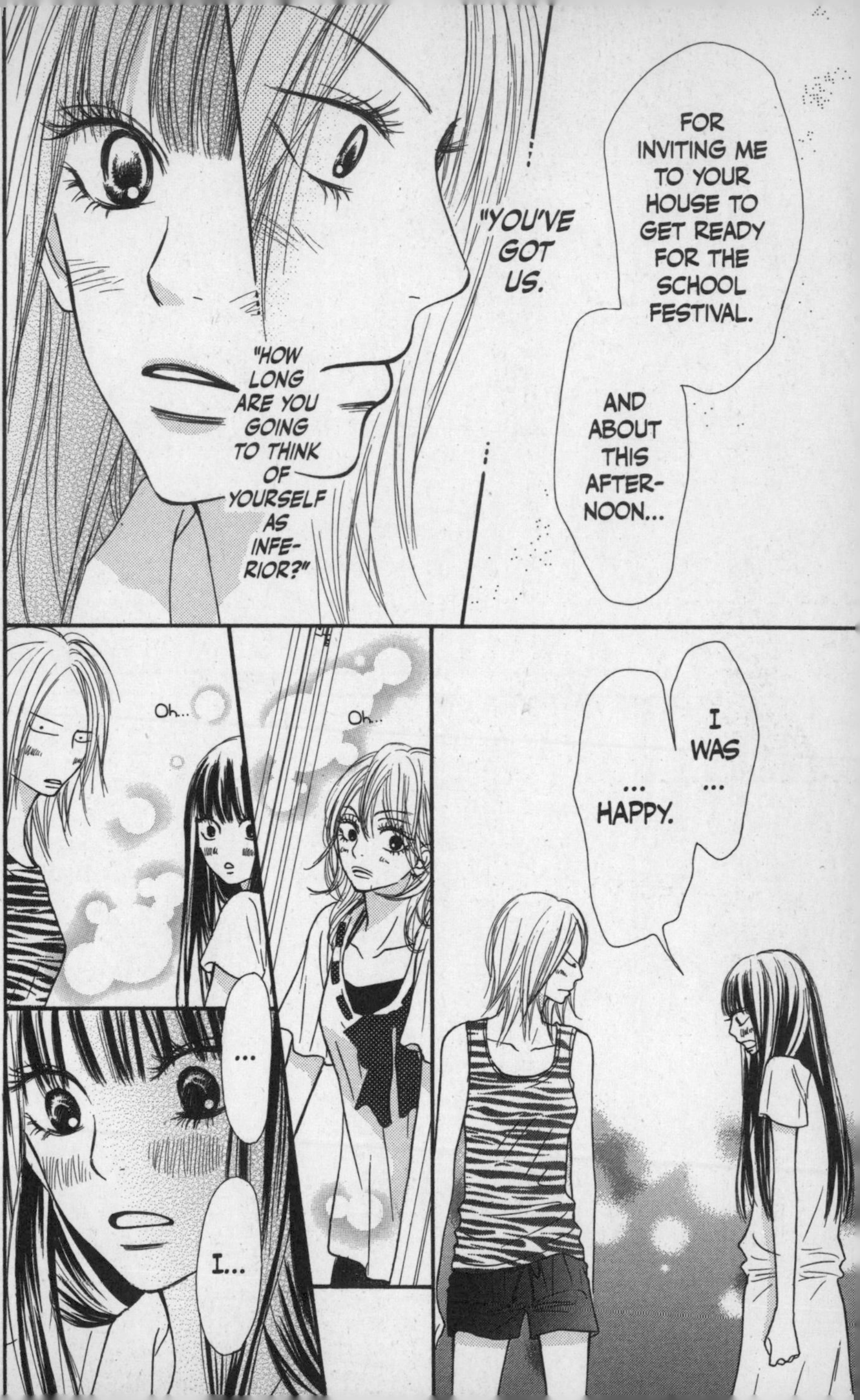

FOR INVITING ME TO YOUR HOUSE TO GET READY FOR THE SCHOOL FESTIVAL.
AND ABOUT THIS AFTERNOON...
"YOU'VE GOT US.
"HOW LONG ARE YOU GOING TO THINK OF YOURSELF AS INFERIOR?"
I WAS ... ... HAPPY.
Oh...
Oh...
...
I...

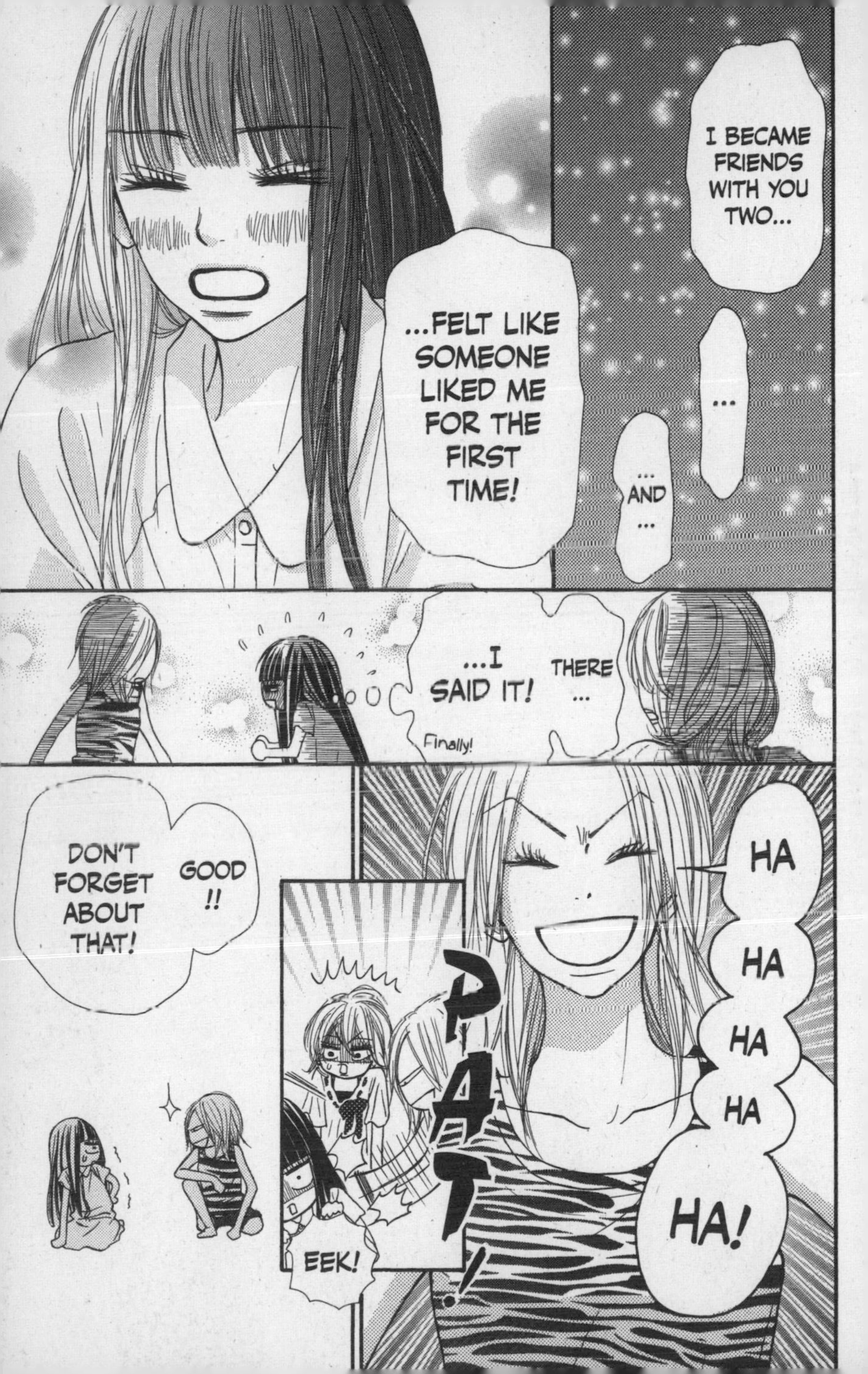
I BECAME FRIENDS WITH YOU TWO...
...
... AND ...
...FELT LIKE SOMEONE LIKED ME FOR THE FIRST TIME!
THERE ...
...I SAID IT!
Finally!
HA
HA
HA
HA
HA!
PAT!
EEK!
GOOD !!
DON'T FORGET ABOUT THAT!

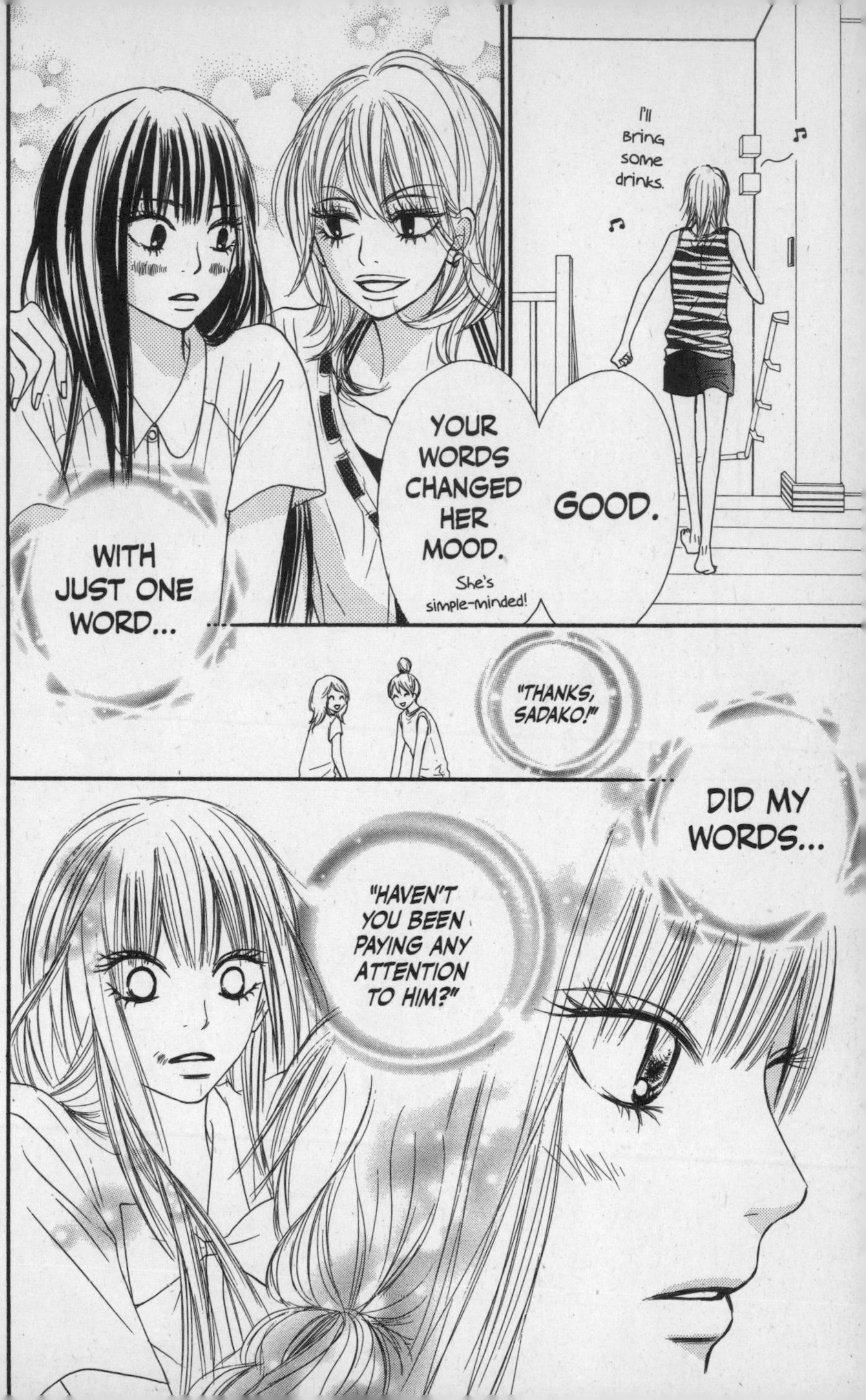
I'll bring some drinks.
GOOD.
YOUR WORDS CHANGED HER MOOD.
She's simple-minded!
WITH JUST ONE WORD...
"THANKS, SADAKO!"
DID MY WORDS...
"HAVEN'T YOU BEEN PAYING ANY ATTENTION TO HIM?"

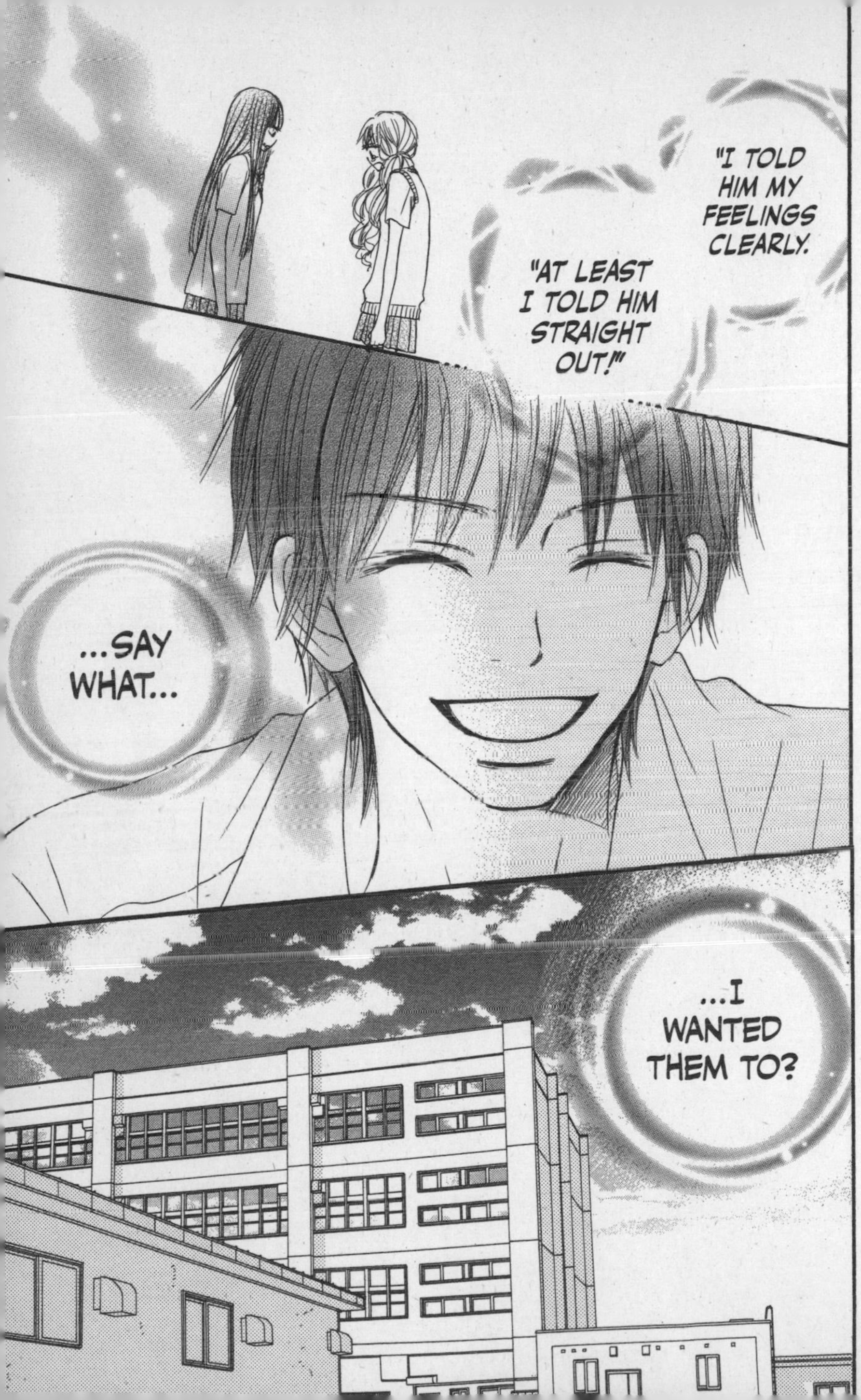
"I TOLD HIM MY FEELINGS CLEARLY.
"AT LEAST I TOLD HIM STRAIGHT OUT!"
...SAY WHAT...
...I WANTED THEM TO?

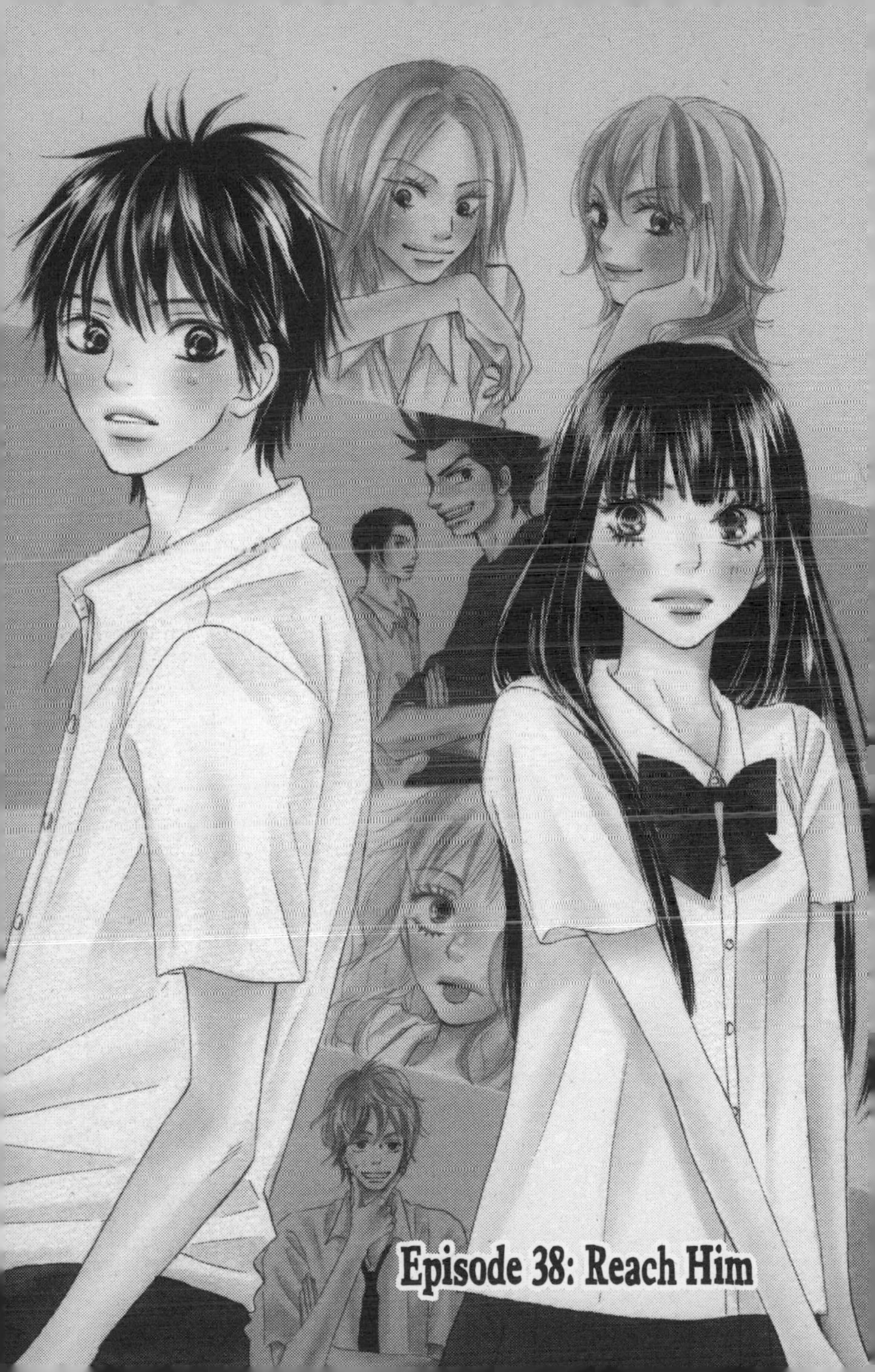
Episode 38: Reach Him

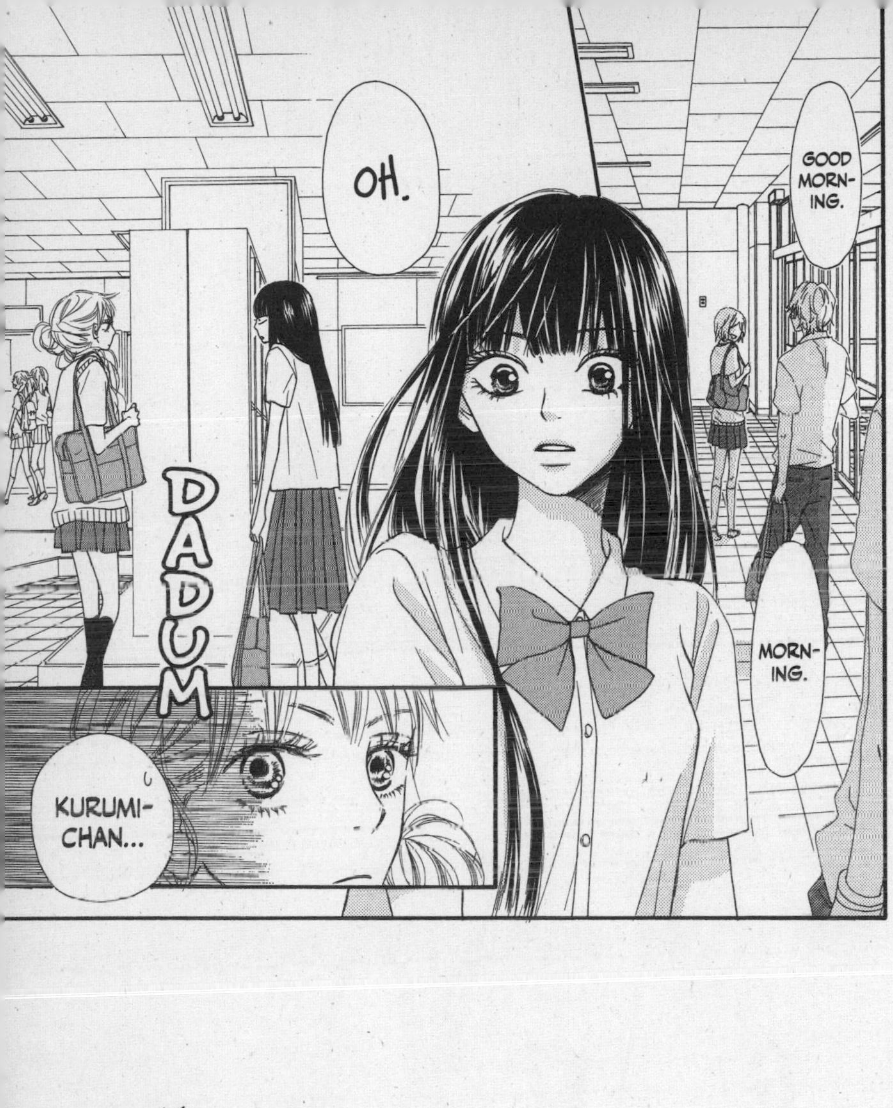
GOOD MORN-ING.
OH.
MORN-ING.
DADUM
KURUMI-CHAN...

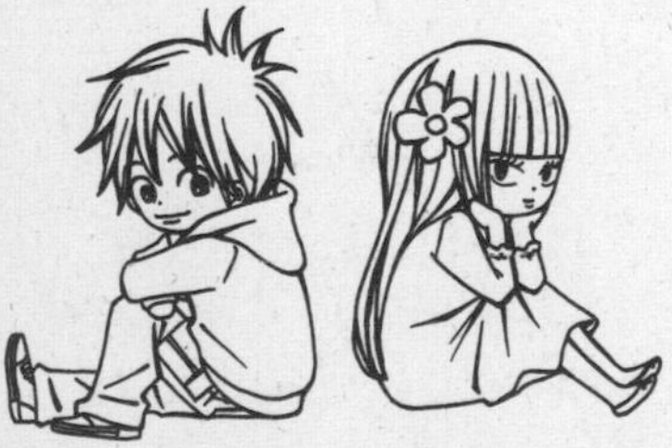

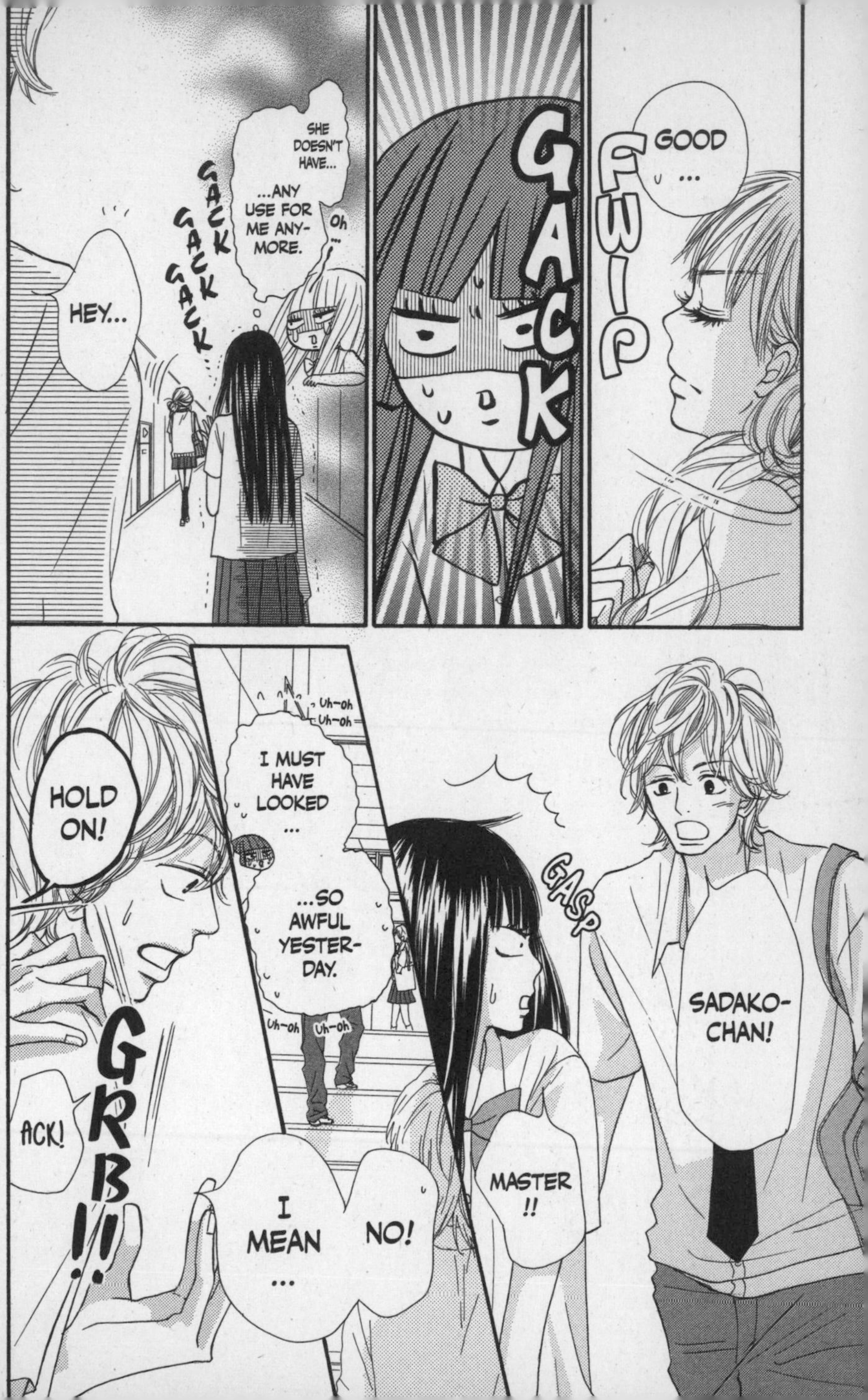
GOOD ...
FWIP
GACK
SHE DOESN'T HAVE...
...ANY USE FOR ME ANY-MORE.
Oh ...
GACK GACK GACK
HEY...
GASP
SADAKO-CHAN!
MASTER !!
NO!
I MEAN ...
Uh-oh Uh-oh
I MUST HAVE LOOKED ...
...SO AWFUL YESTER-DAY.
Uh-oh Uh-oh
HOLD ON!
GRB!!
ACK!

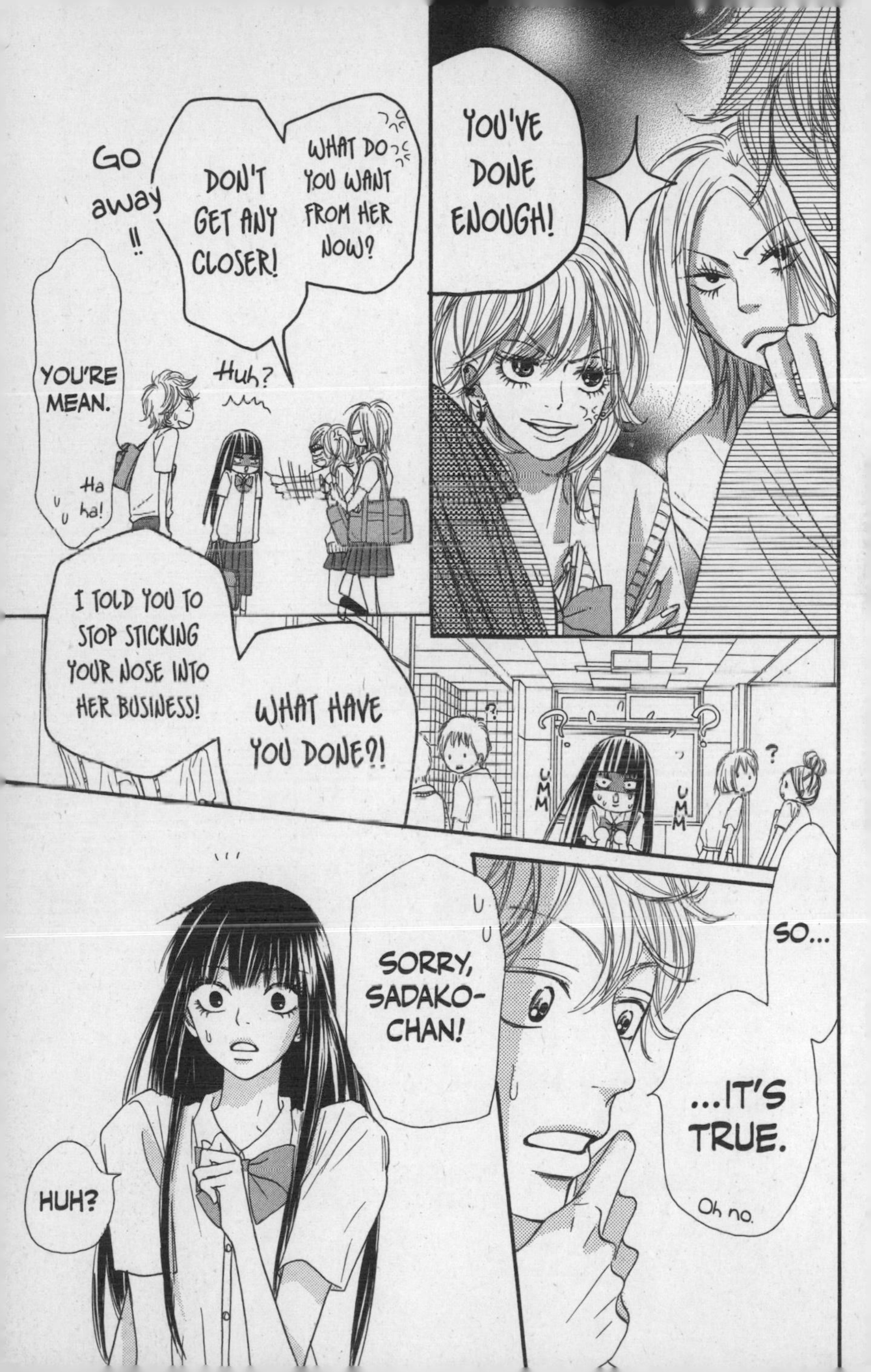
YOU'VE DONE ENOUGH!
WHAT DO YOU WANT FROM HER NOW?
DON'T GET ANY CLOSER!
Go away!!
Huh?
YOU'RE MEAN.
Ha ha!
I TOLD YOU TO STOP STICKING YOUR NOSE INTO HER BUSINESS!
WHAT HAVE YOU DONE?!
UMM
UMM
SO...
...IT'S TRUE.
Oh no.
SORRY, SADAKO-CHAN!
HUH?

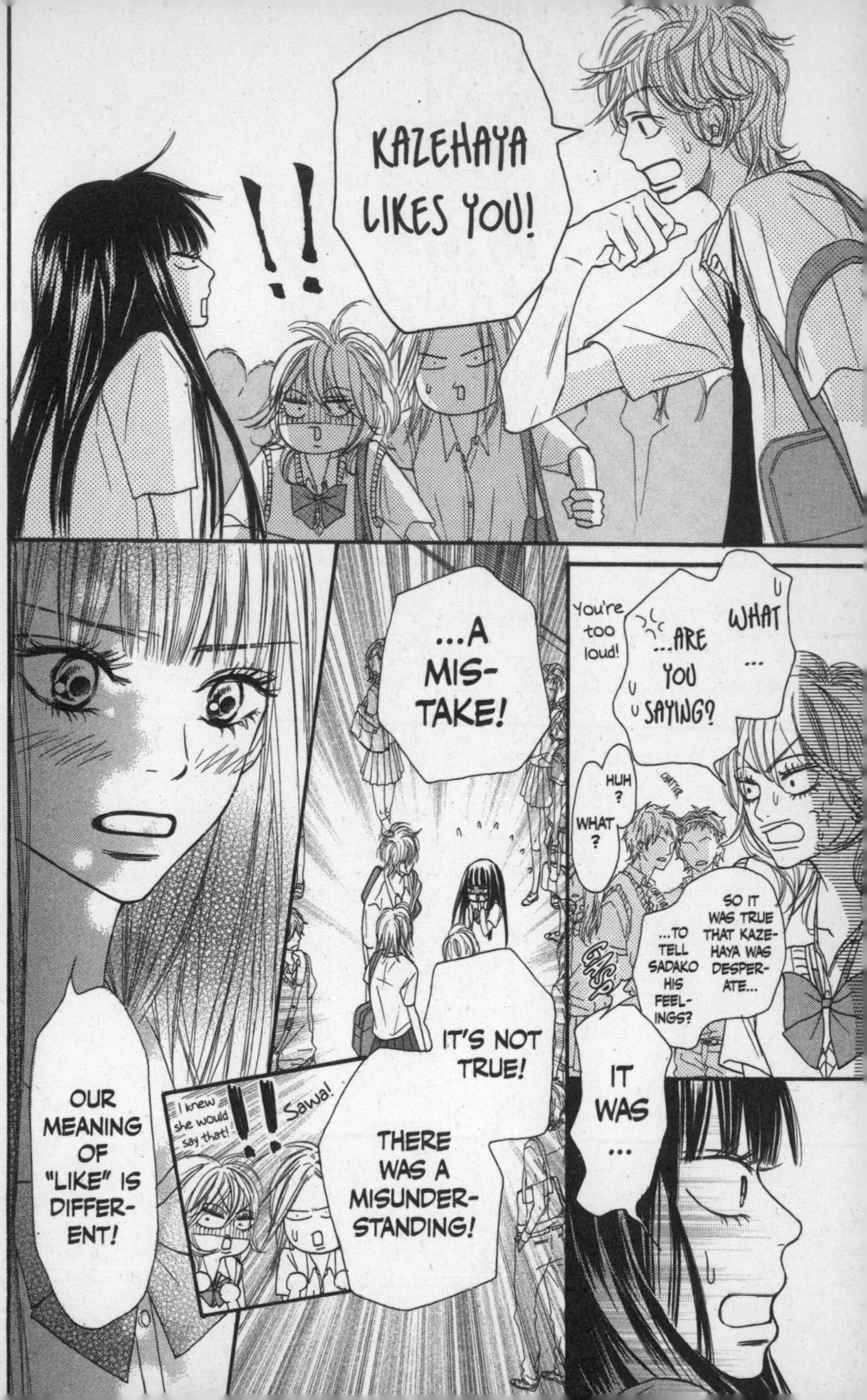
KAZEHAYA LIKES YOU!
!!
WHAT ...
...ARE YOU SAYING?
You're too loud!
HUH? WHAT?
CHATTER
SO IT WAS TRUE THAT KAZE-HAYA WAS DESPER-ATE...
...TO TELL SADAKO HIS FEEL-INGS?
GASP
IT WAS ...
...A MIS-TAKE!
IT'S NOT TRUE!
THERE WAS A MISUNDER-STANDING!
!!
Sawa!
I knew she would say that!
OUR MEANING OF "LIKE" IS DIFFER-ENT!

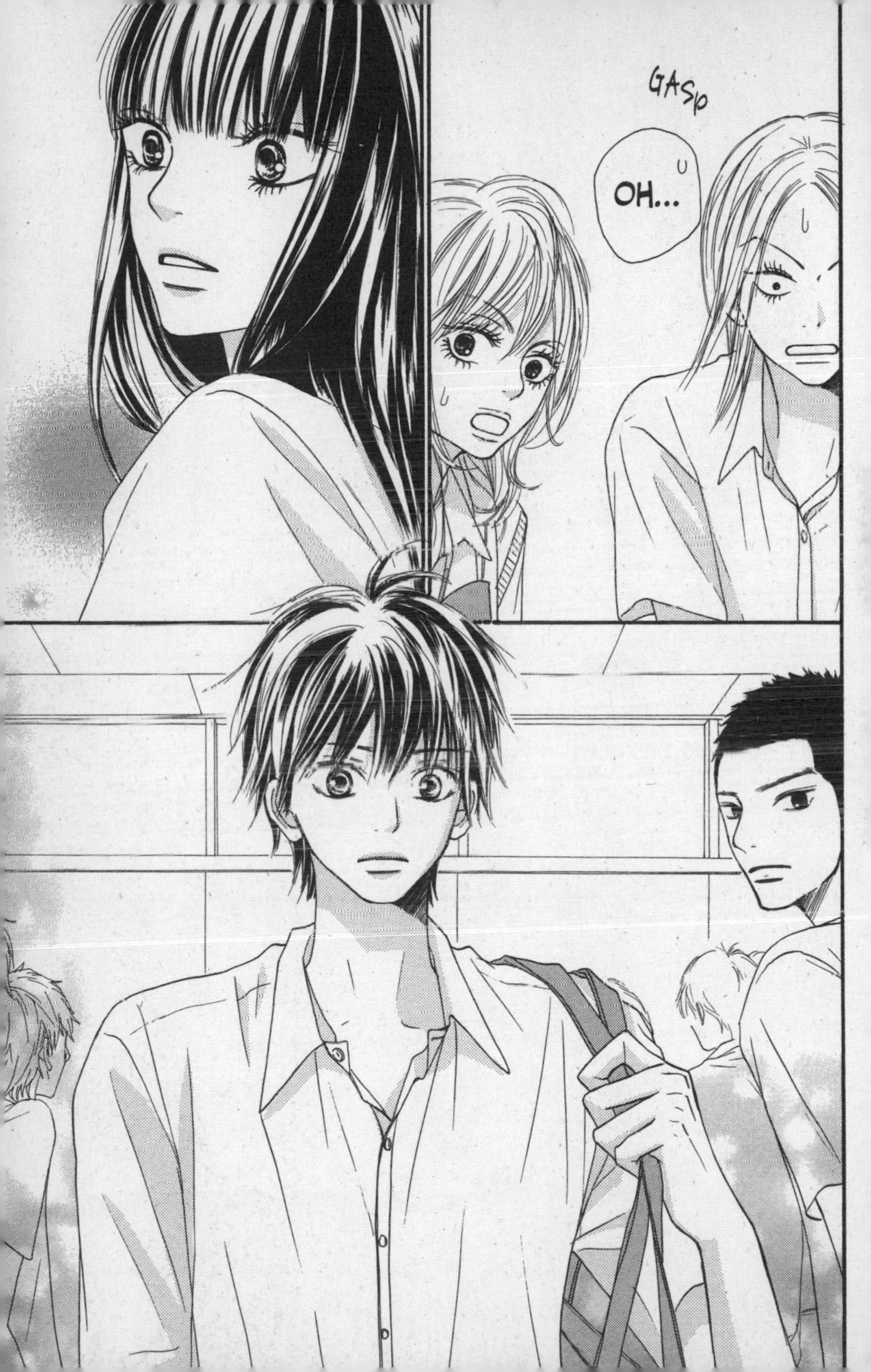
GASP
OH...

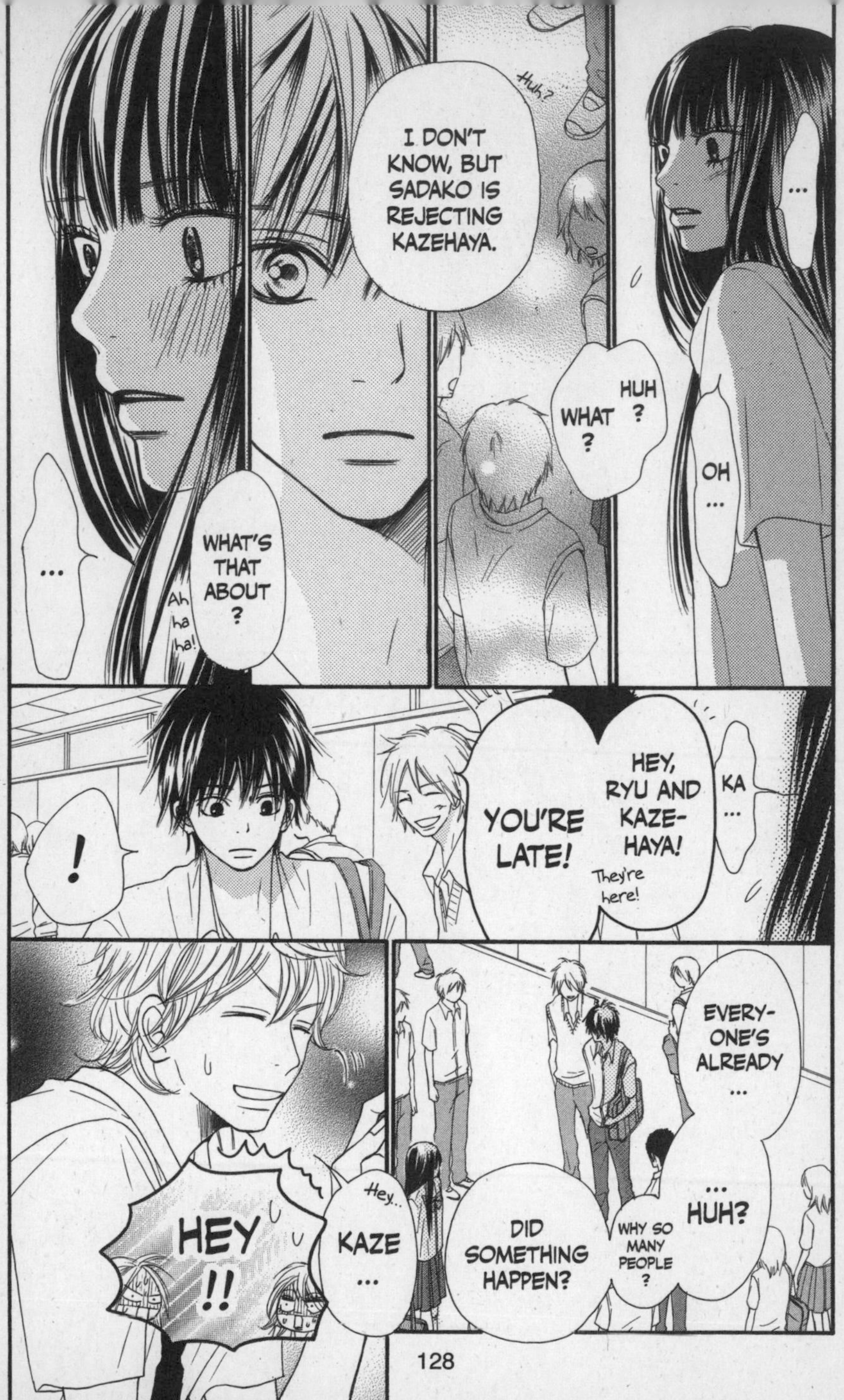
...
HUH ?
WHAT ?
OH ...
Huh?
I DON'T KNOW, BUT SADAKO IS REJECTING KAZEHAYA.
WHAT'S THAT ABOUT ?
Ah ha ha!
...
KA ...
HEY, RYU AND KAZE-HAYA!
They're here!
YOU'RE LATE!
!
EVERY-ONE'S ALREADY ...
... HUH?
WHY SO MANY PEOPLE ?
DID SOMETHING HAPPEN?
Hey...
KAZE ...
HEY !!

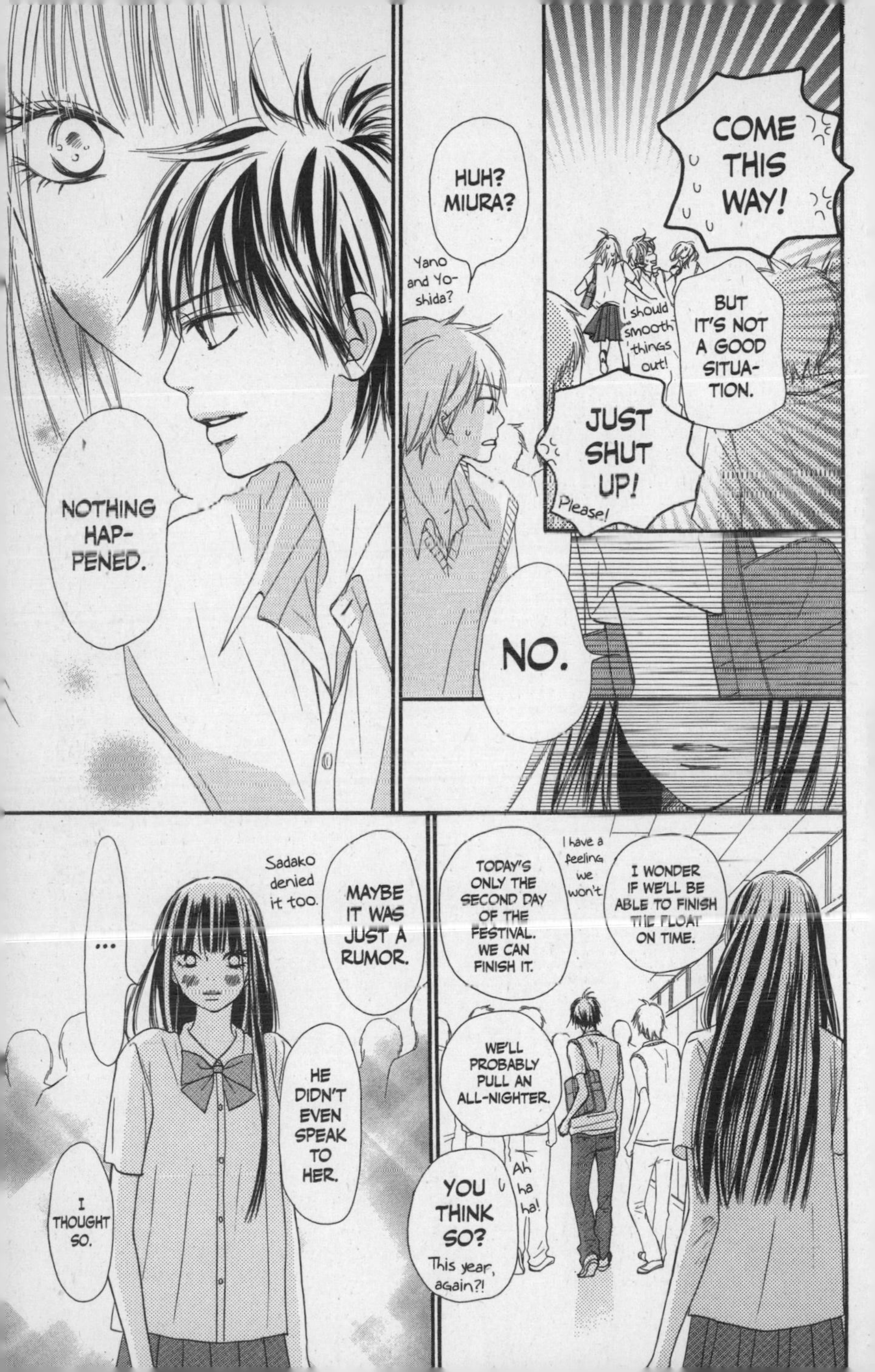
COME THIS WAY!
BUT IT'S NOT A GOOD SITUATION.
I should smooth things out!
JUST SHUT UP!
Please!
HUH? MIURA?
Yano and Yoshida?
NO.
NOTHING HAPPENED.
I WONDER IF WE'LL BE ABLE TO FINISH THE FLOAT ON TIME.
I have a feeling we won't.
TODAY'S ONLY THE SECOND DAY OF THE FESTIVAL. WE CAN FINISH IT.
WE'LL PROBABLY PULL AN ALL-NIGHTER.
YOU THINK SO?
This year, again?!
Ah ha ha!
MAYBE IT WAS JUST A RUMOR.
Sadako denied it too.
HE DIDN'T EVEN SPEAK TO HER.
...
I THOUGHT SO.

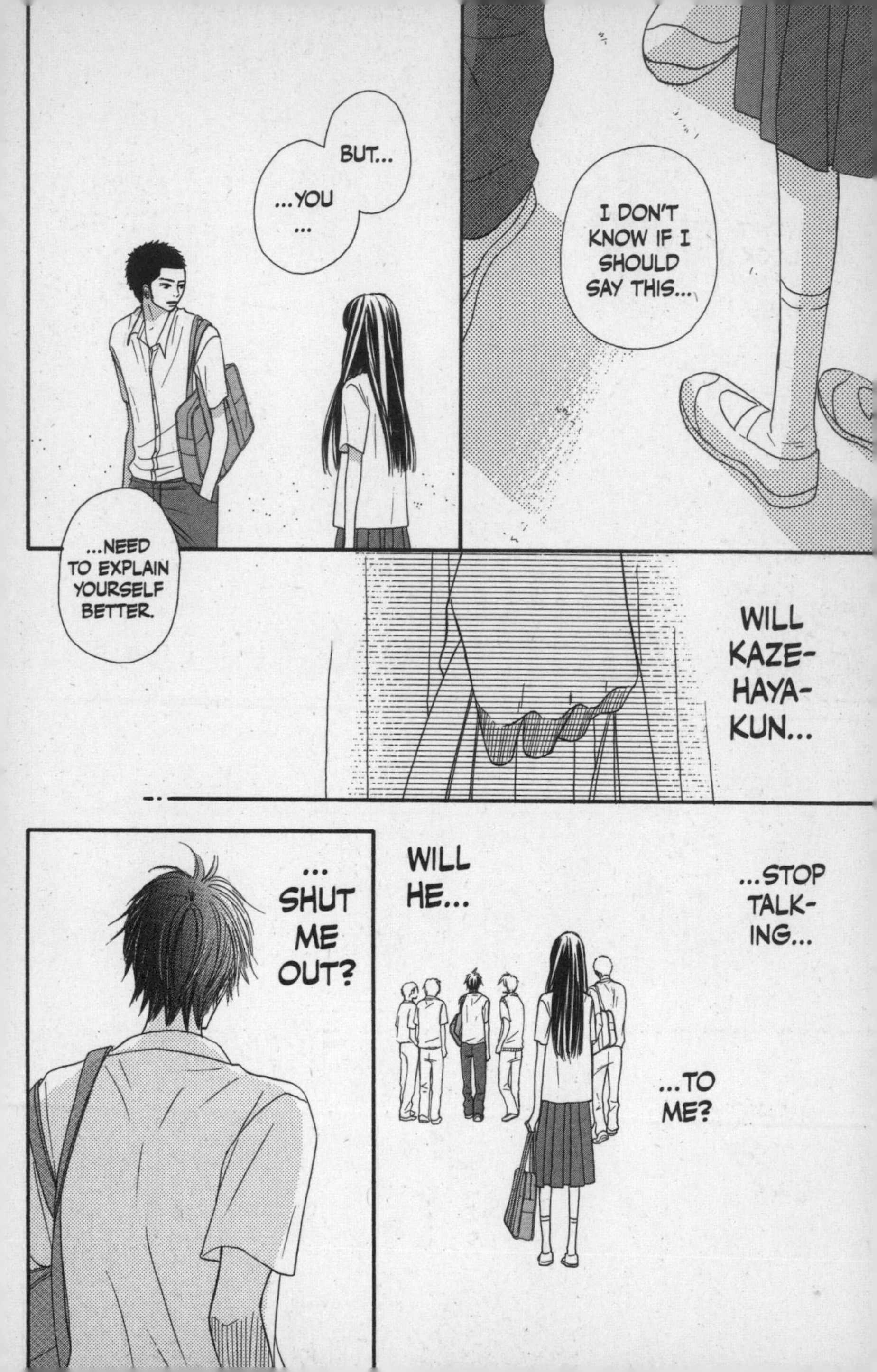
I DON'T KNOW IF I SHOULD SAY THIS...
BUT...
...YOU ...
...NEED TO EXPLAIN YOURSELF BETTER.
WILL KAZE-HAYA-KUN...
...STOP TALK-ING...
...TO ME?
WILL HE...
... SHUT ME OUT?

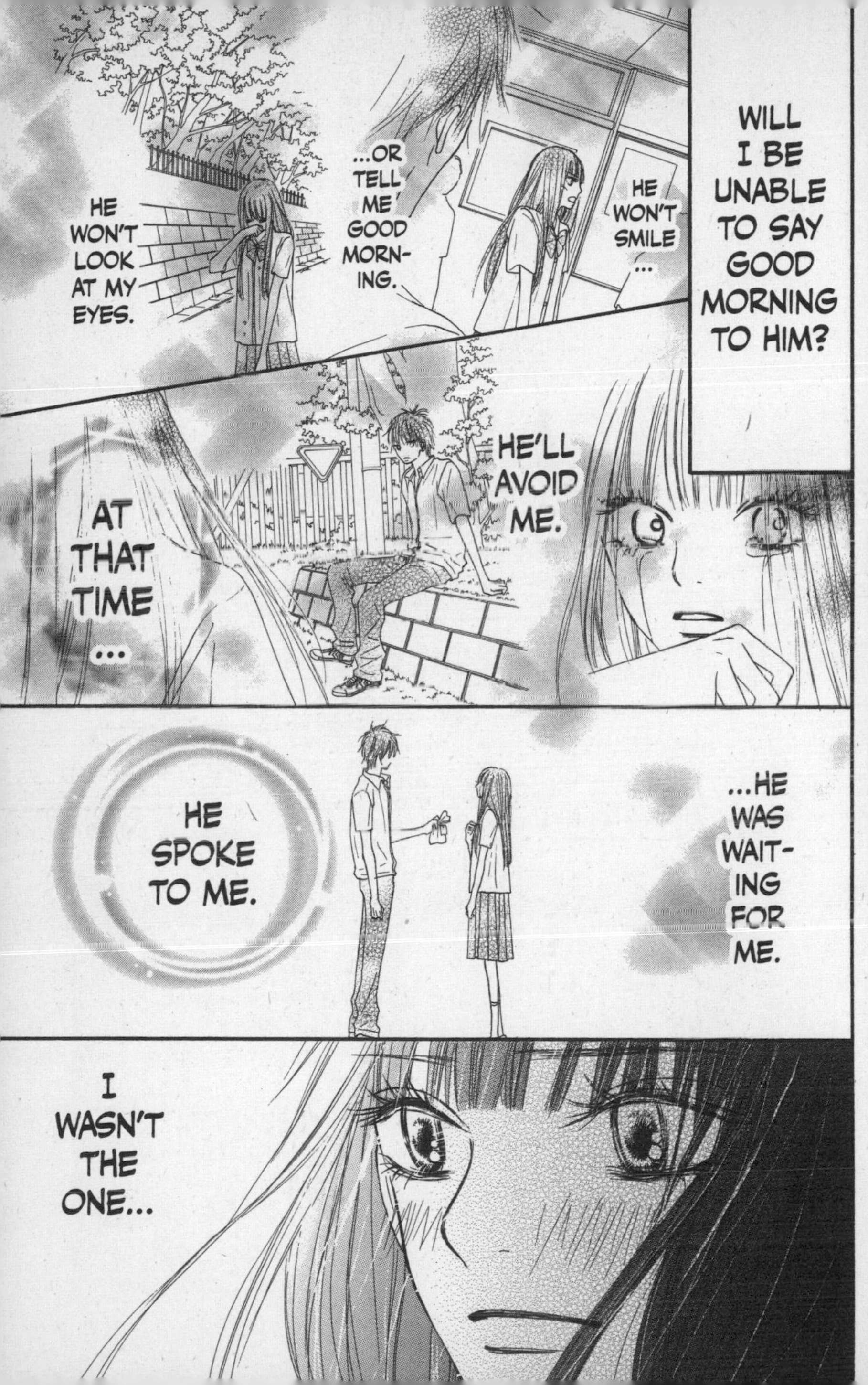
WILL I BE UNABLE TO SAY GOOD MORNING TO HIM?
HE WON'T SMILE...
...OR TELL ME GOOD MORNING.
HE WON'T LOOK AT MY EYES.
HE'LL AVOID ME.
AT THAT TIME...
...HE WAS WAITING FOR ME.
HE SPOKE TO ME.
I WASN'T THE ONE...

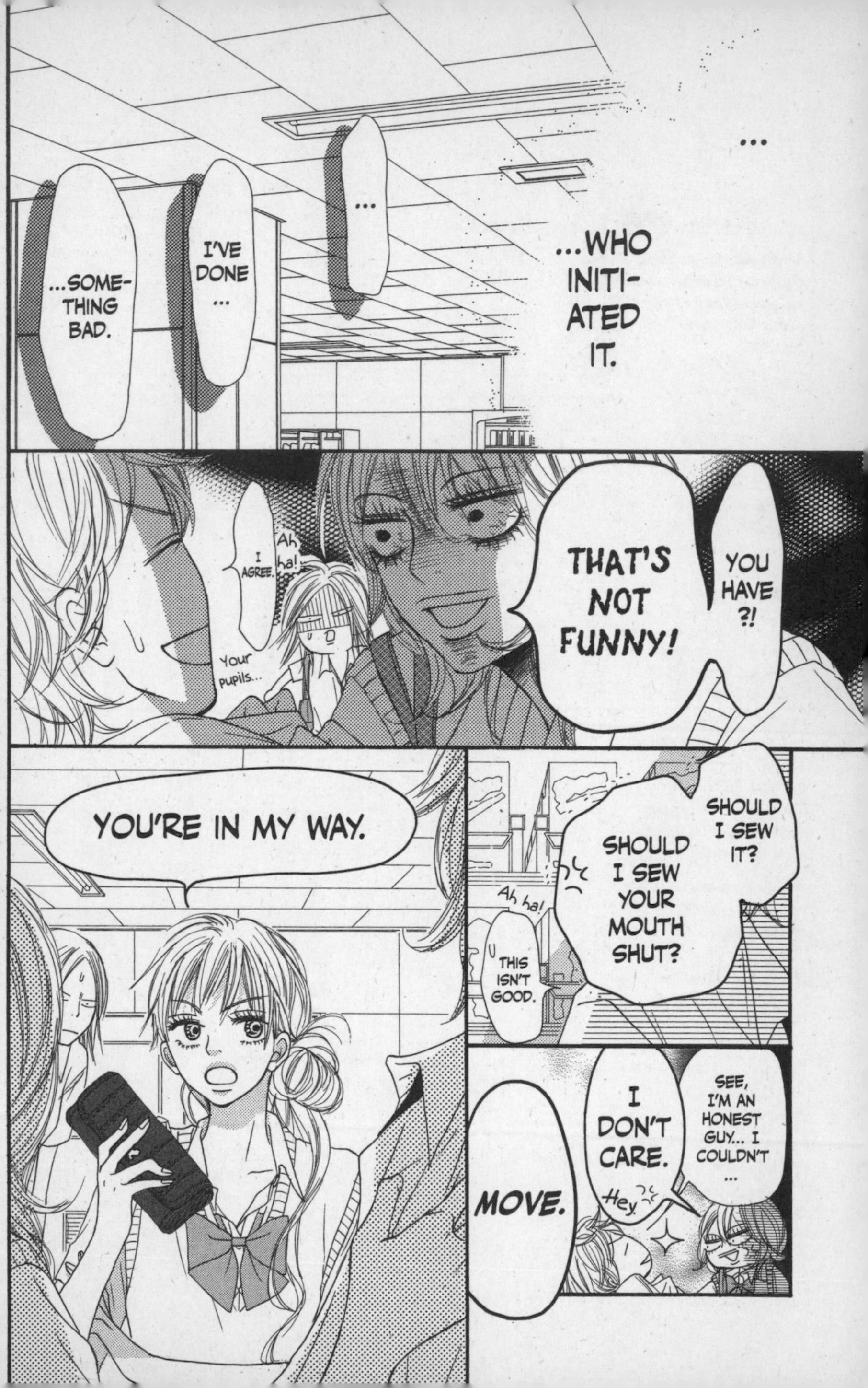
...
...WHO INITI- ATED IT.
...
I'VE DONE ...
...SOME- THING BAD.
YOU HAVE ?!
THAT'S NOT FUNNY!
Ah ha!
I AGREE.
Your pupils...
SHOULD I SEW IT?
SHOULD I SEW YOUR MOUTH SHUT?
Ah ha!
THIS ISN'T GOOD.
SEE, I'M AN HONEST GUY... I COULDN'T ...
I DON'T CARE.
Hey
MOVE.
YOU'RE IN MY WAY.

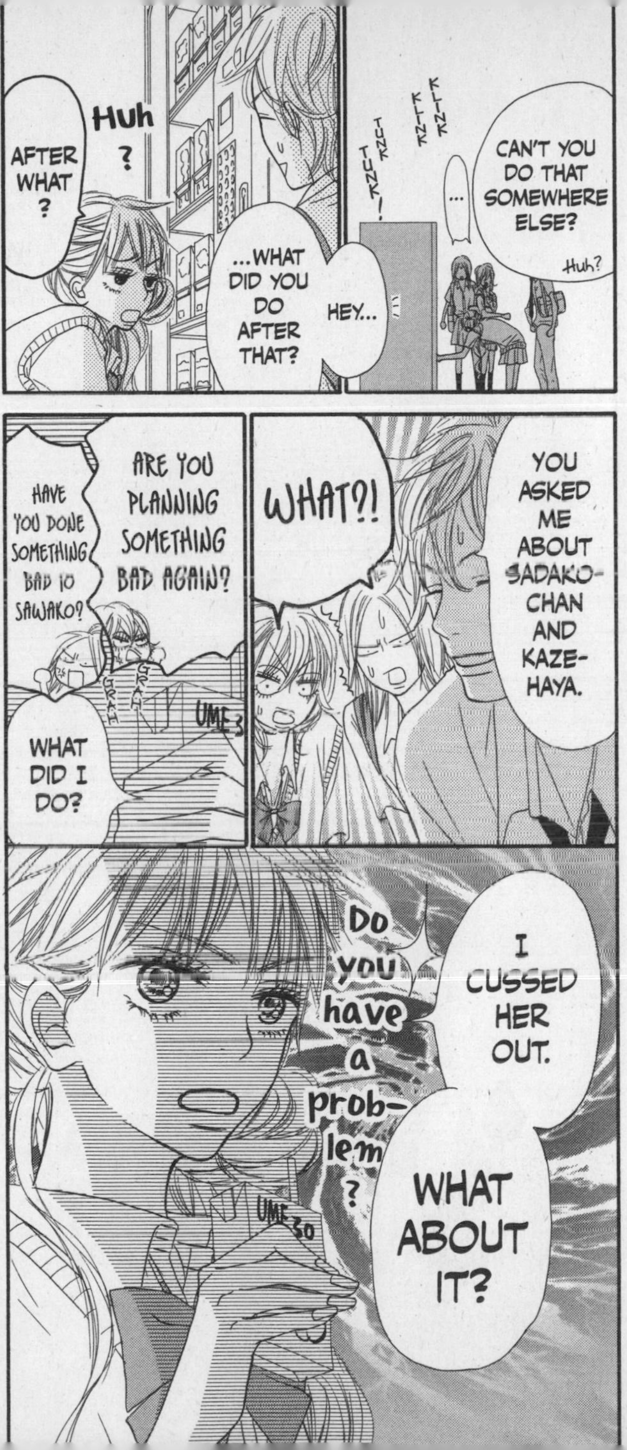
CAN'T YOU DO THAT SOMEWHERE ELSE?
...
Huh?
KLINK KLINK
TUNK TUNK!
HEY...
...WHAT DID YOU DO AFTER THAT?
Huh ?
AFTER WHAT ?
YOU ASKED ME ABOUT SADAKO-CHAN AND KAZE-HAYA.
WHAT?!
ARE YOU PLANNING SOMETHING BAD AGAIN?
HAVE YOU DONE SOMETHING BAD TO SAWAKO?
GRAH GRAH
UME3
WHAT DID I DO?
I CUSSED HER OUT.
WHAT ABOUT IT?
Do you have a prob-lem ?
UME30

KARUPIN on JAPAN 2

While I was taking a break, Ms. Kanae Shimokawa wrote the original novella *Kimi ni Todoke* for Bessatsu Margaret.

Good story! BLOOP

Thank you very much, Ms. Shimokawa! Please enjoy the novels published by *Kobaruto Bunko* and the original novella I mentioned above! ♥ They are very lyrical and wonderful stories! I drew the illustrations!

There will be a game for the Nintendo DS, and the TV anime will start about the time I start writing again! I have enjoyed both since last year. The game and anime are linked to each other... (The voice actors are the same!) Please look forward to them!

The stories in the game are detailed, cute and funny. I'm really looking forward to it. Please enjoy the tutorial as well! ♥ We talked over every detail of the anime, but I'm sure I'm the one who is looking forward to it the most. They made it with enormous care. (I'm impressed!)

I can't wait to play the game and watch the anime! I'm going to spend years playing that game!

One-fourth is already done!

See you in Volume 10! ♥ By Shiina

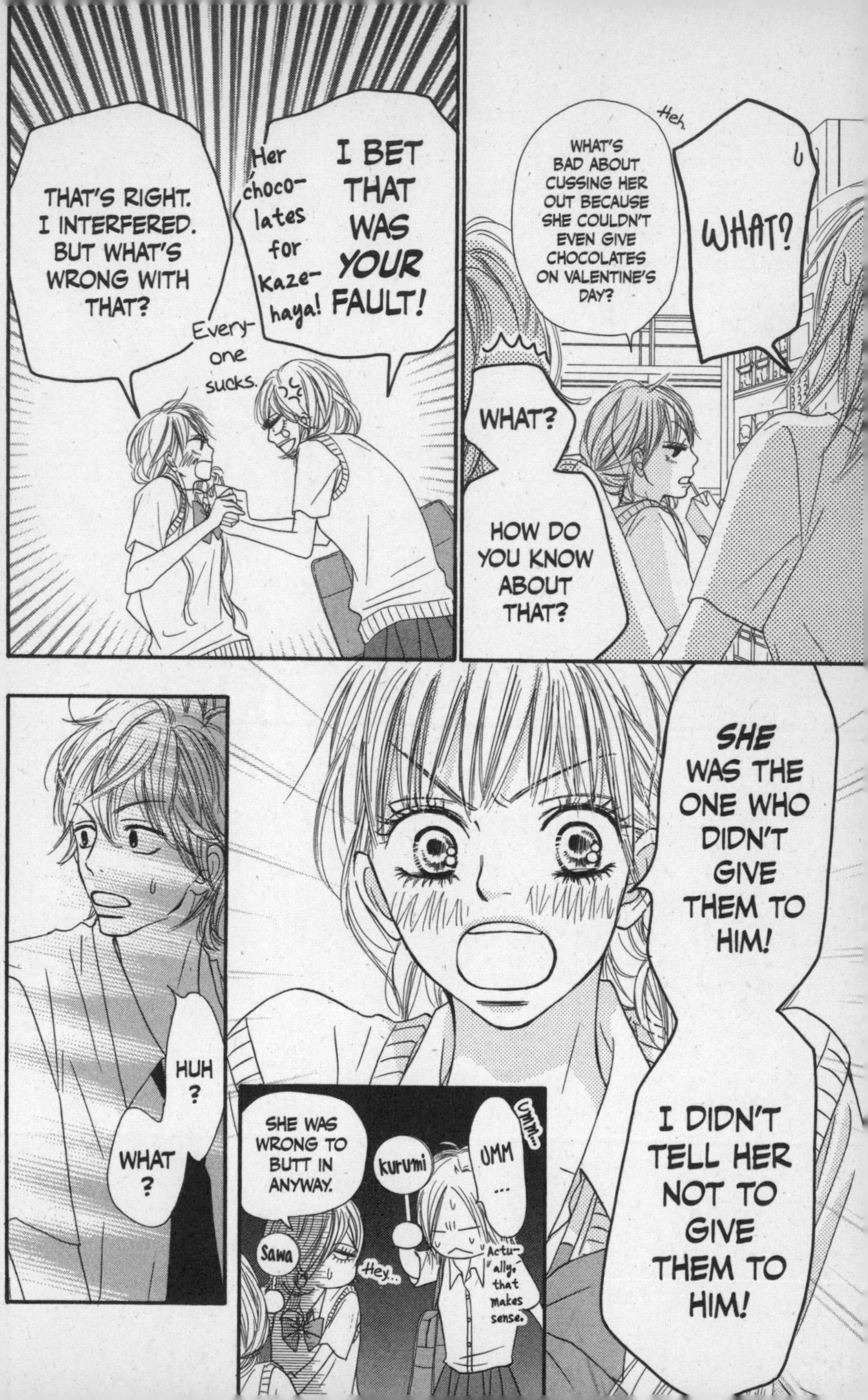

Heh
WHAT?
WHAT'S BAD ABOUT CUSSING HER OUT BECAUSE SHE COULDN'T EVEN GIVE CHOCOLATES ON VALENTINE'S DAY?
WHAT?
HOW DO YOU KNOW ABOUT THAT?
I BET THAT WAS YOUR FAULT!
Her chocolates for Kazehaya!
THAT'S RIGHT. I INTERFERED. BUT WHAT'S WRONG WITH THAT?
Everyone sucks.
SHE WAS THE ONE WHO DIDN'T GIVE THEM TO HIM!
I DIDN'T TELL HER NOT TO GIVE THEM TO HIM!
Umm...
UMM ...
kurumi
SHE WAS WRONG TO BUTT IN ANYWAY.
Actually, that makes sense.
Hey...
Sawa
HUH?
WHAT?

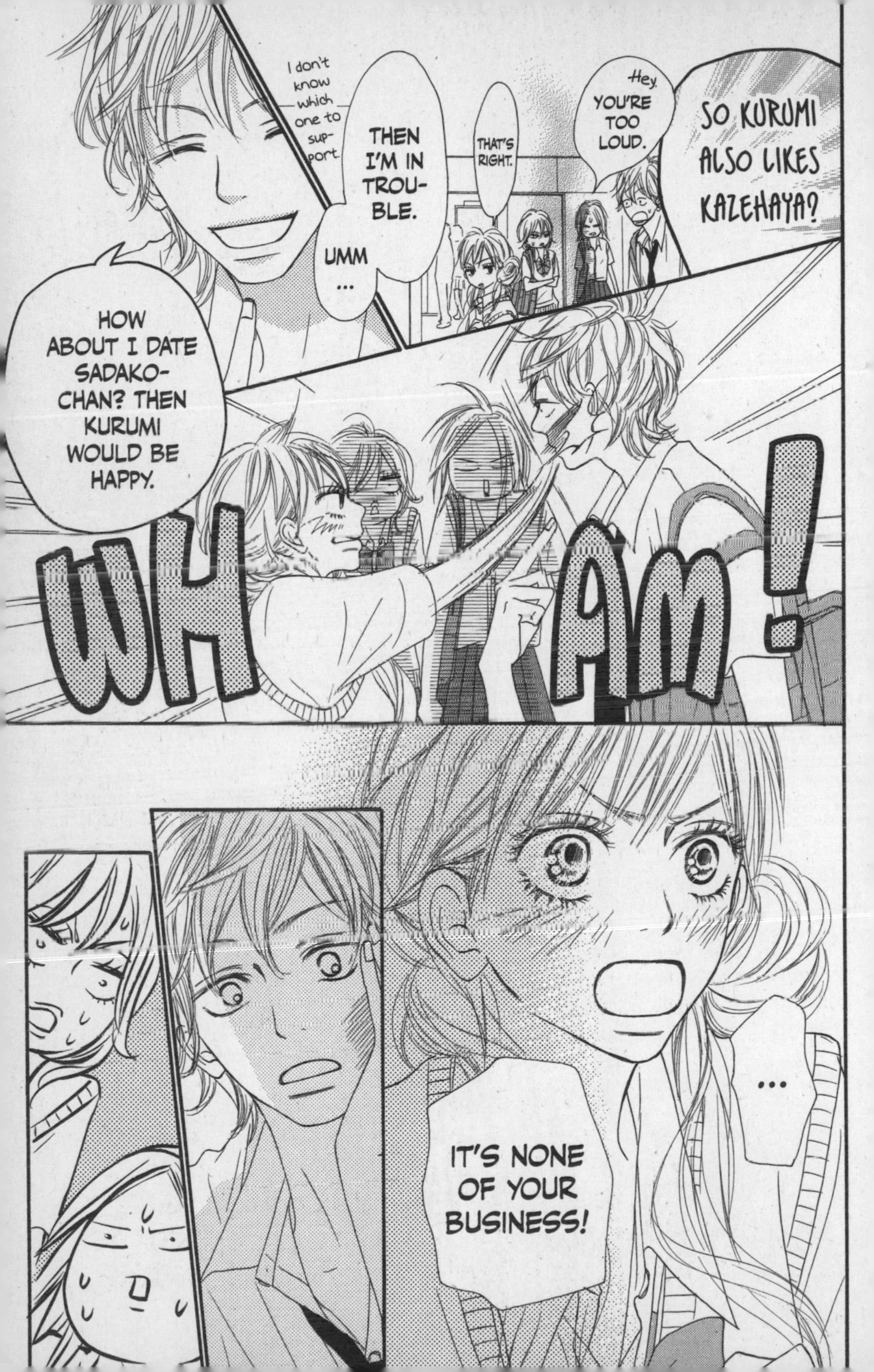
SO KURUMI ALSO LIKES KAZEHAYA?
Hey. YOU'RE TOO LOUD.
THAT'S RIGHT.
THEN I'M IN TROUBLE.
I don't know which one to support.
UMM ...
HOW ABOUT I DATE SADAKO-CHAN? THEN KURUMI WOULD BE HAPPY.
WHAM!
...
IT'S NONE OF YOUR BUSINESS!

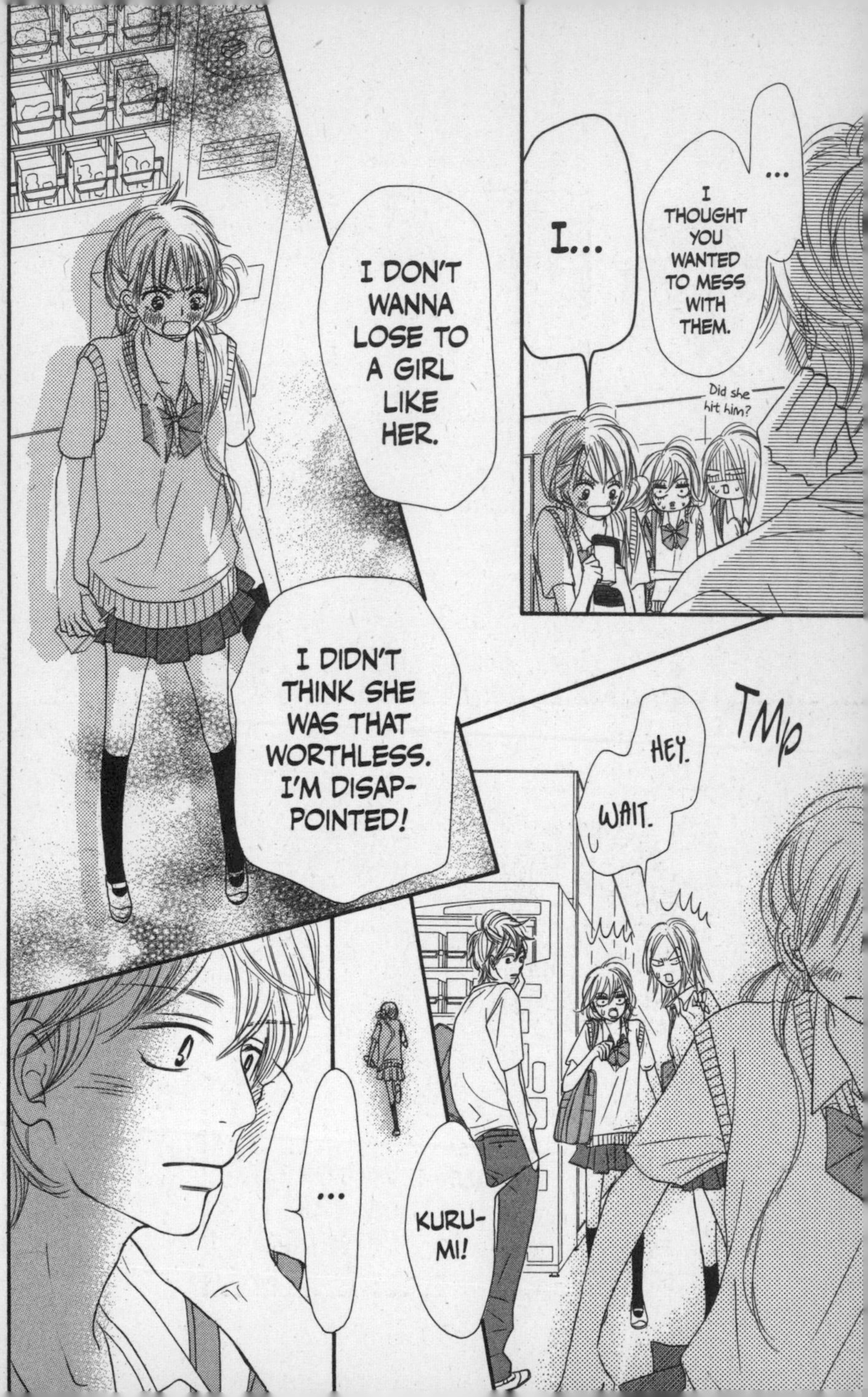
...
I THOUGHT YOU WANTED TO MESS WITH THEM.
I...
Did she hit him?
I DON'T WANNA LOSE TO A GIRL LIKE HER.
I DIDN'T THINK SHE WAS THAT WORTHLESS. I'M DISAPPOINTED!
TMP
HEY.
WAIT.
KURU-MI!
...

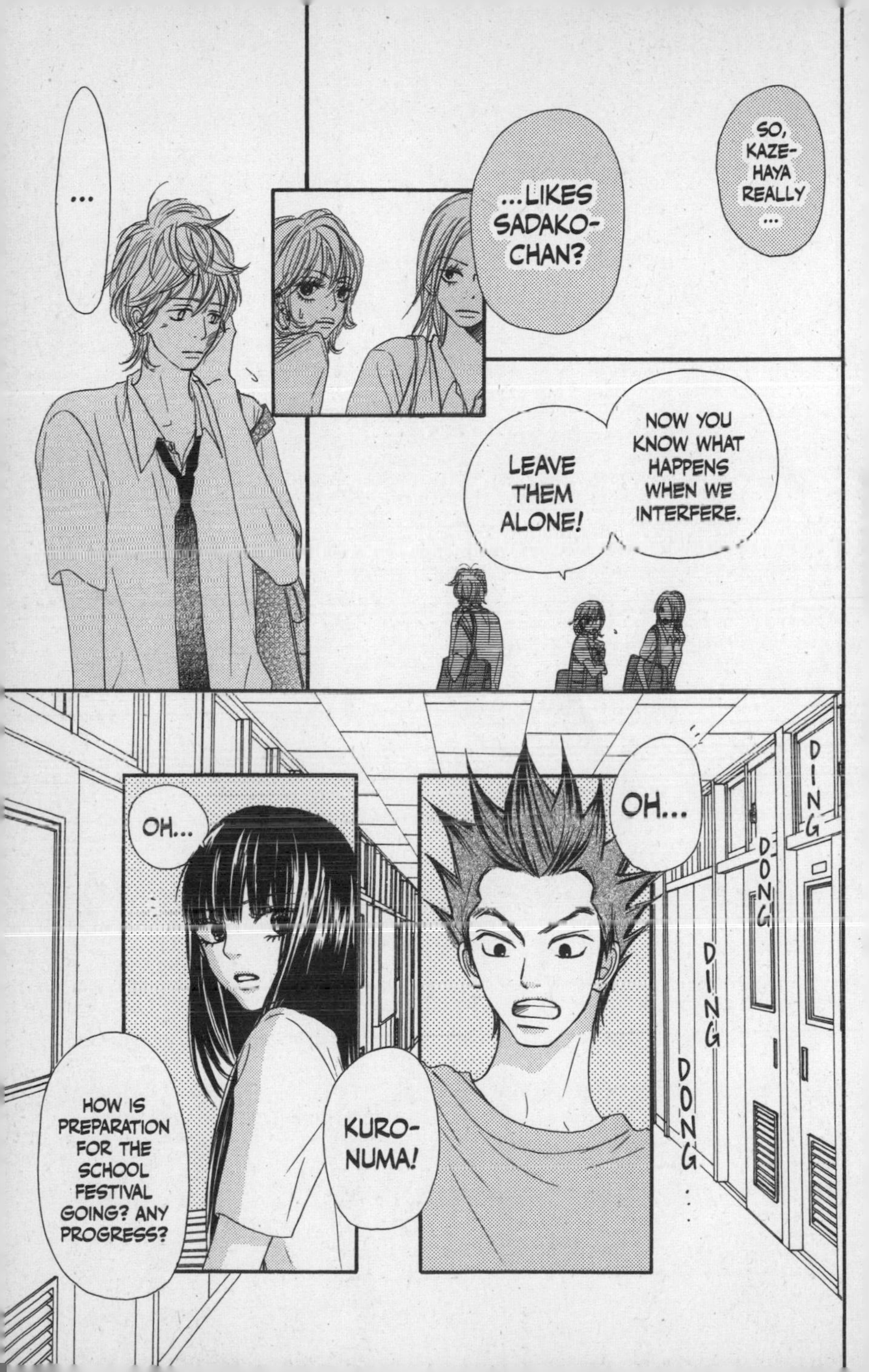
SO, KAZE-HAYA REALLY ...
...LIKES SADAKO-CHAN?
NOW YOU KNOW WHAT HAPPENS WHEN WE INTERFERE.
LEAVE THEM ALONE!
...
DING DONG
DING DONG
OH...
OH...
KURO-NUMA!
HOW IS PREPARATION FOR THE SCHOOL FESTIVAL GOING? ANY PROGRESS?

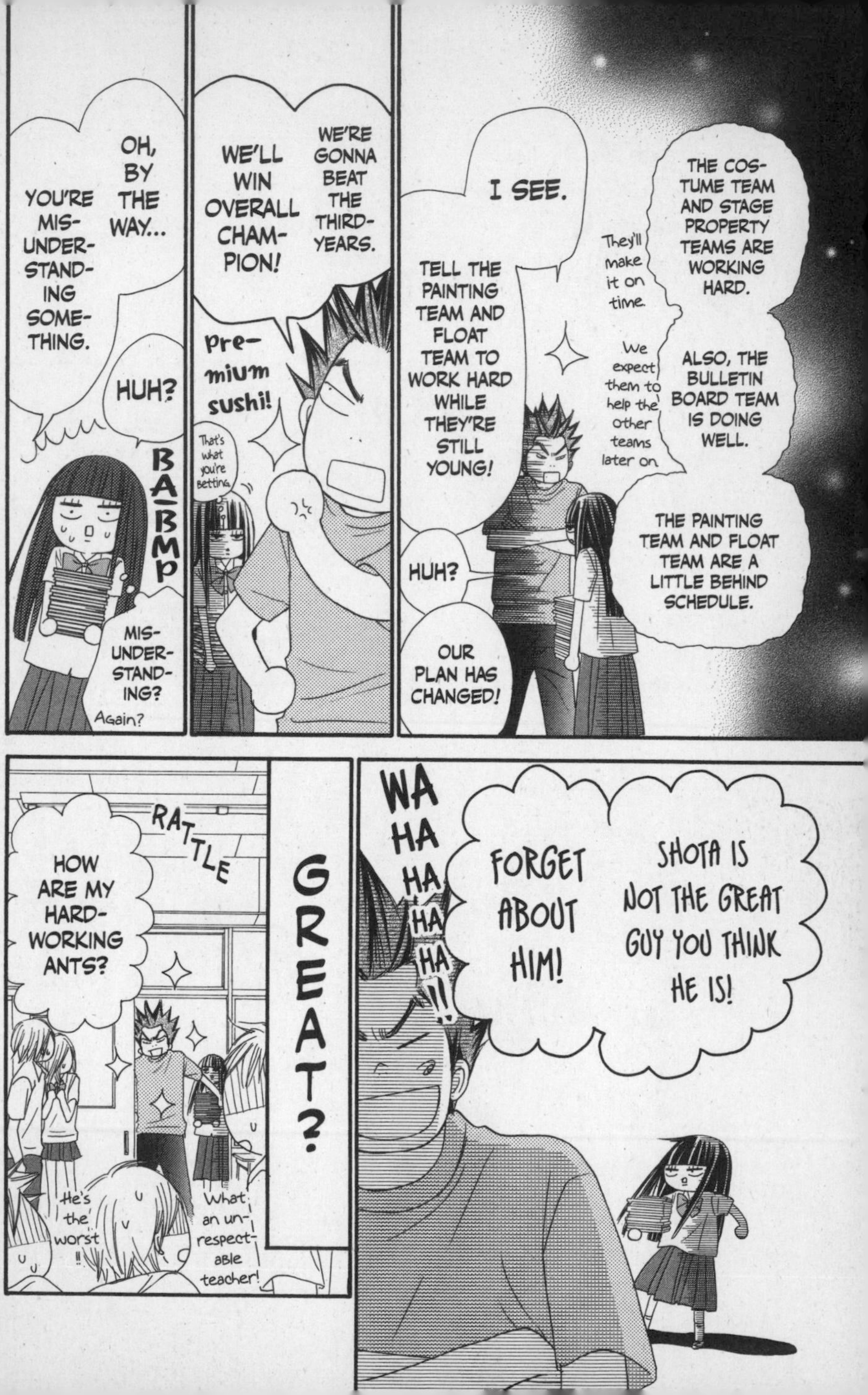
THE COS-TUME TEAM AND STAGE PROPERTY TEAMS ARE WORKING HARD.
They'll make it on time.
ALSO, THE BULLETIN BOARD TEAM IS DOING WELL.
We expect them to help the other teams later on.
THE PAINTING TEAM AND FLOAT TEAM ARE A LITTLE BEHIND SCHEDULE.
I SEE.
TELL THE PAINTING TEAM AND FLOAT TEAM TO WORK HARD WHILE THEY'RE STILL YOUNG!
HUH?
OUR PLAN HAS CHANGED!
WE'RE GONNA BEAT THE THIRD-YEARS.
WE'LL WIN OVERALL CHAM-PION!
pre-mium sushi!
That's what you're betting
OH, BY THE WAY...
YOU'RE MIS-UNDER-STAND-ING SOME-THING.
HUH?
BABMP
MIS-UNDER-STAND-ING?
Again?
WA HA HA HA HA!!
SHOTA IS NOT THE GREAT GUY YOU THINK HE IS!
FORGET ABOUT HIM!
GREAT?
RATTLE
HOW ARE MY HARD-WORKING ANTS?
What an un-respect-able teacher!
He's the worst!!

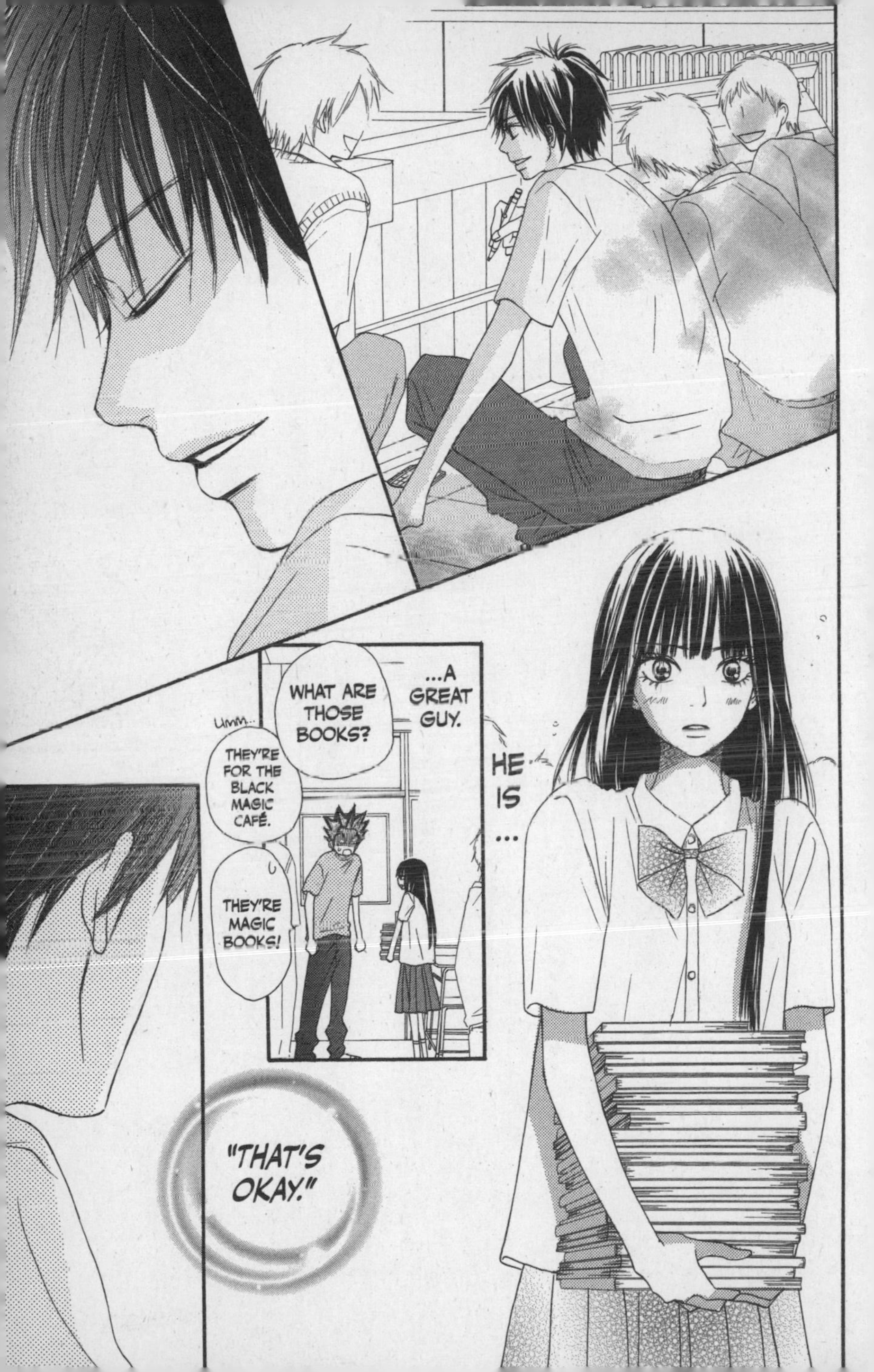
HE IS ...
...A GREAT GUY.
WHAT ARE THOSE BOOKS?
Umm...
THEY'RE FOR THE BLACK MAGIC CAFÉ.
THEY'RE MAGIC BOOKS!
"THAT'S OKAY."

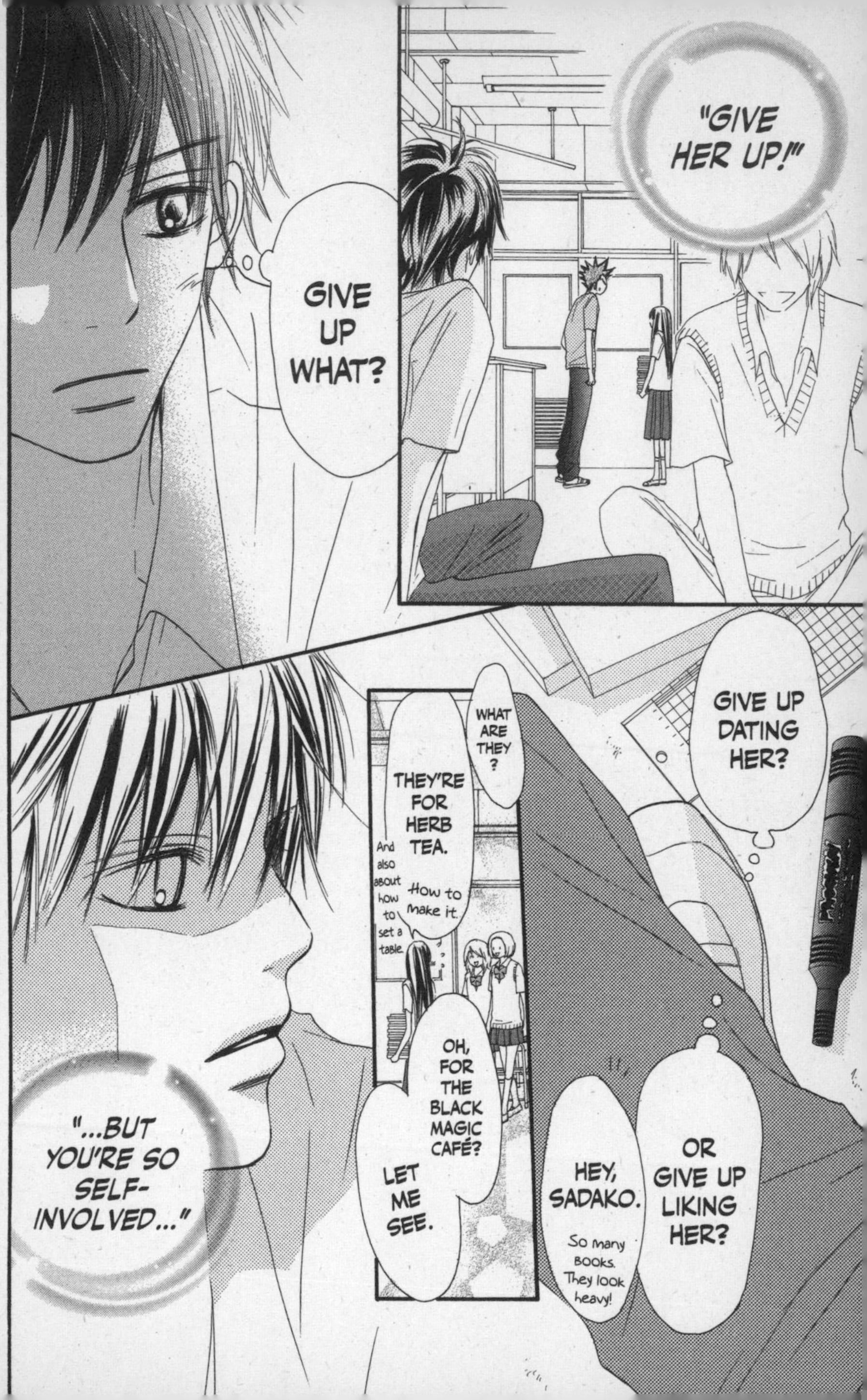
"GIVE HER UP!"
GIVE UP WHAT?
GIVE UP DATING HER?
OR GIVE UP LIKING HER?
HEY, SADAKO.
So many BOOKS. They look heavy!
WHAT ARE THEY?
THEY'RE FOR HERB TEA.
How to make it.
And also about how to set a table.
OH, FOR THE BLACK MAGIC CAFÉ?
LET ME SEE.
"...BUT YOU'RE SO SELF-INVOLVED..."

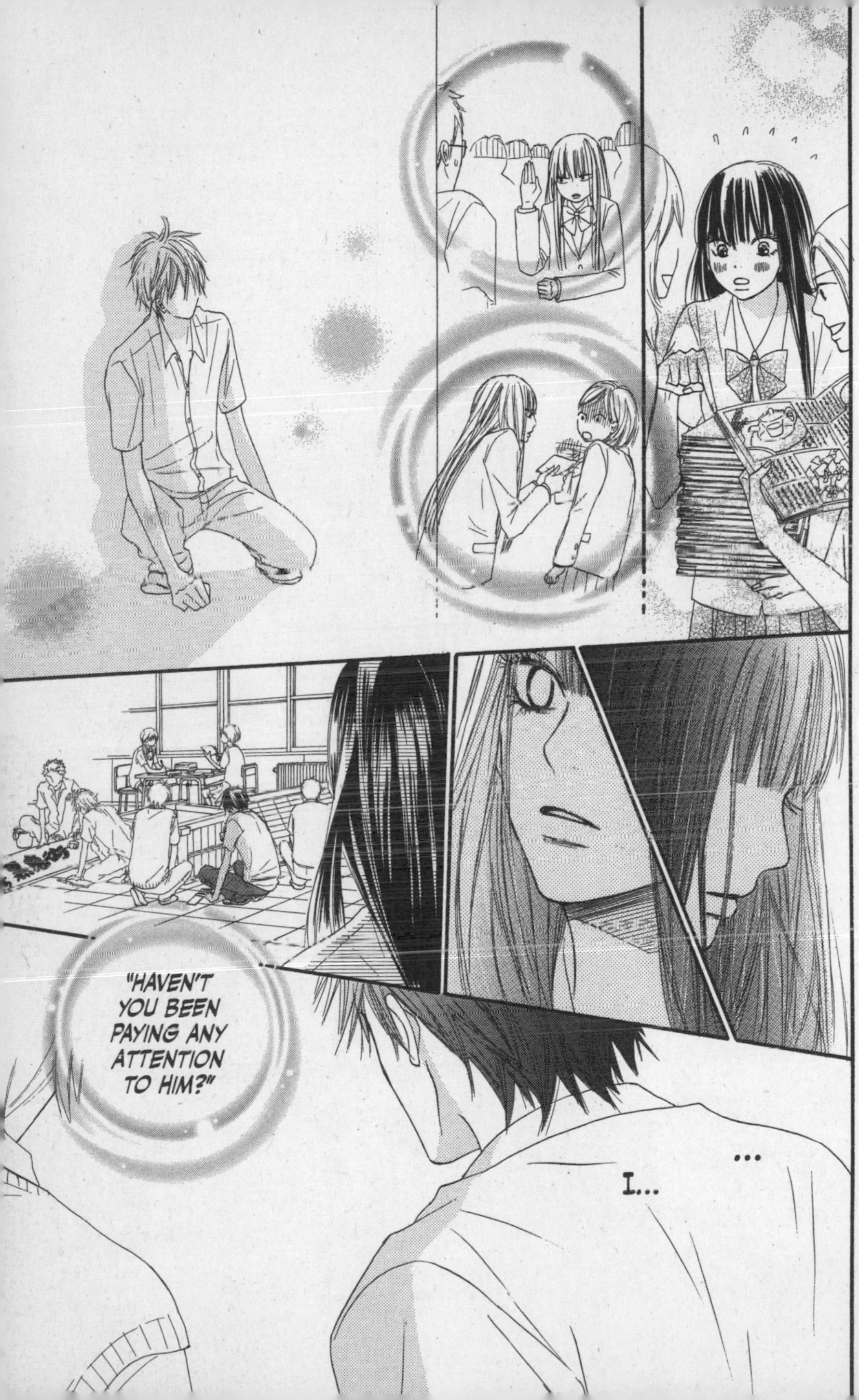
...
I...
"HAVEN'T YOU BEEN PAYING ANY ATTENTION TO HIM?"

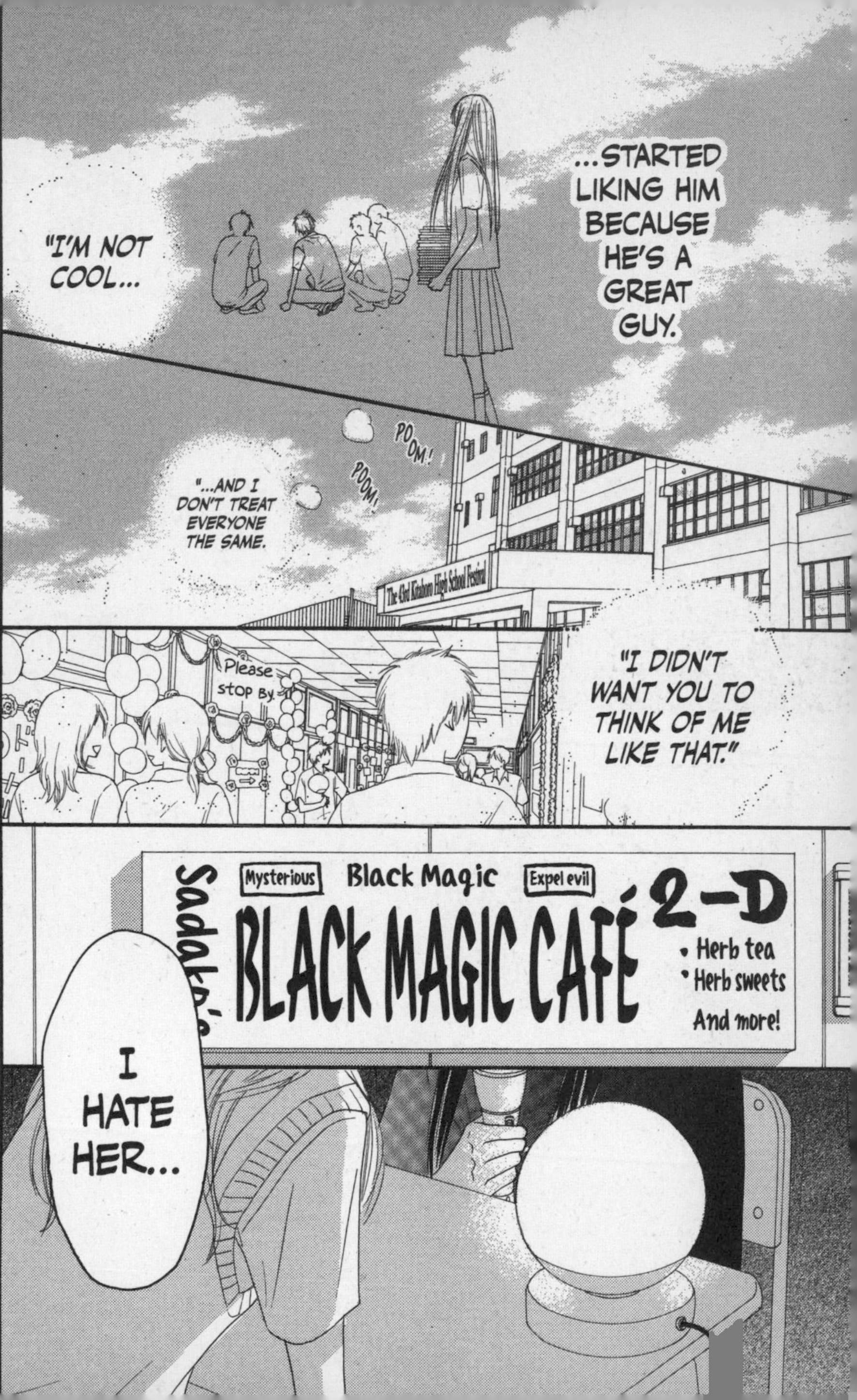
...STARTED LIKING HIM BECAUSE HE'S A GREAT GUY.
"I'M NOT COOL...
POOM!
POOM!
The 43rd Kitahoro High School Festival
"...AND I DON'T TREAT EVERYONE THE SAME.
"I DIDN'T WANT YOU TO THINK OF ME LIKE THAT."
Please stop by.
Sadako's
Mysterious
Black Magic
Expel evil
BLACK MAGIC CAFÉ
2-D
• Herb tea
• Herb sweets
And more!
I HATE HER...

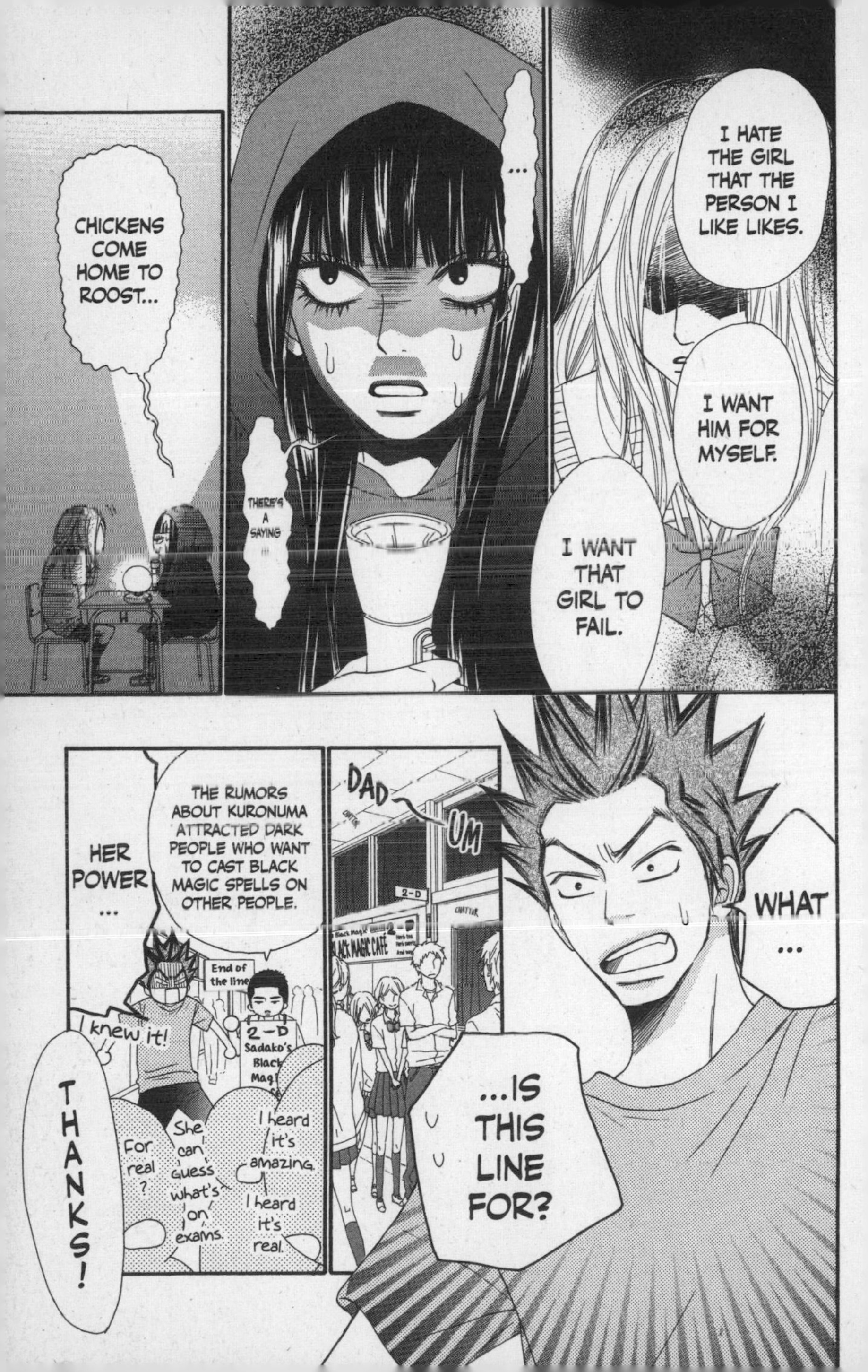
I HATE THE GIRL THAT THE PERSON I LIKE LIKES.
I WANT HIM FOR MYSELF.
I WANT THAT GIRL TO FAIL.
...
THERE'S A SAYING ...
CHICKENS COME HOME TO ROOST...
WHAT ...
...IS THIS LINE FOR?
DAD~
UM
2-D
BLACK MAGIC CAFE
THE RUMORS ABOUT KURONUMA ATTRACTED DARK PEOPLE WHO WANT TO CAST BLACK MAGIC SPELLS ON OTHER PEOPLE.
HER POWER ...
End of the line
I knew it!
2-D Sadako's Black
THANKS!
I heard it's amazing.
She can guess what's on exams.
For real?
I heard it's real.

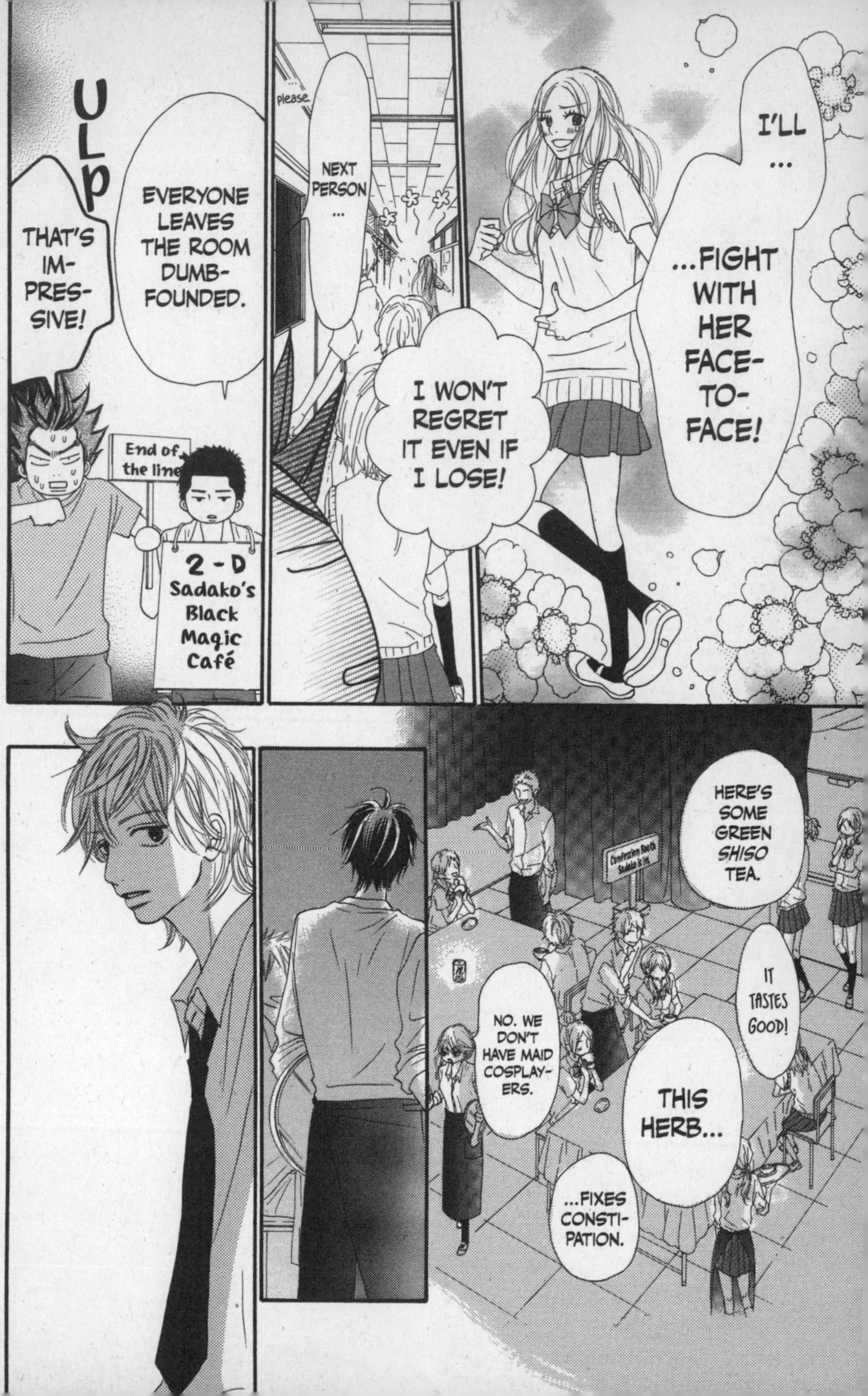
I'LL ...
...FIGHT WITH HER FACE-TO-FACE!
I WON'T REGRET IT EVEN IF I LOSE!
NEXT PERSON ...
... please.
EVERYONE LEAVES THE ROOM DUMB-FOUNDED.
ULP
THAT'S IM-PRES-SIVE!
End of the line
2 - D Sadako's Black Magic Café
HERE'S SOME GREEN SHISO TEA.
IT TASTES GOOD!
THIS HERB...
...FIXES CONSTI-PATION.
NO. WE DON'T HAVE MAID COSPLAY-ERS.

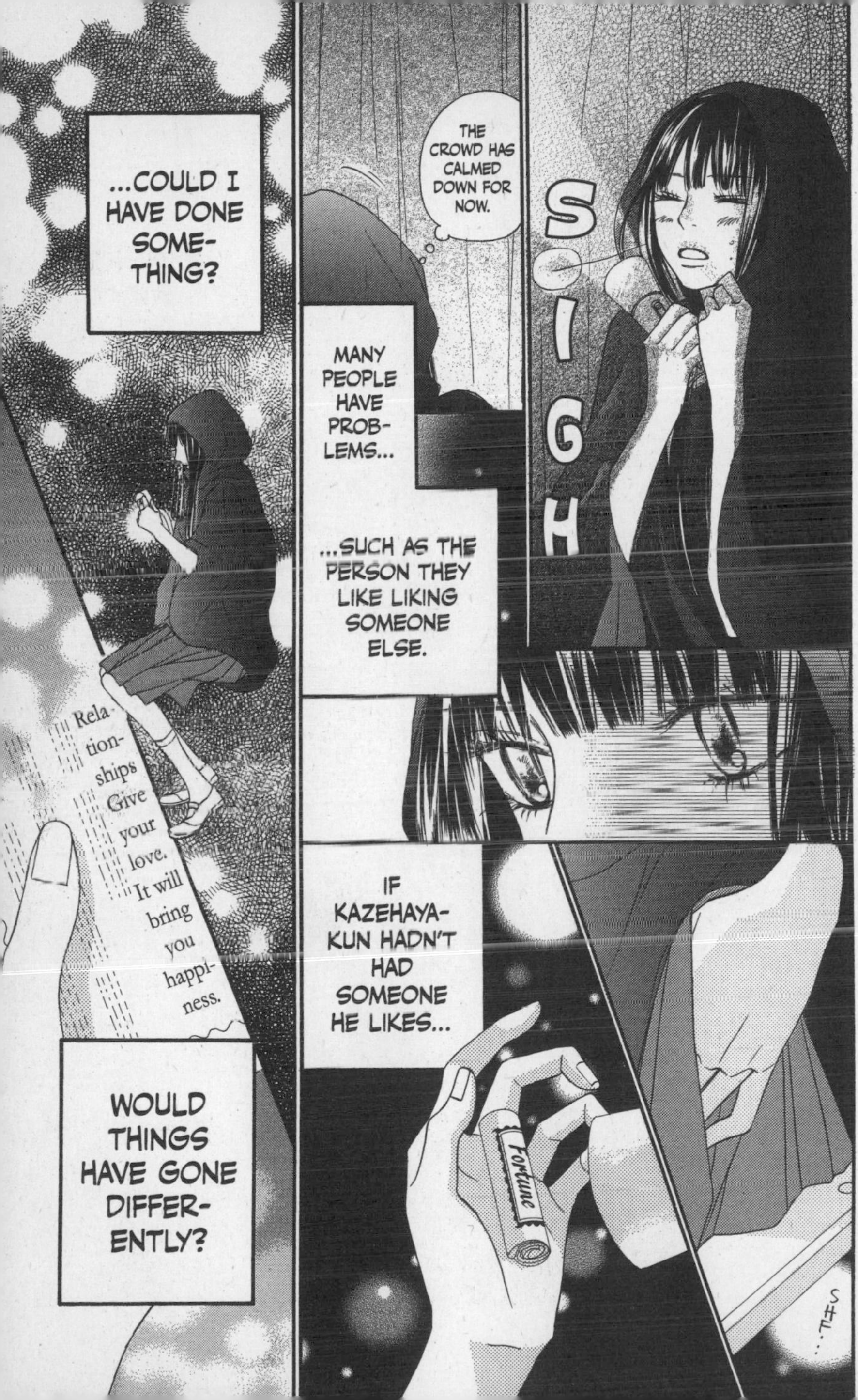
SIGH
THE CROWD HAS CALMED DOWN FOR NOW.
MANY PEOPLE HAVE PROBLEMS...
...SUCH AS THE PERSON THEY LIKE LIKING SOMEONE ELSE.
SHF...
IF KAZEHAYA-KUN HADN'T HAD SOMEONE HE LIKES...
Fortune
...COULD I HAVE DONE SOMETHING?
Relationships Give your love. It will bring you happiness.
WOULD THINGS HAVE GONE DIFFERENTLY?

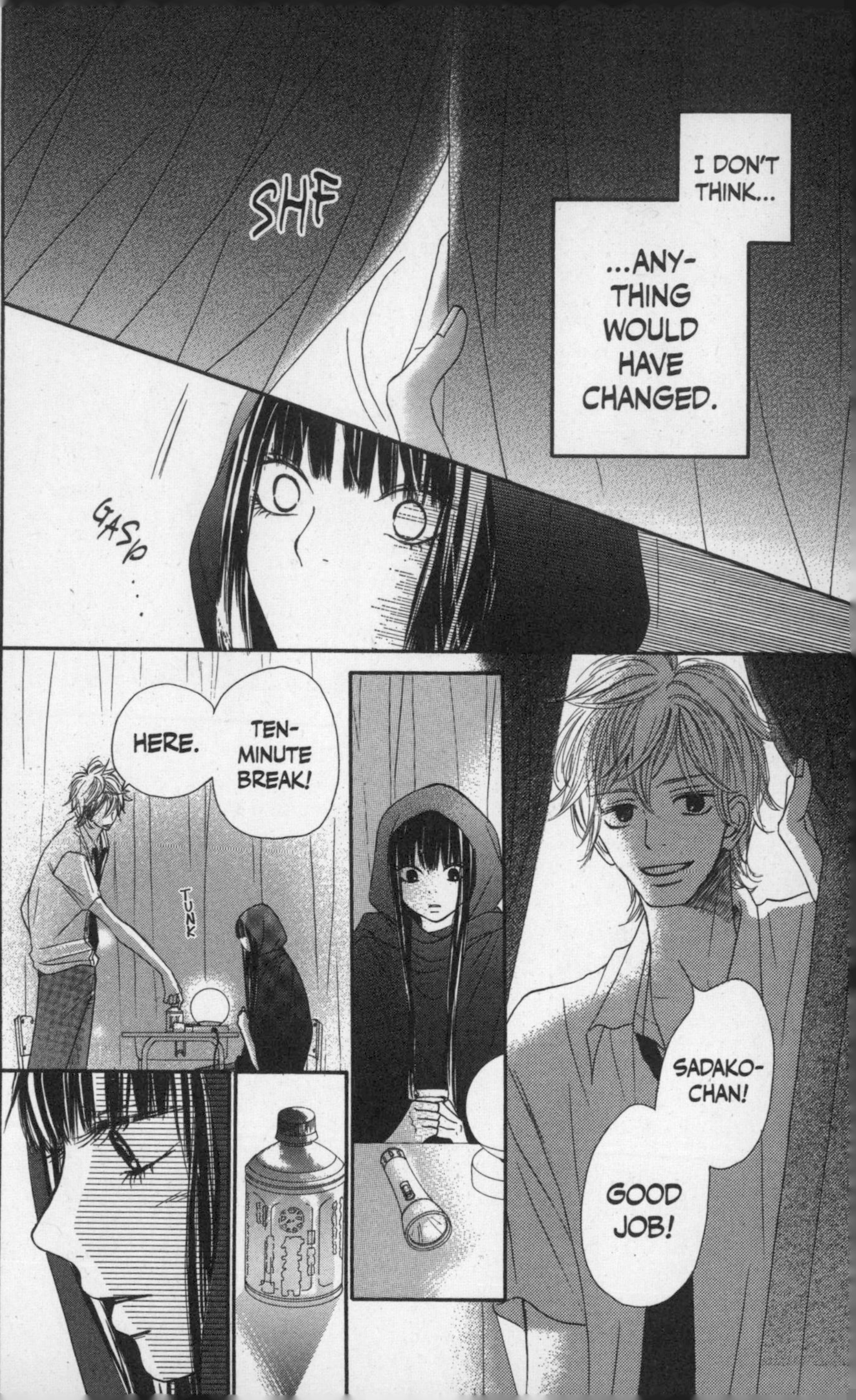
I DON'T THINK...
...ANY-THING WOULD HAVE CHANGED.
SHF
GASP...
SADAKO-CHAN!
GOOD JOB!
TEN-MINUTE BREAK!
HERE.
TUNK

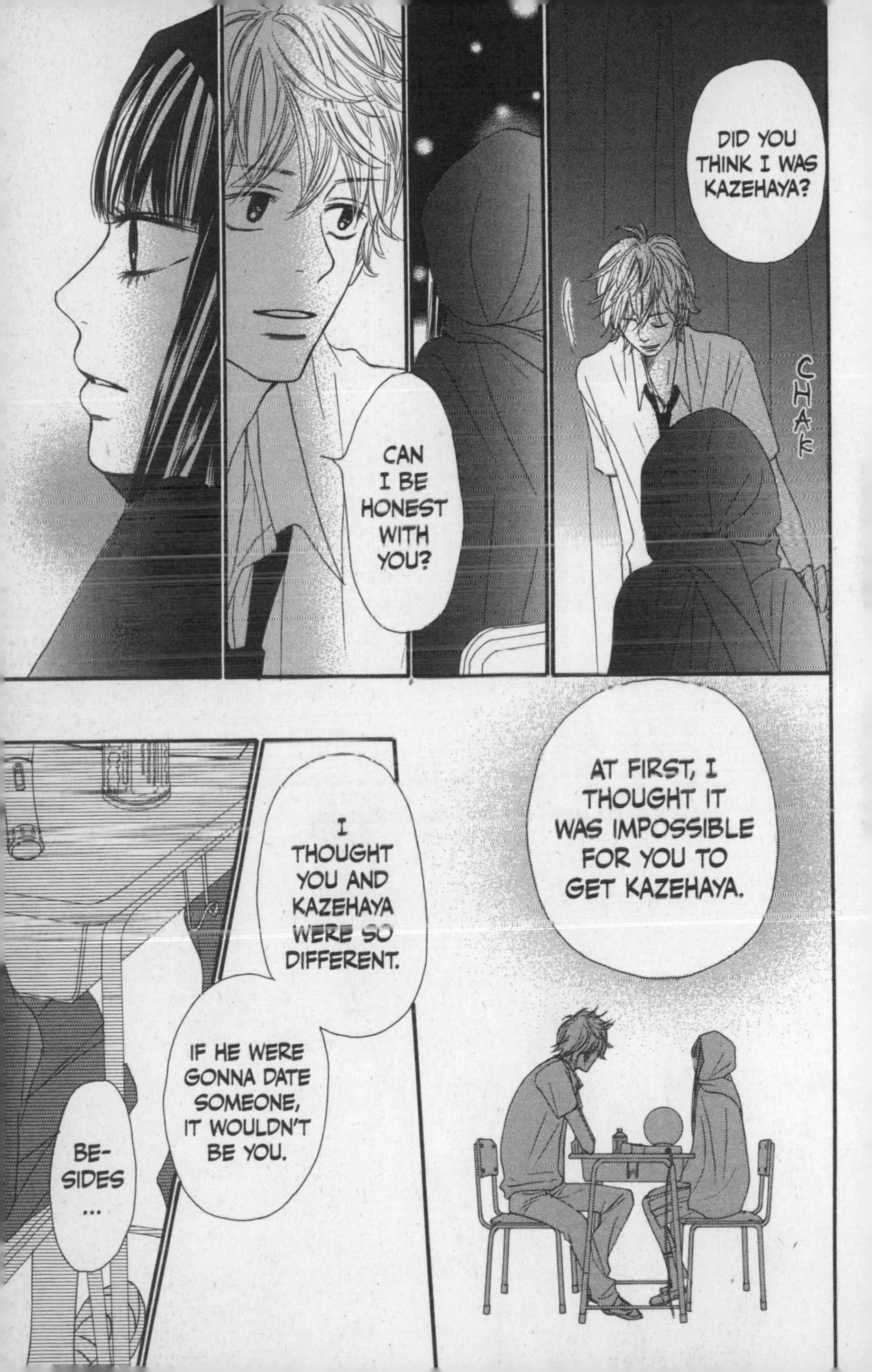

DID YOU THINK I WAS KAZEHAYA?
CHAK
CAN I BE HONEST WITH YOU?
AT FIRST, I THOUGHT IT WAS IMPOSSIBLE FOR YOU TO GET KAZEHAYA.
I THOUGHT YOU AND KAZEHAYA WERE SO DIFFERENT.
IF HE WERE GONNA DATE SOMEONE, IT WOULDN'T BE YOU.
BE-SIDES ...

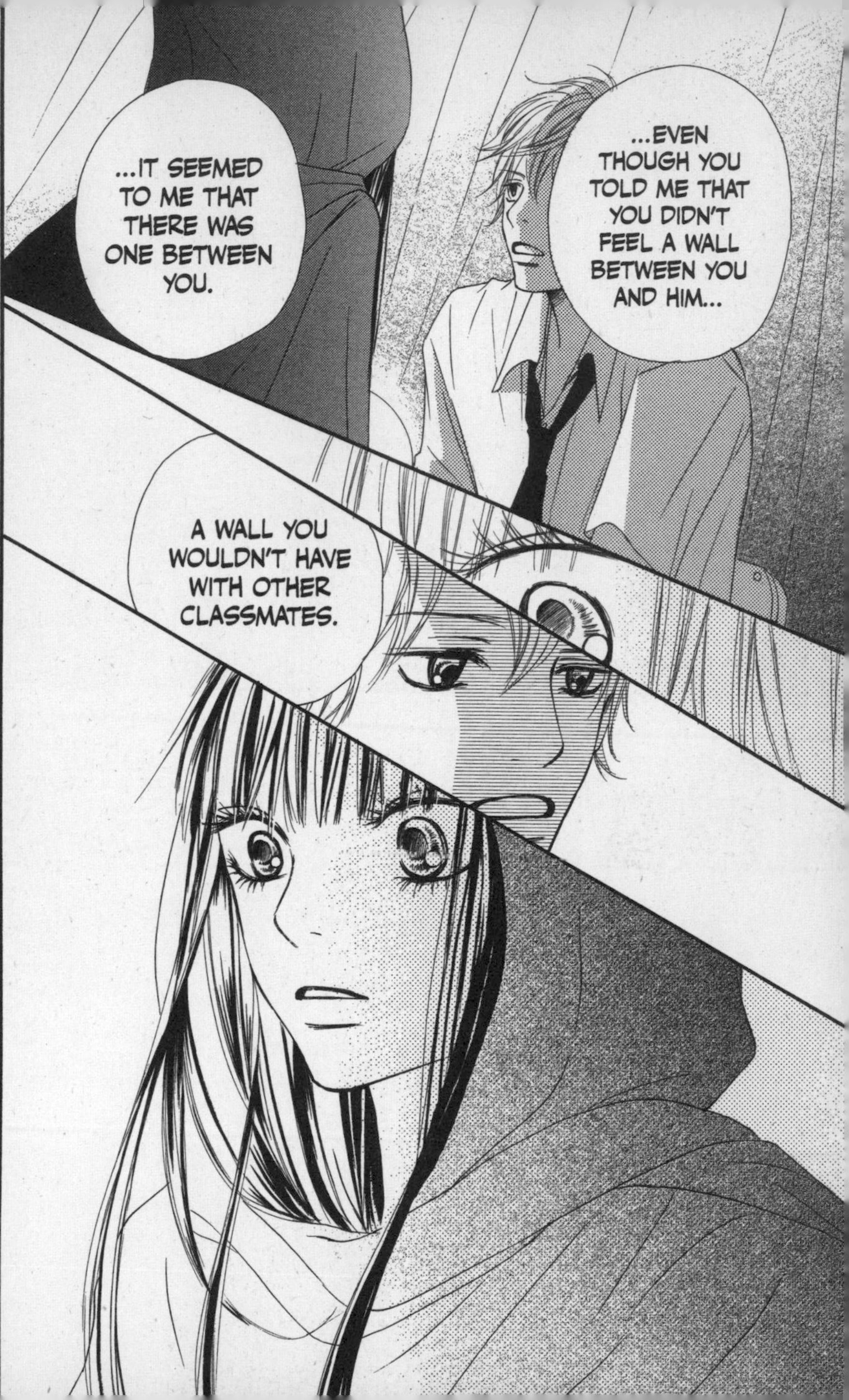
...EVEN THOUGH YOU TOLD ME THAT YOU DIDN'T FEEL A WALL BETWEEN YOU AND HIM...
...IT SEEMED TO ME THAT THERE WAS ONE BETWEEN YOU.
A WALL YOU WOULDN'T HAVE WITH OTHER CLASSMATES.

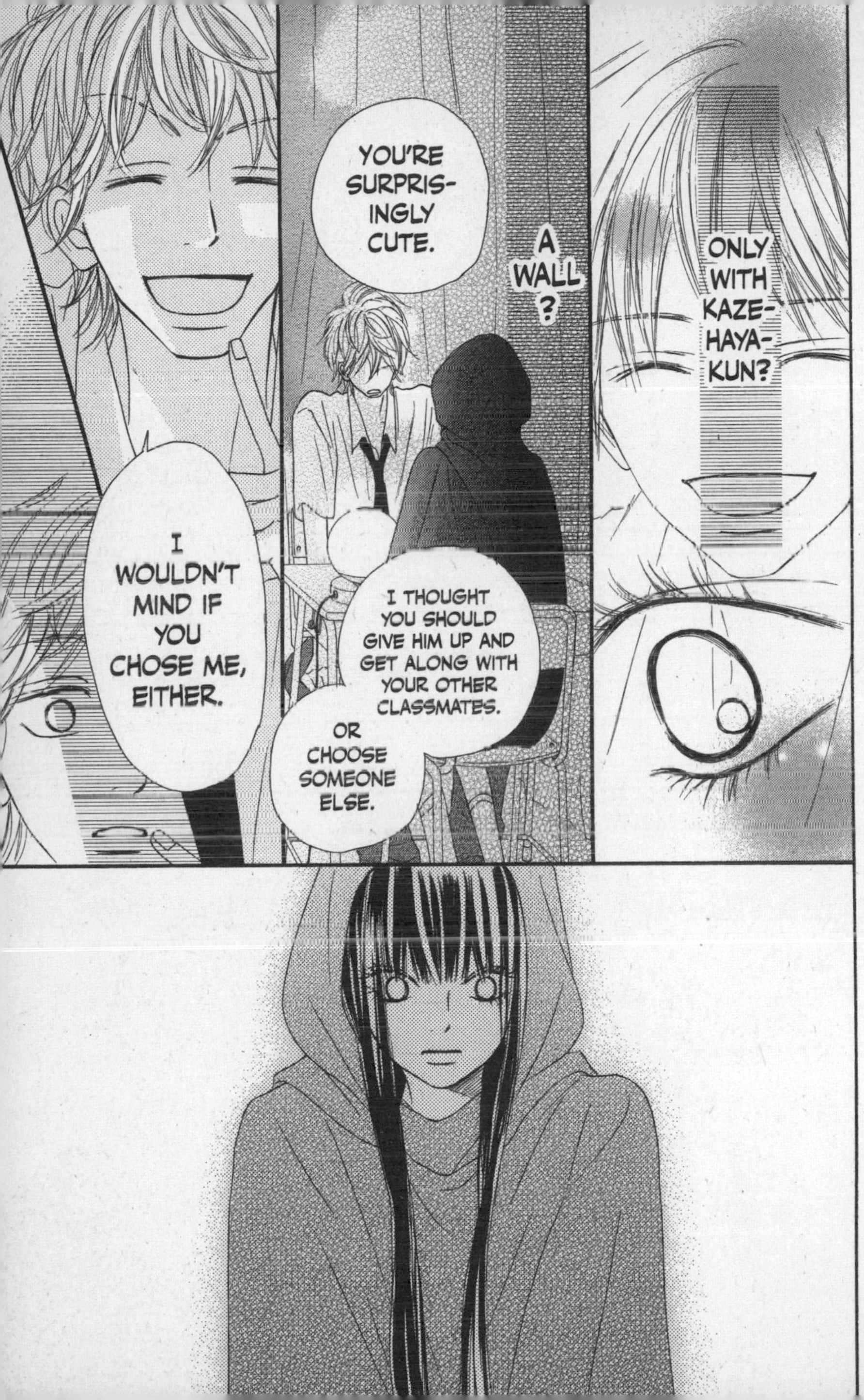
ONLY WITH KAZEHAYA-KUN?
A WALL?
YOU'RE SURPRISINGLY CUTE.
I THOUGHT YOU SHOULD GIVE HIM UP AND GET ALONG WITH YOUR OTHER CLASSMATES.
OR CHOOSE SOMEONE ELSE.
I WOULDN'T MIND IF YOU CHOSE ME, EITHER.

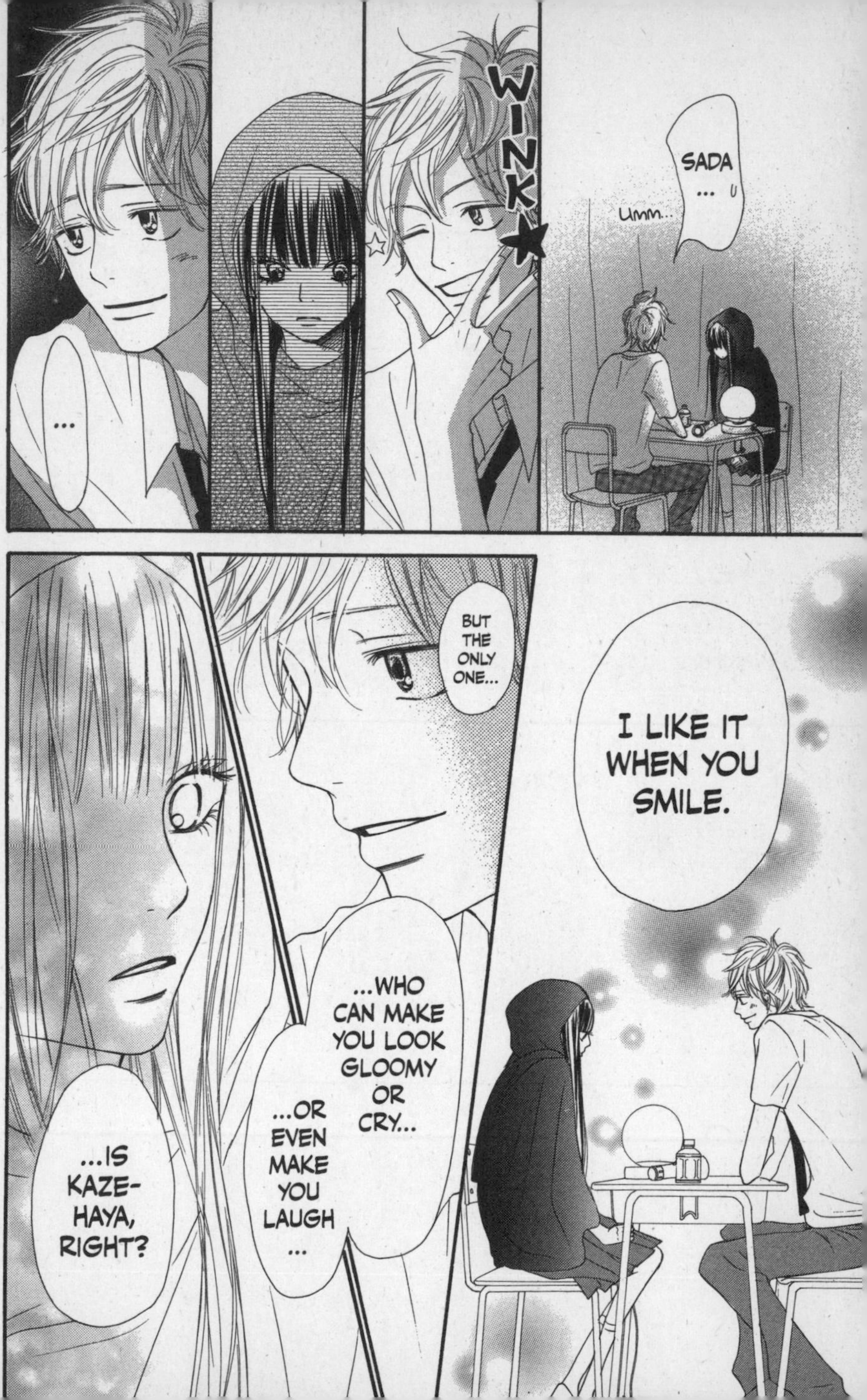
SADA ...
Umm...
WINK
...
I LIKE IT WHEN YOU SMILE.
BUT THE ONLY ONE...
...WHO CAN MAKE YOU LOOK GLOOMY OR CRY...
...OR EVEN MAKE YOU LAUGH ...
...IS KAZE-HAYA, RIGHT?

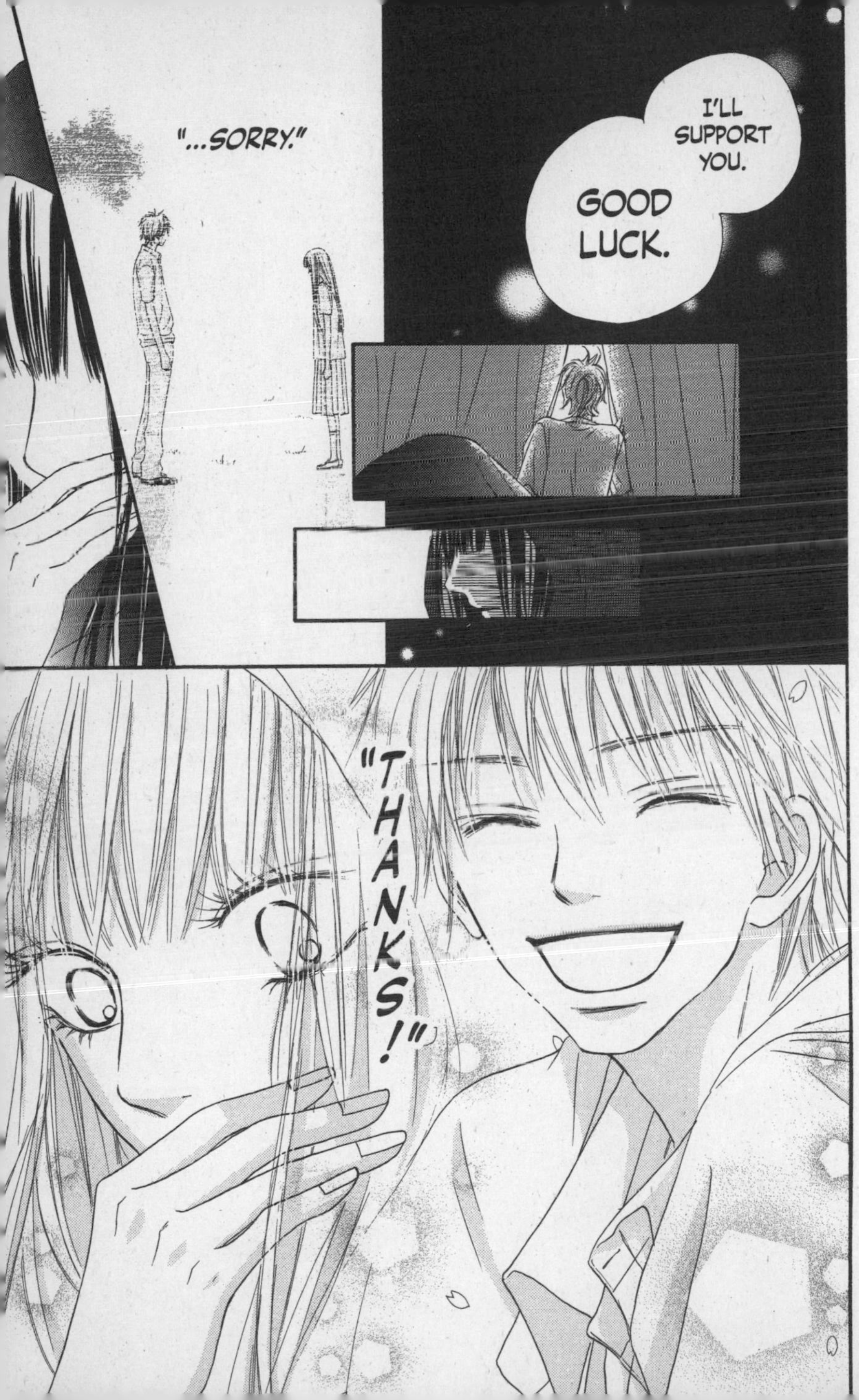
I'LL SUPPORT YOU.
GOOD LUCK.
"...SORRY."
"THANKS!"

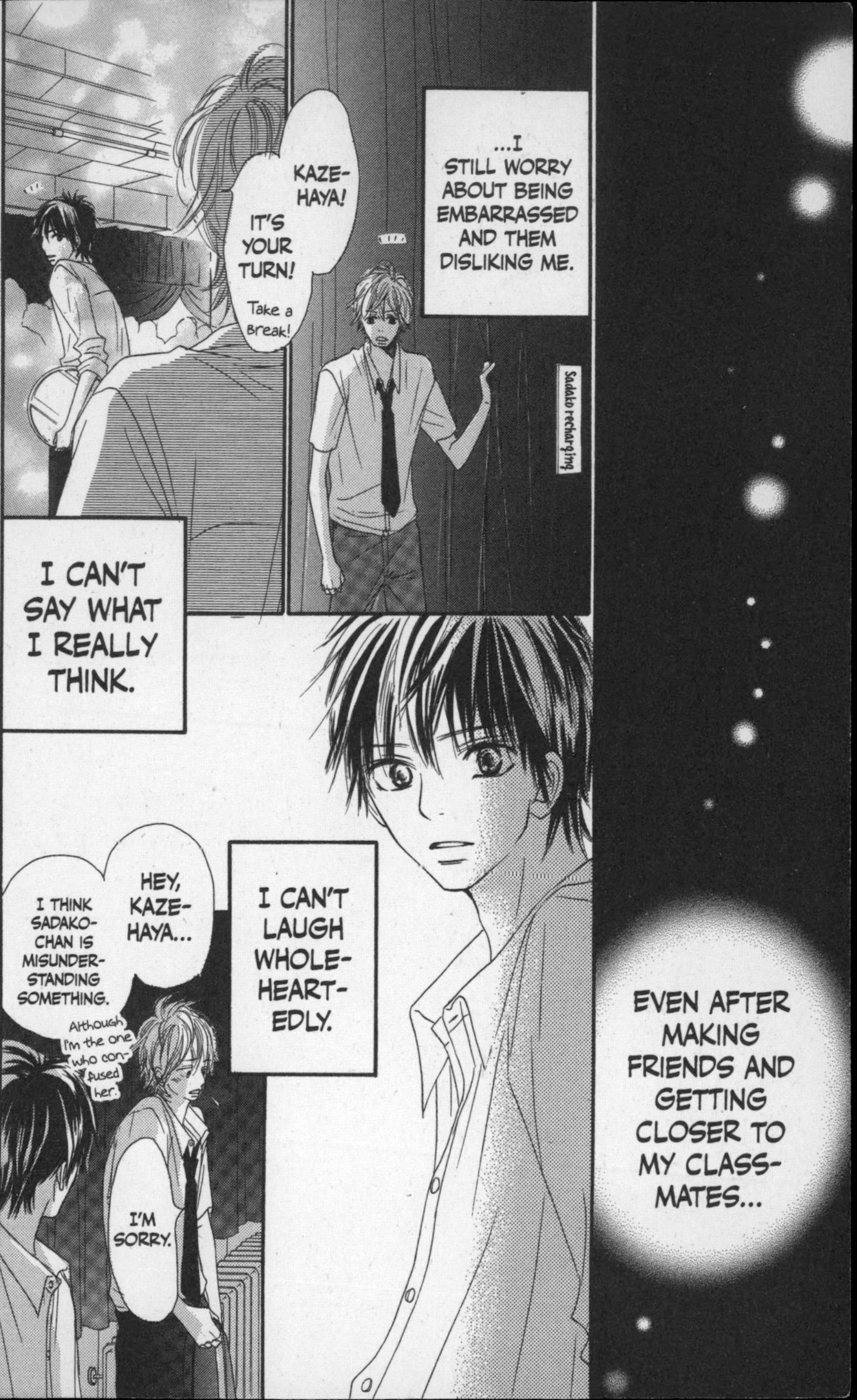
EVEN AFTER MAKING FRIENDS AND GETTING CLOSER TO MY CLASS-MATES...
...I STILL WORRY ABOUT BEING EMBARRASSED AND THEM DISLIKING ME.
Sadako recharging
KAZE-HAYA!
IT'S YOUR TURN!
Take a Break!
I CAN'T SAY WHAT I REALLY THINK.
I CAN'T LAUGH WHOLE-HEART-EDLY.
HEY, KAZE-HAYA...
I THINK SADAKO-CHAN IS MISUNDER-STANDING SOMETHING.
Although I'm the one who con-fused her.
I'M SORRY.

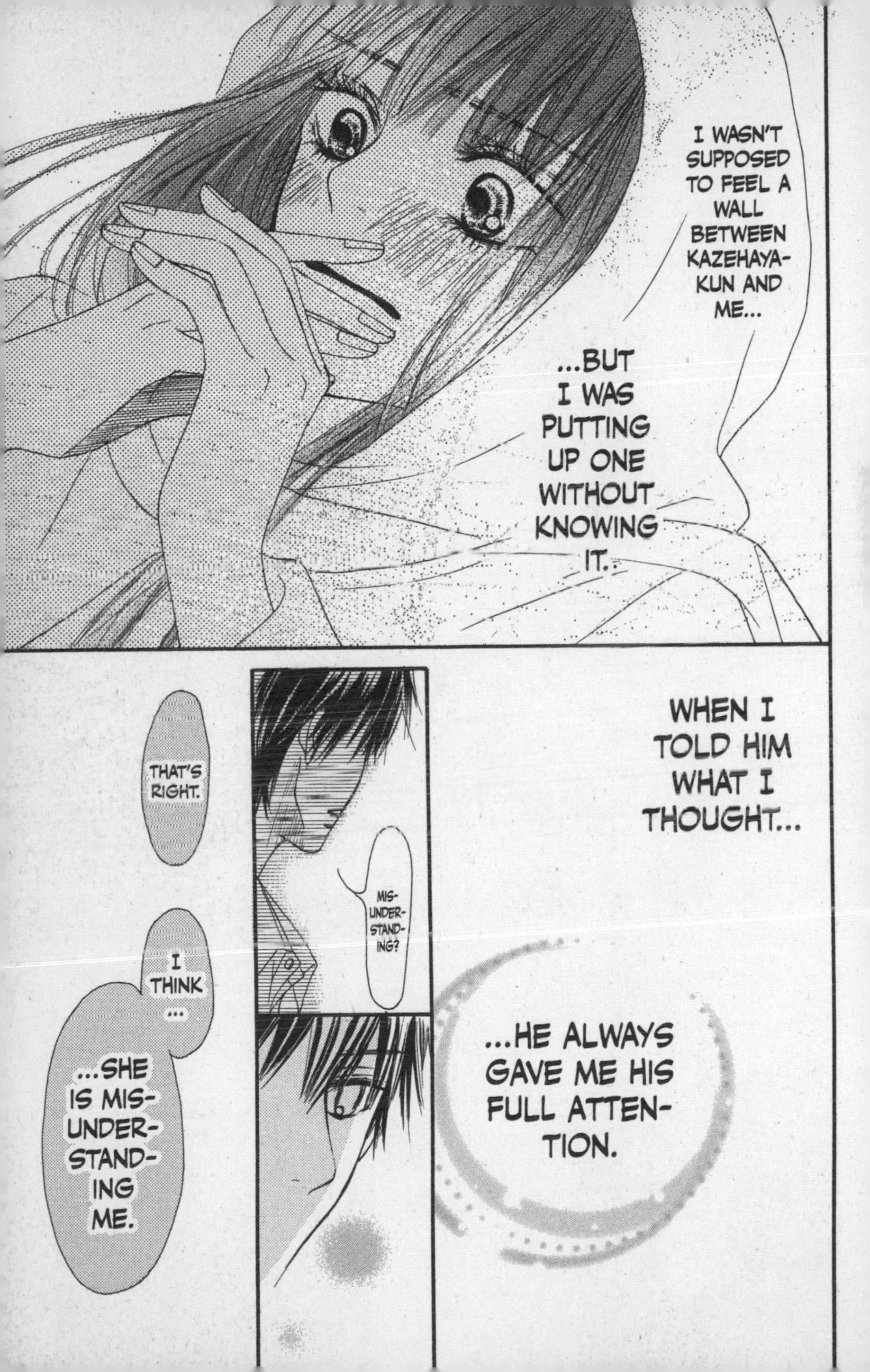
I WASN'T SUPPOSED TO FEEL A WALL BETWEEN KAZEHAYA-KUN AND ME...
...BUT I WAS PUTTING UP ONE WITHOUT KNOWING IT.
WHEN I TOLD HIM WHAT I THOUGHT...
...HE ALWAYS GAVE ME HIS FULL ATTEN-TION.
MIS-UNDER-STAND-ING?
THAT'S RIGHT.
I THINK...
...SHE IS MIS-UNDER-STAND-ING ME.

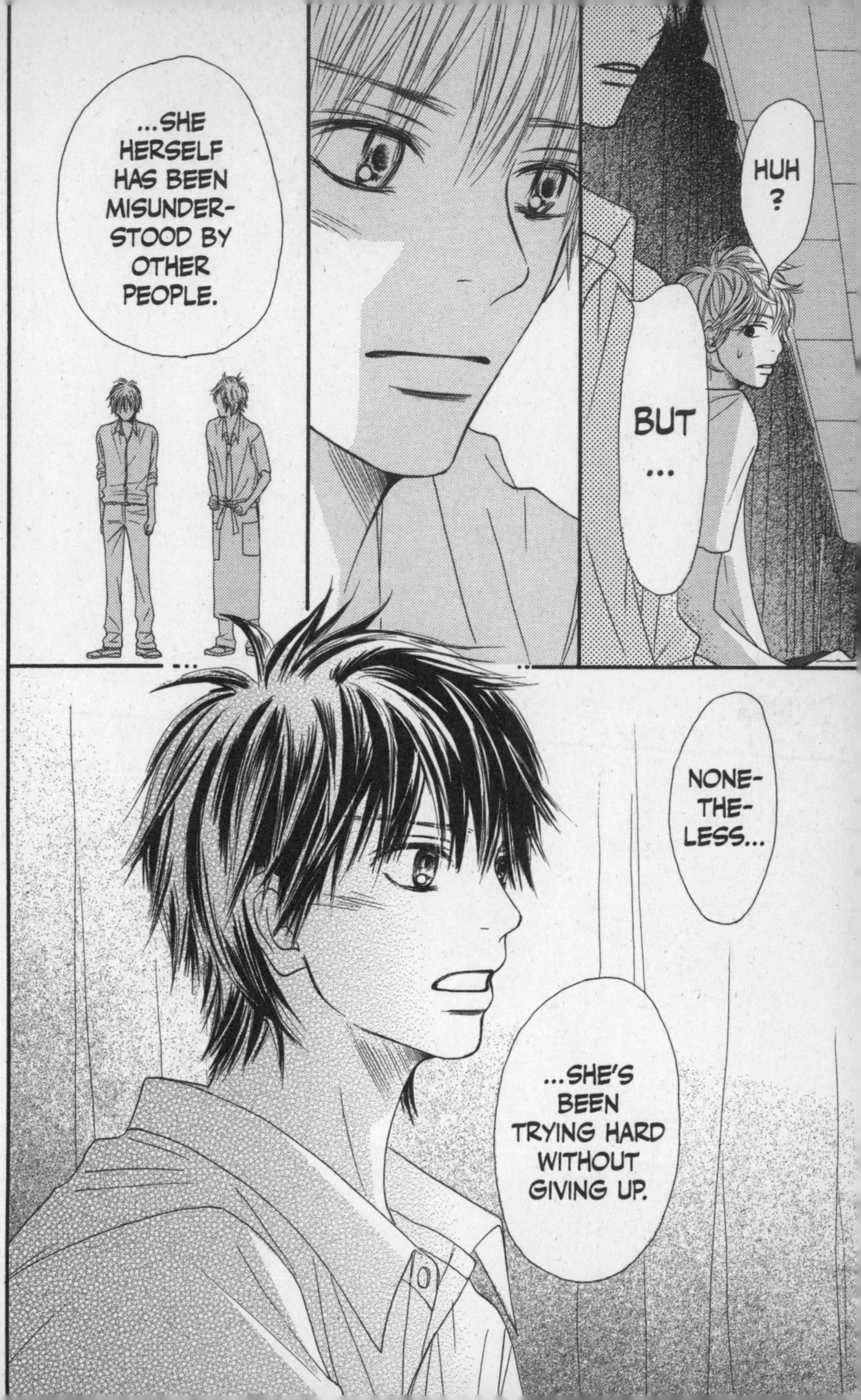
HUH?
BUT...
...SHE HERSELF HAS BEEN MISUNDERSTOOD BY OTHER PEOPLE.
NONE-THE-LESS...
...SHE'S BEEN TRYING HARD WITHOUT GIVING UP.

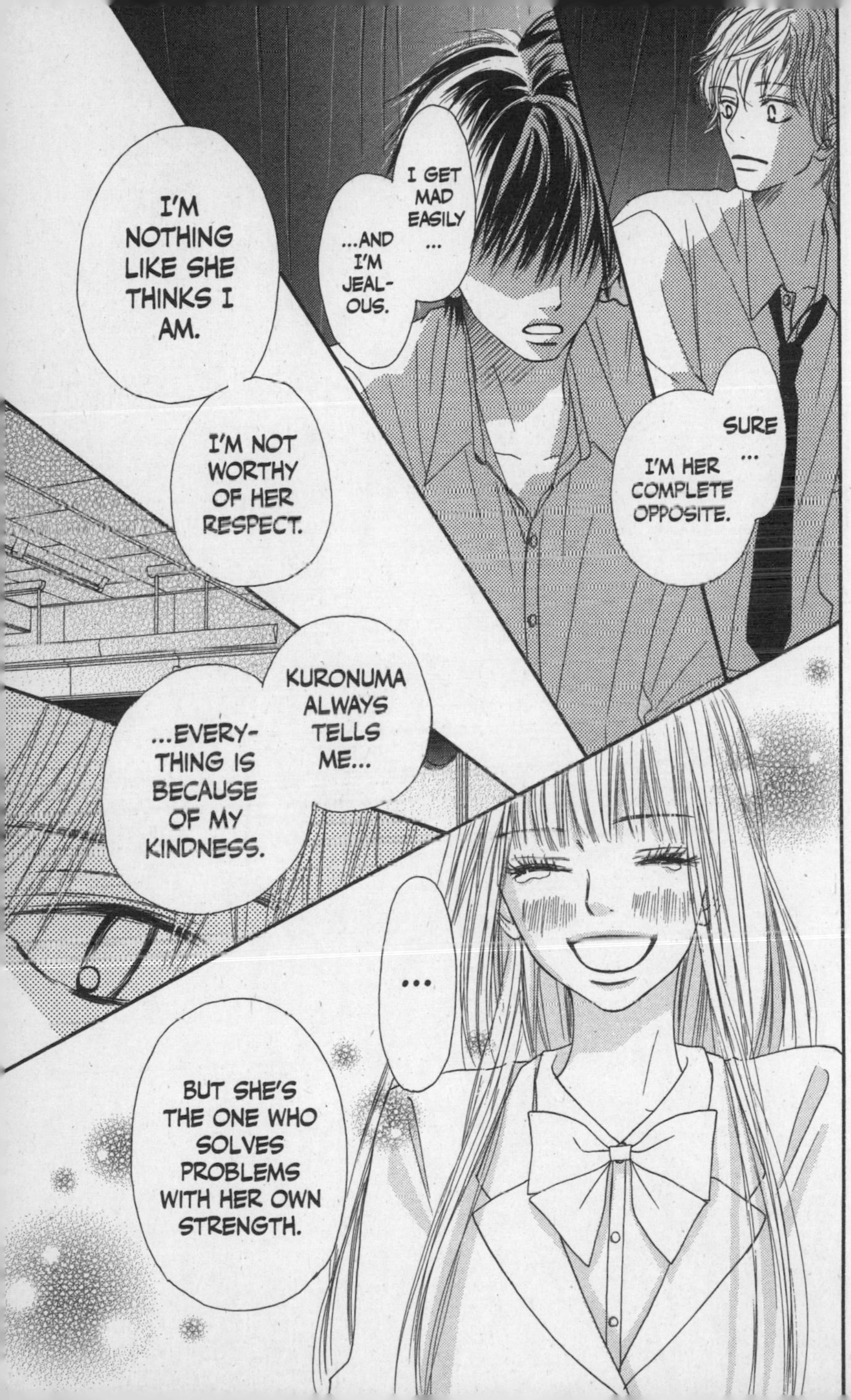
I GET MAD EASILY ...
...AND I'M JEAL-OUS.
SURE ... I'M HER COMPLETE OPPOSITE.
I'M NOTHING LIKE SHE THINKS I AM.
I'M NOT WORTHY OF HER RESPECT.
KURONUMA ALWAYS TELLS ME...
...EVERY-THING IS BECAUSE OF MY KINDNESS.
...
BUT SHE'S THE ONE WHO SOLVES PROBLEMS WITH HER OWN STRENGTH.

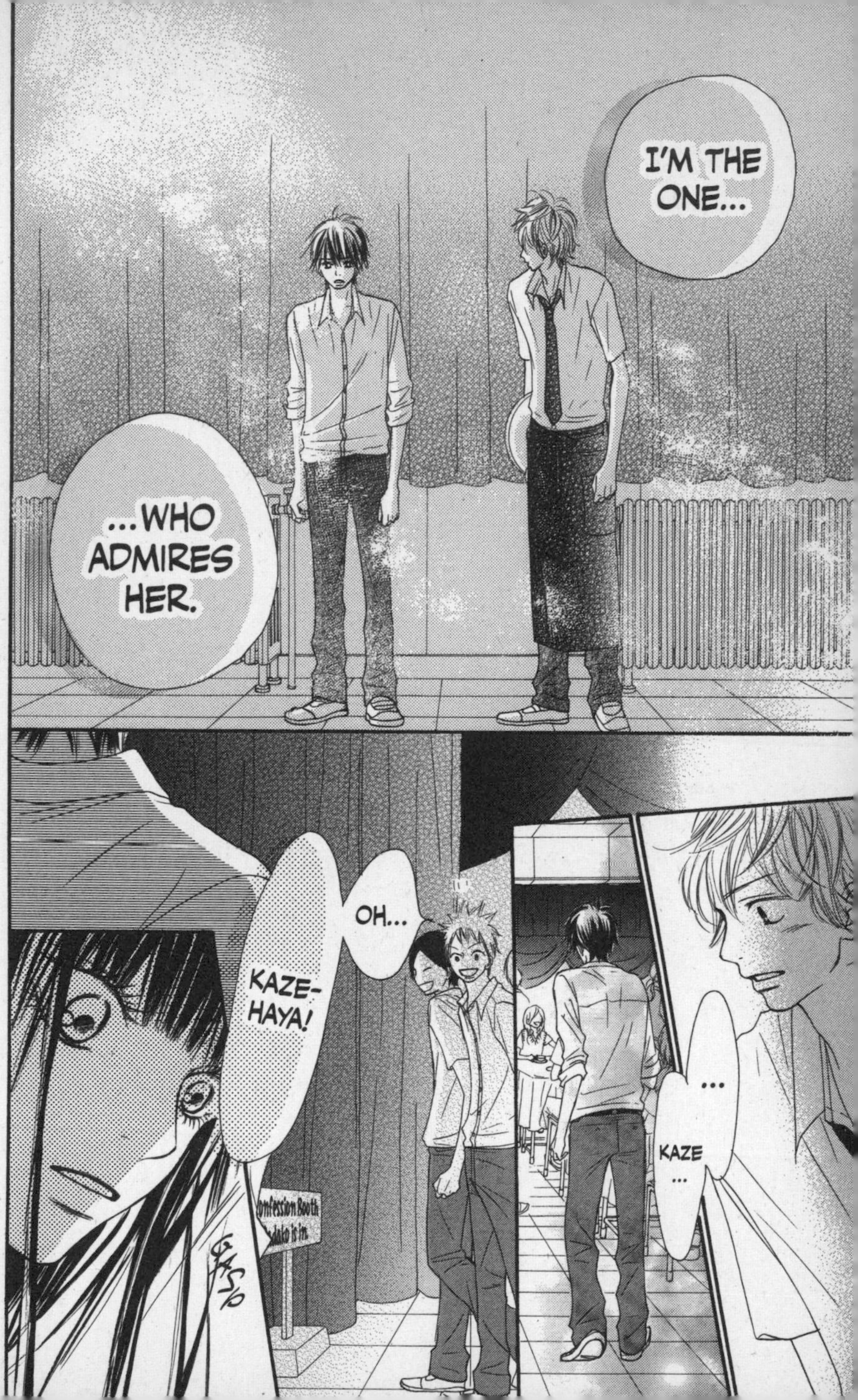
I'M THE ONE...
...WHO ADMIRES HER.
...
KAZE ...
OH...
KAZE-HAYA!
GASP

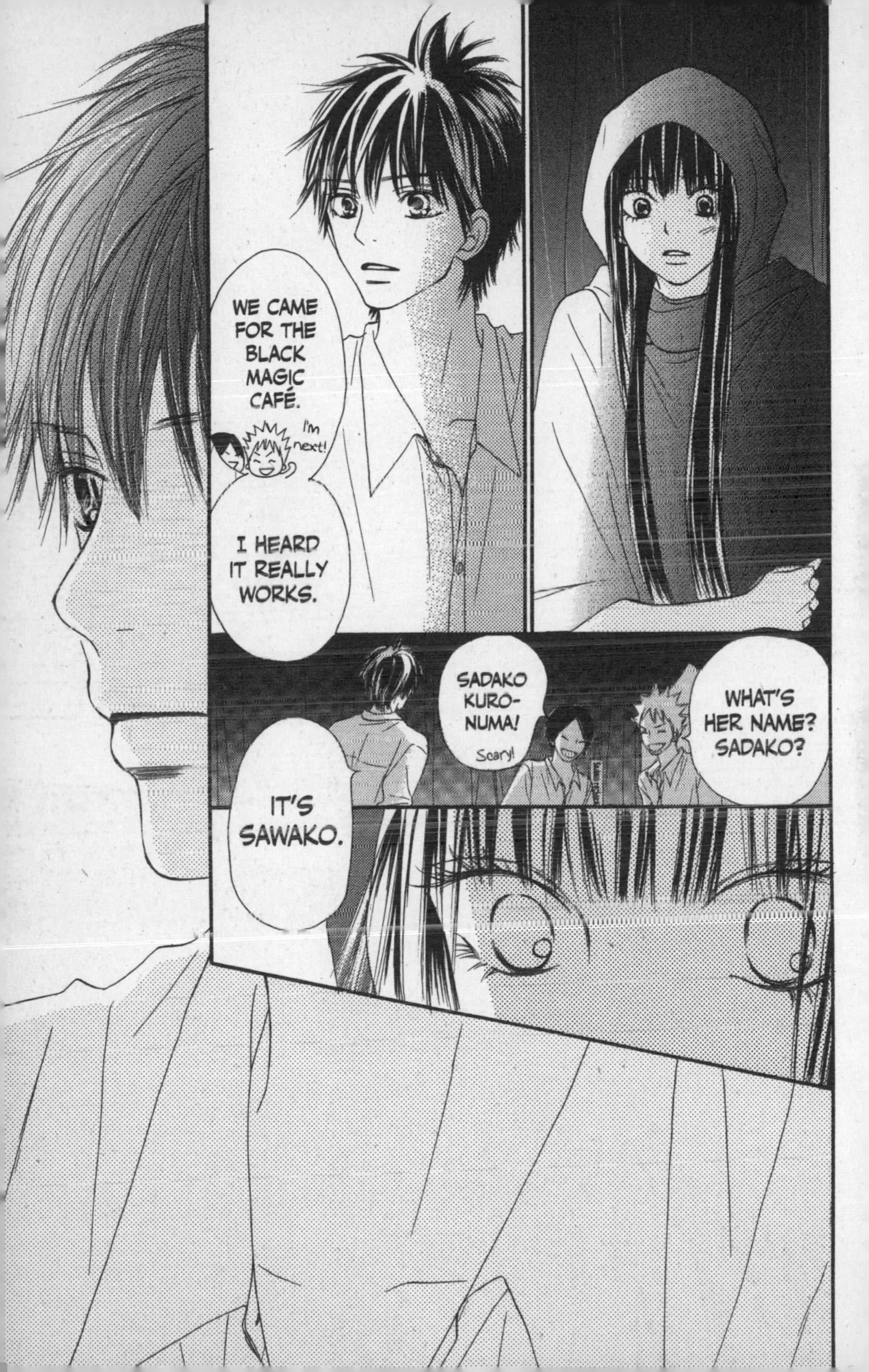
WE CAME FOR THE BLACK MAGIC CAFÉ.
I'm next!
I HEARD IT REALLY WORKS.
WHAT'S HER NAME? SADAKO?
SADAKO KURO-NUMA!
Scary!
IT'S SAWAKO.

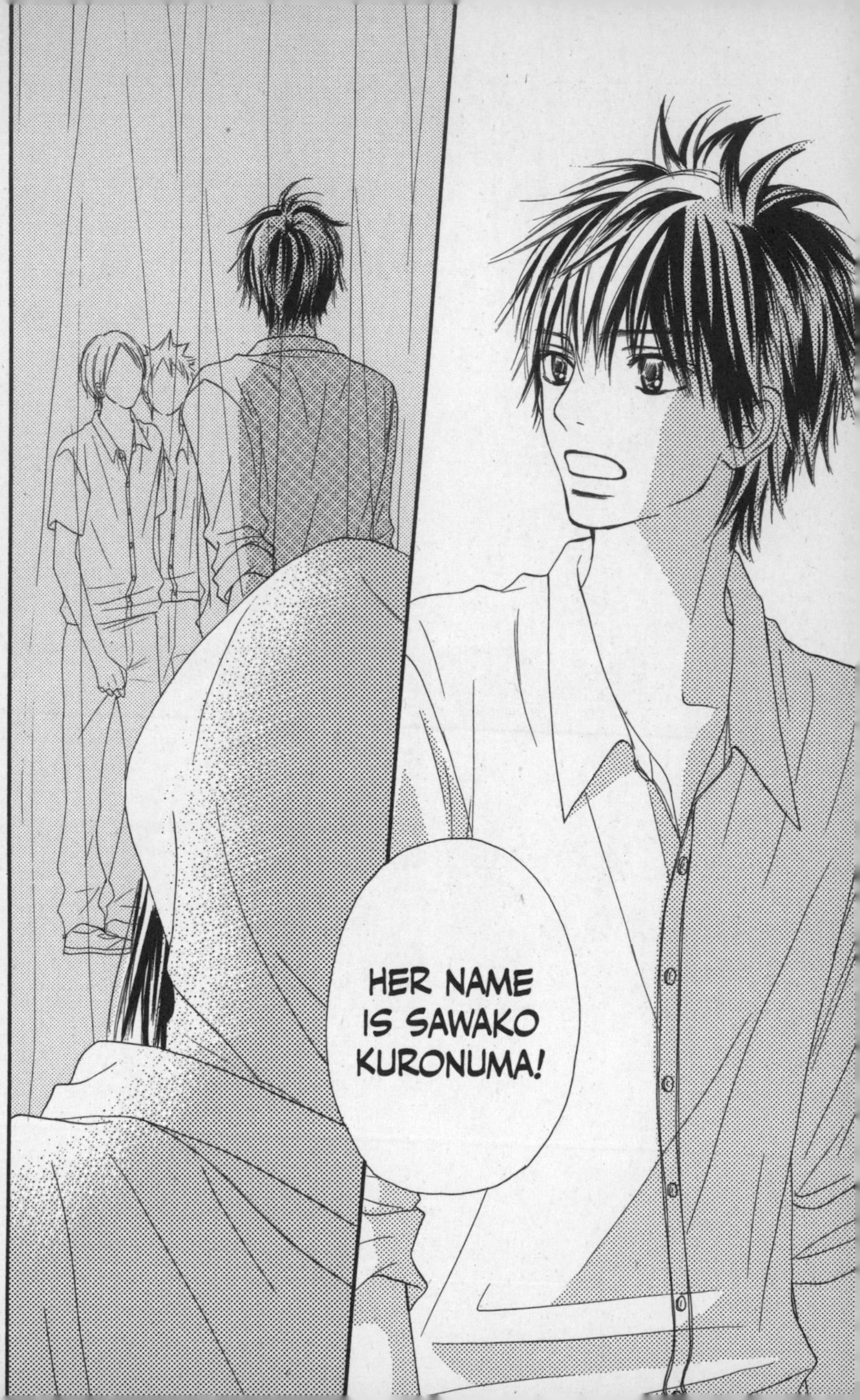
HER NAME IS SAWAKO KURONUMA!

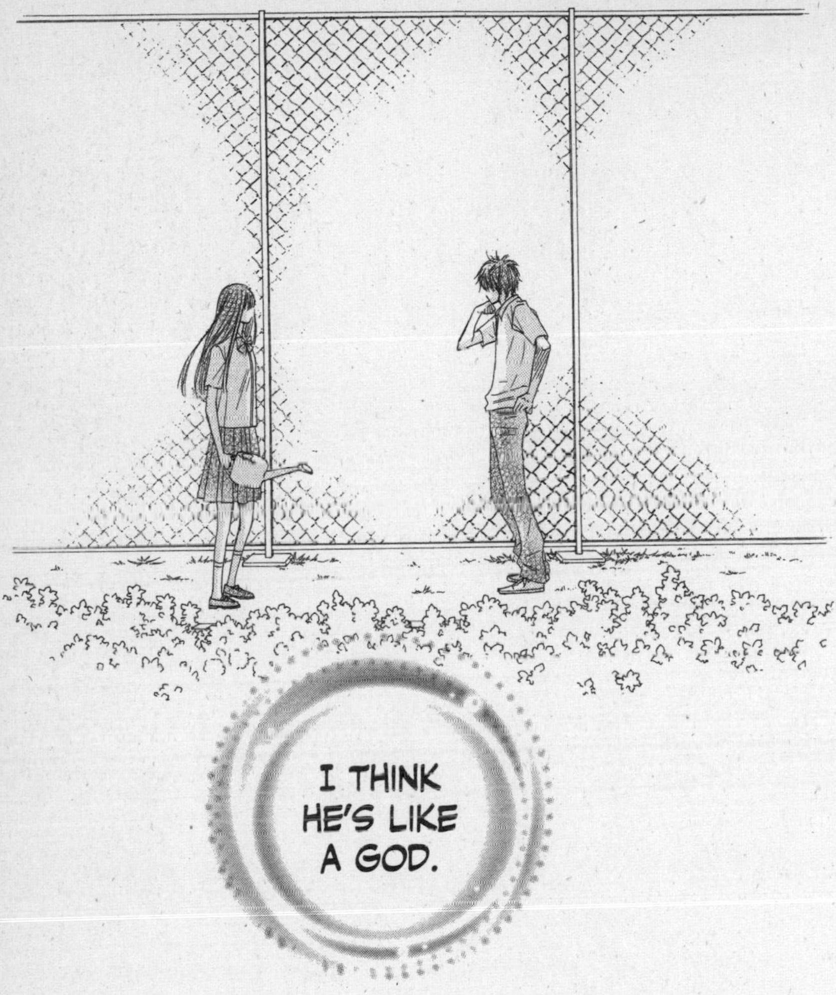
I THINK HE'S LIKE A GOD.

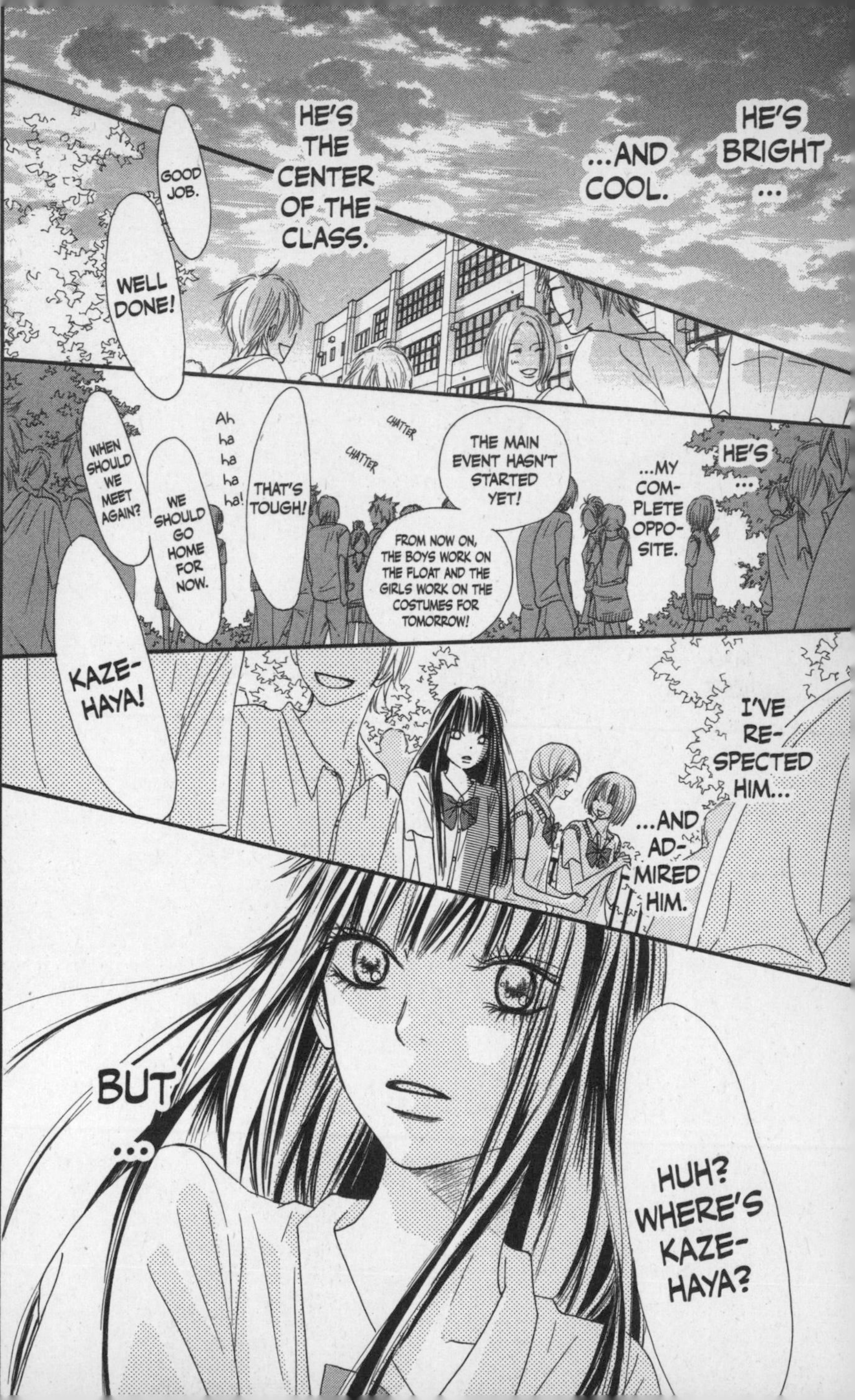
HE'S BRIGHT ...
...AND COOL.
HE'S THE CENTER OF THE CLASS.
GOOD JOB.
WELL DONE!
HE'S ...
...MY COMPLETE OPPOSITE.
THE MAIN EVENT HASN'T STARTED YET!
FROM NOW ON, THE BOYS WORK ON THE FLOAT AND THE GIRLS WORK ON THE COSTUMES FOR TOMORROW!
CHATTER
CHATTER
THAT'S TOUGH!
Ah ha ha ha ha!
WE SHOULD GO HOME FOR NOW.
WHEN SHOULD WE MEET AGAIN?
I'VE RE-SPECTED HIM...
...AND AD-MIRED HIM.
KAZE-HAYA!
HUH? WHERE'S KAZE-HAYA?
BUT ...

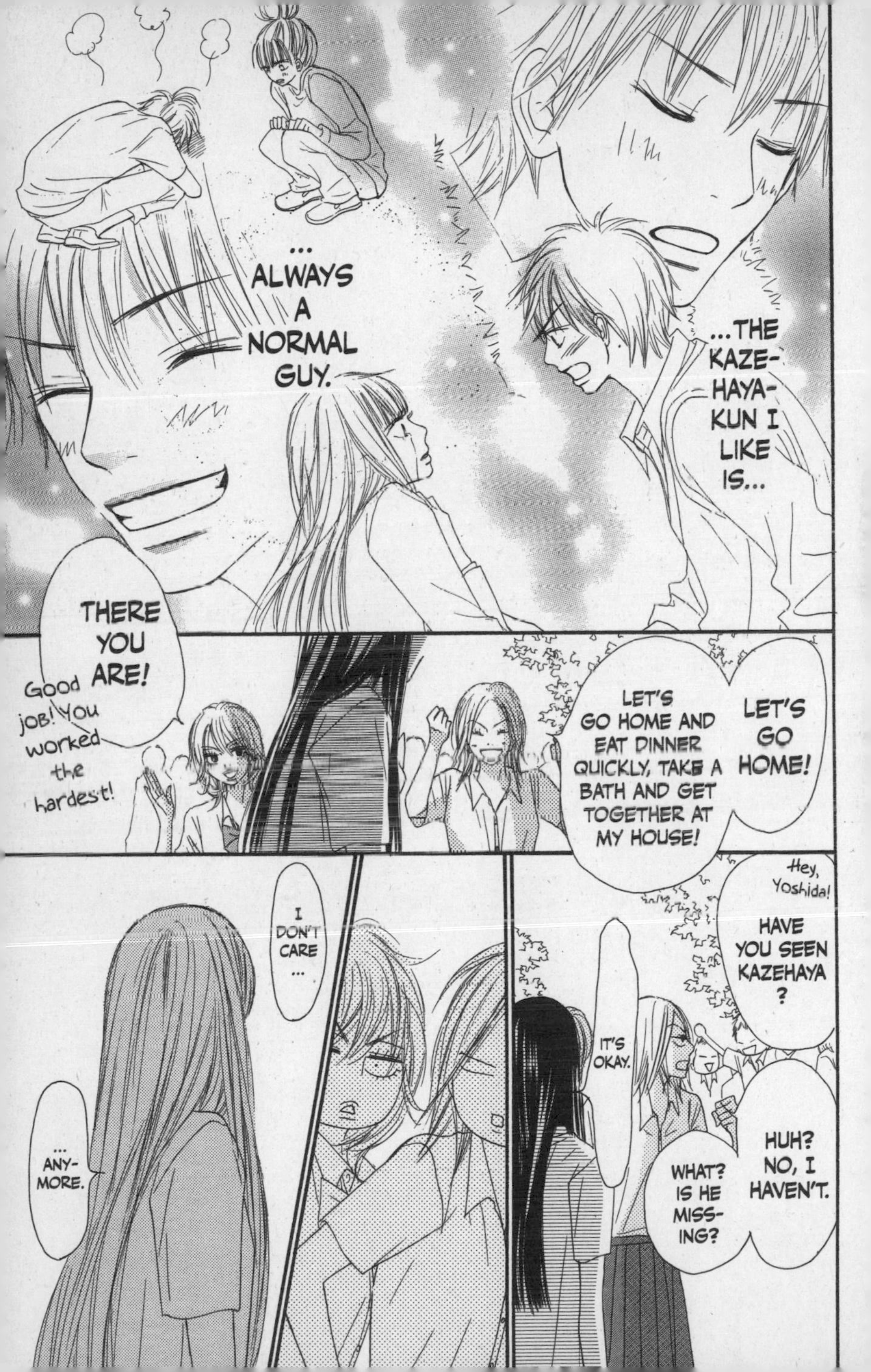
...THE KAZE-HAYA-KUN I LIKE IS...
...ALWAYS A NORMAL GUY.
THERE YOU ARE!
LET'S GO HOME!
LET'S GO HOME AND EAT DINNER QUICKLY, TAKE A BATH AND GET TOGETHER AT MY HOUSE!
Good job! You worked the hardest!
Hey, Yoshida!
HAVE YOU SEEN KAZEHAYA?
HUH? NO, I HAVEN'T.
WHAT? IS HE MISS-ING?
IT'S OKAY.
I DON'T CARE...
...ANY-MORE.

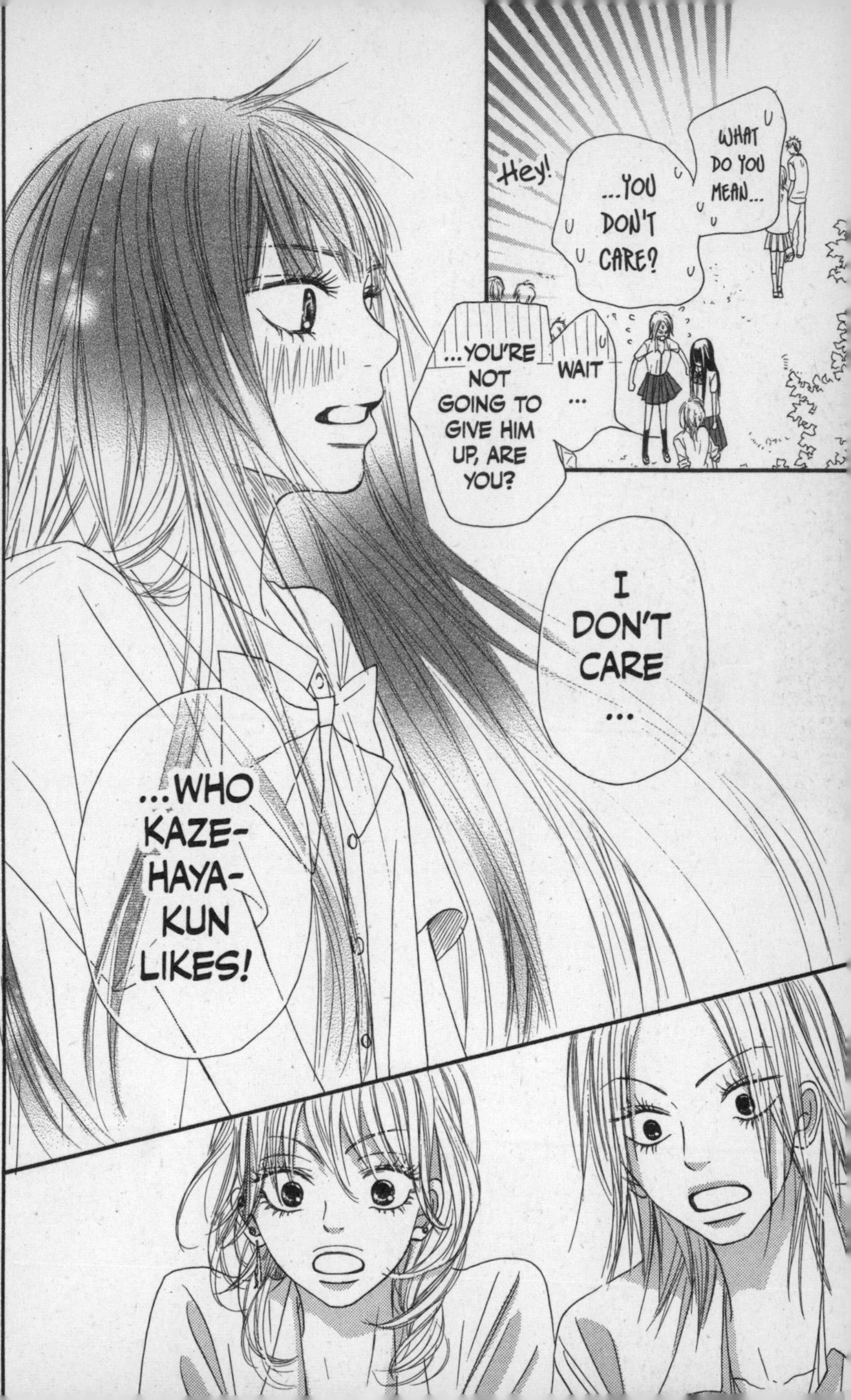
WHAT DO YOU MEAN...
...YOU DON'T CARE?
Hey!
WAIT ...
...YOU'RE NOT GOING TO GIVE HIM UP, ARE YOU?
I DON'T CARE ...
...WHO KAZE-HAYA-KUN LIKES!

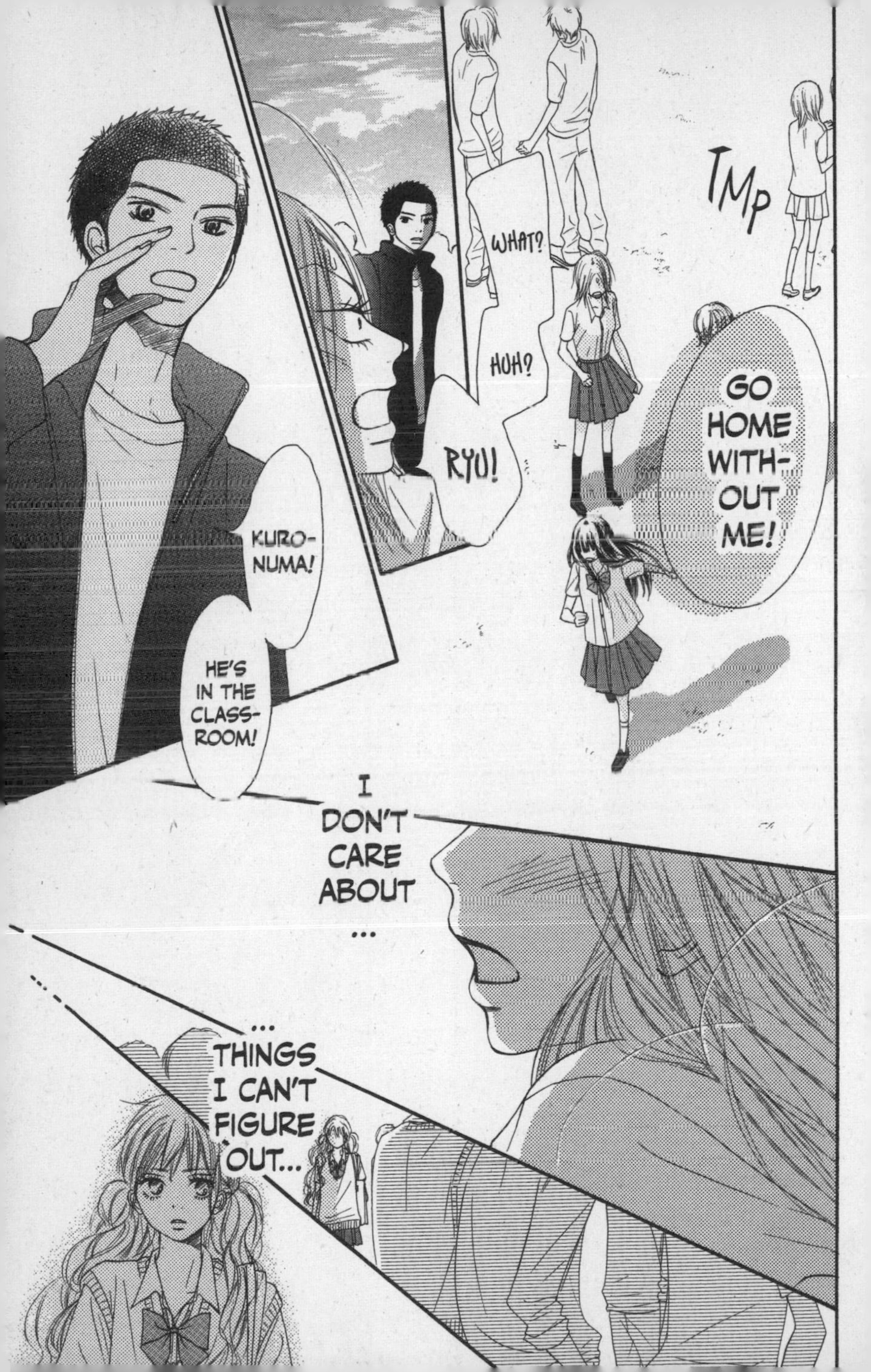
TMP
GO HOME WITH-OUT ME!
HUH?
WHAT?
RYU!
KURO-NUMA!
HE'S IN THE CLASS-ROOM!
I DON'T CARE ABOUT ...
... THINGS I CAN'T FIGURE OUT...

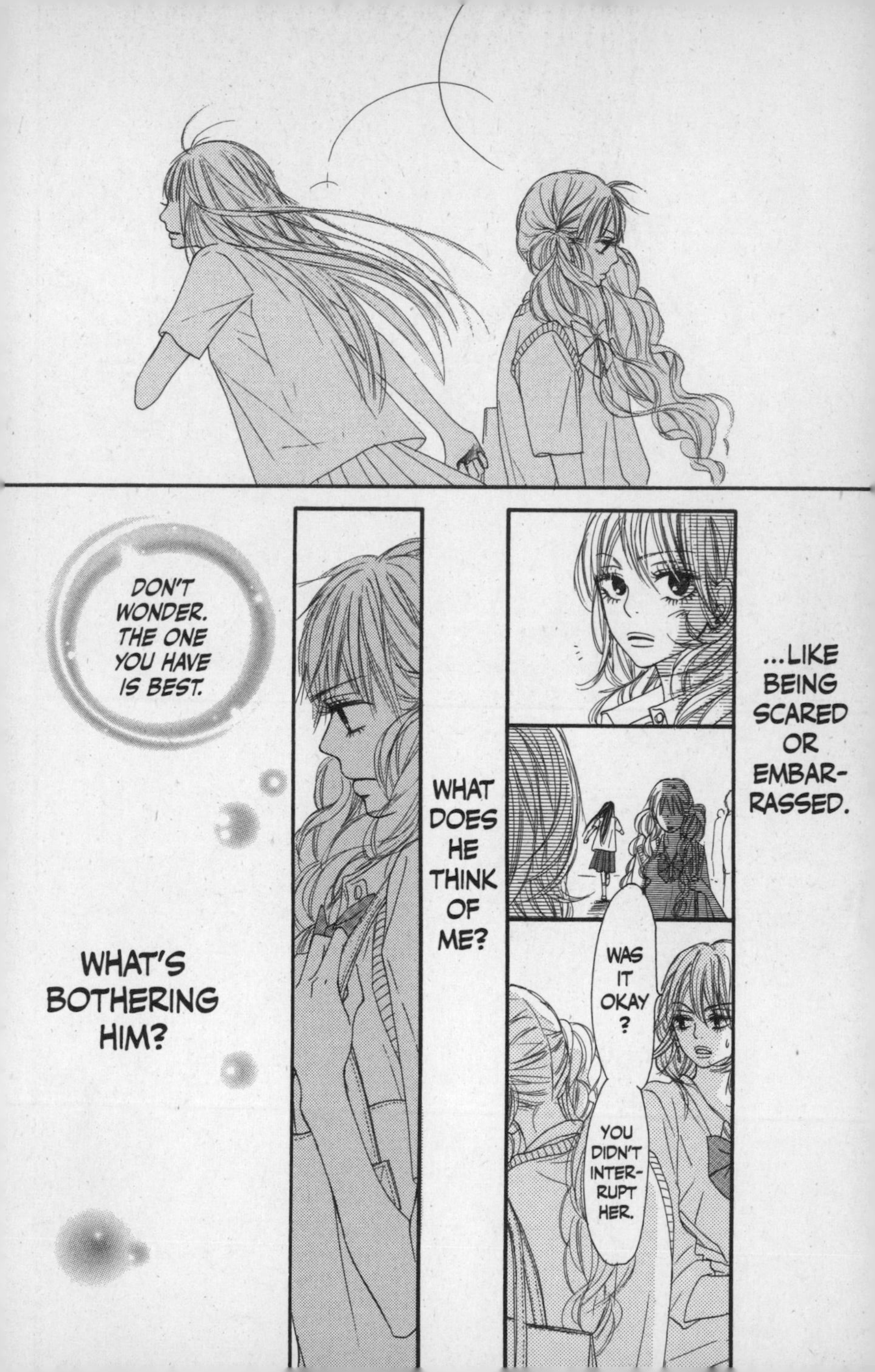
...LIKE BEING SCARED OR EMBARRASSED.
WAS IT OKAY?
YOU DIDN'T INTERRUPT HER.
WHAT DOES HE THINK OF ME?
DON'T WONDER. THE ONE YOU HAVE IS BEST.
WHAT'S BOTHERING HIM?

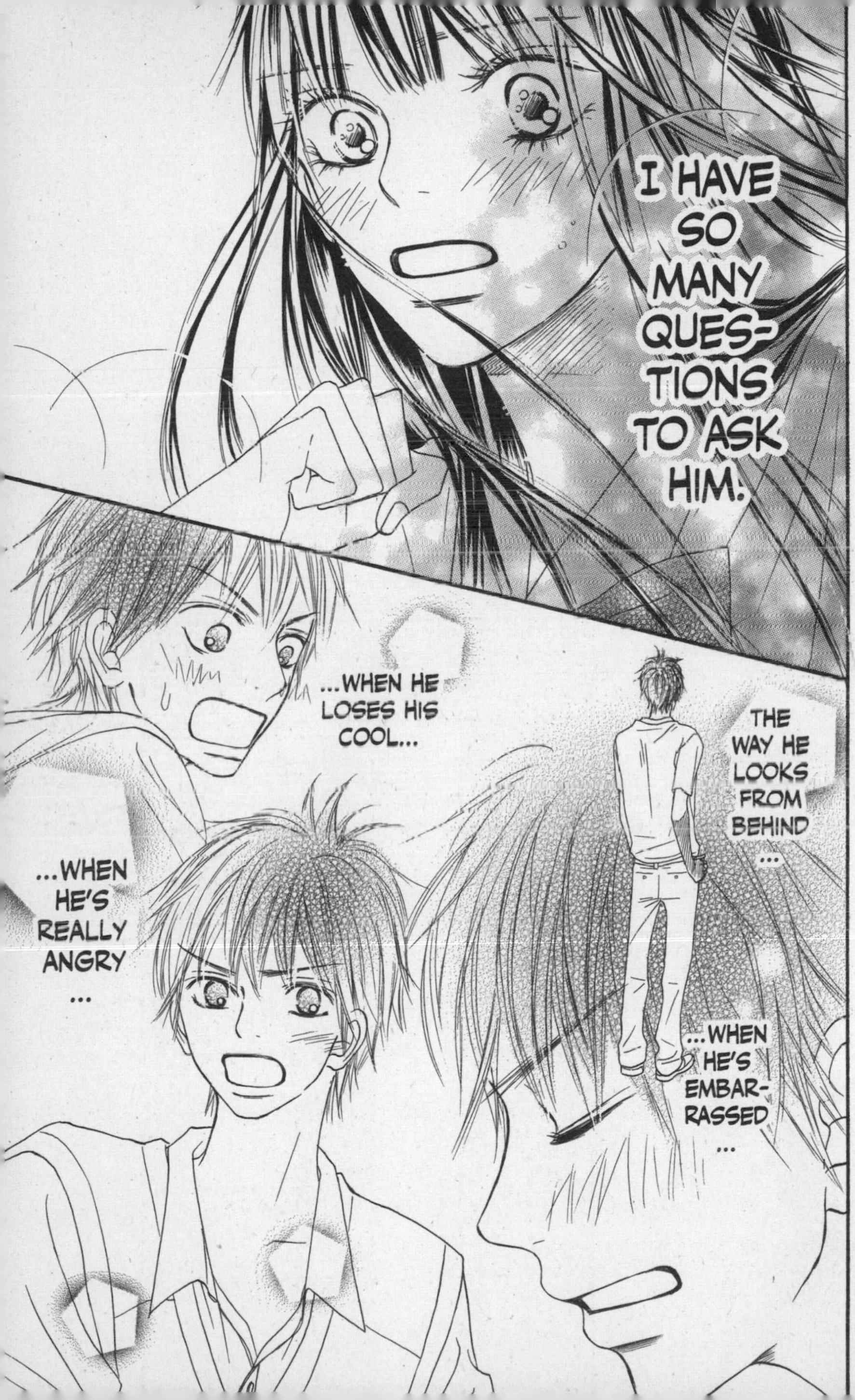
I HAVE SO MANY QUES-TIONS TO ASK HIM.
THE WAY HE LOOKS FROM BEHIND...
...WHEN HE LOSES HIS COOL...
...WHEN HE'S EMBAR-RASSED...
...WHEN HE'S REALLY ANGRY...

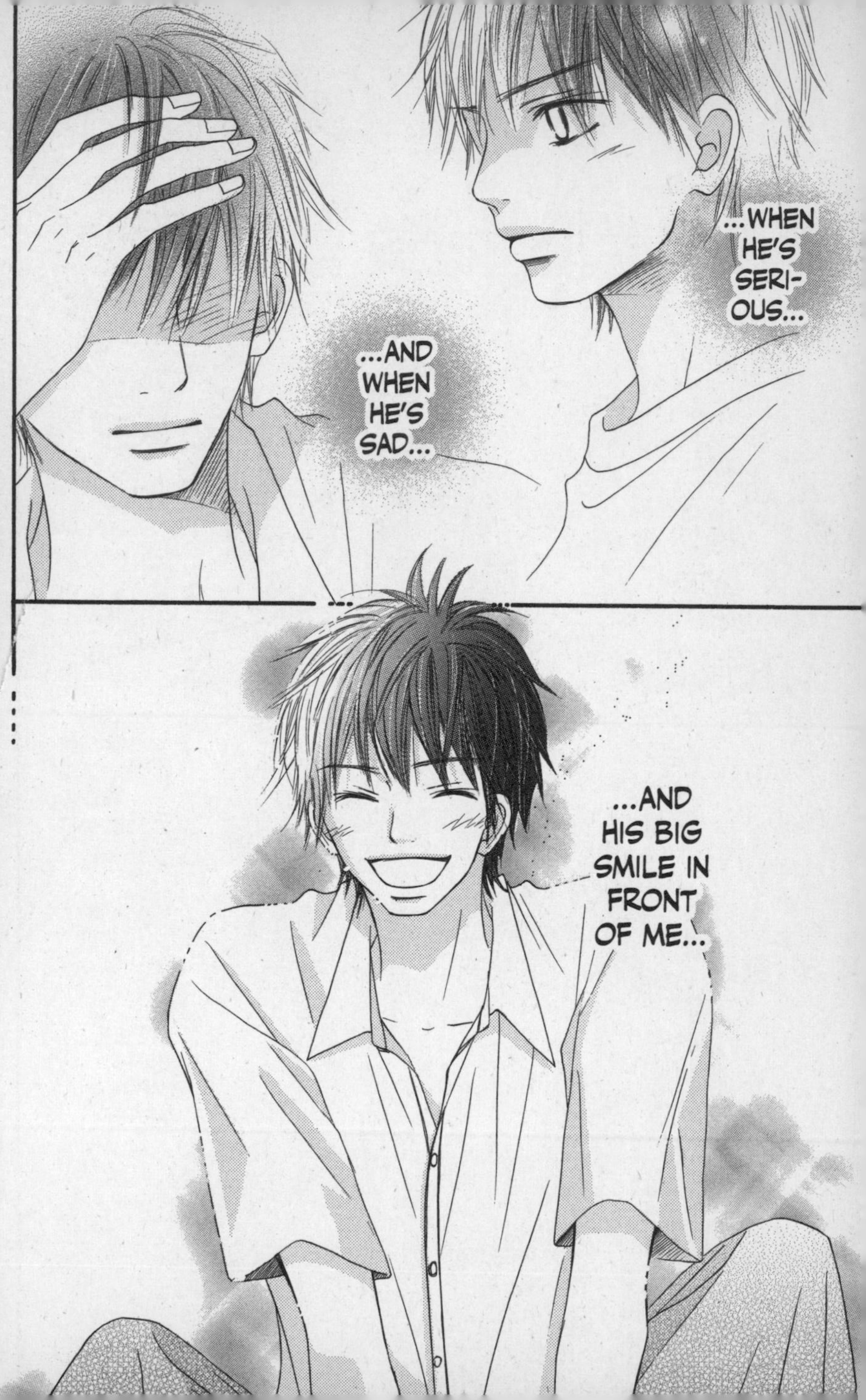
...WHEN HE'S SERI-OUS...
...AND WHEN HE'S SAD...
...AND HIS BIG SMILE IN FRONT OF ME...

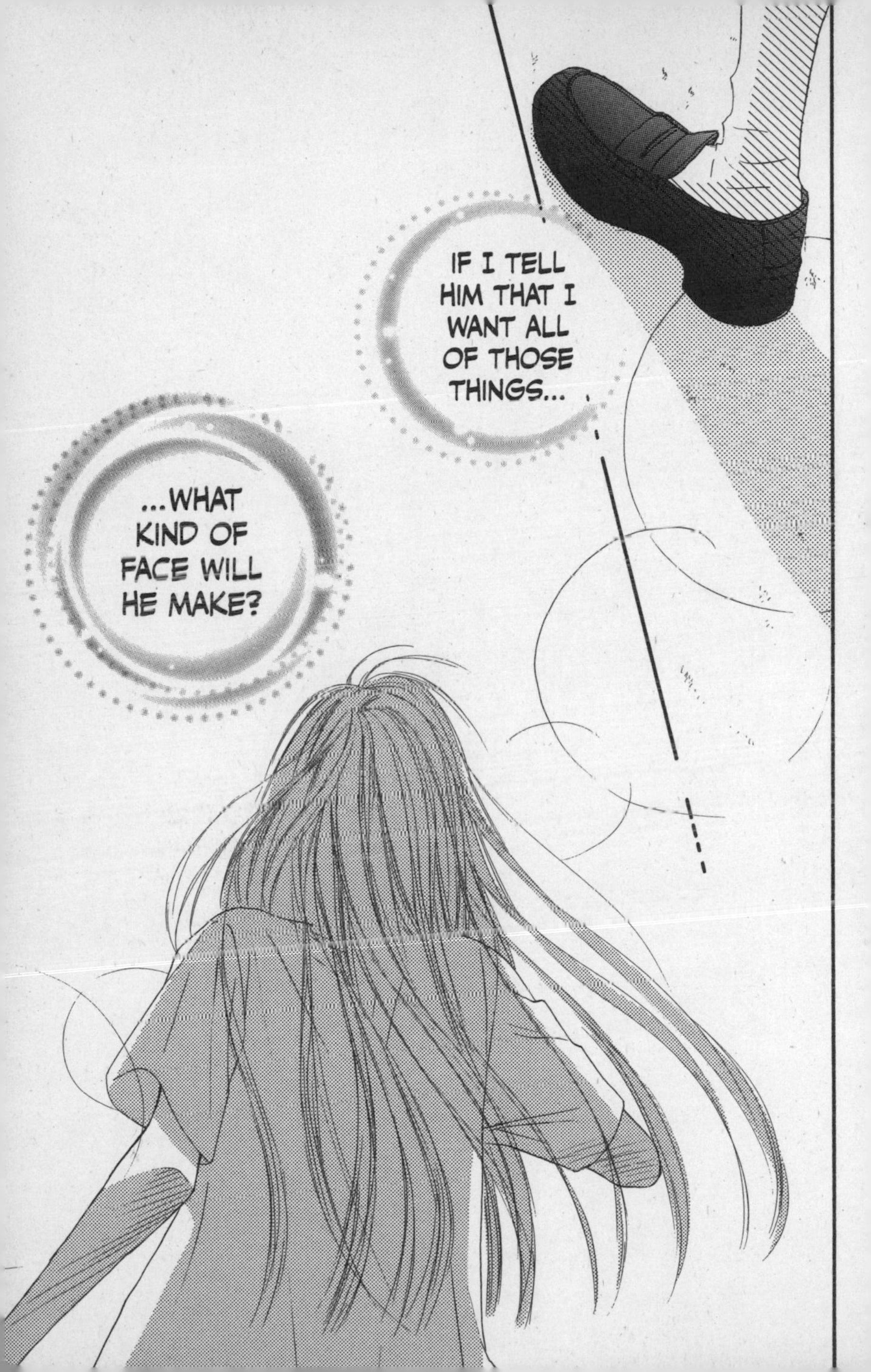
IF I TELL HIM THAT I WANT ALL OF THOSE THINGS...
...WHAT KIND OF FACE WILL HE MAKE?

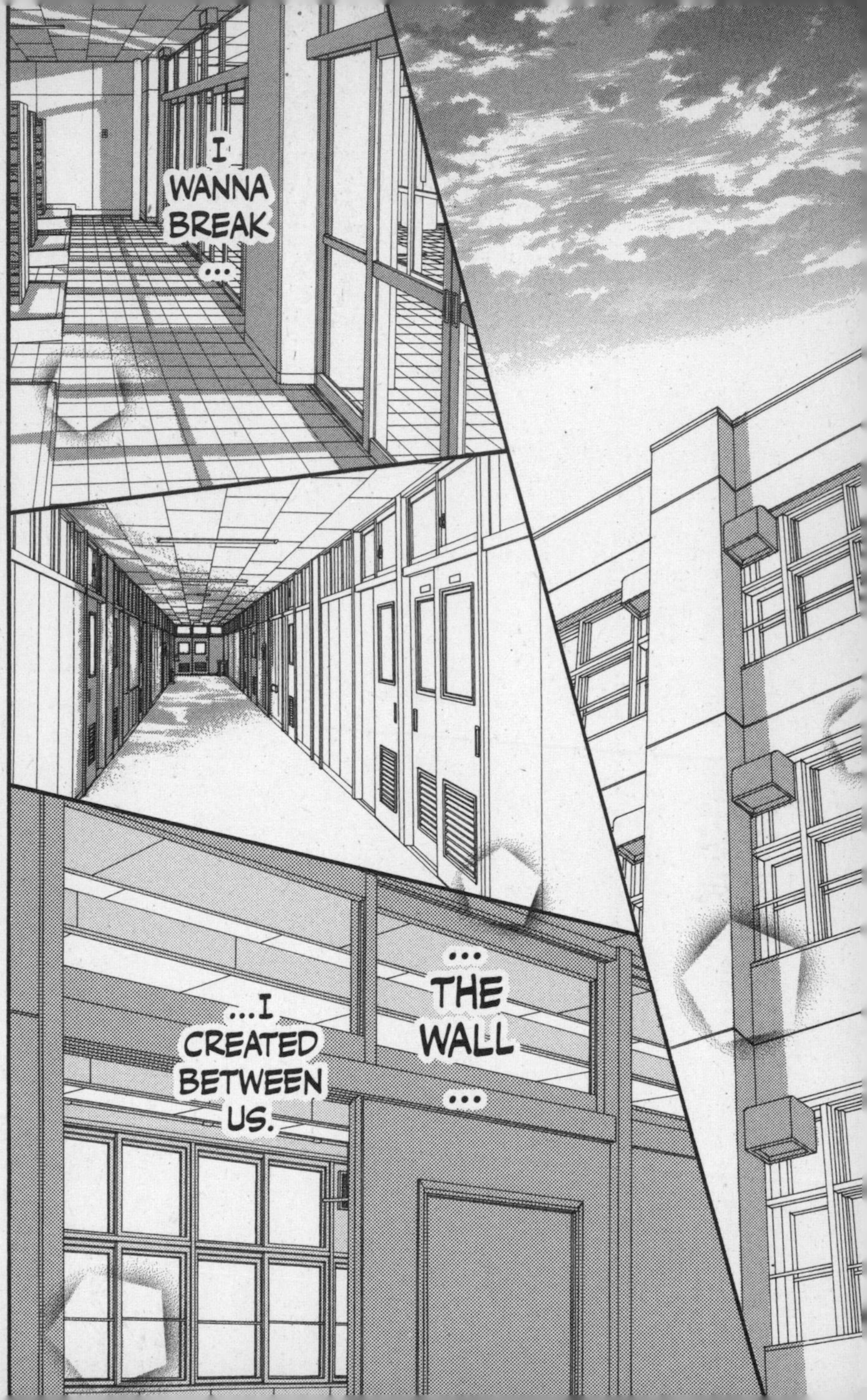
I WANNA BREAK...
...THE WALL...
...I CREATED BETWEEN US.

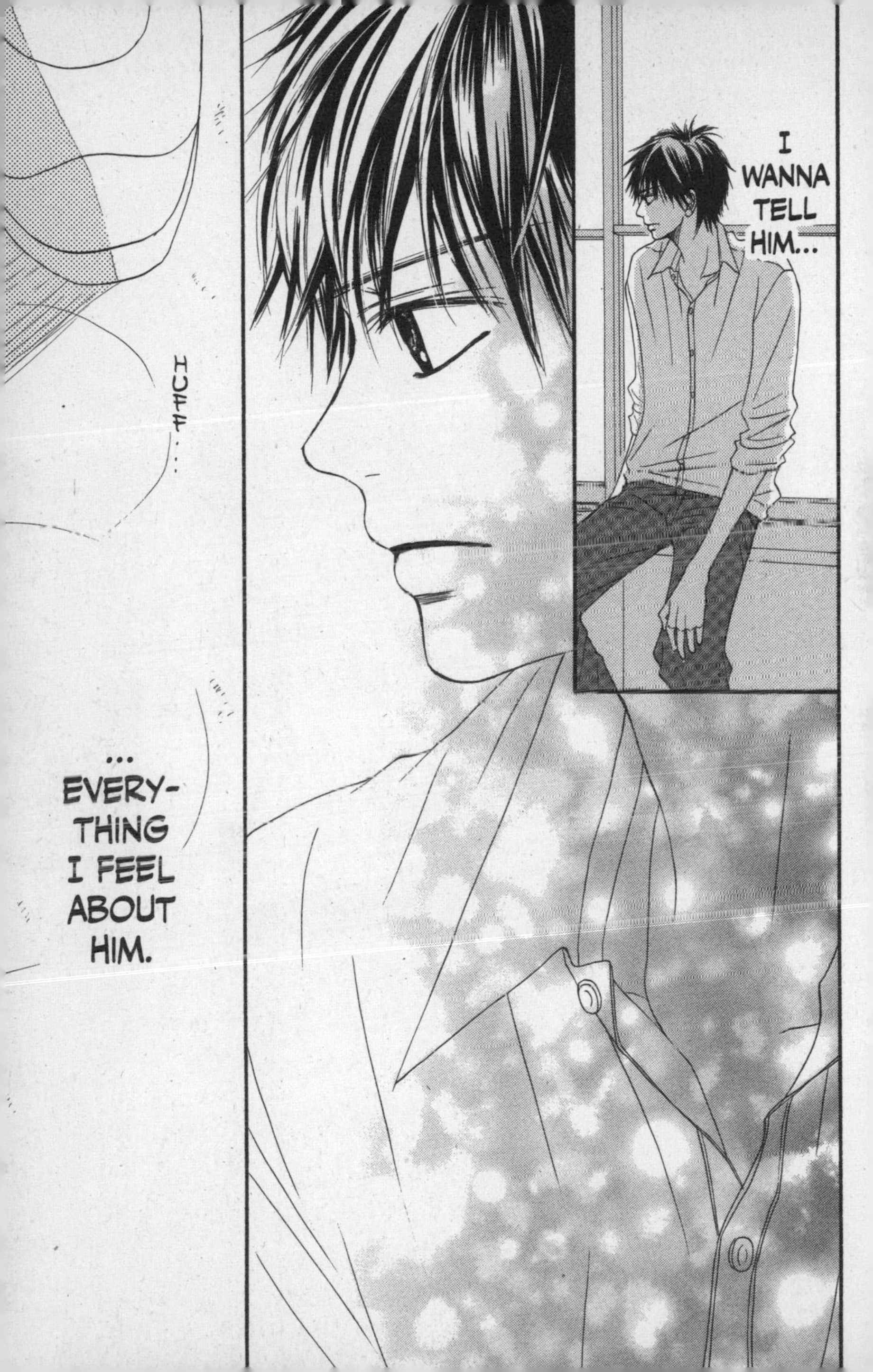
I WANNA TELL HIM...
HUFF...
...EVERY-THING I FEEL ABOUT HIM.

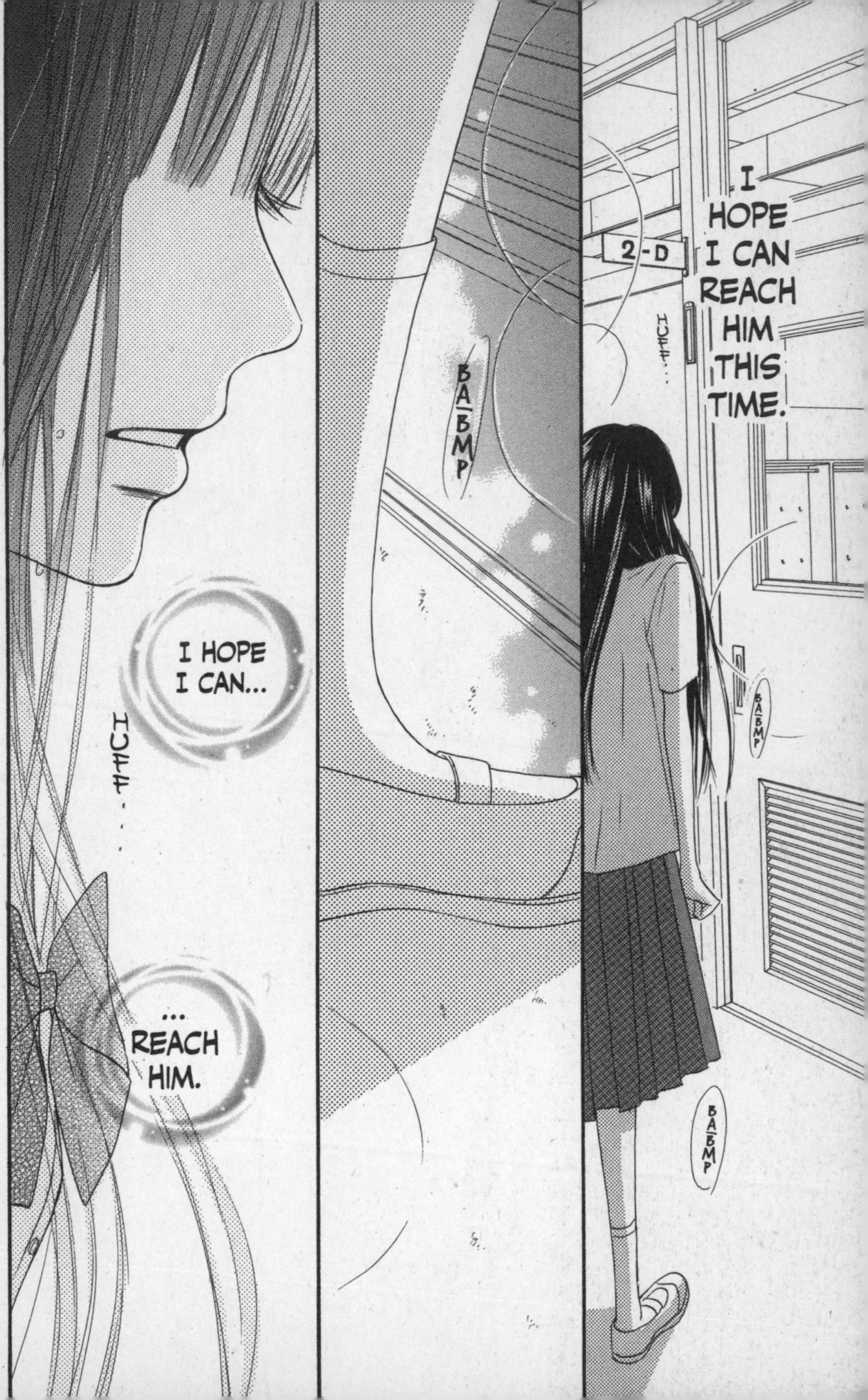
I HOPE I CAN REACH HIM THIS TIME.
HUFF...
BA-BMP
BA-BMP
BA-BMP
I HOPE I CAN...
HUFF...
...REACH HIM.

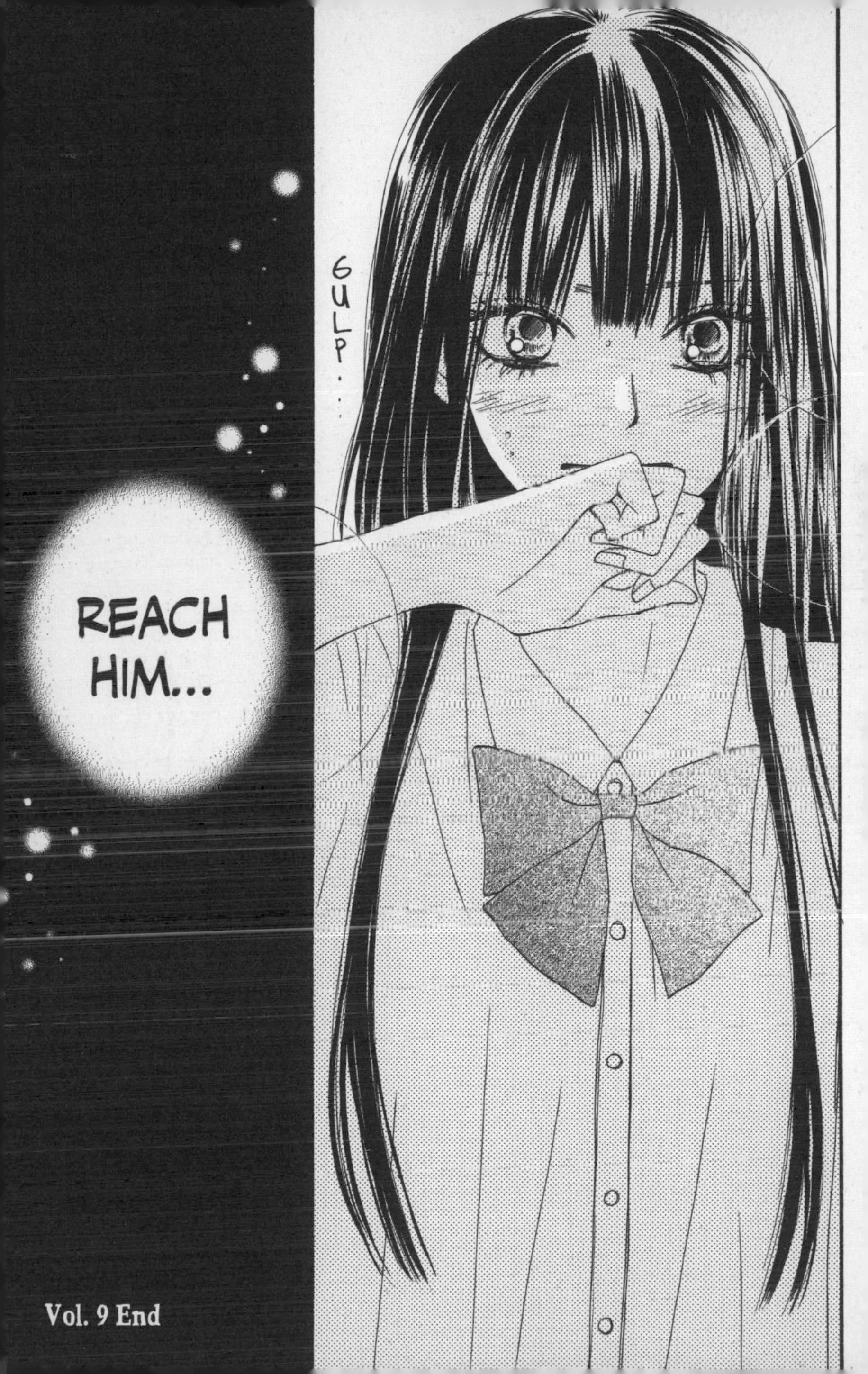
REACH HIM...
GULP...
Vol. 9 End

From me (the editor) to you (the reader).

Here are some Japanese culture explanations that will help you better understand the references in the *Kimi ni Todoke* world.

Honorifics:
When saying someone's name in Japanese, a suffix is often attached to indicate how familiar the speaker is with the person. Some are more polite and respectful, while others are endearing. Calling someone by just their first name is the most informal.
-kun is used for young men or boys, usually someone you are familiar with.
-chan is used for young women, girls or young children and can be used as a term of endearment.
-san is used for someone you respect or are not close to, or to be polite.

Page 75, school festival:
Many schools hold yearly festivals in which classes organize activities, such as class cafés, performances or art exhibits.

B-BMP
B-BMP
B-BMP

Is it possible?

About the time this graphic novel comes out, light novels (one retelling the manga and another with a new story) and a video game for the Nintendo DS will also come out, and an anime will begin airing. Everyone who's been involved with these projects has really paid a lot of attention to faithfully creating the world of *Kimi ni Todoke*. I'm so moved that I even cry a little. When I first started writing this story, and even until recently, I had no idea it would become such a big deal. Thank you, everyone!

--Karuho Shiina

Karuho Shiina was born and raised in Hokkaido, Japan. Though *Kimi ni Todoke* is only her second series following many one-shot stories, it has already racked up accolades from various "Best Manga of the Year" lists. Winner of the 2008 Kodansha Manga Award for the shojo category, *Kimi ni Todoke* also placed fifth in the first-ever Manga Taisho (Cartoon Grand Prize) contest in 2008. In Japan, an animated TV series debuted in October 2009, and a live-action film was released in 2010.

Kimi ni Todoke
VOL. 9

Shojo Beat Edition

STORY AND ART BY
KARUHO SHIINA

Translation/Ari Yasuda, HC Language Solutions, Inc.
Touch-up Art & Lettering/Vanessa Satone
Design/Nozomi Akashi
Editor/Carrie Shepherd

KIMI NI TODOKE © 2005 by Karuho Shiina
All rights reserved. First published in Japan in 2005 by SHUEISHA Inc.,
Tokyo. English translation rights arranged by SHUEISHA Inc.

Printed in Canada

Published by VIZ Media, LLC
P.O. Box 77010
San Francisco, CA 94107

10 9 8 7 6 5 4 3 2 1
First printing, July 2011

www.viz.com

www.shojobeat.com

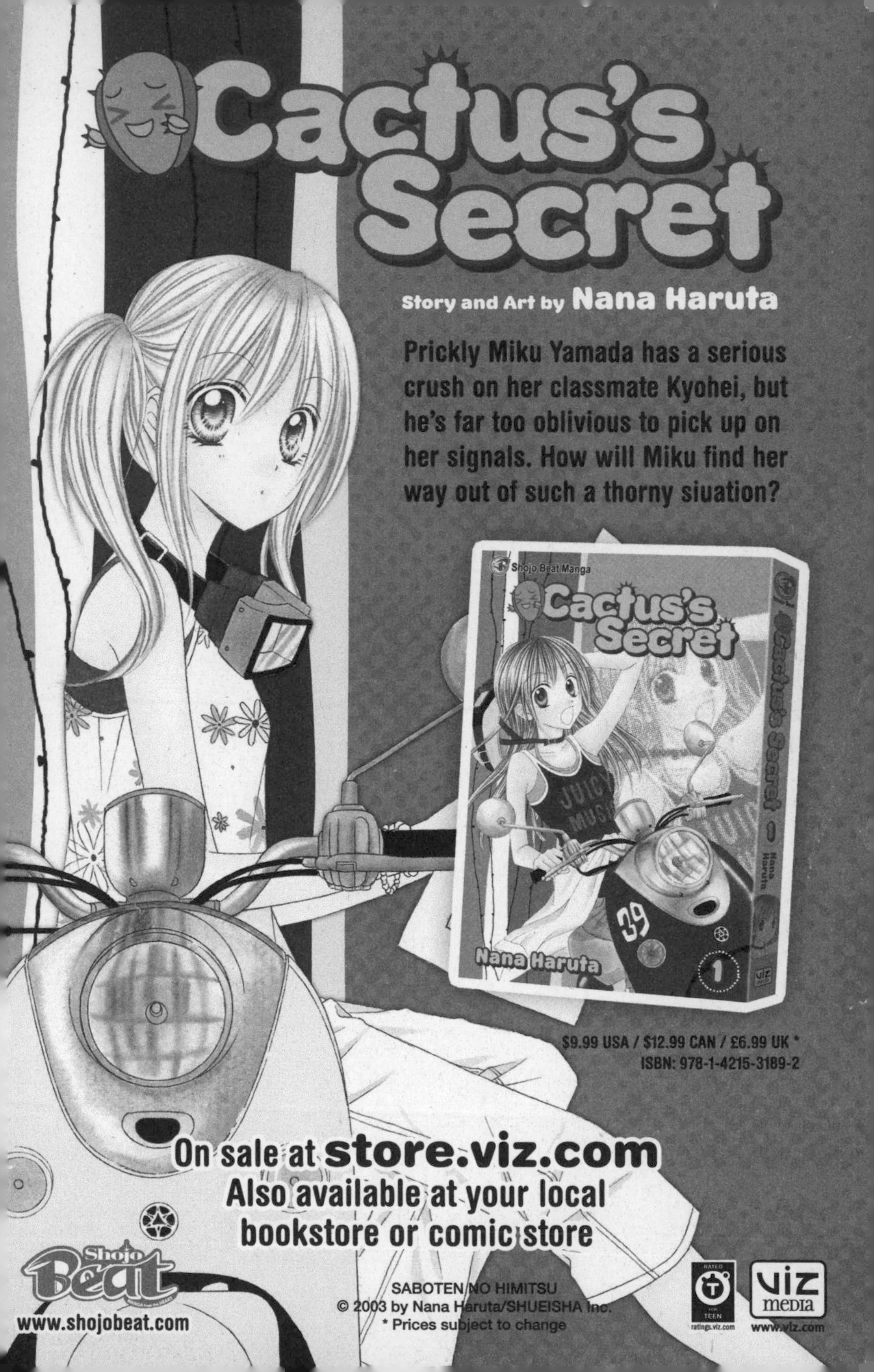
Cactus's Secret
Story and Art by Nana Haruta
Prickly Miku Yamada has a serious crush on her classmate Kyohei, but he's far too oblivious to pick up on her signals. How will Miku find her way out of such a thorny siuation?
Shojo Beat Manga
Cactus's Secret
Nana Haruta
1
$9.99 USA / $12.99 CAN / £6.99 UK *
ISBN: 978-1-4215-3189-2
On sale at store.viz.com
Also available at your local bookstore or comic store
Shojo Beat
www.shojobeat.com
SABOTEN NO HIMITSU
© 2003 by Nana Haruta/SHUEISHA Inc.
* Prices subject to change
RATED T TEEN
ratings.viz.com
VIZ media
www.viz.com